Gottfried Semper

Gottfried Semper by Ernst Kietz, 1850. (Semper-Archiv Zurich)

Gottfried Semper

In Search of Architecture

Wolfgang Herrmann

The MIT Press
Cambridge, Massachusetts
London, England

Gottfried Semper: In Search of Architecture consists of material originally published in *Gottfried Semper im Exil* (Basel: Birkhäuser Verlag, 1978), pages 9–124, and in *Gottfried Semper: Theoretischer Nachlass an der ETH Zürich, Katalog und Kommentare* (Basel: Birkhäuser Verlag, 1981), pages 12–68, 180–190, 196–204, 217–249. These titles are volumes 19 and 15 of the Schriftenreihe des Instituts für Geschichte und Theorie der Architektur [GTA] series of the Eidgenössischen Technischen Hochschule Zürich. The foreword by Adolf Max Vogt, chapters 1 and 3 in part I, chapter 1 in part II, and "Semper's Literary Estate" in part III were written especially for this edition. English translation and new material © 1984 by The Massachusetts Institute of Technology.

This book was set in Baskerville by The MIT Press Computergraphics Department and printed and bound by Halliday Lithograph in the United States of America.

Library of Congress Cataloging in Publication Data

Herrmann, Wolfgang, 1899-
 Gottfried Semper: in search of architecture.

 "Consists of material originally published in Gottfried Semper im Exil (Basel: Birkhäuser Verlag, 1978), pages 9–124, and in Gottfried Semper: Theoretischer Nachlass an der ETH Zürich, Katalog und Kommentare (Basel: Birkhäuser Verlag, 1981), pages 12–68, 180–190, 196–204, 217–249"—Verso of t.p.
 Translated by the author.
 Bibliography: p.
 Includes index.
 1. Semper, Gottfried, 1803–1879. 2. Architects—Germany—Biography. I. Title.

 NA1088.S48H47 1984 720'.92'4 [B] 84-14417 ISBN 0-262-08144-X

Contents

I
Semper's Life and Work

1

2

3

4

II
Semper's Aesthetic Theory

1

5

*A Critical Analysis and Prognosis of Present-Day Artistic Production
(Preface to "Theory of Formal Beauty")   245*

List of Illustrations

Foreword

Text

Foreword

"Table and Tablecloth": Joseph Paxton and Gottfried Semper

On January 28, 1852, several months after the close of the Great Exhibition of 1851, Joseph Paxton gave a speech before the Royal Commission.[1] He tried to explain the structural principle of his exhibition hall, which had become instantly famous as the "Crystal Palace." He compared the support structure and the glass skin of this hall, which he had derived from a hothouse, to a "table and tablecloth." He wanted to make clear to the members of the Royal Commission that the new feature of his building method consisted primarily in the improvement of the "tablecloth" (glass skin), which led to the possibility of the "table's" (the support structure) being "greatly varied to suit changing conditions and changing uses."[2]

This comparison of a work of architecture to a table and tablecloth would have pleased no one more than the German architect Gottfried Semper. Semper was in fact living in London at the time of the exhibition, but as a political emigrant who had fled Dresden after his participation in the unsuccessful 1849 revolution, he now had to fight for professional recognition in England—a country whose language he had not yet mastered in 1851. Although he was invited to participate in the design of the Great Exhibition that year, his role was limited to minor building and interior decoration.

I assume that Semper would have been pleased and satisfied by Paxton's descriptive formula table and tablecloth, on the grounds of his unique theory of the fundamentals of architecture, which he had brought along from Germany and which—despite his forced emigration—was published there in 1851 under the title *Four Elements of Architecture*. Semper's basic theory held that the walls of the primitive house of ancient times were not made of stone but consisted of hanging cloth—rugs or woven "mats." In other words, Semper also maintained the thesis of tablecloth and table, but he advanced it as a *historical* theory of the "original conditions of human society." He now found, curiously enough, in the Great Exhibition, that is, in Paxton's Crystal Palace, an excellent proof for his theory. There he discovered a "Caribbean Hut" (figure 1), which confirmed his theory of the textile-wall.

This bamboo hut evidently made a lasting impression on Semper, for he discussed it first in a London lecture of 1854, "On Architectural Symbols"; then in section 143 of his main work, *Der Stil*, he illustrated it and described it under the heading "The Primitive Hut." He found in it "not an imaginary construction but a completely realistic instance provided by ethnology . . . which could be seen in the Great Exhibition of 1851. In it appear all the elements of ancient architecture in a highly original manner and without adulteration: the hearth as the center, the earthen platform surrounded by the pilework as a terrace, the roof on columns (pillars), and the woven bamboo mat (fence) as a space divider or wall." Here we find listed in full the four elements that constituted a house in Semper's view: the hearth, "the first and most important, the moral element of architecture," then the earthen platform (terrace), on top of that the roof on columns (supporting system), and finally the wall, which is to be understood as a textile hanging.[3]

Semper assigned a "technical skill" to each of the four elements present in the hut, that is, he presented the four elements of his scheme as crystallizations of the early building professions. For the construction of the hearth were employed "the ceramic and subsequent metallurgical arts"; for that of the earthen platform (terrace), processes involving water and masonry; for the columns and the roof, the art of joinery; and, finally, for the walls, "the art of weaving mats and rugs."

It goes without saying that this is a highly idealistic scheme. Yet it is not easily forgotten, for two good reasons. First, to conceive the wall as texture, as a mat and a textile hanging, also means to include in the archaic household from the very beginning ornament and color—two elements of future *picture making*; and second, Semper was ready and willing to *verify* his idealistic scheme, as his reception of the Caribbean hut proves. This "completely realistic instance provided by ethnology" thereby became a lesson for him, too, and enabled him to abandon his idealistic point of departure and to find the pragmatic anthropological approach that later on became the distinctive feature of *Der Stil*.

From this point of view, the Crystal Palace of 1851, together with its exhibitions, was a unique phenomenon. For the Caribbean hut

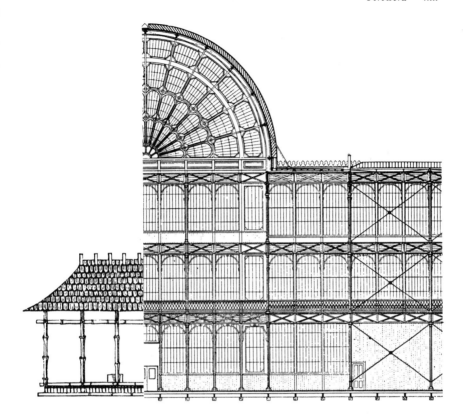

1

Wall and structure, primitive and modern. The Caribbean hut as represented in the Great Exhibition of 1851 compared with Paxton's Crystal Palace, which housed the exhibition.

exhibited there represented the original form of the principle table and tablecloth, which Paxton propounded as his own. In other words the germ of primal form, the seed for the Crystal Palace, was exhibited within its own structure. To date I have not been able to find any evidence that Paxton became aware of this strange coincidence. As far as I know, Semper did not notice this connection either, simply because in his opinion Paxton's work, regardless of how much admiration it received, did not belong in the category of architecture.

The Function of the Hand in the History of Production

In the third part of this book Wolfgang Herrmann presents five manuscripts that are to be found in the Semper-Archiv of the Institut für Geschichte und Theorie der Architektur of the Eidgenössische Technische Hochschule, Zurich. The first three of these five handwritten texts, published here for the first time, are part of "Comparative Building Theory," a final masterwork Semper had planned. Although in his draft for the preface (MS 55) he emphatically criticized the existing theories of Durand and Rondelet and set down his own goals, he interrupted his favorite project in order to write another book (*Der Stil*), "devoted exlusively to the industrial arts." We have to ask why he thus left the field of architecture proper in favor of the industrial arts, including textiles, ceramics, carpentry, masonry, and metalwork. The answer is to be found in a lecture he gave in the London years, that is, before receiving a professorship at the ETH in Zurich.

The crucial passage reads as follows: "A great part of the forms used in architecture thus originate from works of industrial art, and the rules and laws of beauty and style . . . were determined and practiced long before the existence of any monumental art. The works of industrial art therefore very often give the key and basis for the understanding of architectural forms and principles." These two sentences are clear evidence for the transformation of the idealist Semper into an anthropologically oriented pragmatist, who no longer sought explanations from "above"—that is, derived from the monumental—but who found them in the applied arts, in the so-called simple or "lower" genres, and thus in that genre that in his times was called industrial art (*Kunstindustrie*). He justified this decisive fundamental change in standpoint, doubtless also influenced by the impressions left on him by the Great Exhibition and its Caribbean hut, in the first of the sentences quoted above: "beauty and style . . . were determined *long before* the existence of any monumental art" (italics added). This insight and conviction resulted for him in a logical chain of connections: *because* he believed that the monumental was chronologically a secondary phenomenon, he discovered the vast sphere of the industrial arts; *because* this sphere represented the earliest production of the human hand, he wanted to discover its rules of production; *because* these rules of production were determined by the properties of the material and the properties of their intended use, he discovered thereby the early stages of Functionalism.

Thus it becomes understandable that he analyzed in great detail hundreds of examples of industrial art of many countries and periods, but it is nevertheless astonishing that in this two-volume work by an architect for architects, the entire first volume (approximately 480 pages) is devoted to textile art. In the second volume follow approximately 200 pages on ceramics, 132 pages on carpentry, and 120 pages on masonry—all in all, the most circuitous route ever taken by an architectural theorist to arrive finally at the theme of architecture.

In section 3 of *Der Stil* he distinguished between "four categories of raw materials . . . (1) elastic . . . , (2) soft . . . , (3) of . . . a relative solidity (ductile), (4) hard . . . of retroactive (tensile) strength. Correspondingly, there are four main activities of industrial art. . . (1) textile art, (2) ceramic art, (3) tectonics (joinery), (4) stereometry (stone building), etc."

Thus in *Der Stil* Semper followed the development of the human hand from its processing of elastic and soft materials to that of ductile and hard ones, in the sense of an evolutionary process of "technical skills." From our perspective it is striking that he conceived this theory of the evolutionary history of production by the human hand at the very moment when in the countries of the western world so-called machinery became dominant, when the work of the hand was copied and at the same time supplanted by the machine.

Semper and Nonverbal Semiotics

For the most part, Semper was conscious of his own motivation. In the London lecture mentioned above he stated: "When I was studying in Paris I used to walk in the *jardin des plantes*, and there I always felt drawn as if by a magic force away from the sunny garden and into the rooms where the fossilized remains of the animal kingdom of prehistory . . . are arranged in long rows. In this magnificent collection, the work of Baron Cuvier, one finds the types of even the most complicated forms of the animal kingdom." This "magnificent collection" of Cuvier's suggested to him, apparently once and for all, the framework of his theoretical work. It triggered the question: "From the observation of (animal) nature . . . shouldn't we be allowed to conclude by *analogy* that in the *creations of our hands*, in the *works of art*, approximately the *same kind* of process is to be found?"

It is this analogy to Cuvier's classification of the forms in the animal kingdom that made Semper's work fascinating for his readers for many decades. Berlage in the Netherlands, Otto Wagner in Vienna, the followers of the Bauhaus, the architects of the Chicago School, among them Sullivan especially, were all influenced by it. Seen in retrospect, Semper created a concept somewhat parallel to Darwin's— not inspired by Darwin, however, but by Cuvier, who had advanced his typology forty years earlier.

An example of Semper's precision in his observation and differentiation of the early manifestations of "industrial art" is his distinction between knotted and plaited work. In section 52 of *Der Stil* he described the knot, which "at first had served as the device of tying together the two ends of a thread" (figure 2); in section 54 the plaited work (figure 3), which interested him especially because it "creates a two-dimensional fabric" and thereby also makes possible woven mats and thus, finally, the textile-wall.

Viewed in light of present-day semiotics, and in particular zoosemiotics, which points out similar phenomena (plaited, however, not by human hand but, for instance, by the beak of a weaver bird), Semper appears as a pioneer (figure 4). He was the first to deal with

2
Knot. (*Der Stil* 1)

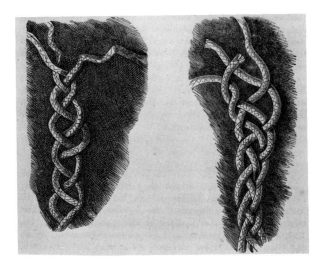

3
Plaited work. (*Der Stil* 1)

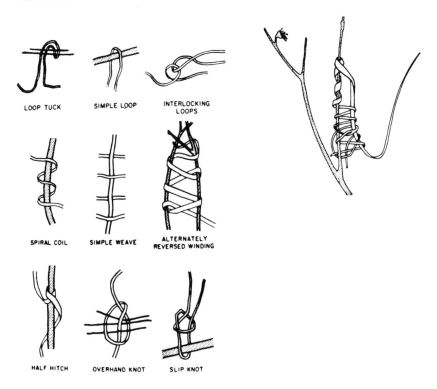

LOOP TUCK   SIMPLE LOOP   INTERLOCKING LOOPS

SPIRAL COIL   SIMPLE WEAVE   ALTERNATELY REVERSED WINDING

HALF HITCH   OVERHAND KNOT   SLIP KNOT

4
Plaited work built by the weaver bird. (From Thomas A. Sebeok, *Prefigurements of Art*, 1979, after Hancocks, 1973)

some questions whose relevance for today and the near future needs to be discovered anew—as soon as nonverbal semiotics has regained its independence from verbal semiotics. For as long as the phenomena of industrial art are examined exclusively insofar as they allow analogies to language—as in the case of French Structuralism—they yield only limited aspects. The totally different analogy, which fascinated Semper and was triggered by the work of Cuvier, grants to the human hand its own "language" that is independent of verbal structures and receives its own dignity and importance from the very fact that it is structured in a way that is different from the human capacity for verbal language. The Anglo-Saxon semiotic scholars, Thomas A. Sebeok for instance, have always been skeptical of the predominance of the linguistic model and have pointed out its limitations and one-sidedness. There is no doubt that Gottfried Semper belongs to the circle of those pioneers who recognized the nonverbal sign and its own specific nature and began to interpret it.

Adolf Max Vogt
translated by Radka Donnell

Acknowledgments

I wish to express once more my deep-felt gratitude to Adolf Max Vogt, whose resolute efforts made the prospect of an American edition come true. My thanks above all to my wife, Anni, who helped with the translation as gladly and well as she did with the initial research at the Semper-Archiv, to Barbara Weinberger, who took an early interest in the translation, revising it with much care, and to Robin Bledsoe, who never tired of struggling with Semper's (and my) prose.

Editorial Method

Translating one's own writings has its advantages: communication between author and translator is close, the principle of considering the original text as almost sacrosanct less of an impediment. Naturally, I have tried to convey the meaning of the original as truthfully as I possibly could, but I had no scruples about clarifying passages that now, some years after I had written them, seemed ambiguous or about making corrections and additions when recent research called for them. But apart from this and the addition of short introductions to the three main parts, the American edition is basically the same as the German ones, with this distinction: the texts of the first two parts, here combined into one volume, were originally written and published five years apart.

The identity of author and translator ceased, of course, when it came to the translation of Semper's theoretical manuscripts. The text is at times difficult to understand even for someone whose mother tongue is German. Semper affects, in Pevsner's words, "a literary style which can be horrible." To make it not only understandable but also palatable to the English-speaking reader, long intertwined phrases had to be broken up and simplified. Even emended, the English version is no easy matter to read. This, I am afraid, could not be avoided. It would have been wrong to try to modernize Semper's style. These manuscripts were written in the middle of the last century, and Semper conformed to the more ornate and involved literary style of the time. In addition, he often left the meaning intentionally vague, so a translator would not be justified in deciding arbitrarily on a specific interpretation. Should the reader find one or the other wording odd, it very often sounds odd in German, too. The objective not to indulge in a radical purification but, on the contrary, to retain something of the flavor that his writings convey to the German reader fills in the portrait that I have tried to give of Semper in the first two parts of this book.

Some items that date from Semper's London years—official documents, certain correspondence, manuscripts for lectures—were written in English. This made a deviation from the German edition advisable since I now could cite verbatim what I often had preferred to paraphrase for the benefit of the German reader. To this class of documents belong Semper's London lectures and letters he wrote to Henry Cole. Quoting from these, I did not correct his peculiar and often faulty English.

Furthermore, the manuscripts for his published works as well as for lectures and treatises exist in different versions. As I had done in the German edition, I selected those versions for quotation that best formulated a particular thought or contained some additional information. This explains why at times two quotations that echo one another are in fact not identical. In addition to writing different versions, Semper also frequently revised what he had considered to be the final manuscript. The revisions of the preface and introduction to his "Theory of Formal Beauty" (MSS 178, 179, reproduced at the end of the book) were particularly extensive. I choose for incorporation into the main text those revisions that help to clarify the meaning but, not wishing to burden the text with notes, I did not indicate where a passage in its revised form was adopted in preference to the original one.

The freedom I enjoyed in deciding on the best presentation of the manuscripts, the opportunity I had of updating the main text, of rewording passages where necessary, and of correcting errors—all these fortunate conditions give me hope that the translation of the original edition was worth the long hours spent on it.

Gottfried Semper

I

Semper's Life and Work

The Beginnings: Semper in Dresden, 1834–1849

Semper was offered the post as head of the school of architecture at the Academy of Fine Arts in Dresden when he was thirty-one years old. He had never taught before, nor at the time of his candidacy had he built or published anything. Yet he was finally appointed. No doubt he owed his success in some degree to the strong recommendation of his teacher Franz Christian Gau who, born in Cologne, had moved to France, like many artists of his generation, and had settled in Paris as an architect.[1] Semper had studied under him intermittently for three years, from 1827 to 1830. But the facts that Gau had even been approached by the director of the Academy, Graf Vitzthum, and that his recommendation was taken up so eagerly in Dresden point to another reason for the decision in favor of Semper.

The repercussions of the French revolution of 1830 (which Semper witnessed) brought about the start of a liberal trend in Saxony. Reforms were demanded and at least partly carried out—in the political field by the grant of a constitution drawn up by the chief minister von Lindenau, in the cultural field by a more enlightened policy. This also affected the Academy, as von Lindenau and Graf Vitzthum wished to see the changes necessary for the accommodation of progressive ideas. For this reason they had hoped to persuade Gau to accept the post for himself and, when he declined, had rightly assumed that a student recommended by him would be inspired by French liberal ideas and be well qualified to carry through the much-needed art educational reform. They were not disappointed.

As soon as Semper arrived in Dresden in September 1834, was officially installed in his post, and took the oath as servant to the Crown, he submitted proposals for a reorganization of the teaching method in his department. There were to be no separate classes but instead a close collaboration of all students on one given project.

Another essential feature of his system was close interrelation of theoretical and practical instruction. (Twenty years later he was to apply the same method successfully at the Department of Practical Art in London.) Soon after his arrival he gave his inaugural lecture, which served also as an introduction to a course of lectures on the history of architecture.

There is every reason to suppose that all went well: Yet, when the first excitement about the appointment had passed and Semper became aware of the many duties he was expected to discharge, he was beset by doubts as to whether he was equal to the task. He turned to Gau, who in reply tried to restore his self-confidence, telling him that his predecessor, Joseph Thürmer, far from being superior to Semper, had lacked, like all German architects, Semper's great ability "to accommodate high artistic aspirations . . . to the reality of practical needs."[2] These reassuring words helped to allay his doubts.

Semper received further encouragement, of far more consequence, from an unexpected quarter. During the first months of the year following his appointment he was occupied with completing a design for a large theater, which he had probably been working on when still at home in Altona.[3] The value of such an exercise must have been pointed out to him when on a visit to Berlin the previous year by Graf Brühl, the superintendent of the royal theaters in Berlin, because when the set of designs was completed he sent them to Brühl. Brühl asked for more copies, which he presented to the royal dilettante architect, the crown prince, and to Karl Friedrich Schinkel. Thereupon Schinkel recommended Semper's plan to Brühl's counterpart in Dresden, Wolf Adolph von Lüttichau.[4] Only then, it seems, did the authorities in Dresden fully realize the great talent of the young man whom they had had the good sense to appoint as teacher at the Academy. To us, who take Semper's fame for granted, this circuitous form of recognition seems strange. But it is really quite understandable. Here was a young architect with very little practical experience apart from a small private gallery that he himself belittled as "a hothouse for statues."[5] At the same time there were many experienced architects holding official appointments who would have been, and in some cases were, the obvious choice when it came to the execution of an important building. It is a sign of Semper's superior talent that his project was given preference.

Semper was not content with simply submitting a plan for the Hoftheater and indicating a suitable place for a monument dedicated to the memory of a former king. His plan went far beyond what had been requested of him (figure 2). He incorporated the famous baroque

2
Semper. Design for Zwingerforum, Dresden, 1842. (Semper-Archiv Zurich)

building the Zwinger by making its splendid open-ended courtyard the festive entrance to a wide space, reaching down to the Elbe. The space was flanked on one side by a guardhouse designed by Schinkel, by the baroque Catholic Hofkirche, and by parts of the royal palace, and on the opposite side by his new theater linked to the Zwinger by a low wing containing the orangery. By means of this loose assembly of various buildings (to which at a future date a monumental Picture Gallery would be added) he intended to provide Dresden with a cultural center that was fashioned in spirit though not in form after the urban forum of antiquity, where no building dominated but all related to each other as parts of a total organism. He once told his students that the most difficult but also the most essential part of architecture was to create a harmonious whole, which meant that "the architect must take into account the environment which should, as it were, blend with the building as much as possible. . . . In recent times little attention has been paid in Germany to this aspect of architecture; as an art it has been confined to a beautiful facade planted there without any attempt at integration."[6]

Following these principles, Semper created a masterpiece. The site he chose for the theater clearly indicated an interrelation with the existing structures, but the building itself had an individual character. He achieved this by adapting, though in no way imitating, the festive and rich quality of the surrounding monuments and by consciously rejecting the contrasting stylistic forms then in fashion, a style he had

3
Semper. Hoftheater, Dresden. Watercolor by Christian Gottlob Hammer, ca.
1845. (Potsdam-Sanssouci, Aquarellsammlung no. 4012)

recently described as "meager, dry, severe, and lacking in character."[7]
He "consistently followed the principle of making [the theater's] exterior
appearance dependent throughout on the needs of the interior organization."[8] In this way he achieved a composition of great diversity:
the outer display of the semicircular auditorium with its two bands
of deeply recessed arcaded windows was the dominant feature; rising
above it were the walls and roofs of the upper tiers and the stage
house, flanked by prominent entrance pavilions; the whole was adorned
with a structural display of the then unusual motives of the Italian
Renaissance and by ample figurative decoration as a prelude to the
festive interior decor by three leading French designers, Edouard Des-
pléchin, Jules Dieterle, and Charles Séchan. When the Hoftheater,
Semper's first major work, was opened in 1841 with a performance
of Goethe's *Torquato Tasso*, it made a deep impression and established
his reputation in Germany and abroad (figure 3).
 By then Semper was engaged on another important project, the
design for a new museum. Several locations were proposed. The one
Semper most favored was to place it, a free-standing monumental
building, near the Zwinger where it would form an integral part of

the assembly of buildings, thus lending the forum still greater significance. However, for financial reasons this site was turned down. Reluctantly Semper accepted the final decision to make the Picture Gallery the fourth side of the Zwinger court, although the spatial unity of Zwinger and forum and with it his grand plan of urban development were thereby destroyed.[9]

Semper's position as head of the department of architecture at the Academy and the fact that he had been charged with the planning of important public buildings led to private commissions. In the same year in which work on the theater began, he built two homes for the banker Martin W. Oppenheim: the Villa Rosa, its plan a skillful adaptation of the Palladian villa, and a more substantial town house in the style of a Florentine or Roman Renaissance palazzo.[10] When in 1837 the Jews in Dresden were allowed to erect their own synagogue, it was no doubt through Oppenheim, who was Jewish, that Semper's design was accepted. The building was centrally planned, left plain except for a few Romanesque features.[11] When he took part in a competition for a synagogue in Paris ten years later, he repeated the plan but gave the exterior a much richer "Byzantine" decoration, as he called it. In view of the interest Semper was later to take in industrial art, it is worth noting that he designed the furnishings and interior decoration of the Oppenheim houses and Dresden synagogue as well as the furniture of the theater.

Within less than a decade the name of the inexperienced young professor had become well known in Germany and abroad. When the duke of Mecklenburg decided in 1843 to have his medieval castle restored and partly rebuilt, he asked Semper to submit plans. Although in the end they were not accepted, the extensive project, on which Semper spent considerable time, is of interest not least because it gave him the opportunity to lay down in a memorandum his remarkably advanced ideas on the principles that should guide restorations of ancient buildings. Read in connection with the views expressed by his contemporary Viollet-le-Duc they are especially interesting.[12]

It was natural that Semper, a native of Altona, was invited to compete in planning the rebuilding of Hamburg, in great part destroyed by fire in 1842. Again he saw as his task the integration of the main buildings, the town hall, and the church into one organic whole with the provision of new open spaces, streets, and living quarters.[13] He did not win. Even more frustrating were, two years later, the circumstances connected with the competition for the rebuilding of the church of St. Nicholas in Hamburg, a sad story that will be related in more detail below in "Semper's Position on the Gothic."

In spite of these failures, Semper must have been well satisfied with life. As the architect in charge of a building program that would give new life to Dresden, he had become a respected member of the community; his teaching went well, and there was a prospect of his lectures being published; more important still, a splendid publication about the Hoftheater was already in the press. In 1835 he had married Bertha Thimig, seven years younger, who at times, it seems, had a steadying influence on his rather erratic temper. With his growing family he had settled down to an apparently comfortable life. But there was a cloud on the horizon—the political situation. The liberal trend that had brought Semper to his position proved to be short lived. The men who had set their hopes on reform either accepted the fact of their waning influence or withdrew from the political stage altogether. This Semper could not do. For him political and professional attitudes were closely linked, one the expression of the other. After a revolution rocked the monarchy in Berlin in March 1848 and storm clouds began to threaten Dresden, Semper openly joined the opposition forces that prepared to fight reaction. In May 1849 the storm broke loose. The ensuing uprising ended in the defeat of the democratic forces—and brought the most successful and productive phase of Semper's life to an abrupt end.

In Exile: Semper in Paris and London, 1849–1855

Flight from Dresden and Stay in Paris, 1849–1850

On May 9, 1849, after a six-day battle, the uprising in Dresden collapsed and Semper fled. The consequences were catastrophic. His family life broke up, his career was in ruins, and work as an architect was impossible for many years—he had gambled away almost everything. How deeply had he been involved in the struggle?

Semper never made a secret of his political beliefs. As a committed republican and supporter of the radical wing of the bourgeois opposition,[1] he sided openly with the cause of the revolutionaries. "When the uprising broke out," he wrote later to a friend in New York, "I found it impossible to deny my republican convictions."[2] In his first letter after his flight he declared categorically to his brother Karl, "Everybody must know what his sense of duty demands of him and must act accordingly." Proud to have stood up wholeheartedly for the cause, he despised the noncommital attitude of the better-educated classes "who, even when taking sides, were not willing to sacrifice anything for their party." Still under the influence of the exciting battle that had taken place only a few days before, he declared, "I feel free of blame." He also freely admitted instantly obeying an order to build a barricade "in submission to a power that had to demand unconditional obedience if it was to win the battle in which it was involved."[3] He was probably referring to the barricade erected in front of his own house. Later it was testified, not only by those who had fought on Semper's side, that the high quality of the main barricades was due to his expert instructions.[4] Richard Wagner also mentioned that Semper told him of his concern about the "extremely faulty construction" of the first barricades, and that on Wagner's advice Semper joined the defense committee and thus became authorized to safeguard the places of importance.[5] He carried out his duties so conscientiously that, according to a report by a Prussian officer, the barricades of the inner city were of a quality probably never before encountered in street fighting; they could not be taken by storm but only by being outmaneuvered.[6] Moreover, according to later testimony, Semper had urged young people of the Technical Legion to join the fight and before the uprising had attended preparatory talks at the home of Wagner, as one of the leaders confessed at the trial.[7]

Apart from his political response to the uprising, Semper was undoubtedly attracted by its strategical opportunities. When, at age twenty, he had chosen mathematics as his main field of study, he had considered directing these studies toward military science. This special interest always remained alive in him. During the exciting days of March 1848, when he heard of the armed uprising in his native Holstein, which would inevitably lead to war with Denmark, he had given his brother Karl advice about the necessary defensive measures—first for the whole province and then, in great detail street by street, for Altona. "Our corner on Prinzenstrasse," he remarked finally, "is a critical point. The weakest part of this position is the area around the Jewish Cemetery from where we can reasonably expect an attack by the troops from outside. I hope that it will not come to this extreme. But should it come to this, you must resist. Nowadays there is no other way."[8] If he could be intensely alarmed about the defense of a country hundreds of miles away, how much stronger must have been his reaction when, in a city where he had settled for fifteen years, conflict arose over a cause that affected him as deeply as the pressing political situation at home. The letter is equally revealing in another respect: in an explosive situation, driven to fateful activity, Semper would intervene without consulting others, least of all his wife. He wanted his brother to know that he did not tell Bertha about the events in Altona "so as not to frighten her, but also to be saved from unnecessary counterarguments, etc., etc., should I suddenly decide to take action."

All the evidence indicates that Semper helped plan and carry out the uprising, though not as a leader. He had every reason to flee.[9] The first days of flight were full of dangers, but also of lucky escapes. A warrant for his arrest, issued on May 14, made his situation dangerous as long as he remained in Saxony or in territory controlled by Prussia.[10] He succeeded in getting in touch with his brothers, whom he asked for money. A middleman informed one of them on May 29 that "H.S."—he did not dare write Herr Semper—"arrived safely in Heidelberg."[11] After a democratic government rose to power during the first days of May, Baden became "the refuge of the German revolution" where the "leaders of the uprising in Saxony . . . met again."[12] On May 30 Semper arrived in the capital, Karlsruhe.

Hardly four weeks had passed since the fateful step that cost him so much. At the time he had not thought of the consequences. "But God knows I then felt a noble emotion that I could not resist," was the explanation he gave to Bertha for his seemingly incomprehensible act.[13] In the politically congenial climate of the Badensic democracy, he believed that this feeling had been justified. "If I were twenty years younger, had no wife and six children, and were rich, you all would have heard more of me."[14] But as things were, he now refused an offer to join the resistance.[15] He restrained within the bounds of reason his political interest, which so recently an overpowering impulse had burst open into frantic activity. For him the events of those six days did not mean the unforgivable failure of a revolutionary act, which must be repeated until it succeeded; just as for the majority of the bourgeois democrats and the republicans of 1848, so for Semper the uprising was little more than an extreme political discussion after which one would take up again one's professional work.

Immediately after his arrival in Karlsruhe Semper asked Karl: "Write to my wife to request Herr Architect Krüger to collect everything that relates to my lectures on architecture, partly in my own hand, partly copied by others, to be found on my desk; he should make a parcel of it so that I can eventually receive it. I want to make good a promise I gave a long time ago and turn the collected material into a book." There followed exact instructions of what he wanted to receive: "1. several papers inside a blue envelope. The latter, the envelope, can be recognized by a large ink blot that covers the whole page. 2. two exercise books about houses in my own hand. 3. several exercise books written by others lying on my desk. 4. several finished drawings. . . . They are prepared for woodcuts. Some of these drawings (tracings from the publication on Nineveh) are in one of the drawers of my bookcase."[16] To get hold of these papers quickly mattered so much to him that, a few days later from Strasbourg, he asked his colleague and former pupil Bernhard Krüger directly to do him this favor. In particular the envelope with the ink blot was important, for it contained letters to his publisher, Eduard Vieweg.[17]

Upon his arrival a week later in Paris, Semper reminded Karl of the request made in his previous letter "because it matters a great deal to me to have a serious occupation."[18] A serious occupation—this had to do with architecture, not with politics. He felt the same way as his comrade-in-arms on the barricade, Wagner, who about this time assured Liszt that he would never again get involved in a political catastrophe, adding, as if freed from a nightmare: "What I am glad about and what I can promise is that, striving hard, I have become an artist again."[19] Although Semper did not have Wagner's resilience and optimism, he surely shared with him the relief of being able to do intellectual work again.

His reaction to the warrant for his arrest is also significant. Semper had fought the power of reactionary authority, not the state, whose firm foundation in bourgeois society and bourgeois ethos he endorsed. That he, professor at the Dresden Academy, was on the wanted list seemed to him outrageous and wounded his pride. When he suggested to Vieweg "Letters of an Outlaw" ("Briefe eines Geächteten") as the title of a pamphlet, he may have chosen the word in defiance of the reactionary forces; however, the way in which he talked in letters home about himself as the "outlaw," makes it obvious that he felt being outlawed was a disgrace and cruel fate, not an honor. From then on he suffered from the feeling of being an outcast, deserted by everybody.[20]

After a short stay in Karlsruhe Semper traveled into Alsace and spent a few days in Strasbourg. On June 6 he left for Paris in a stagecoach, high up on an uncovered seat, pinned down between two recruits, exposed during the day to heat, and to storm and cold during the night—an agonizing journey that lasted two and a half days and two nights.[21] He probably decided to go to Paris when he and his comrades realized that reactionary forces would gain the upper hand in Germany. Paris was an obvious choice: as a young man he had worked there under Jakob Ignaz Hittorf and Gau and was sure of being welcomed with open arms, above all by Gau with whom he had always kept in contact, but also by the architect and designer Léon Feuchère and by Desplechin, Séchan, and Dieterle, who, ever since the commission for the interior decoration for the Dresden Hoftheater, were not only obliged to him but had become fast friends.[22]

Yet once in Paris he became acutely aware of being an exile; only now did he recover his senses. He—who after his successful flight had written to Bertha pretending, or possibly believing, that "this thorough shock of our situation may be our greatest blessing" because he had started "to become lazy"; who at the end of the same letter had exclaimed, "Away from here and let us set sail for America"—now became subdued and sighed, "Now *you* can console me, because I am really getting quite scared."[23] His main worry, which weighed heavily on him, was to build new life and to reunite his family.

He thought of Paris as only as interim stop. Like many men of 1848 he was eager to leave behind him a Europe that politically had become hateful to him, and to make a fresh start in the New World where "not only does the stigma that sticks to an exile in all European countries not exist, but one even can be sure of arousing special sympathy."[24] He seemed determined to carry out his plan, to burn his bridges behind him. "If I could raise enough money . . . to pay for the journey to America, then I would try it over there. I can never return to Dresden, and there is nothing for me in Paris either."[25]

Bertha on the other hand did everything to make a return to Dresden possible. When she wrote in her first letter after Semper had fled that she intended to make an approach in high quarters on his behalf, he did not want to have anything to do with it. "I do not want to owe my freedom to special considerations and His Majesty's clemency. Nothing can make me disown my party and my faith . . . in what light would I be seen by my fellow sufferers. . . . Either acquittal or voluntary banishment forever!"[26] But weeks later, when she blamed him bitterly for his irresponsible behavior during the uprising, heedless of the consequences and indifferent to the destruction of their family life, Semper felt guilty and declared his willingness to return to Dresden for her sake. "In this respect I retract the declaration I made in my last letter, I retract it and am willing to submit to the humiliations of the victorious party as far as my honor allows, since you regard it as a test and proof of my love for you."[27]

The secretary of the Academy, consulted by Bertha, was of the opinion that Semper should submit a petition to the king of Saxony in which he should "admit his wrong and ask for pardon."[28] Semper was willing to approach the king, but not to ask for clemency. In his petition he speaks first of his political convictions—the idea of a united strong fatherland—of the shock of seeing all the beautiful expectations of a "great national future vanish one after the other"; stresses, without going into details, his subordinate role in the street fighting; and ends with the "most humble plea" not to look upon his "absenting himself as a voluntary banishment arising from a self-imposed judgment, but rather to consent most graciously to my conducting my own defense from abroad, as well as to graciously issue a command to the effect that the replacement of my post as professor . . . and of my office as architect of the new museum be deferred until after a judiciary verdict."[29] The petition was indeed not a plea for clemency, yet Semper feared that it was inconsistent with his passionately held convictions and that it could easily lead to suspicions and dangerous animosity on the part of his fellow sufferers.[30] Hardly had he sent off the letter to Bertha when he regretted it and asked her to hold it back.[31] But she had already passed it on to the court's minister, Zenker.[32] As Semper had predicted, "the step proved completely useless."

He had agreed to the petition only for Bertha's sake. This did not mean, however, that in his heart he did not count on reinstatement through his own rehabilitation or a general amnesty. It was therefore of the greatest importance to make sure that there were no new appointments. Even before there had been thought of a petition, he had asked Krüger to make inquiries of the secretary of the Academy: "I am completely in the dark about my situation . . . I should very much like to know whether I could still hope or should give up everything . . . especially with regard to my professorship."[33] At the same time, Gau tried to intercede on his behalf with Johann Gottlob von Quandt, collector, patron of the arts, and member of the academic council.[34] Semper himself decided to approach privy councillor H. W. Schulz directly. "Maybe the step was risky," he told one of his brothers. "I have somehow provoked a decision that would make my return forever impossible—but the present state of uncertainty is unbearable."[35] Only when Quandt bluntly refused to mediate and Schulz did not respond at all, did Semper send to Bertha his petition to the king.

A few days later Schulz's reply arrived, having been merely accidentally delayed. In contrast to von Quandt, Schulz was sympathetic and full of understanding for Semper's unfortunate situation, willing to help wherever he could, although he had to admit that "all that I have been able to do for you is nothing more than so far preventing the new appointment to your post by making arrangements for a substitute at the Academy as well as at the building site of the museum." He explained that he had tried to find out at court something about the reaction to Semper's petition and generally about the court's attitude toward him and his guilt—all in vain. He could not advise him to return to Dresden; the penal sentence would be more severe against him, a servant of the Crown, than against an ordinary fighter on the barricades. Although he did not want to dash Semper's hope for a return following an amnesty, he strongly advised him that should there be a chance for "a pursuit commensurate with your talent, you should seize it energetically."[36]

Undoubtedly this friendly yet realistic advice made it easier for Semper to sever his emotional ties to Dresden. At about this time he wrote to his mother: "I cannot get used to the idea of ever returning to the old situation again. . . . Only a complete rehabilitation would, as it were, oblige me to take up my old situation, though only for the present. . . . I am seriously thinking of letting my family come and turning my back on Dresden forever . . . it would at present even upset me, should I have to go back to Dresden immediately."[37] In spite of his high-spirited tone it was a long time before he definitely ruled out the possibility of a return. Again and again he hoped for an amnesty that would end his distressing life in exile. Even as late as November, hearing that he might be included in a forthcoming amnesty, he asked Bertha to take certain steps that would effectively delay "a decisive new appointment."[38] But in the end he realized how futile these hopes were, and at midnight of the last day of this fateful year 1849 he could write to his mother, "I have given up all my hopes for Dresden," and two months later to Vieweg, "I do not think any more about a return to Dresden. And that is that!"[39] When Bertha urged him in March to submit a petition for a pardon, he firmly rejected it: "After they have robbed me of everything, I should ask for mercy? You cannot want that. It is impossible."[40]

Thus Dresden was barred to him. A successor would teach at the Academy, someone else would finish the building of the Picture Gallery. Yet one work remained that in fact he could do better in Paris than in Dresden—writing his long-planned book, "Gebäudelehre" (Theory of Building Types). His 1844 contract with the publishing firm Vieweg was his only remaining asset, the only possibility for income by his own effort; though only just enough to cover his most urgent expenses for a while, with luck at least this little sum would soon be available. Apart from the wish to take up his profession again, financial need had been another reason that he had insisted from Karlsruhe that his papers be dispatched as quickly as possible.

Vieweg's negotiations with Semper had started in the summer of 1843. At first the intention had been nothing more than a revised edition of David Gilly's *Handbuch der Landwirtschaft*, but Semper suggested a larger scheme; this led in August of the following year to a contract by which Semper agreed to hand in, for a sum of 1500 guldens and in a comparatively short time, an original work, "Die Lehre der Gebäude."[41]

Although Semper had found in Vieweg a publisher who showed understanding for his ideas, which were, as Vieweg stressed after a crucial meeting in January 1844, "in accordance with [my] own"; a publisher who admired Semper as "one of the most intelligent and foremost living architects," convinced that no other German architect was as competent for literary work; a publisher prepared to start printing as soon as possible ("I am dying to read the first Mss."); and a publisher who constantly encouraged him to make a beginning— in spite of all these favorable circumstances, for almost five years from the signing of the contract, Semper continually put off starting to write.[42]

Once in Paris, Semper sent Vieweg a long letter to make sure that the publisher still stood by the contract in spite of the delay, for which he pleaded guilty.[43] Vieweg reassured him and agreed with him that what mattered now was to prevent his name from being forgotten. This, Vieweg argued, Semper could achieve only through writings, since as an architect he was forced to inactivity. "The *Theater* [the publication about the Hoftheater] should be published as soon as possible, and it will be up to you to make it possible for me to have 'Lehre der Gebäude' follow quickly." He would also be willing to take up Semper's suggestion to publish his collected thoughts on art and politics, the "Briefe eines Geächteten," "provided that it does not interfere with your more serious work, 'Lehre der Gebäude.' " As a first step Semper should draft some of these letters, which would make it possible for Vieweg to find a correspondent as Semper had requested. "And now, my dear friend," he ended, "I beg of you to tell me in detail, openly and without reservation, about the circumstances that caught you in this wretched uprising, about the extent of your involvement, and, honestly and without being sanguine, the hopes you may perhaps have of coming to a reconciliation with Dresden. You are in need of a friend—and I offer myself as one." Semper should tell him everything, what could vindicate him and also what incriminated him. "I shall then consider what should be done and will, if I can see the slightest glimmer of hope of reconciling you with the future, go to Dresden myself, intervene for you with the ministers, with the king, and with Prince Johann."[44]

Semper must have supplied this information because in his next letter Vieweg reported that his inquiries in Dresden had so far not been answered, but that immediately after publication of the book on the theater he personally would "take further steps." No more mention is made of "Briefe eines Geächteten," but instead Vieweg was willing to publish Semper's translation of a French edition of an ancient text.[45]

Nothing came of either project: Semper never wrote drafts for the "Briefe," and he began but never finished the translation of François Mazois's *Le Palais de Scaurus*.[46] He gave them up for good reason: by the middle of July his papers from home arrived at last. Now he was in possession of the manuscripts and lecture notes for "Gebäudelehre," as well as a number of exercise books containing his lectures in detail as recorded by different students. All this material was to be turned into a comprehensive book. He started at once but soon realized that if he wanted to obtain his fee soon, he had to use every available moment of his spare time, which was at best limited because of his need to earn a living.[47]

It was indeed a vast program that he had set himself: A survey of all possible building types, arranged into eleven groups. To give an idea of the ambitious scope of "Vergleichende Baulehre" (Comparative Building Theory, as the title read from now on) here are some of the many building types with which Semper wanted to deal "according to different epochs": first, dwellings, to be followed by temples, churches, mosques, synagogues; schools, libraries, museums; hospitals, orphanages, hostels; post offices, market halls, stock exchanges; town halls, parliaments, archives; law courts, police stations, prisons; fortresses, arsenals, barracks; triumphal arches, monuments, tombs; theaters, concert halls; finally, towns and planning new quarters.

In the main preface he explained his aim:[48] while many books treated architecture from a philosophical or historical point of view, such as aesthetics or the history of architecture, or dealt only with specific aspects, such as dwellings for town or country, or were treatises on building materials or design, until now there existed no work that showed "the combined effect of all actual or potential factors of an intellectual or material kind in the creation of architectural works of art."[49] In this connection he gave a critical survey of the different trends in contemporary architecture—"the eclectic school," "schematism," "the dynamic-technical trend"—a classification that from then on repeatedly appeared in his writings until finally in *Der Stil* it was crystallized into distinct groups. He saw as his task "to pursue the development of architecture and the embodiment of its basic principles, also to trace the law hidden under the artistic covering back to its simplest expression."[50] This sentence echoes the views on architecture that he had set out in 1843 in his first letter to Vieweg, a copy of which he now found in the "envelope with the ink blot."[51] He incorporated almost verbatim the main passages of this letter into the last page of the preface, which he wrote only a few days after receiving his papers.[52]

After the preface comes the section on dwellings, the first of the eleven groups. In the introductory paragraphs, which again repeat almost verbatim the text of lectures given in Dresden, he justified the unusual arrangement of the text. He would begin with dwellings and not with buildings consecrated to religious service because the dwelling was "the simplest and most basic form within the sphere of architecture." In the next part, which takes up the "differences in the basic idea of the dwelling," he still kept to the Dresden lectures but broadened them by introducing the basic elements of architecture—fence, roof, and hearth. He also stressed the value of the comparative method. He did not finish the third part about "the dwellings of the Assyrians, Chaldeans, Medes, and Persians"; the manuscript breaks off in the middle.[53]

This, then, was the "serious occupation" he had longed for. Yet it could not resolve his grave situation. Weeks grew into months, and there was no position in sight, although he had followed up any chance that presented itself. Soon after his arrival in Paris in June 1849, he had asked a friend in Basel, the painter Adolph Mende, what prospects might exist for him in Switzerland.[54] A few weeks later he asked Reichsminister August Jochmus, whom he knew from his travels in Greece, to let him have "letters of recommendation for the Orient, perhaps Constantinople, Athens, or Alexandria" because he had in mind "to seek refuge in these parts of the world."[55] He also sent an application to the Greek government for an appointment and had applied for a post as professor of fine arts at the University of Bern.[56] All these attempts, certainly undertaken with high expectations, came to nothing. Then, by the end of September, the first apparently well-founded prospect appeared: G. H. Geill, a Belgian architect who had been working at the Picture Gallery in Dresden, informed him that a post as director of the Academy of Drawing in Ghent was being advertised and advised him to come and present himself. Semper left Paris on October 20. A month later he was back, disappointed and deeply hurt by the way he had been treated. The journey had been a complete fiasco. "Herr Geill had recklessly persuaded me to go there and has done hardly anything for me. He asked me once for dinner and introduced me to a boorish Flemish gentleman who was not interested in me at all." Moreover, Semper became seriously ill in Brussels and ran into trouble with the police.[57]

Shortly before leaving for Ghent he had received a letter from a stranger. A Dr. Friedrich Krause, headmaster of a boys' school in Dresden, told him in words of warm and sincere sympathy that, convinced Semper needed help and encouragement, he had organized a collection among people who were well disposed toward him. Semper, deeply touched by this friendly and brave gesture, expressed his gratitude and accepted the money, though only as a loan.[58] This contact grew into a friendship that lasted over many years. Dr. Krause helped in any way that he could, above all by an offer to accept in his school the two elder sons on terms that saved Semper and Bertha much worry. In the future, whenever they were faced with an important decision, they could rely on Dr. Krause's well-considered advice.[59]

When Dr. Krause sent the money he told Semper that, through a personal connection, he might be able to help him to some employment in England. In the next letter he mentioned the name of his English acquaintance, which he had withheld so far because he knew that "at some time you have been his opponent." It was William Lindley whose plan for the rebuilding of Hamburg, destroyed by fire in 1842, Semper had as member of the adjudicating commission violently opposed. In order to forstall Semper's feeling of awkward embarrassment, Dr. Krause cited a letter from Lindley: "The difference of opinion about the rebuilding of this city can have no effect upon my mind." Besides, Lindley was really "a good man through and through and politically of your opinion." It seems, however, that in practical terms Lindley had nothing to suggest except that Semper "could work in London under an architect"; in case this was of interest to Semper, he would gladly put letters of recommendation at his disposal.[60] Writing to his mother, Semper assured her that to be subordinated to another architect would not scare him but that "without a firm prospect he would not dare to cross the Channel."[61]

This prospect seemed to materialize when at the beginning of the following year 1850, his friend Dieterle recommended him as a highly qualified draftsman to a Mr. Graham who was the owner of a well-known London firm of interior decorators. "I have a good chance for private employment in London," Semper wrote on February 3 to Krüger and asked him to send "sketches by his own hand for the Theater and the Palais of Herr Oppenheim . . . above all the drawing for the sideboard . . . but also for the colored ceilings as well as the sections of the halls of this house. . . . Of the Theater I want to have all the decorations in my own hand that can still be found, for instance the main ceiling, those of the foyers of the entrance halls, of the proscenium, etc. . . . also the best sketches from Pompeii . . . for instance, the blue room, the yellow room, etc." He would submit all these drawings together with a "sample drawing of an interior decoration and furnishing." Speed was necessary—"within four weeks all must be decided."[62]

Now, when he seemed to have a chance in London, Semper turned to Lindley for advice. Lindley's answer was delayed by his temporary absence from Hamburg until April—by which time this so eagerly seized offer, like so many projects before, had "dissolved like a phantom into thin air."[63] Lindley took the opportunity to assure Semper that their quarrel had not been personal: "I believe both of us as artists can in every respect be tolerant." He then gave a detailed and well-considered account of English conditions and pointed out the difficulties that Semper would encounter should he decide to move to England. In his opinion, in spite of his talent Semper would "have to overcome two big obstacles—ignorance of English business practice, and political prejudices. The well-off architects and artists as well as others are, with few exceptions, averse to all revolutions or anything akin to them; unfortunately, in England, as anywhere else, most people are not educated enough to be as tolerant in political as they are in religious matters. Your talent will be recognized, but one will feel more at ease with conforming though less gifted colleagues. What would be in this regard an advantage for you in North America would in England count against you."[64] Discouraging words, which Semper certainly had not forgotten when six months later he was faced with a momentous decision, and which he may also have remembered later in London at a time when, deeply depressed, he mistrusted other people's motives.

While he was working on the sample drawings for Graham, Wagner arrived in Paris; his report about Zurich impressed Semper. "I have aroused in him a new longing for Switzerland, specially for Zurich," Wagner wrote to his friend Jakob Sulzer, Staatsschreiber of the Zurich canton. "Would it be possible to offer him a post at the University with a salary even if for the time being only a small one? He has refused offers from England because they would make him too dependent on others."[65] Sulzer's reply must have been negative. Still, Semper did not give up the idea of settling somewhere in Switzerland, mainly because there would be no language difficulties, not even in the French part; though he could understand English, he did not speak it.[66] The reports he received from old friends in Switzerland were not encouraging.[67] An architect with whom he had studied under Gau, Rudolf von Stürler, regretted that the chances for political exiles had worsened since the last election. Semper's troublesome position of being on the wanted list also prevented him from applying to his native Altona for the post of town architect that had been advertised at the beginning of the year, however tempting it had been.[68] Hermann Köchly, a comrade in the Dresden uprising whom Semper had approached about his chances in Geneva, was being told officially that "there were already many architects in Geneva and . . . a chance of success existed only for an architect who would buy large parts of land around the bastions and build houses there on speculation."[69]

Of course, Semper was also trying to find a job in Paris. His French friends, much concerned about his misfortune, did all they could to ease his plight. Dieterle and later Séchan let him stay with them, gave him the opportunity to participate in their decorative designs, helped him to smaller commissions, and passed inquiries on to him. Wagner met Semper "in Desplechin's hospitable home, where he tried to make his disturbed life bearable with minor artistic work."[70] When the international competition for the building of the Great Exhibition of the Works of Industry of All Nations in London was announced, Semper obtained letters of introduction to an influential member of the French commission. Whether Semper took part in the competition is not known—if he did, he shared the fate of the 245 contestants whose designs were rejected without exception.[71]

Dieterle and Séchan had been able to help Semper when they received a commission for a decoration for the Paris Opera. They handed the design for a perspective view of an Egyptian town on to him, and he proudly told Bertha that "it had been accepted and must now be finished at all speed."[72] How eagerly he longed for a turn for the better is proven by the splendid plans for the future that such a modest job made him dream of. "It is possible," he made himself believe, "that this temporary collaboration will develop into a close business connection, more honorable and more profitable for me," that eventually he would "rise to a position of an associé" by passing on to the partnership commissions which had been given to him personally.[73] In late 1849 he wrote more confidently to Bertha than for a long time: "I begin to hope that in time I might be able to start a modest existence here. I am fairly busy and even have prospects for substantial commissions. Literary work would be sufficient to keep me occupied all the time. But it is badly paid. . . . Anyway, I have more courage since I have plenty of work."[74]

The "prospects for substantial commissions" may refer to an introduction to Count Larochefoucault-Liancourt, who around this time "more or less" promised to commission an extension to his chateau, a promise that made him hope to gain a footing in France as an architect. But he had learned to be skeptical, knowing full well that until spring, when the work was due to start, the count could change his mind "ten times over." This was in fact what happened.[75]

Toward the end of his stay in Paris, in the late summer of 1850, another member of the French aristocracy approached him. The Comtesse de Villeneuve sought his advice about the decoration of a small salon in her chateau at Boil-le-Roi. He sent two designs, and the work was carried out according to them as far as can be judged from the correspondence.[76]

Real prospects for a commission turned up when the Jewish community of Paris decided to build a new synagogue. Semper had heard of this project soon after his arrival in Paris. The banker Oppenheim, his former patron, sent him a letter of introduction to Baron de Roth-

4
Semper. Design for synagogue, Paris, 1850, detail. (Semper-Archiv Zurich)

schild who in turn recommended him to the president of the con-
gregation.[77] To his disappointment Semper had discovered that only
a renovation of the old synagogue was wanted and that an architect
had already been appointed. In March 1850, however, he heard quite
by chance that the members of the community had changed their
minds and that they now wanted a completely new synagogue built
at a different site. The executive, his "patron," promised to propose
him as second competing architect; he also let him know that "the
council was going to inquire from the Dresden community whether
their synagogue was solid and well planned." Semper wrote at once
to Dresden requesting that, with the help of his Jewish student Si-
monsohn, care be taken "that the report will be . . . favorable and that
above all the misfortune with the cracks is not brought up, which
really was not my fault but that of the executive for whom the house
could not be light and cheap enough"—a somewhat devious, but
under the circumstances pardonable, request.[78] He submitted a design
(figure 4).[79] A few weeks later he was pessimistic: "With the synagogue
I face a tough competition, and it is hardly reasonable to count on
it."[80] Indeed, this well-founded hope also came to nothing. The synagogue was not built until the 1860s, and to another design.[81]

The misery of his exile—separation from his family, financial worries, repeated failures after high expectations—weighed heavily on Semper. In the first year, and more so in the following years, he wavered between deep despair and bold determination to assert himself. Arriving in Paris, he was so downcast that he wrote to Bertha: "The best would be to leave this world"; but a few weeks later he wrote home almost as if to encourage himself and to keep his family's spirits up: "I cannot despair, this mood is contrary to my nature; although there are no prospects in sight, I still feel confident that all will turn out better than we fear."[82] Shortly afterward he was fainthearted and so desperate that he finished the letter to his mother about the planned new synagogue with these words: "I have no confidence in myself and my luck anymore."[83] The useless journey to Ghent, his undignified treatment there, made everything look black; only other people's confidence could help him through this slough of despair. "Oh Bertha," he sighed after his return from Belgium, "if you knew how all this hurts, how sick I am at heart—but, courage!—as you say, it will all get better."[84] Later he again encouraged her, told her that he was used to negative answers, but "all the same one must not leave anything untried and not lose heart." The vague prospect of an academic post in Geneva made him dream: "How wonderful it would be, if we could lead an honorable life in beautiful Switzerland. . . . I begin . . . to believe that my lucky star rises again."[85] Despondency and exuberance, reasonableness and self-deception, followed in quick succession.

The safest thing was still his literary work; it was also a tempting escape from the awful present. But even here a wave of depressions from which he could not free himself made it difficult for him to concentrate on historical and seemingly irrelevant problems. Thus to Bertha in November 1849: "As soon as I am alone, I fall back into my gloomy suffering that makes mental work difficult, and yet so much depends now on my staying power."[86]

At times work on "Vergleichende Baulehre" became an unbearable burden, seemed an encroachment on his time. Once, not having heard from Vieweg, he declared: "I would be quite pleased should he not reply. Then I would be free of any obligation concerning the book which will tie me to Europe for quite some time."[87]

When he wrote this, in March 1850, he had not touched the manuscript for many weeks. His time had been taken up by other work, which he hoped each time might lead to a permanent rewarding occupation. "My literary work," he had written at the beginning of the new year, "has been interrupted for many months because of my journey to Belgium and a commission for the Opera. I hope soon to be able to start again. But I do not have the necessary peace and leisure, nor the inner security that is more necessary for a man of practice when dealing with unwonted academic work than when engaged on work of his own art."[88] By the end of January he was free enough to "think about the long-neglected work for Vieweg."[89] But then he had to work full steam on the order from Jackson & Graham, so that February passed before he could take up writing for Vieweg again.

There was another reason for the delay, a reason that led him to discard all he had written so far or, at least, to revise it thoroughly. In Dresden he had already learned, mainly through a detailed article in the *Allgemeine Bauzeitung*, about the exciting excavations carried out by Botta in Khorsabad and Layard in Nimrud, and he had seen the first part of Botta's book on Nineveh.[90] Yet it was a very different experience to stand in front of the originals. "I live like a hermit," he wrote to Krüger in August 1849, "and come to Paris only to study either in the Louvre or the Library"; and a short time later to Johann Andreas Romberg, publisher and editor of the *Zeitschrift für praktisches Bauwesen*: "I have been granted special admittance to the collections of the Louvre and even to those treasures that are hidden and inaccessible to the public because I was lucky enough to get to know the director, who has been very friendly toward me."[91]

Semper was greatly impressed by the Assyrian reliefs in the Louvre as well as by the editions of Botta, Layard, and Costa, the final parts of which appeared during the year 1849. Thus, in February 1850 he gave Vieweg two reasons for the delay: first "the wretched fact that I have to earn my living" and second that "the works by Botta, Costa, and by Layard on Assyria and Persia and by von Lassen on India were sufficiently ready only a few weeks ago for me to use them properly. I had to revise the first part on Assyria, Babylon, Persia, and India completely."[92]

These excuses were indeed true, but for the moment they served the purpose only of asking Vieweg for an advance and financial assistance to buy blocks for woodcuts. Three weeks later Vieweg agreed to send payments, "though only from time to time," and also authorized Semper to buy blocks although he doubted whether he could find suitable ones:

Single picturesque views of castles may occasionally be not out of place but, for God's sake, beware not to lose the practical direction; we must not aim at a picture book. Let us begin; send me the manuscript, drawings, and blocks for a definite part, and you will not be short of further payments.

But the thing must, for your own sake, commence well and make steady
progress. Therefore undertake the completion of one part because nothing
is achieved with only the preparatory work. You are now engaged for almost
a year on these preparatory works and those are again only a revision of
your older drafts. . . . Do not take me as selfish, because I am not and I
believe I can serve you best in this way. . . . Only, for God's sake, a beginning
first, then your courage and enthusiasm will revive![93]

Perhaps courage and enthusiasm did revive—anyway, two months
later Semper sent off a bulky manuscript: 380 tightly written pages;
a preface and a long introduction followed by seventeen chapters
dealing with dwellings in ancient Mesopotamia, China, India, and
Egypt.[94] He had difficulties with the preface; he had "already revised
it twice" and eventually decided not to trouble with it any more and
to take it up again only at the very end.[95] The preface was essentially
the same as the one written a year before; only the beginning was
new. It sets out his basic attitude toward "architectural science," which
he believed had reached a point in its development where—like any
other science—it would have to pass from the stage of analysis to that
of synthesis. He hoped that his treatise would at least stimulate this
development. What was new in the text was a precise formulation of
the "four elements of the earliest art of building—the roof, earthwork,
enclosure, and, as the spiritual center of the whole, the social hearth"—
"the embryo of every social institution." Searching for the basic elements (*Urelemente*) was a new direction in his theory of art, evident
too in the chapters on dwellings. Above all, stimulated by the newly
found Assyrian reliefs, he gave his first exposition of his "Bekleidungstheorie," or "theory of cladding," which from then on became
an increasingly important part of his architectural theory, until it finally
assumed a central position in *Der Stil*. The whole manuscript, including
the space estimated for the illustrations, when printed would have
come to about twelve sections out of the sixty to seventy envisaged
for the total work. Much remained to be done.

At least he was freed from the pressure of this work, if only temporarily. In all other respects, nothing had changed; everything seemed
as hopeless as ever. "I really do not know what will become of me,"
he complained in the same letter in which he announced the dispatch
of the manuscript to Vieweg. One way to escape this misery remained:
emigration to America. For a long time he shied away from this
decisive step. The question of money came into it of course, but with
the backing of his brothers and sisters this was not crucial. They were
ready to let him have a loan large enough to cover the journey, initial
living expenses, assistance for his family left behind, and the purchase

of books for a school of architecture he was planning to start over there.[96] The real difficulty was himself, his indecision. He hoped from one prospect to the next that they might lead to something permanent, that he would be spared the hardship of being transplanted into a completely unknown, even though free, country. Yet with every new failure he fell back again on this "extreme step"; he rejected arguments against emigration as invalid, only to have doubts immediately afterward, arguing that "in view of the young children such a decision would be risky." Responsibility for wife and children made it twice as hard for him to come to a decision. "Bertha seems almost rooted in Dresden," he complained in July 1849. "She has an aversion to America, so that I may have to give up this plan."[97] Nevertheless, he told friends and acquaintances that he thought about emigrating to America; most of them encouraged him, and some regretted losing him but did not dissuade him. For all sides he received letters of recommendation. He asked a former pupil, Wilhelm Heine, who had also fled to Paris and in the summer of 1849 emigrated to America, about the opportunities over there.[98] Heine's report that he and his friends "after a short time had found plenty of work" made him more and more inclined to think seriously about emigrating.[99] "Particularly since the news . . . that my professorship has already been assigned to Nicolai," he wrote to Bertha in March 1850, "all my thoughts are again turned toward America whence, with God's help, I intend to go this summer." He only awaited the outcome of the synagogue project. "Should that come to nothing, I will definitely go to America. I have reasons to fear that there is no future here for me."[100] Ideas of what he could undertake over there were either vague—a school for architects and engineers, partnership with an established architect—or fantastic, suited to the country of all possibilities—speculative house building, a candle factory, public bath- and washhouses.[101] Although in May he comforted Bertha by telling her that his "decision to go to America" was still not definite, he asked her in the same letter to take immediate steps to obtain an important letter of recommendation to the head of the House of Astor, as well as letters of recommendation promised by Dr. Krause, Oppenheim, and friends in Hamburg.[102]

By the middle of July he had given up hope of succeeding in Europe. A planned meeting with Bertha did not materialize. On August 1 he wrote to her, and he sounds somewhat disappointed: "I have fixed my departure for August 15 since there is nothing of importance to keep me here and you do not come. I shall probably travel via London . . . and thence via Liverpool away by steamer. But I may leave directly from Le Havre." His agent, Louis Pusinelli, recommended the *Baltimore*, which was to sail on August 19, as "quite a good sailing ship which for the last crossing took only twenty instead of the normal thirty days."[103]

"But before that I have to go on business to London," he had explained to Pusinelli.[104] The business seems to have been connected with his idea of establishing washhouses in New York. His friend and colleague, the architect, engineer, and chemist Jakob Kreuter, had given him advice on candle production and washhouses and also the address "of the architect of public baths in London . . . Pritchard Baly."[105] It seems almost certain that Semper made the journey in order to visit this expert. He left Paris on August 26 and was back on September 1.[106]

Ten days later he told his brother Karl that he would sail on September 18 or 19 from Le Havre where letters, addressed to his agent, would reach him. He left the same instructions with Séchan with whom he lodged, sent his seven pieces of luggage in advance, and on September 18 boarded the *Wilhelm Tell*, which was to depart the following day. Then, on the evening of the eighteenth, he received a letter from London, forwarded by Séchan, dated September 16.[107] The writer was Dr. Emil Braun, secretary of the Archaeological Institute in Rome, whom Semper might have known by name but had never met.[108] While on a visit to England Dr. Braun had heard with regret that Semper intended to leave Europe. "As an admirer of your fine talent and your wonderful works I should like to try everything possible to keep you here with us. I believe I am able to offer you, or at least to suggest, a field for your artistic activity, a field that promises to become no less brilliant than the one you have left behind." He would be in Paris within two or three days and asked Semper to let him know where he could meet him. Although the letter contained nothing concrete, and despite the erstwhile offer from Ghent that had sounded just as tempting and yet ended in failure, Semper hesitated. "What should I have done?" he asked Karl several days later. "I was already registered as a passenger; my luggage was on the way from Hamburg to New York; there my arrival is expected, announced as certain. Against that—the possibility of a happier state of my affairs and the ease with which I could clarify this matter by simply postponing my departure." Had he been alone in the world, he would have ignored the letter, he wrote; but to spare his family the dreaded journey he felt duty bound to follow up any offer. Consideration for his family might have played a part, but in the end it was what he read into Dr. Braun's letter, the prospect of a position equal to that in Dresden, that made him leave the ship, give his hand luggage to his agent, and return to Paris to await Dr. Braun's arrival.

Instead of Dr. Braun a letter from him arrived from Scotland, where he had been called by the sudden death of his father-in-law. He believed that under the circumstances it would be best for Semper to depart immediately for London where he, Dr. Braun, would have great pleasure in helping him to settle down. In greater detail than in the first letter he then explained why he assessed Semper's prospects in England so highly. What he wrote was, with one exception, vague: the best English architects were only engineers "and hardly know where the realm of art lies. As soon as a building is completed, the walls usually remain without decoration and give the impression, from inside as well as from the outside, of a makeshift container. Yet the need for refined forms is now frequently felt; perhaps no moment is as favorable as the present to win a good part of the educated English classes to a higher culture." Besides, he had arranged with a "learned architect," a Mr. Falkener (who had told him of Semper's intention to emigrate), to let him have a room in his office. For a start Braun could commission "several designs for furniture"; it was possible that Semper could "join him in greater enterprises and, in case of success, would have a nice income." What seemed to have more substance was the information that the "Board of Health has just attained important legislation and has decided on the creation of several large cemeteries" and that Braun, asked for his advice, had already sent in a report. "What I suggest in it has been accepted; maybe you would be willing to carry out my ideas."[109]

Understandably, Semper was disappointed. "Letter No. 2," he wrote Karl, "considerably lowered the expectations . . . that the first one had raised." He consulted Hittorf, Gau, and other friends, then wrote to Dr. Braun: "After careful consideration, long hesitation, and with the unanimous approval of my friends here . . . I have decided not to accept your kind invitation, but to proceed with the postponed journey to New York on the 29th . . . my money for the journey is getting short; besides, the unending state of doubt and uncertainty . . . have mentally and physically exhausted me; I have lost the cheer and confidence needed for what I still want to achieve on European soil where, however, the ban weighs me down . . . and therefore the best I have achieved, my reputation as an artist, will bear no fruit."

At least this was what he drafted. Then he overturned the decision once more.[110] "After long hesitation," he wrote to his brother, "I decided to go to London." He arrived there on September 28 at eleven o'clock in the evening; as on his previous short visit, he stayed at the Hotel d'Allemagne et du Commerce in Leicester Street.

Struggle for Professional Recognition in London, 1850–1852

Dr. Braun called at the hotel, in spite of Sunday rest, immediately after Semper informed him of his arrival. He was accompanied by two gentlemen. One was a German by the name of vom Hof, who had somehow managed to act as a go-between without contributing anything; the other was a man of importance, Edwin Chadwick.[111]

Here now was the man for whom he had given up his journey to America at the last minute, the man who as Dr. Braun had indicated could give him what he ardently longed for: work as an architect. To understand the events of the next few months and to make comprehensible Semper's hopes and disappointments that followed, it is necessary to summarize Chadwick's activity.

Because of the industrial revolution the living conditions of the working population in Britain's abnormally fast-growing cities deteriorated to such a degree that demands for remedy were voiced with ever-greater urgency; among those actively working for reform, Chadwick took a leading part. The Poor Law of 1834 was to a great extent based on his findings. As a member of the commission charged with the implementation of this law, he surveyed the sanitary conditions of the slums and in 1842 submitted a report of fundamental importance. In spite of its gruesome details and supporting statistics, the government would hardly have decided on the necessary far-reaching reforms had the reformers not been helped by a new ally: cholera. By the autumn of 1847 it was evident that the epidemic, ravaging the European continent, would reach England. At the last hour, in August 1848, Parliament passed the Public Health Act that Chadwick had carefully prepared and demanded for ten years. In October cholera reached Scotland and soon spread throughout England. The epidemic lasted fifteen months, and at its height there were 345 deaths a day in London alone. The problem of interment became acute.

Under the Public Health Act a Board of Health was set up. Chadwick, the directing member, realized that its most urgent task was the reform of interment. He had already in 1843 dealt with the plight of "interments in towns" and had warned that continued use of the old cemeteries, intended for a much smaller number of people and situated now in densely populated areas, would unquestionably bring about really scandalous conditions. Now that the cholera dramatically proved this state of affairs, he saw the possibility for the Board of Health to force through the reform he had demanded; to this end, he prepared a new report about the health risks incurred by intramural burials.

A comprehensive plan that would end these deplorable conditions was finally drawn up by him and two colleagues. Burial, "a most unfit subject for commercial speculation,"[112] would become a public service for which charges would be legally fixed on a rising scale for different classes. All intramural churchyards and cemeteries would, after reasonable compensation, be taken over by the Board of Health and, with the exception of Kensal Green, be closed. Kensal Green, enlarged, would then form one of the national cemeteries of which at least one more would immediately be needed. Chadwick thought he had found the right site for this new national cemetery, outside town yet close to a river, in Abbey Wood downstream from Woolwich. The transportation of bodies could take place on the river, "the silent highway"; eight buildings, established at equal intervals on both banks, would serve for the reception of coffins and the bereaved.

Before these proposals had been worked out in detail, two members of the board had visited the cemeteries of Berlin, Munich, and Frankfurt; what they learned about Continental practices certainly had some influence on the report. It was submitted to the government in December 1849. Because the warnings of the first report six years before had been only too drastically confirmed during the cholera epidemic, this time the government unreservedly accepted the proposed reform. The Metropolitan Interments Bill was laid before Parliament in April 1850 and, after lenghty debate, finally received royal assent on August 5.

Counting on the long parliamentary process, the members of the board had taken certain preliminary steps even before the bill became law. Among these was the resolution passed at a meeting on July 9 to request Dr. Braun (perhaps recommended to the board by Chadwick) to "visit and inspect the Chief existing Cemeteries in the Metropolis . . . and point out such improvements upon them as may appear to him to be practicable [and] to give the Board such observations on the Architectural arrangements . . . as may aid the Board in the consideration of the selection and decoration and management of new sites."[113] On August 5, the day the bill was passed, it was again stated that "Dr. Braun be requested to complete his examination of the existing Cemeteries, to report on the improvements in decorative arrangements and on the improvements in the application of the Fine Arts thereto."[114] A few weeks later Dr. Braun submitted his report, whereupon on August 30 he was informed "that the Board will be glad to receive further detailed suggestions for Art Decorations."[115]

At the same time the board had begun to take other measures, above all the valuation of the cemeteries to be acquired. This proved to be an unexpectedly lengthy undertaking, made more difficult through the antagonistic attitude of the cemetery companies. While waiting for the negotiations to be resumed the board sent a delegation, under Chadwick, to Paris to study the arrangements there; they returned by the middle of September.

Matters had reached this stage when Semper sat facing his visitors: Chadwick, energetic and full of optimism, glad of the lucky chance to meet this first-class architect, one who was even familiar with the Continental practice so important for his project; and Dr. Braun, archeologist, known and recognized by the profession, delighted when he could make plans far removed from scientific research, always convinced that with sufficient perseverance they would lead to financial success. Both men explained to Semper the public burial service as envisaged, talked of the national cemeteries, of the immense chances the plan would offer the architect. Chadwick presented a memorandum for a cemetery chapel drafted by him and his colleagues; it contained detailed "instructions . . . for designs in respect to the construction of a Church for the celebration of Divine Service at the National Cemetery," of which the most important ones were these:

The structure must be governed by the especial requirements of the Cemetery. In the first place to avoid the worry and painful impression by the rapid performance of successive separate services it will be generally necessary to have simultaneous services over several bodies . . . but . . . by architectural arrangements each party of mourners may be kept private and separate from the others. . . . Their place in the Church will be a sort of stall capable of holding twelve persons [Semper's copy gives the number of persons as eighteen]. . . . For the avoidance of precedence and distinction, each stall and each coffin should be equidistant from the pulpit. This would render a semicircular arrangement of the stalls necessary. Behind the pulpit which should be within the centre of the semicircle, would be the choir and the organ. . . . These places and arrangements might make it necessary to complete the circle, unless a horseshoe form were found preferable. The stalls should be so arranged that the separate sets of mourners would be in complete privacy and would not see other parties or other coffins than the one in respect to which they attended as mourners . . . for the preservation of order and silence as the service concludes, the coffin would be lowered through the floor of the chapel into a crypt beneath. . . . These suggestions set forth the objects to be sought by the architectural arrangements. They are open to any variation or improvement. . . . Probably a circular dome would be the best form of roof. As it would be necessary to throw light into or upon the stalls, the roof might be made of glass with iron ribs. . . . Probably the building though circular would be low and the dome not high.

All these conditions would make great demands on an architect's ingenuity and experience.[116]

The magnitude of these ideas overwhelmed Semper. By the next morning he was writing to Karl about the "immense burial ground of 600 acres," about the "round chapel in which one hundred bodies should be consecrated daily, in three sections, therefore thirty to thirty-five simultaneously," about the subterranean passages into which the coffins would be lowered to "correspond with the different levels of the cemetery's terraces that contain the graves," about the halls near the entrances in which to celebrate the wake "of course with everything that is needed, anterooms, scullery, kitchen, etc." "I have," he con-cluded, "already added something of my own to these ideas."[117] And, indeed, a document, "Instructions for the preparation of the Cemetery," drafted by Chadwick in his own hand soon after the meeting,[118] might well owe something to Semper's suggestions, as perhaps the appre-hension that "the addition of a third gallery would give the edifice too much the appearance of a theatre. Even in making [one] gallery, care should be taken to divest it of any appearance which might suggest such a resemblance."

All this made Semper's head spin. Yet, "tempered and hardened by so many disappointments," he was determined to examine every-thing well before committing himself. "They really seem to have the intention of charging me now with the preparatory work and probably later with the execution of these ideas," he wrote Karl. "The only question is how far the authority and reliability of these gentlemen go who pretend to have found the right man in me." But when, next morning, he was introduced in the office of the Board of Health to the other members, he was convinced of their sincerity and dared to admit, "It seems my affairs look good. . . . they have already discussed what my position should be."[119] Much would depend on the impression his drawings that Krüger had sent him to Paris would make, and they unfortunately were on the way to America, except for a few which, sent from le Havre, would arrive within the next few days. Much depended also on how acceptable he would be to "his Lordships and other noble members of the Board"; here Baron Bunsen, his former patron and colleague at the Society of Antiquities in Rome, could be of great help, unless Bunsen thought it incompatible with his official duty as Prussian ambassador in London to aid a political refugee. Dr. Braun, on the eve of his departure from London, visited Bunsen; later, from Rome, he let Semper know that Bunsen would not answer the visiting card Semper left with the embassy but would be willing to help him should Semper ask by letter.[120] Semper may have suffered under this degrading treatment, but, in fact, Bunsen's reserve was of no importance. Difficulties there were, great difficulties, but they had nothing to do with Semper personally; they were entirely political. That Semper could not judge the situation was only natural; at that time even the members of the Board underestimated the dangers that threatened their grand project, and they asked Semper to start preparing his plans.

He threw himself eagerly into this work. For the first time—apart from the competition for the Paris synagogue—real prospects were before him. He made quick sketches on odd pieces of paper—on the back of a draft for a letter to Dr. Braun announcing his arrival in London, on the last page of his copy of the memorandum, on an unfinished letter to Chadwick, and at the bottom of a copied letter to Karl. He hesitated between a rectangular room with the stalls placed along one of the short sides or around exedras, and a circular room with the stalls, numbering sixteen, all around; he then tried to combine both schemes by placing the circular chapel within a rectangular building that would contain the rooms needed for the funeral service, a solution for which he designed the exterior and the low dome crowning the whole (figure 5).

No doubt Chadwick had told him of his journey to Paris, and of his unsuccessful attempts to obtain information about the form and appearance of funeral processions and ceremonies there. In any case, shortly after their first meetings Semper wrote to Séchan and, since he put 200 francs at his disposal for buying and copying engravings, it is likely that Chadwick had commissioned Semper to acquire French material and also to have designs made that would be suitable for English conditions.[121] Although Séchan met with the same uncooperative attitude from the director of the Service des Pompes Funèbres de Paris as had the English delegation, through his many connections he succeeded in having other architects supply him with documentation about official funeral processions, for instance, "Monsieur Labrouste le résumé mis au net par lui qui est relatif à l'empereur."[122] It took until the middle of November, however, before he could report having received from the obliging director of the "entreprise des pompes funèbres de la banlieue" lithographs and tracings illustrating ordinary funerals, a "série des diverses classes de services comprenant les tentures mortuaires de la maison, de l'église et la char de chaque classe." In the end, having waited in vain for a safe opportunity, Séchan entrusted the whole material to the train. The parcel contained a complete collection of illustrations of all the objects necessary for the funeral

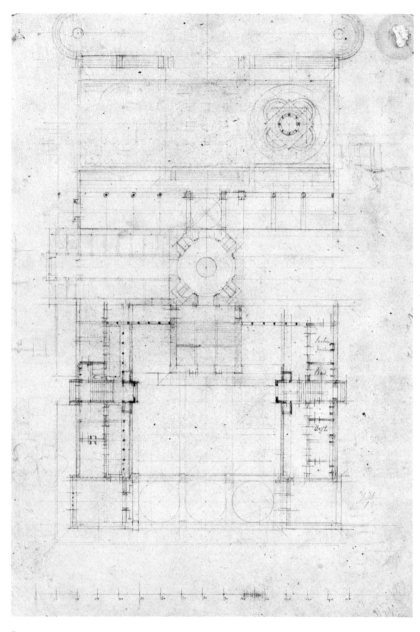

5
Semper. Sketch of chapel for National Cemetery, London, 1850. (Semper-Archiv Zurich)

services of different classes, including illustrations of the mortuary and the exterior and interior of the church.[123]

By then many weeks had passed since the promising conference, and Semper's relation to the board was still not clarified. Replying on November 30 to Karl's letter written six weeks before, he excused his long silence: "I would have much liked to say something definite about my position but, even now, this unfortunately is still not possible. The Board of Health is too occupied with preliminary steps . . . and above all with the purchase of land to think about examining plans, etc. Yet I am busy with designing a plan, which, once it is finished, should help me with an application for employment; the secretary of the Board of Health, Mr. MacAuley [sic], (brother of a well-known writer and statesman) promised to draft it for me. He does not doubt its success, since I enjoy the goodwill of all members of the Board."

Charles Macaulay and his superiors were certainly sincere and acted in good faith when they held out hopes to Semper. However, the resistance they quite unexpectedly had to overcome grew so strong that they thought it advisable to defer the plans that concerned him until the situation became clearer. In December Semper complained to Dr. Braun that since his departure things had not improved: "I am not quite sure about my relationship with the general Board of Health. The matter of the cemeteries is altogether shrouded in mystery, which I cannot penetrate . . . Mr. Chadwick . . . carefully avoids giving me a proper commission or even a hint about how he intends to make use of me."[124] Had Chadwick told him about the struggle that the board was waging with the government, Semper would certainly have thought these explanations only feeble excuses to get rid of him. Brought up in Germany, familiar with French customs, he must have taken for granted public administration of cemeteries, and felt that by introducing a new Interment Law now, the British government had only caught up with the times. But what must have been incomprehensible to Semper was that the same government that had steered the bill successfully through Parliament now obstructed it, backed by the powerful influence of the Treasury, and, whenever possible, created difficulties for the board. It needed a long familiarity with British politics to find it credible that only the fear of cholera had driven ministers to accept the law and that now, in October 1850 with the danger passed, they thought it unpardonable to have acted against their political conviction that the greatest possible passivity of the state in the social and economic sphere, and unrestricted laissez-faire in private business, were the ideal state of affairs.

The conflict dragged on for months. By the end of December Semper was alarmed because of Macaulay's hint that "difficulties have arisen about the realization of the cemetery plans." The always optimistic Dr. Braun reassured him: "You do not need to worry at all; since the matter has become a necessity, it has to be carried out. Chadwick has pushed through more difficult projects and McAully [*sic*] tends to be pessimistic."[125] Chadwick was indeed a tough fighter, but the sides were not equally matched. In March 1851, after many months of delaying tactics, the Treasury momentarily relented, but when new difficulties arose about raising funds, ministers and special interests who hated the law and the attitude it represented exploited the difficulties until toward the end of the year they killed off the whole project. Semper's hopes were thus dashed by a short-sighted, reactionary policy. Under more favorable circumstances he really would have had the opportunity for work that would at least have given him the chance to prove himself as an architect in England.

Yet long before the final defeat, Semper had given up his work on the design for the main project, the cemetery chapel, probably on Macaulay's or Chadwick's advice. Instead he worked on plans for a reception house, which he was going to submit when applying to the Board of Health for an appointment. Macaulay had offered to draft the application, but he too, Semper complained, "evades entering into a more serious discussion about the cemetery affair."[126] Planning the reception house stretched over many weeks; even months passed before the board examined Semper's plans. Here, therefore, is a good place to pursue Semper's other activities during this period.

Chadwick was still sincerely convinced that one day he would give Semper a leading role within the whole national cemetery project. But not long after the first, optimistic meeting he must have realized that the difficult negotiations would drag on for a long time and so felt duty bound to help Semper, whose financial situation was precarious, in some other way. "Mr. Chadwick has made great efforts to find me some work," Semper wrote appreciatively to Karl, and he assured Dr. Braun that Chadwick's kind disposition toward him could not be doubted.[127] After an introduction to the philanthropist Montefiori and one, sent him from Paris, to a member of the London House of Rothschild proved unfruitful, and Semper reported with annoyance that both had put him off with polite phrases,[128] Chadwick tried to encourage him: "I regret that the Jews are not ready to give you any engagement. I will make enquiries, in other quarters, as to projected edifices, in order to gain you opportunities of employment."[129]

Above all, there was the structure of glass and iron that was rising in Hyde Park before the eyes of a steadily growing number of spectators. Chadwick knew well the man who had designed it, Joseph Paxton (figure 6). On Semper's behalf he arranged a dinner party to which, besides Paxton, Chadwick's enthusiastic colleague Lord Ashley had also been invited. "I have asked [Paxton] to meet you. If you can do me the favour to dine with me and bring your drawings . . . that will give a favourable opportunity . . . I have asked Lord Ashley to dine with us, and we shall have that honour if you can come."[130] Paxton thought it "a pleasant dinner [with] Lord Ashley and other nobs there."[131] He did not mention Semper, although he had been shown his drawings and Chadwick had brought up the idea of employing Semper as draftsman. As often happens on such occasions, it occurred to Semper only afterward that he should have sought Paxton's patronage for obtaining a much more interesting job; whereupon early the next morning he sent a short note to Chadwick: "the idea occurs to me that if you could have the kindness to see [Paxton] and recommend me for the decoration of the Building for 1851, it might have great effect." Chadwick obliged and contacted Paxton just before he left the same afternoon for Chatsworth. "He replies to me," reads Chadwick's note of the same day to Semper, "that the task of painting and decorating the edifice is in the hands of Mr. Owen Jones under the direction of a Committee, and though the work is not done exactly as he Mr. Paxton could wish, yet that he has no control over the matter."

There was now only the prospect of working as draftsman for Paxton, a job that had little attraction for Semper. "Though I have never been an office worker, necessity knows no law," he wrote a few days later to Karl.[132] But when weeks passed and he had not heard anything from Paxton about the job, while the hardship grew, his pride was broken: "I would have liked to accept the job even at a small salary, but I have not heard from Mr. Paxton since . . . and find it so difficult to solicit."[133]

Dr. Braun also tried to help Semper, not only because his overoptimistic report had kept Semper from his journey to America, but also because it was his nature to organize other people's lives, to give advice, and to develop new projects in which he confidently expected all difficulties to be surmounted. Edward Falkener had indeed followed up his offer to share his office with Semper, even though in the end it amounted to nothing more than putting a room and address at Semper's disposal and exploiting his talent for making competent designs, an arrangement that made Semper complain, "I sell not only

6
Sir Joseph Paxton by S. W. Reynolds after O. Oakley. (National Portrait Gallery, London)

my hand but also my ideas and lose the authorship into the bargain."[134]
Dr. Braun repeatedly urged Semper to offer Falkener a formal partnership,[135] but because of their incompatibility, they never even discussed the idea. When Dr. Braun inquired about it, Semper complained:
"I do not know why, but the coldness of this man makes it impossible
for me to broach the proposition suggested by you. I am also afraid
of his despotism. I believe he has good prospects for receiving an
important commission (a corn exchange) and will take good care not
to have to share the benefit arising from it. Maybe he would employ
me as draftsman and this only out of consideration."[136] Without giving
up the idea of a partnership with Falkener, Dr. Braun recommended
Semper to George Scharf, "a man well versed in art. . . . Perhaps you
could go together in establishing a drawing school. . . . Scharf would
be an excellent famulus for you. The good taste he will learn from
you he will spread among the people and thus with his help you may
gain much ground."[137] When Semper, depressed by the hopelessness
of his situation, wrote a desperate letter a few weeks later, Dr. Braun
was "greatly concerned and dejected." Trying to restore Semper's
confidence, he replied that when he himself had been in similar situations, courage and resolution always quickly revived. So it had been
this time; after long deliberation an idea had occurred to him. As
Semper knew, he was the owner of a galvanoplastic factory in Germany
and for the English market collaborated closely with Elkington in
Birmingham. This kind of business would be given a considerable
boost if an artist like Semper joined it in a leading position. Dr. Braun
would let him have half of his own share in the Birmingham firm
and, of course, also half of the eventual profits. "Galvanoplastic," he
continued, "has already reached a point at which it can be as useful
to sculpture as engraving, lithography, and woodcut are to the art of
drawing. The reason that so little has been achieved with this process
until now is due solely to the lack of artists capable of taking over the
direction of those products that have now become technically possible.
Great things could be done with it in England if a man like you
investigated on the spot what luxury demands and initiate a thorough
reform of taste. At the same time this would be the best way to make
you known as architect." He should make himself familiar with the
trade and prepare a well-planned campaign. "Then, at the opening
of the exhibition we shall be ready for action."[138] Nothing came of
this ambitious plan. The same thing happened, though this time not
through Dr. Braun's fault, with his offer for partnership in another
project—an officially registered cemetery office, a plan he had submitted to the Board of Health on the day of Semper's arrival.[139] No

doubt Dr. Braun was honestly trying to help Semper, but he was in Rome and as a foreigner was hardly more familiar with English conditions than was Semper.

Chadwick, on the other hand, moved in the center of British public life, among influential people, and was therefore in a much better position to take steps that could be successful. Through him Semper, still impatiently awaiting Paxton's offer, was asked to present himself to a man who later was to influence decisively his stay in England (figure 7).

On December 1 Rachel Chadwick, writing for her husband, advised Semper to go the next evening with his portfolio to the home of Henry Cole: "Mr. Cole is a leading member of the Commission which directs the works of the 'crystal palace' and he says that he thinks the Society of Arts might be got to publish your view of the restored Acropolis and your paper on Polychromy." To Semper's great disappointment, the visit had to be postponed for a few days, since just then he was confined to bed.[140] On December 5 Cole entered in his diary: "Mr Semper Dresden Architect came introduced by Chadwick."[141]

Semper probably spoke about himself, of his activities in Dresden, of his views on the use of color in ancient architecture, and of his theories on art. That might have sounded too abstract and dogmatic for Cole, yet, perhaps out of courtesy and encouragement, he gave Semper hopes that he could help him with the publication of the paper on polychromy when translated into English. At the end of the meeting he kept Semper's portfolio.

Semper had probably written the paper soon after his arrival in England, because Rachel Chadwick started with the translation at the end of November.[142] Shortly after the meeting with Cole and possibly stimulated by it, Semper decided to enlarge the paper by adding his ideas on architectural theory. This work helped to take his mind off the enervating uncertainty about the outcome of the cemetery project. "My affairs have still not made any progress," he complained to Bertha in early 1851, adding, "For six weeks I have worked on a paper that I hope will cause a stir."[143] On the same day he sent the manuscript to Vieweg; it was published in the autumn under the title *Die vier Elemente der Baukunst* (*The Four Elements of Architecture*).[144]

Semper had a compelling reason to join two loosely linked themes—an archeological polemic about polychromy and theoretical reflections about basic architectural elements—into one book. Since spring of the preceding year when he had dispatched the first installment of "Vergleichende Baulehre" to Vieweg, he had had hardly any time for writing, being busy with preparing to emigrate to America, even though

7
Sir Henry Cole by Samuel Laurence, 1865. (National Portrait Gallery, London)

it was clear to him that, if at all, he could finish the work only in Europe where all the necessary research material was at his disposal. From Paris he had written to Vieweg in February 1850: "Had my commitment to you not retained me, I would already have departed for America. But, as it is, I either stay here or go to London; both places are the only ones where I can continue the book."[145] But the work did not make much progress in London either, although the art treasures and the library of the British Museum were now easily accessible. As in Paris, "the wretched need to earn a living" and repeated, always unsuccessful, attempts to find employment intervened; he lacked the inner peace that work on such a far-reaching subject demanded. If the publication of "Vergleichende Baulehre" was so far off—admittedly his own fault—would not other writers anticipate his basic ideas? He was afraid—certainly quite unjustifiably—of a "literary theft" that would rob him of the fruit of his intellectual work.[146] It was urgent to present his ideas as quickly as possible to the public. To add them to the article on polychromy had the advantage of turning the short paper into a book, while the theoretical study was made more attractive by current interest in the subject of polychromy. "The manuscript," he wrote to Vieweg, "was really written for England where at present the problem of polychromy is vigorously debated. But it will certainly also be read in Germany, especially since it does not lack polemic and other piquant matters. At the same time it serves as an example of how I intended to arrange my 'Vergleichende Baulehre.' "[147]

Understandably, Vieweg was annoyed: All he had seen of "Baulehre" after years was "a meager parcel of manuscripts . . . with which, not knowing at all whether the work will ever be finished, I cannot possibly start printing"; now, instead of a further delivery of "Baulehre" he received "another small article of six sections."[148] Nevertheless he promised to publish quickly "Vier Elemente," and Semper's mind was put at ease with the knowledge that this pamphlet, which was an important milestone in the development of his theoretical viewpoint, and which contained original unpublished ideas, would soon be in print. Still, the article was written in German, and what mattered to him was to become known in England. Dr. Braun, convinced that the pamphlet would help him there, advised having Vieweg publish an English translation at the same time. He brushed aside Semper's objection that the publisher might find this difficult: "We shall easily manage the translation of your brochure on polychromy."[149] However, that was easier said than done, and Semper, reasonably, tried only to place the paper with an English periodical.[150]

Since the day that he had presented himself to Cole, many weeks of silence had passed. Eventually he decided to go to the Crystal Palace, still under construction, in order to bring about a meeting with Cole, who visited the hall almost daily. Having tried several times to gain entry without success ("Mais n'ayant pas été si heureux pour vous y recontrer ou d'être admis"), he wrote a letter in French, with which he was more conversant at that time than English and asked him "de bien vouloir charger quelqu'un en mon nom pour me faire parvenir les dessins qui sont chez vous depuis quelque temps." But then he came to the real reason that he was so eager to see Cole: all his attempts to find adequate employment had been in vain and had only resulted in brusque, offending rejections and waste of time. People did not know him here, or pretended not to know him, so that to be successful and once more make a name for himself, he would have to begin all over again. Very carelessly, with empty promises and under false pretenses, someone had made him come to England and had kept him from emigrating to America. He now thought about opening a school for architects after the model of the one in Dresden that he had directed for over fourteen years, from which during that time a number of notable architects had come. But it was difficult for him to find in London the necessary number of pupils. "En attendant . . . je vous demande la faveur de bien vouloir me soutenir avec votre influence dans ma tâche énoncée. . . . A ce but je prendrai la liberté de vous soumettre sous peu de jours mon programme et je vous prie de bien vouloir le communiquer aux Messieurs de vos connaissances."[151]

The year before, Semper had talked about his then vague intention to open a school for architects and engineers in America. Now that the prospects of ever again working as an architect became more and more dim, he came back to the idea and began to draw up a detailed plan. The longer he thought about it, the more promising it seemed to him, so promising that at the beginning of March he let pass a chance for a well-paid job as Paxton's assistant at Chatsworth because it did not fit in with his plan for a school.[152] He wrote Bertha that he intended to combine a boardinghouse with this institute, run by her and their oldest daughter; it should cater first of all to young architects who wished to study in England and whom he would teach in his studio. He could make a start if he had eight or twelve students. "I have taken my final, firm decision to hold out in England if at all possible." Already the belief of having overcome the nerve-racking indecision gave him courage. With the call "Now all hands to the wheel, let's start without delay," he ends the letter.[153]

A boardinghouse for his students—that sounds very modest. But in fact he had a very ambitious program in mind for the "Deutsche Atelier für Architekten und Ingenieure in London," under which name he wanted to advertise it in German newspapers.[154]

To a German friend he had set forth the guidelines by which the institute would be run. The interesting program, instructive too about the way he had taught in Dresden, covers the art of building as a whole:

The institute should serve the common study of architecture and civil engineering, and exercises should play a major part in both subjects; thus, skill and knowledge [*Können und Wissen*] will be gained at the same time. At these exercises . . . the close relationship rather than the difference between the two . . . subjects should be stressed; according to this principle they should be jointly taught so that, for instance, one student may be working on a project for a house while the one next to him is designing a bridge. . . . It would be necessary to have assistants . . . in particular to interest an experienced English engineer in this project. I know two who, at least, could give me advice and information. The institute should be divided into two classes: the first as "Bauschule" would be preparatory to the second, the "Atelier," where right under my eyes and next to my study students would carry out designs. That is how I ran it in Dresden where, of course, I was never short of work. The best students could later claim payment for their assistance.

The exercises in the Bauschule would proceed from projection, the first combinations and elements of "fine" architecture, drawings of construction in stone, wood, and iron to first attempts of designing plans for civil architecture and engineering, and finally to the execution of larger projects; practice in ornamental designs, perspective, freehand drawing and drawing picturesque architectural objects, first after pattern books and later by invention, were also included. "The students of the 'Atelier' class should not be given a fixed program for their exercises, which will be of a more practical nature and should, if possible, immediately follow the design stage as was the case in Dresden." Simultaneously with these exercises there would be lectures. He set out the first course, on comparative architecture, in greater detail: "All building types will be dealt with separately, from the historical as well as functional point of view, and will be arranged in related groups. This course extends over several terms." Other subjects were construction, mechanics, road building, bridges and canals, geometry, physics, and applied chemistry. In conclusion, he stresses two advantages that a visit to a school in London under his direction would have for young Germans: "1. My practice in Germany extending over many years and, in addition, my knowledge of French and English ways of building, the characteristics of which must be of special interest to Continental architects who so far neither know nor apply them. 2. The supremacy of the Englishman in everything that has to do with practice and construction, which I will always aim to point out."[155]

This was written on Christmas Eve 1850. Two months later he was ready to announce the institute publicly. He drafted advertisements, asked friends to revise them, and tried to have them placed with German and Swiss newspapers. He asked Chadwick, as well as Cole, to recommend his institute, and asked Dr. Krause for his opinion. The reaction of all three was discouraging.

To Semper's long and in many ways pitiful letter, Cole replied the following day with a four-line note: "Dear Mr Semper, I return your portfolio with thanks. If I can aid your views I shall be happy and will try to do so. In haste Yours faithfully Henry Cole."[156]

Chadwick also doubted whether Semper was ready to take charge of a school of architecture in England: "I should imagine that for its success more knowledge of the habits and wants of the class of architectural students would be required than you would be likely to obtain readily."[157] Dr. Krause too pointed out the obstacles he would have to surmount for such an undertaking in a foreign country: "Your dear wife would be too much of a novice to cope with a large household, in a country moreover whose customs, requirements, and peculiar habits demand some knowledge and tact." More sensible and experienced than Semper, who easily yielded to daydreaming, Dr. Krause bluntly declared the project unsuitable "since its success depends on so many Ifs and Whens and since the risk is too great." He proposed if not dropping the plan at least postponing it until the end of July when they could talk it over (probably on the occasion of his visit to the Great Exhibition).[158]

Before Semper had to decide whether these objections were justified, he received an offer for a job in the exhibition building that stopped him from thinking about vague plans for the future. As late as February, he had received from Cole the short and noncommittal reply just quoted, and yet it was Cole, as Semper later affirmed, to whom he owed the job in the exhibition building.[159] Probably Cole had recommended him when asked by a foreign agent for the name of an experienced interior decorator.[160]

Within the framework of the Great Exhibition the task given to Semper—to arrange the exhibits of Canada, Turkey, Sweden, and Denmark—was not of great importance. "On m'a employé pour arranger quelques divisions de l'édifice, voilà tout"—so Semper wrote to a French manufacturer who had addressed him in his letters as "architecte du Palais."[161] Whereas the big countries employed their own staff for work that could only be carried out on the spot, the smaller ones handed this task over to their consuls, who had neither time nor inclination to look after the detailed arrangements of the exhibits. Once these facts are understood, it is possible to assess Semper's work correctly. He was appointed not by the exhibition commission but by the London representatives of the countries involved; to these men he was accountable, from them he received instructions. The tone of the Swedish consul's note was no doubt typical: "Mr. Semper will not fail to be on Saturday at 10 o'clock in the Swedish Department . . . to the command of Mr. Tottie." This is why Semper's name was not mentioned in the daily papers and publications that appeared in ever-greater numbers from the start, nor in the official catalogue. Only the commissioners, officially appointed by their governments, were responsible for their national stands, and therefore only their names were mentioned in the catalogue; Semper was in constant contact with the representatives of the four countries but only occasionally, if at all, with the official management.[162]

However that may be, for the next few weeks he worked in the exhibition building, designing and supervising the arrangement of the four comparatively small stands of which the Turkish one had the greatest number of exhibits (figure 8). We have a description of it from the pen of a German visitor:

The Turkish collection gains considerably through being arranged and decorated with great care and in good taste. The stand opens out to the transept and therefore demands special attention. It displays a tent in the shape of a light and elegant mosque made of gauze shot through with gold and red and is surmounted by a half-moon; from the posts fly flags and horsetails with Turkish inscriptions and along the walls hang carpets in colorful splendour. As this was finished only the day before yesterday [May 8], a new attraction has been created which increases the effect of the transept and earns universal praise. The exhibits too are sensibly and clearly arranged.[163]

Contemporary illustrations and drawings of the Canadian stand exist in Semper's hand: several illustrations of the so-called Canadian Trophy, a very effective free composition in which the various kinds of Canadian timber used for shipbuilding form the support for a large canoe; and also some drawings for the structural decorations of the three walls with their glass cabinets, designed by Semper whereby, he said later, he "had applied his principle of an architectural decorative order" (figure 9).[164]

8
Crystal Palace, London, 1851. Interior: transept looking north. (Semper-Archiv Zurich, from *The Illustrated London News*, June 7, 1851)

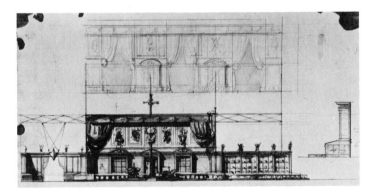

9
Semper. Design for the Canadian stand, Crystal Palace, London, 1851. (Institut für Denkmalpflege, Dresden. Deutsche Fotothek Dresden)

If his work in relation to the whole could necessarily have had only limited effect, the Great Exhibition by contrast was of decisive importance for him and the development of his architectural ideas. Here he found an unusually wide-ranging survey of man's industrial arts from raw material, machines, and tools to finished products and works of art. He noted at this time his "almost daily perambulations through the Hyde Park palace." It became clear to him that the obvious inadequacy of European industrial art was deep rooted, as evidenced by the sequence of displays chosen by the exhibition commission. In his opinion it was incorrect to begin with materials and tools instead of with needs and functions; modern science and speculation had turned things upside down ("needs do not go any more to the market, but the market creates new needs"). To bring order into this chaotic Babel of an exhibition his special study, the theory of architectural principles, would have been uniquely suited to underline the unifying bond, to act, as it were, as "major domo and steward of comparative history of culture."[165]

The exhibition with all its faults taught him much; it gave the impetus to a reorientation of his "Vergleichende Baulehre." The contrast between the lack of style in modern products and the natural and instinctively sure feeling for style that primitive people had—"the Persians, Indians, and Arabs . . . the Chinese and even the Canadian savages"—led him increasingly to realize that his great work would make sense and be of value only if it were preceded by a detailed description of the technical arts.[166]

He intended to write several articles for German magazines, recounting his impressions of the exhibition.[167] However, only one article was published, soon after the opening, in the German edition of the *Illustrated London News*.[168] The closing of the exhibition led him to write a summary of what he had seen in a pamphlet, *Wissenschaft, Industrie und Kunst* (Science, Industry and Art), the genesis of which will be discussed in the following pages.

His work at the exhibition temporarily eased his financial situation, but there was no sequel; to judge from his letters, Semper did not seem to have expected that it would lead to a more permanent job. A vague prospect of being appointed by a German state (possibly Hamburg?) to be its representative on one of the juries fell through, and with it "vanished a good opportunity of becoming better known."[169] When, therefore, the installation of the four stands was completed, the prospect of finding permanent work was more doubtful than ever.

Under these circumstances his best hope was still the Board of Health, although many months of inactivity had passed since the first contact. As mentioned, he had worked since the end of the previous year on plans for a reception house. By the middle of February 1851 he received a letter from Henry Austin, the board's secretary, at present on sick leave in Brighton. Austin thought that in view of the board's financial difficulties he should not wait any longer to tell Semper what he would already have told him in London but for his illness. "Mr. Chadwick informed me," read Semper, "that you had been preparing some sketches for Reception Houses for the dead, and I was desirous of ascertaining to what extent you had understood his instructions on the subject, so that you might not proceed beyond what was at present prudent or desirable. If you have not seen Mr. Chadwick lately, perhaps it would be well that you should devote but little further time to the subject, until I have an opportunity of explaining to you the position of the Board with regard to their points of re-numeration, as under present circumstances difficulties may arise upon this point." This ominous letter no doubt dampened Semper's high expectations, but the biggest shock was still to come.

When, after long resistance, the Treasury authorized in March the purchase of two existing cemeteries, Chadwick believed—as it proved, mistakenly—that they would soon be in public ownership. On April 17 he wrote to Paxton asking him to visit the two cemeteries and thereafter, as the board's expert, to testify before the arbitration tribunal as to the reasonableness of the proposed purchase price. "In respect of one of them," he continued, "the Brompton Cemetery, which is very badly laid out, it strikes me that it would be of value, & if it were properly done, very effective, to give a bird's eye or isometrical view of the Cemetery as it is; & prepare another on the same scale and exhibit it, as it ought to be? Might not Semper aid or be tried in getting out such a view? He is at present engaged in arranging the goods at the Great Exhibition, & will continue there until the open-ing."[170] In the same letter Chadwick was full of optimism about the acquisition of the national cemetery in Abbey Wood; obviously he still felt strong enough to fight the constantly growing opposition. One month later it was decided to start planning Abbey Wood.[171] In con-nection with these preliminary steps, Semper was at last, on May 14, asked to submit his plans for a reception house.[172] Because at the next meetings more important matters were being discussed, it took until the end of June for the board to examine the plans.

There were two sets of plans, one from Semper, the other from an employee of the board, the architect Edward Crecy. "The Board," the minutes of June 26 read, "considered the subject of the proposed Reception Houses for the Dead, and examined the designs prepared by Mr. Semper and Mr. Crecy."[173] Semper was known to all the members, who were aware that he was Chadwick's protégé and that his reputation as an excellent and experienced architect was undisputed. In spite of these circumstances, which placed them under some obligation and, in any case, were favorable, the board arrived at this devastating conclusion:

The design of Mr. Semper for a Reception House appeared to the Board to be wanting in appropriate Character. It conveys no religious or appropriate impression of its object, either in arrangement of ornamentation; with the exception of some symbolism of objectionable character, the external features might serve for a Bath or for many other objects.—The Board had expressed a desire that the Edifice should be of a Christian Style of Architecture, and preferred that of Norman Gothic.[174] Although Mr. Semper's design exhibits some striking Architectural effects, there appear to be many objections in the arrangement shewn. The plan covers four or five times the space of ground required for the number of bodies proposed to be accommodated, and very unnecessary expense would be thereby incurred, both for site and for building. There appears to be no arrangement for the privacy of the mourners and the admission and removal of the bodies would in this Design be attended with great inconvenience, and would apparently be conducted entirely in view of the public.

In short, Semper's design was wrong in every respect: the style was inappropriate, the layout too extensive, the planning impracticable.

The first objection did no more than express the prevailing view that for religious buildings only a style derived from the Middle Ages was appropriate. "From the architecture, from the decorations, everything belonging to pagan structures or periods should be strictly excluded. The style & decoration should be Christian" had in fact been clearly stated in one of the programs for the cemetery church, even though it then continued: "If it can be so it should be of the present period. If nothing characteristic, solemn, & yet cheerfully impressive can be devised of the present period, which will give satisfaction, then a selection may be made of the styles in use which appears to give the greatest satisfaction to the largest body of the members of the Church of England."[175] This allowed the architect a certain degree of latitude, yet Semper had had doubts from the start whether it would not be better to follow Chadwick's oral advice and change his design— far removed from "Norman Gothic"—into Gothic. In the end, advised by Dr. Braun, he had decided against it.[176] Having taken this risk by his own free will, he could accept the objection to the stylistic form, without taking offense. The two other criticisms hit him harder, for they questioned his competence as architect.

It was a definite defeat. Perhaps it would have been less wounding if Semper could have blamed it on an unfair preference given to Crecy, the board's employee. But Crecy's design was equally judged to be "deficient in appropriate character and in suitable arrangements" and also rejected in its entirety. Nor would the rejection have been so offensive had he and Crecy been asked to submit revised plans. Instead, it was decided at the same meeting "that Mr. Austin be directed to prepare further Plans . . . more in accordance with the instructions and views of the Board." The constantly growing financial difficulties most likely forced the board to save the considerable cost of commissioning private architects; the same reason caused them a month later "to discontinue preparations involving expense of Plans of Reception Houses."[177] This would have given Semper little consolation, if he knew anything at all about these reasons. The awful fact remained: the design on which he had set so much hope had after careful examination been rejected, the grand project had suddenly collapsed.

The rejection hurt him deeply and affected his spirits, which were already shaken from the distress and misery of the last years. He swung from one emotional extreme to the other, from optimistic confidence to unreasonable despair. Shortly after the opening of the Great Exhibition, he was in high spirits;[178] but the confident mood did not last long; a sympathetic German friend soon afterward found him so dejected that she implored him not to doubt himself.[179] The shock of seeing his work condemned hit Semper when he was in this state of mind. His despair erupts in a letter written to the same friend: he felt deserted by everybody, was even suspicious of well-meaning people close to him: "I have heard nothing from Mr. Chadwick. . . . Mr. Paxton to whom I offered myself body and soul left me without an answer. . . . the same with my friend Dr. Braun in Rome; first he lures me to come here, then he departs and leaves me to my fate; now he does not even answer my letter." His inclination to suspect other people's motives turned under the influence of this setback almost into paranoia: "I cannot remain in London any longer. The Continent is too close and invisible powerful hands reach out from there to ruin us outlaws once more. English people . . . soon notice when you go downhill and then the smallest faux pas, every sin of omission, is intentionally misinterpreted; people are glad to have found a reason for withdrawing their help."[180] He wrote of "intrigues . . . from his homeland [*Heimat*]" that wrecked his effort of finding work,[181] believed that "slanders are being spread among English people"[182] so that even those who had shown a genuine interest in him lately behaved coolly; trying to get to the bottom of this, he found that "agents of the German governments, among whom some scholars and professors were the most dangerous ones," made it their business to show in the most glaring light his disloyalty and his ingratitude toward the king of Saxony.[183] He was worried that the passport he needed for a planned meeting with Bertha would not be issued "because of the terrible mania of persecuting us poor refugees";[184] he felt so insecure, was so oversensitive, that the tone of a French manufacturer's letter, somewhat resentful about Semper's belated reply, sent him into such a state of anxiety that he implored Dieterle and Séchan to rescue him from this threatening situation. They both contacted the manufacturer, whose next letter reverted to a neutral, courteous tone without hinting at the intervention.[185] The incident would be of no significance but for Dieterle's and Séchan's soothing replies that reveal Semper's really alarming state of mind. "Tu t'es exagère," wrote Dieterle, "le sens et l'importance des expressions de sa missive, enfin je crois que tu as bien tort de te tormenter de cette affair et d'y attacher quelque importance," to which Séchan added: "il est évident que cette lettre ne voulait pas dire ce que vous avez cru."[186]

Thus, in the summer of 1851, he imagined he was being persecuted on all sides, lost faith in his own ability, suffered under constant failures. The confidence with which he had pursued the project of a school of architecture in the spring had given way to the disappointing realization of its impractibility—at any rate, no more was said about it. In this hopeless situation he had, as before, only one way out—emigration to America.

He had never given up this lifeline. He had considered even the move to London temporary, at least in the beginning. "I shall probably remain in London during the winter," he declared shortly after his arrival,[187] and he was still hesitant at the new year: "I cannot yet decide whether to stay here." "I will wait to the end of the summer . . . and if by then the plans [of the Board of Health] are unsuccessful will definitely move to America with the whole family."[188] In February, misled by the rosy vision of a school of architecture, he took his "final, firm decision" to remain in London.[189] As his intensive work in the Crystal Palace also drew him away from brooding miserably, he felt more confident for a while and ordered his luggage, still in New York where it had been sent in advance in September 1850, to be returned to him.[190] But now, after the fiasco of the design for the reception house, he was impatient to leave London behind him. He told friends of his decision and obtained letters of recommendation from them. When he heard that a professorship of civil engineering at the University of Toronto had been advertised, he applied for the post.

Yet, just as in the previous year, he found it difficult to make the final break with Europe. Perhaps he could still make use of his talents in some form or another and keep his head above water. The Great Exhibition gave him an idea for a plan, which needed the collaboration of his Parisian friends. He wanted to open an agency for industrial art designs, "un bureau de renseignement et de consultation pour l'art industriel" where private clients could choose from collections that would include the whole range of industrial art ("la céramique, la verrerie, les meubles, la tapisserie, le papier peint, les dessins d'étoffes, etc., etc.,"), and where his own task would be that of an "intermédiaire entre les artistes et le public"—in short, he had in mind a "design center," to give it the title of today's British institution.[191] Dieterle thought the idea interesting, though several things would have to be sorted out first.[192] The plan was not mentioned again, but it was obviously not abandoned, for the *Zeitschrift für Bauwesen* referred in November/December to a communication sent in by Semper: the reader was informed that a newly founded international society of artists intended to hold an art exhibition in London next February "where mainly industrial-art designs, drawings, and models inclusive of those for architecture ... will have their place."[193] Among their members were four French artists: Jules Klagmann, Dieterle, Michel Liénard, and Hector Horeau, of whom the first three were prominent in industrial art and decoration, while the fourth had made a name for himself with a design for the Great Exhibition that gained an honorable mention from the jury.[194] This idea also remained on paper, yet the interlude is interesting because it reveals not only Semper's hesitation to leave for America, but also his isolation as an artist in England: he succeeded in procuring the collaboration of French artists, tried to obtain it from German artists, but none of the leading British artists, if they had been approached at all by Semper, had offered their assistance.

Wavering between the wish to come to a decision and the fear of its finality, having nobody but himself to consult when weighing up the pros and cons, he longed for a talk with Bertha. "I simply must speak to you," he wrote to her on August 30, "and propose ... a meeting in Belgium. ... I believe a discussion is necessary." After more letters full of joyful expectation and anxious apprehension that something might go wrong, their meeting took place in Bruges after a separation of more than two years. Semper spent two weeks there with Bertha and the two older boys.[195]

On October 3 he was back in London. The parting from his family and the close of the Great Exhibition a few days away put him in a sad mood. To fight the feeling of emptiness he worked on a series of articles aimed for publication in a German newspaper. "Only a few more days and the great world bazaar is closed, the summer has lost its glory, autumn mood prevails." This, written on the first day after his return, was the first sentence of the introductory article. What he had planned as a retrospective review of the exhibition—from the "enthusiasm aroused in spring by the powerful first impact" to "sober examination and detailed comparison"—changed during the next two weeks into a critical statement about the repercussions and lessons of the exhibition. Following the advice of friends, he decided to publish it as a pamphlet; six days after the end of the exhibition, on October 17, he sent the manuscript to Vieweg.[196] This was the first version of the book that was published the next year under the title *Wissenschaft, Industrie und Kunst* (Science, Industry and Art). It was considerably shorter than the final text, consisting only of the first three chapters. The length and contents of the first version are known in essence from a copy that Semper himself wrote when, just before he was going to dispatch the manuscript, he received an offer for an English edition.[197] He took this opportunity to improve the text, mainly stylistically. Hardly had he finished the copy when it was suggested to him "to propose improved teaching methods for young technicians with special consideration for the formation of good taste."[198] Thereupon he wrote four more chapters and made additions here and there to the first part. This explains the dichotomy of the brochure, in which the two parts are only loosely connected, as in *Die vier Elemente*: in the first three chapters a concise and imaginative presentation of what he considered to have been the important consequences of the exhibition and their significance for the future; in the concluding four chapters an informed discussion of art educational problems.

Having complied with Semper's request to start printing immediately, Vieweg now had to wait two months for the final manuscript, and was then forced to discard the already completed type of the first manuscript and start afresh. The pamphlet finally appeared in spring 1852.[199]

The reunion with his family helped Semper to see things in a less gloomy light. Bertha, who had always dreaded the idea of America, may have persuaded him to persevere in England. His time was now fully taken up with writing: the enlargement of *Wissenschaft, Industrie und Kunst* kept him busy for many weeks, as did its translation, which he hoped would make him known in English circles. He was also shortening the manuscript of "Vergleichende Baulehre," sent eighteen months before from Paris, as agreed between himself and Vieweg when the publisher visited London. A new version of the introductory chapters, on which he worked around this time, the end of 1851, is indeed less diffuse, and the ideas they contain, after the experience of the exhibition, are further developed.[200]

Semper also had encouraging news. In the first letter from Dresden after her return, Bertha told him that his friend Franz Hanfstängl was, at Queen Victoria's request, coming to England soon. "He will," she continued excitedly, "talk about you and your affairs when he goes to see the Queen and her husband . . . a new ray of hope that may bring about an improvement and easing of your situation. He can perhaps introduce you to the Queen whose husband is known to favor and support the arts and that means also the artists. With God's blessing you may be given a job or at least commissions which will be useful to you."[201] Semper, who knew more about English conditions than Bertha, might have reacted to the news less enthusiastically and have hoped only that the advice a colleague from Hamburg had given him some months before, "to seek the patronage of Prince Albert for the school of architecture," might after all become a real possibility, at least for the planned "design center."[202] Since Semper never mentioned the episode or Prince Albert during this time, it can be assumed that either Hanfstängl's recommendation was ineffective or that he had promised more than he could deliver. What is clear from Bertha's letter, however, is that Semper had had no contact with the prince, neither when he moved to London nor when he was commissioned to work for the exhibition.

All the same, some of Semper's acquaintances, if not so high ranking, were still quite influential. His friendship with the Chadwicks was not affected by the loss of the cemetery project. Edwin Chadwick saw him from time to time, sought his expert advice, and obtained official letters of introduction for him; his wife Rachel also tried to pass commissions on to him.[203] The Bonham-Carters, with whom he was on friendly terms, introduced him toward the end of the year to Lord Ashburton, head of the Baring family.[204] Lord Ashburton thought about enlarging his country seat, The Grange, and asked Semper for advice. After Semper had inspected the place, Lord Ashburton sent him a present for his trouble, which Semper said in his letter of thanks "je n'ai vraiment pas mérité n'ayant pas été dans le cas de vous rendre aucun service." The hope, certainly cherished by Semper, of working for Ashburton at some time was, however, not fulfilled. The enlargements were carried out by C. R. Cockerell, who together with his father, had several years before done some work at The Grange.[205]

The plans for emigration may have been pushed into the background, but until his situation radically improved they were never dropped altogether. A former colleague, now in New York, wrote at the beginning of January that in his opinion Semper would risk very little by coming to New York: "Much is being built here. One begins to give buildings a rich decor, that of the Renaissance style . . . New York would certainly be the place where with regard to money you would be all right." As he heard, Semper had been recommended to Astor. "You could not do better. Astor himself builds continuously."[206] Thereupon Semper was going to write to Astor explaining that he would have presented himself eighteen months before but for a strange incident that called him back when he had already boarded a steamer to bring him from Le Havre to New York. At this time he also again told friends of his resolve to sail to America with his family.[207]

It seems therefore that in January and February 1852 he was doubtful whether he could hold out in England. And yet no less a person than Cole had already helped to make Semper's name more generally known, or at least to make potential clients aware of it. The *Journal of Design*, a periodical edited by him, carried in its December number a short article under the title "On the Study of Polychromy by Gottfried Semper"; it consisted of excerpts from Semper's archeologically oriented study published several months before, *Vier Elemente*, which could have been of interest to the readers of the journal only because the use of color in modern buildings was at that time being widely discussed.[208] More important for Semper was the concluding editorial remark: "Mr. Semper it was who so skilfully arranged the Canadian Court in the Great Exhibition. His knowledge both of architecture, and generally of decoration, is profound, and his taste excellent. It is men of his acquirements from whom our manufacturers would be likely to obtain great help."[209]

It is strange that Cole thought it appropriate to reprint excerpts from a paper five months after its publication. However, at about this time he was pulling every string in order to be put in charge of reforming the schools of design. As he was using the *Journal of Design* for the promotion of his ideas on the organization of art education in general (and had even launched the *Journal* for that purpose six years before), it can be assumed that, with future developments in mind, he wanted to make Semper known as a contributor to the journal. This would mean that he was planning to make use of Semper's experience and talent as a teacher, unless he intended no more than helping him to commissions by alluding to his capability as architect and decorator. For the moment, this article did not lead to anything.

However, it indicates that Cole's relationship to Semper became more personal than it had been so far. When he heard that Semper was ill, he sent him, possibly on Rachel Chadwick's initiative, a check for £5 "to keep until you get rich enough to repay it to me" and offered him the admittedly minor job "to draw some very simple outlines of objects in a large bold way"; as an entry in Cole's diary indicates, these were to serve as models in drawing lessons.[210]

Vitally important information reached Semper during January. For weeks now the public had discussed the question of how to make the best use of the considerable surplus from the Great Exhibition. The commissioners had accepted a plan, Semper heard, that included the formation of an art school. Here was at last what he had longed for for almost three years—the possibility of permanent employment appropriate to his knowledge and experience as architect and teacher. He was all the more hopeful because he knew that Cole was in constant touch with the commissioners. On January 29 he applied to Cole, in English. "Having heard," the letter begins, "that the High Commission appointed for the Exhibition of all Nations is now preparing the Establishment of a School for art and industry I take the opportunity to declare that I would feel most happy, if my services should appear to the High Commission of some utility in the accomplishment of this their most important task." As former director of a school for architects—a position he held for many years—he believed himself familiar with the subjects in question. In Dresden he had reorganized the school and had given the instructions a more practical orientation by introducing "ateliers" where his own activity as architect proved to be of great value. He had been responsible for every decorative detail and even for the furniture of all public and private buildings constructed by him in Dresden and other parts of Germany. He could therefore rightly say that the decorative part of architecture was his speciality. He had made designs for silversmiths and for manufacturers of chinaware and was therefore familiar with the technical requirements of porcelain manufacture; he had also supervised the casting of the bronze statue of the late king of Saxony standing in the Zwinger. Furthermore, at the Dresden Academy he had given lectures dealing, apart from theoretical and applied geometry, with the history of architecture and comparative architecture, which included all applied arts. The major part of his drawings, among them details of antique bronze vases and a collection of decorative engravings, was here in London; he would be glad to make use of them once again as teaching material—they were, of course, at the disposal of the High Commission. As proof that he had been seriously studying his special subject, he enclosed

"the first part of an elemental treaty [*sic*] on China picture" that he
had written in Sèvres (obviously an essay on porcelain painting, which
he wrote in June 1850).[211]

It might be thought that Cole himself had prompted him to write
the application. But much contradicts this assumption. Had the suggestion come from Cole, no doubt he would have explained to Semper
how matters really stood. The commissioners had indeed decided to
build a cultural center on the ground south of the Crystal Palace, still
to be purchased; yet these plans could be realized only after the sales
negotiations had been completed, and they dragged on until 1853 and
beyond.[212] The "school of art" that Cole might have mentioned and
that was the only possible place of employment was the "School of
Design," the direction of which Cole would soon take over under the
explicit condition of changing it into a new department under the
Board of Trade. The commissioners had, therefore, nothing to do with
this school and its management. Besides, there was no need for an
application—the usual procedure, which Cole later observed, was for
the director to choose as teachers those who seemed to him best
qualified and for the Board of Trade after consultation to confirm the
appointment officially. What clinches the argument against Cole having
known of the application in advance is his reply: "Upon my return
from Yorkshire," he wrote on February 4, "I find your letter. If I have
an opportunity I will endeavour to promote your wishes. I have forwarded your Mss which interested much to the Editor of the Athenaeum." This short note, which dealt with letter and article in the
same courteous, noncommittal manner, leaves no room for doubt:
Semper had acted on his own initiative when applying for a teaching
job at the "School for art and industry."[213]

It was six full weeks before Cole asked Semper to come and see
him. Although Cole did not hold out any prospect for an engagement,
the fact alone that he entrusted him with a job no doubt filled Semper
with hope. In his application he had stressed his knowledge of porcelain
manufacture; Cole now suggested that he give a lecture on this subject,
but before doing so visit Minton's, the leading English ceramic factory,
at Stoke-on-Trent.[214]

Semper was there by March 20. Three days later Herbert Minton
wrote to Cole: "Mr. Semper is now here & in very comfortable lodgings.
You request me to 'assist him all I can.' In which way do you wish
me to assist him & what are yr Views in sending him here? I understand
he is to give a Lecture, upon Ceramic Manuf at yr request. Is it on
behalf of the Soc of Art or the School of Design? I fear he has much
to learn but he is a clever man and I think has good taste. I have

introduced him to Arnoux [his French manager] who has taken great fancy to him."[215] It seems therefore that Cole had given neither Semper nor Minton a clear indication of his intentions, which obviously were to get an expert's opinion about Semper's ability and to be assured that in fact he was, as he had said, "acquainted with the exigencies of China fabrication et [*sic*] . . . all the procédés used in that important branch of Industry."

Semper remained several weeks in Stoke. At the end of his stay he sent a report to Cole. He apologized for not having written before but he first wanted to form his own opinion about the many new things he had seen in this center of English industry. Then follow remarks that are instructive as to Semper's attitude toward applied art: he had found Minton's "decorative floor-and wall tiles" most interesting; in his opinion their influence on architecture and art in general would be considerable. The encaustic process employed in their manufacture could of necessity use only a limited number of colors, which had the salutary effect of restraining decorative extravagance. For this reason he found it regrettable that the new process of printing tiles was increasingly favored among artists, not so much because of lower cost but for the freedom given in the choice of colors. He had always found that restraint imposed by material helped to safeguard good taste. Minton's majolica ware lacked the rough, sandy clay of Urbino that forced the potter to produce simple, large forms and prevented him from abusing the decorative elements of his art. These problems, briefly hinted at, should be discussed in the advanced courses of the School of Design. Right from the start, in addition to drawing lessons, the students should be given tasks that related to their chosen profession. That was how he did it in Dresden: after short instructions in the use of drawing material and exercises in projections, the students started at once with designs for architectural details, and thereafter proceeded to designing the interior and exterior of a simple cottage; they were permitted to draw "leaves, flowers, figures, etc." only if they needed them" for some decorative parts of their compositions." It would be desirable for schools like the pottery school here to be given a complete collection of vases and other vessels assembled not so much from the usual aesthetic point of view as from an emphasis on material, size, and function.[216]

Semper's intentions behind this letter were obviously to stress his long experience as teacher and his ability to form his own judgment, and to make clear that his practical ideas accorded with Cole's attitude. The letter was written on Thursday, April 9; the following day he left

Stoke and returned via Liverpool and Birmingham. "I shall be back in London on Saturday or Sunday morning."

On Monday he met with Cole. There was no mention of lectures and ceramic art, but instead Cole made him an offer so exciting, so promising, that Semper wrote Dr. Braun about it the next day, asking him to contribute to the success of the work he had been offered.[217] Details are given in other letters, above all in one Semper wrote to Vieweg: "I should deliver a kind of illustrated 'catalogue raisonné' about the whole field of metallurgy that should include the most important things that man has created in metal, from the oldest to our own time."[218] The fact that he had been offered for this work £180, in no way a negligible amount, meant his first real, if only literary, success in England; but what made the meeting a momentous event was Cole's hint that the catalogue, if satisfactory, might earn him a professorship at the Board of Trade's newly established Department of Practical Art. Cole had probably given only a slight intimation, for Dr. Braun advised, "Let Cole come out into the open with his offer and make him increase it as much as possible by telling him what you have in mind to include in the catalogue."[219] Semper followed this advice and submitted a plan more to his liking, which "would include also the principles of architecture as a result and a working together of the different other branches of art," but was then quick to assure Cole that he would do anything Cole wished him to do.[220] Cole did not take up these proposals but must have been more explicit about Semper's prospects because on May 20 Semper stated without reservation, "I am a candidate for the post as professor at the local drawing school and for the moment have at least been given a commission by the director which . . . should serve as an introduction to a more permanent official position."[221]

Nevertheless, Semper was still not sure whether Cole would keep his promise in the end. Probably in order to put some pressure on him and to make clear the urgency for a decision, he added to a progress report on the catalogue the unrelated information that a friend in New York had advised him to come over, as several German architects had found more work there than they could cope with. He, Semper, knew that things look different when seen from nearby but he was afraid that in England "Continental influences and the jealousy of the English artists and architects" would never let him succeed here.[222] Cole, it seems, was not willing to commit himself, for in a letter to Bertha many weeks later Semper was still skeptical. Though he repeated what he had told Vieweg at the outset, that much depended on this work, he still had doubts: "I do not believe it will help me to a secure position; when asking for definite information I have been given only evasive answers." Doubtful again about his prospects in England, he came back, as so often before, to his old plan of emigrating to America:

This work, which under different circumstances I would welcome, is very embarrassing now. Without it, I would have not the slightest doubt what to do. With all of you I would at once board a ship to New York, and that still is the idea to which I always come back in the end. Here, in overcrowded England where the architects do not let a foreigner gain ground, I do not believe that I am ever going to build again. Heaps of English candidates are after the teaching jobs—national jealousy alone does not allow the principals to appoint foreigners to these posts. So my prospects are slight and I shall never thrive here.[223]

Even taking into account that Semper was by nature skeptical and after so many setbacks did not want to raise false hopes for Bertha's and his own sake, it is evident that Cole had not made a firm offer and that Semper had to be content with the promise that a satisfactorily finished catalogue might bring him a more permanent position. In his situation this was important enough for him to make the utmost effort to hand in a first-class work.

Because he had been given only two or three months to complete it and because there existed hardly any literature on the subject, or at least no comprehensive study, he had to throw himself into this work energetically and without losing any time. He wrote to all the friends he had on the Continent: to Séchan in Paris, Dr. Braun in Rome, Vieweg in Braunschweig, to his old friend Theodor Bülau in Hamburg, to an old acquaintance, Julia von Zerzog, to his successor at the Academy in Dresden, Hermann Nicolai, and no doubt to many more. He asked them all for information about local works of art in metal—ancient, medieval, or modern—and if possible for drawings or engravings. "For me everything is important and interesting that more or less belongs to art, for instance, even weathervanes, balls from a church spire, door knockers, signboards, etc." The main thing was that information and illustrations were sent to him as quickly as possible. "Speed is everything . . . belated help is of no use to me."[224] His friends and acquaintances on their part approached other experts in other places so that in the end a host of people contributed to the birth of the catalogue—Dr. Braun promptly, Julia von Zerzog tirelessly. The former was in his element. Here was a field of activity for his flair for organizing, was the possibility of giving advice and guidance to his protégé. By May 4 he had sent Semper a "first draft for a systematic survey of old and new metalwork"; organized into four main groups (Egypt, Orient, Antique, and Middle Ages) and many systematically arranged subdivisions, it contained an amazing number of objects and included some relevant literature—a scheme which, as Dr. Braun wrote, "can serve as framework to be filled in." He seemed to have in mind a magnum opus on metalwork over which he would have overall control. "To think of cataloguing is possible only when the plan has been fixed and the preparatory work is proceeding."[225]

During May contributions arrived from all sides. Particularly useful were Dr. Braun's references to articles that contained descriptions and illustrations of important metalwork. On May 22 Semper asked the director of the British Museum library, Anthony Panizzi, for permission to make drawings from Agincourt's and Willemin's works, "being charged by Mr. Cole to work out an illustrated Catalogue for a projected collection of metalworks." During the next few weeks he worked regularly in the Reading Room of the museum.[226] On June 9 he decided to submit to Cole a few finished drawings. Failing to see Cole, who was away on an official journey, he explained in the interim report mentioned above how far the work had progressed and the difficulties he had encountered. To make the catalogue interesting, he believed it ought to include objects that had not been published, and of the published ones to include at least one illustration drawn from a different angle, in some cases even in color. With this in mind, he had turned to his Continental friends, who now expected to be reimbursed for expenses. Would Cole be so kind as to grant him an expense allowance. He himself had already spent considerable money on books and had to employ a draftsman to speed up the work. "But I am poor and cannot . . . go on without being supported. . . . I showed my drawings to Mr. Owen Jones who was satisfied, but who believed, that it would be better to make them [on] a larger scale." Of course, this would be determined by the size of the publication; until Cole ordered otherwise, "I shall continue in the same way, as far as I can do without assistance."[227]

Nearly three weeks passed before Cole found time to see Semper, who now submitted not only the drawings but also part of a first draft for the introduction.[228] Cole, it seems, did not respond to the question of an expense allowance;[229] on the other hand he was satisfied with the work so far, and that, after all, was the main thing. "Mon travail a plû à mon homme (qui me protège)," Semper reported to Séchan, but added ruefully, "mais il m'a chargé en oûtre d'illustrer le système que j'avois adopté, pour démontrer les affinités et les différences qui existent entre les ouvrages de métallotechnic (selon leur distinction, leur origine commun ou différent, leur âge, etc., etc.) avec quelques dessins sur bois. C'est encore un travail énorme." He hoped he would at least be well paid, but was still skeptical about the prospects of a possible engagement: "Je ne vois pas bien le but et la fin de tout cela."[230] For the next weeks he worked hard at finishing the text. To allay Bertha's suspicion about his long silence, he wrote: "You know, I am leading the most lonely, miserable life in my lodging. I only leave in the evening at seven or eight for a meal; I have nothing before but a piece of bread with my tea."[231]

By the end of July he handed over the first sheets to the copyist.[232] But even at this time he had little hope and was very depressed: "I cannot describe how much I long to get away and how much I hate my life here." In the same breath he visualized the opportunities waiting for him and his family in America: "If I am paid for my catalogue as I hope I shall be, find someone who will see to it that further drawings are obtained, then I can leave at once having enough for our crossing to America and will be free and happy. Because, I repeat, the air here depresses me."[233]

Because of the deadline set for the completion of the catalogue he was constantly under pressure. He had had little more than three months to make himself acquainted with a material new to him. It was an enormous work, which his habit of digressing did not make any easier. It is therefore understandable that the manuscript in its final form was to some extent inadequate. Much, however, is re-markable—the plan for an ideal museum, the system of classification based more on the "Urmotiv" (basic motif) than on material, and the related theory of cladding (*Bekleidungstheorie*), as well as, for the first time, thoughts about the function and form of ceramic vessels.[234]

He delivered the manuscript in the middle of August, and anxiously awaited the judgment.[235] Cole was obviously satisfied; until then always reluctant to make any promises regarding an engagement, he now declared his firm intention to speak about it to the minister, the pres-ident of the Board of Trade. In fact, before Semper had shown him the first drawings and part of the manuscript, he had already consulted Chadwick, who knew Semper better than he did, and then, a few days later, had seen the minister and had obtained his approval for Semper's appointment.[236] Semper would have been spared many anx-ious hours had he known that the first draft had already secured his position. Whatever might have been the reason for Cole's reticence, he now told Semper outright that he would endorse his appointment as teacher in the Department of Practical Art. On August 17 Semper could at last announce the long-awaited good news: "It seems my work has made a better impression than I hoped because it made director Cole speak to the minister, explain to him my situation, and ask him whether he would object to my appointment although I am an alien and refugee; the minister had laughed and declared that he did not care at all to which faith and to which political party I belong as long as I know my métier and that he hoped I was not appointed because but although I was a refugee, etc., etc." Semper was relieved: his constant suspicion that he would never be allowed to gain ground in England had proved to be unfounded. At last, the nerve-racking time was over—the long years when one hope after another had been dashed, when he had doubted himself and his ability. For the first time since he had fled from Dresden he would have the means for a permanent home, in a city that would no longer be only a temporary refuge on the flight from his homeland. "Under these circumstances it would be foolish to leave . . . I reckon with a salary of about £200 . . . if on top of it I earn £100 we shall manage though perhaps only just because the guinea is spent here like the thaler in Saxony. . . . Cole has promised to pay me an advance on the catalogue." Even the ever-suspicious Semper trusted him now. "I do not doubt his good intentions anymore and am sure he won't desert me." The years of separation were over, the family could be reunited—he hoped by the end of the month.[237] The removal took longer than he had expected, and Bertha and the children arrived in London only at the end of September; but the main thing was the certainty that a new life had begun.

On September 8 Cole had another meeting at the Board of Trade, at which he made definite arrangements for Semper's professorship; two days later Semper was informed of the conditions and accepted them.[238] The following day he received the deed of appointment: "I am directed by the Lords of the Committee of Privy Council for Trade," it begins in formal bureaucratic terms, "to inform you that they propose to establish a class in order to afford instruction in the principles and practice of Ornamental Art applied to Metal Manufactures, and that they have been pleased to appoint you to conduct the same."[239] Full of joy and pride, he wrote to Bertha: "Since Wednesday I am professor at the Department of Practical Art and have already moved into my office. Though my salary is not big (£150 and part of the lectures and consultation fees, etc.) the position is nevertheless quite advantageous because it opens up prospects for other works and for a new sphere of activity. Since the main part is done, the rest is a mere trifle, and this trifle is the considerable expense that I will have to face. But I am resolved to pass the test like a true philosopher and not let this thought spoil the joy of our seeing each other again after this long separation."[240]

The decision was made for England as the country where he and his family would settle for good—or so he thought in September 1852.

Teaching at the Department of Practical Art, 1852–1855

From the moment he joined the Department Semper's life was transformed: his future was secure, his days ran in a well-ordered rhythm. As soon as his family arrived, he moved from the "miserable dirty den" in University Street to an apartment near Hyde Park in keeping with his improved circumstances.[241] From there he walked during termtime across to Marlborough House for the daily (later, also evening) classes; prepared his lessons and public lecture courses; dealt with inquiries from manufacturers and private clients who sought his advice; and worked on commissions, mostly small ones, which came to him through the Department or individuals. To do justice to his change of lifestyle, the style of the narrative will change, too. For the remaining three years of Semper's exile there will be no reports of hopes and disappointments, of financial trouble, of plans, of reproaches, excuses, or warnings. The tale will be limited to the most important of his teaching, designing, lecturing, and writing activities at the Department.

The Department of Practical Art had been formed in February 1852, mainly at Cole's intiative, as the central administration of the Schools of Design, then in existence for fifteen years.[242] Cole and Richard Redgrave—superintendent and art superintendent—were charged with carrying out a far-reaching program: the reform of industrial art education in England, with the London school playing a leading part as a matter of course. To make the planned extension of the London school possible, the Department moved in May from Somerset House to Marlborough House, put at its disposal by the Crown. Apart from an expansion of the school's museum, more space was needed above all for additional technical classes. Cole wanted to discharge an obligation, imposed on the Schools of Design many years ago, to introduce classes for the study of production methods.[243]

To take charge of these classes additional staff was needed. Cole had approached Owen Jones, whose name and personality would have helped to overcome the unavoidable growing pains,[244] but he was not interested in a teaching post. Another suitable person would have been Matthew Digby Wyatt, who had recently completed a large book on metalwork and was the obvious choice for the head of a metal class.[245] It was probably because Digby Wyatt turned down Cole's offer, preferring the lucrative job for Paxton of rebuilding the Crystal Palace at Sydenham, that Semper was commissioned with the metal-work catalogue, although Cole certainly knew that it duplicated Wyatt's work. It was meant as a kind of test, to make sure that with Semper the Department would gain an expert of equal standing. The failure to obtain Wyatt's collaboration might also have been a reason that Cole suddenly changed his plans and assigned the metal class to Semper; an additional reason might have been Minton's doubts about Semper's knowledge of ceramic production. It explains the strange fact that the Department had no ceramics class.

Seven special classes were set up, of which four—Wood Engraving, Lithography, Anatomy, and Painting on Porcelain—had little to do with industrial art;[246] the head of the fifth class, Architectural Details and Construction, resigned after a few months so that there were really only two classes where the guidelines set for the lessons— constant reference to industrial production—could be put into practice: Semper's class for metalwork and Octavius Hudson's for textile fabrics.[247]

Semper was the only teacher with practical experience in the prob-lems of the special classes. For everybody else—the Board of Trade, Cole, Redgrave—they were something radically new. So far the Schools of Design had been drawing schools: drawing exercises formed the basic element, skillful mastery of ornamental grammar the ultimate aim in the training of craftsmen. No wonder that they all thought the intended reform necessary but daring and, while hopeful, were not at all convinced of its success. They considered "the direct practical application of the arts to manufactures" and the special classes to be an experiment, advised the heads of the classes to proceed with much caution, and advocated a trial period of at least two years.[248] Semper did not have these doubts: what had been successful in Dresden could not be impossible in London.

Three months after school started, he submitted a report about his teaching method, asking Cole for official sanction, and also made proposals for broadening the lessons. His "System of Instruction" is a surprisingly progressive document.[249] He advised instruction based on workshop practice, not the conventional system of school classes; no neatly separated lessons or classification of students by age or individual progress, so that by watching the work of advanced students, the beginners could learn more easily; students to assist the professor in his commissions, thereby having the best opportunity of getting practical knowledge and experience; above all encouragement to work creatively, an important side of the instruction at present too much neglected: students passed their time copying without trying creations of their own. "Many a talent has been spoiled by having been too long a time engaged with copying a studying from models and even from nature"—a true observation that threw sharp light on the weakness of art education of the day. The advice was too sharp for Cole. Wishing to publish Semper's "System" in the Department's first yearly report, he revised the text. He changed imprecise phrases, improved the style, softened expressions here and there, but he thought the final criticism went too far: he crossed out the sentence and inserted in its place the inoffensive observation that "those copies . . . would have much more interest for the student . . . if done in connexion with some idea which the student had in his mind."[250]

To keep up the students' eagerness to learn, Semper proposed competitions. Traditionally prizes were awarded once a year for the best school and the best works. In contrast Semper's competitions would take place every two weeks, be closely related to the lessons, and subjected to the criticism of both professor and students. Moreover, he also suggested semiannual competitions, with a traveling grant for the winner of the Gold Medal, obviously modeled after the Grand Prix of the Ecole des Beaux-Arts. Cole was too much of a realist to let this idea stand. The printed report reads only that "to that medal might be attached, by the Board of Trade, certain contingent advantages to the student in the prosecution of his studies."

The most important principle of Semper's teaching was the application of theoretical instruction to practical work. This had caused no difficulties in Dresden; there he had his own large commissions that gave students the opportunity to assist. In London he had only few small commissions,[251] so it was fortunate that a few weeks after school started, the Department gave him work that was especially suitable for encouraging students of the metal class to work with him: a funeral car constructed mainly out of metal.

The duke of Wellington had died on September 14.[252] For political reasons, a solemn funeral procession on a grand scale was called for. Lengthy preparations and the wish to avoid having the official funeral take place during parliamentary recess were the reasons for postponing it to the middle of November. On October 21 the Lord Chamberlain's office inquired whether the Department was ready to undertake the construction of the funeral car. "The Board of Trade considered that the Department was not yet adequately organized to undertake such work officially, but permitted the assistance to be given . . . as a private transaction."[253] Redgrave immediately started making a number of sketches; the same evening Cole entered in his diary, "sketching car."

10
Semper. The duke of Wellington's funeral car, 1852. (Photo Frank Herrmann)

Semper also did some drawings; the illustrations of the "Pompes funèbres" that Séchan had sent him the year before no doubt proved useful. Cole and Redgrave presented these sketches two days later to Prince Albert. "Settled and approved," noted Cole after the audience. "The Prince liked many parts of your design," he told Semper the next day and arranged a meeting for the following morning at Marlborough House.[254] There it was decided to start immediately on the design approved by the prince, which was Redgrave's design incorporating those details of Semper's that the prince had liked. The text to an official lithograph published on the day of the funeral clearly specifies what share various people had in the work: the basic idea had come from superintendents Cole and Redgrave, the design proper from Redgrave, the construction and ornamental details from Semper, those of textile fabrics and heraldry from Hudson. In a public lecture Cole was quite generous in his recognition of Semper's contribution: "The general design of the car was chiefly suggested by Mr. Redgrave, but the successful realization of the structure, with its ornamental details, was due to the ability of Professor Semper."[255] It seems from all the evidence that, while Semper's assistance had been called for at the design stage, his role was limited to the construction and ornamental execution and to overall supervision. He himself never claimed to be responsible for more than the execution (figure 10).[256]

Ettlinger has dealt with the funeral car from an art historical and typological viewpoint. To prove his thesis that the design of the car was due mainly to Semper, he remarks: "His sensitive character would have hardly allowed him to supervise a work designed by another artist. If a considerable share in the design had not been his, he would not have collaborated."[257] When Ettlinger wrote the article little was known about Semper's life after he had fled from Dresden. The quotation serves to show how easily lack of information about Semper's situation could lead to wrong conclusions. The ever-recurring theme in this narrative about Semper's years of exile is his longing for security, and it allows only one conclusion: Semper was neither in a position, nor would he have dared, to refuse the job he had been assigned.[258]

The funeral car for the duke of Wellington was the most important commission received by the Department. Only two more are documented, and again Semper's class was called upon to deal with them. One was a design for a large sideboard for which the client, Sir James Emerson Tennant, had offered a prize of £25 for the best design;[259] the other was for a kiosk where telegraph messages could be handed in, to be erected in the center of Oxford Circus by the Electric Telegraph Company, which also offered a prize.[260] Semper's sketches for the kiosk have survived; they show a small, square building of two stories, as specified, with a roof overhanging on all four sides and a small clock tower to give the small building greater emphasis in its isolated position. It is questionable whether the cost of such a building could have been kept down to the specified sum of £500; whatever the reasons, it was never erected.[261]

At times Semper made use of private commissions for practical teaching.[262] In his tax return for 1853 he declared, apart from his salary of £150, a sum of £100 "from the profession of making drawings," which probably were done in connection with this kind of commission; to these may also belong some designs for furniture that have survived. He received a sum of £20 from the Department for the design for the official school certificate, the original of which was attached to the minutes of the Board of Trade (figure 11).[263]

Designs for three buildings from this period would also have been instructive for his students: a pottery school, a hostel for immigrants, and a bath and laundry establishment.[264] It is quite unlikely that they were done for definite commissions because Semper never mentioned them; the good fortune of having been commissioned with large projects would have found some echo in his correspondence. Since, on the other hand, it is known that in April 1853 he took part in the competition for the "Potteries School of Design, Staffordshire" (figure 12), it can

11

Semper. Design for Department of Practical Art certificate, 1853. (Public Record Office, London)

12

Semper. Design for Potteries School of Design, Staffordshire, 1853. (Institut für Denkmalpflege, Dresden. Deutsche Fotothek Dresden)

be assumed that the other two projects were also done for competitions.[265]

We know of only one larger architectural design on which Semper worked during this time—an engine house and manufacturing building in the Royal Arsenal at Woolwich. The work can hardly have been pure joy for him. The Royal Engineer Corps, to which the Arsenal belonged, gave its officers architectural training and could thus provide the state with cheap personnel whenever the help of an architect was needed. Semper's officer also had architectural ambitions; he returned Semper's design for an engine house with these words: "I have altered the lower elevation in the manner in which I propose it should be built. It is taken from the outline of a cannon & I should like to give the chimney some resemblance to that suitable Object. . . . You will see that I have altered the roof into a parapet."[266] Only the need to supplement his salary could have induced Semper to persevere to the end.

The teachers were under an obligation to give public lectures. Courses of five lectures were foreseen for Semper, one course for 1853, two for 1854.[267] Several manuscripts for them have survived. After Semper's death the most important ones were translated into German, edited and published in *Kleine Schriften* by his sons. In these lectures Semper often repeated what he had said in two treatises published only a short time before in Germany; but much is new and of interest today for the development of his theoretical ideas.[268] One lecture will be singled out because it deals with a problem toward which his standpoint differed from that of the Department.

Because work on the funeral car and preparation for the start of classes did not leave time to work out the lecture course, one inaugural lecture was arranged for Semper and Hudson. On May 20 he gave this, his first public lecture in England, at Marlborough House. Several incomplete manuscripts have survived, among them an interesting fragment which, written partly in German, probably represents the first draft. It is headed, "Draft for the lectures on the relation of the various branches of industrial art to each other and to architecture. 1st lecture."[269] The opening sentence reads: "The decorative arts arise from and should properly be attendant upon architecture." This principle, he declared, was well known to his audience, for it "heads the few rules which the Department has drawn up as a teaching norm" and is—as he wrote in another fragment (this time in English)—"the first of those which are fixed on the walls of Marlborough House."[270] The group of rules to which he referred had been worked out by the Department with Semper's, Hudson's, and probably also Owen Jones's help before school had started.[271] The first rule was taken from a lecture by Jones on June 5, 1852, three months before Semper was engaged.[272]

Therefore the first sentence of Semper's lecture is a quotation from Jones, not coined by himself as the reprint in *Kleine Schriften* implies. Moreover, he could not even agree with it in this form; in fact, the purpose of his lecture was to show that in his opinion the historical evolution of applied art and architecture was the reverse of Jones's axiom. "Everybody who has thought about this sentence," he emphasized at the beginning, "will agree that it needs elaboration so as to make one aware of its consequence and to make its practical application possible, and secondly to prevent being led to wrong conclusions." In a kind of dialogue of question and answer he makes clear where he stands: he asks whether before architecture had developed its laws and main elements, these had been unknown and not applied, and answers: certainly not. He asks whether the influence of architecture on practical arts was the older and more important or, the other way round, the influence of practical arts on architecture, and answers: certainly the latter. He asks whether the other arts borrowed the processing of material, their forms and ornaments, from architecture or whether the forms and rules of architecture could be traced back to those that the practical arts had applied long before, and replies: certainly the latter—questions and answers that a few years later were to form the base upon which he built *Der Stil*. All this, however, conflicted with the view taken by the Department to such an extent that he did not dare, in his first official lecture, to pronounce it in this programmatic form. In the final version he suppressed the provocative formulation, remembering the obligation imposed on him "to make the practice of Art conform to the General Principles recognised by the Department,"[273] and developed his argument in a way less likely to arouse opposition—a justified caution, especially since Cole attended the lecture and found it, as delivered, "thoughtful and suggestive."[274]

If Semper suppressed, or at least toned down, the basic reservation he had about the validity of the axiom the Department had set up, he nonetheless presented his own views incisively. "A great part of the forms used in architecture," he declared, "thus originate from works of industrial art, and the rules and laws of beauty and style . . . were determined and practiced long before the existence of any monumental art. The works of industrial art therefore very often give the key and basis for the understanding of architectural forms and principles."[275]

It was a novel idea. Further developed and explained in later lectures and, no doubt, in conversation, it was food for thought and may have convinced Cole and Redgrave that teaching applied art without any reference to architecture could hardly lead to the desired rebirth of "good taste." In any case, it was wrong to leave Semper's great experience as an architect untapped. When the Department was reorganized in October 1853 under the new name Department of Science and Art, the opportunity was taken to appoint him head of a class for "Practical Construction, Architecture, and Plastic Decoration."[276] The inclusion of architecture meant a fundamental change, which certainly affected his status within the school.

At the same time, he was charged with training candidates for teaching posts at the various Schools of Design supervised by the Department, so that he now had three groups of pupils: fulltime students, evening classes for working students, and teacher candidates. The number of pupils steadily increased. He had started with seven; in the end he had thirteen full-time students, twenty-two in the evening classes, and about fifty candidates.[277]

Although the Department made great demands on him, he still found time for writing; not, as one would expect, for revising and completing "Vergleichende Baulehre," badly needed by Vieweg, but for a mainly mathematically orientated tract to prove that "the Greeks . . . had seriously studied the laws of nature and had created their own forms independent of any imitation." He chose for this research a simple example, ancient slingshot missiles, and tried "to demonstrate the absolute efficacy of their forms derived from the laws of dynamics."[278] The work that he had hoped to finish within a few days dragged on for months: he had to tackle difficult mathematical calculations, the extent of which is evidenced today by six thick manuscript volumes; he discarded, revised, and started all over again. But he was in his element; mathematical problems fascinated him all his life. "I have been working for a whole year on a damned difficult problem that I now at last cast off and surrender to you unconditionally," he wrote to Dr. Krause in January 1854 when he sent him the manuscript for his appraisal. "It has cost me some failings in my duty. . . . The paper . . . grew out of a notion that I had hoped to formulate within a few days . . . but the subject overwhelmed me—I spent many a night over it to produce, perhaps, nonsense or something trivial."[279] Dr. Krause handed the paper to the mathematics teacher at his school who, after proposing some corrections, sent a report to the *Poggendorfsche Anzeigen*, and finally returned it.[280] Semper revised it again, so it was eighteen months before Vieweg received the manuscript, titled "Über die Schleudergeschosse der Griechen" (On Greek Slingshot Missiles). Thereafter events delayed its publication for several years, a misfortune to which we shall return in "The Genesis of *Der Stil*, 1840–1877."

It was just as well for Semper that he finished the tract because a few days after its dispatch he received a commission that was incompatible with pondering over mathematical equations of complicated curves. Paxton inquired whether he could undertake the arrangement of one of the commercial "Courts" inside the reerected and enlarged Crystal Palace at Sydenham. Cole, consulted by Semper, gave his permission willingly; no doubt Semper pointed out the advantage the Department would gain by having the opportunity to provide students with practical instruction.[281]

His official contract for the design and execution of the "Mixed Fabric Court" is dated February 4, 1854. A sum of £2000 was put at his disposal; he was instructed to complete the court on April 24, a full month before the date of the opening. This did not leave much time for preparing the plans and obtaining contracts. From the first day, the directors urged him on; at the end of March they still had not received the plans, and in April they found the work lagging behind schedule.[282] But apparently Semper was not the only one to be late, since the opening fixed for May 24 had to be postponed to June 10. Even then his court was not completed, and when work came to a halt in June only the shell and the most essential decoration had been executed.

The seven commercial courts, including Semper's, all were the same size: 73 by 48 feet. Contracts and accounts, many of which survive in the Semper-Archiv, make it possible to get an approximate idea of what the Mixed Fabric Court looked like. It was a freestanding installation with four walls and a ceiling and was accessible from the hall through eight doors. Inside were twenty freestanding columns in front of the walls, which were decorated by pilasters. Glass display cabinets probably stood in the recesses between the columns. The only architectural decoration mentioned are two cornices, one at the height of the columns, the other the main cornice below the ceiling, both repeated on the outside as well. The sculptured decoration consisted of figures, festoons, and ram's heads in the pediments over the doors; putti and crests in a large pediment (probably over the main entrance door); lion's and ram's heads as decoration of the pilasters; crests on the lower cornice and figurative decoration over the glass cabinets. Semper's budget turned out to be insufficient to provide further decoration as planned; in mid-May he had applied for a supplement of £500, which was rejected.[283] Only when the stream of visitors after the opening celebrations had slowed down did Paxton find time to see about the commercial courts. No doubt he had to admit that Semper's court could not be left half finished, and on July 22 he authorized an additional sum of £800. The next day Semper wrote to Séchan that, lacking sufficient funds, he had not been able to finish the colored decoration but was now in a position to pass on this job to him and Dieterle; they should come over to London for discussion.[284] A few days later they arrived and worked out a program with Semper. Again the budget was too tight, but Paxton refused another increase and, on the contrary, demanded a guarantee from Semper "stipulating that the amount sanctioned by him shall not be exceeded."[285] Therefore, the program had to be cut back and savings had to be made on material. The work was shared between Paris and London—Séchan and Dieterle took over the painted decoration (a large ceiling painting 14 3/4 by 11 1/2 feet) as well as panels, soffits, and twelve wall panels with figures representing the various nations and their textile products; London handled the making of the wooden paneling, the marbling in black, gold, and lapis lazuli, and the gilding and bronzing of friezes, capitals, beadings, and figures.[286] Thus, through

rich and colorful decor a typically French shop was created, the elegance
of which English artists could scarcely have designed. Without Semper's
connections this work would not have been accomplished; he alone,
with the small amount at his disposal, could have secured out of
friendship the cooperation of two leading French decorators.

Because London could start with the decoration only after the work
done in France had arrived, it was October before Semper could order
the painting work and the end of the year before all was completed —
fully six months after the reopening of the Crystal Palace.[287]

Although this delay is one reason why Semper's court is hardly
mentioned in the literature of these years, even completion on time
would have made little difference. This assignment meant more to
Semper than the effective and tasteful arrangement of exhibition stands
three years before in the first Crystal Palace, but the situation was the
same: the best work had gone to other artists. The big attraction was
the "Fine Arts Courts," most of them designed by Owen Jones and
Digby Wyatt. Next to these grandiose diplays of exact reproductions
of great monuments, the commercial courts were hardly noticed. One
of the few reviews that appeared after the completion of Semper's
court concluded a detailed and appreciative description of all the won-
ders that were displayed to the public in the new Crystal Palace with
this remark: "For the class of visitors to whom we have hitherto
addressed ourselves, what is called in Crystal-Palace phraseology 'the
Exhibitors Department' will offer at first but little attraction. Many a
day will they spend in the building without knowing . . . that there
are shops or exhibitors at all, or that they have anything to do with
the Musical Instruments' Court, the Printed Fabric Court, or the Hard-
ware Court, except to pass by on the other side."[288]

When Semper had turned to Séchan, he explained that "ce petit
travail, qui dans soi même, n'est pas grande chose . . . pourra conduire
à d'autres travaux plus importants," and mentioned a project for an
"Odéon ou Halle musicale" on which he was working. It follows from
a second letter that this structure was to stand in the great transept
in the center of the Crystal Palace.[289] The assignment was for the
reconstruction or adaptation of an ancient theater. Some sketches —
studies for the color view now in the Semper-Archiv — have survived
(figure 13).[290] Marginal notes on one sketch indicate that Semper took
as model the theaters in Pompeii, known to him from his travels (the
Odeon and the Great Theater). Whether the reproduction of an ancient
theater was his idea or, more likely, belonged to the main program
culminating in the fine arts courts, it was in any case an honorable
commission, far more important than that for the commercial court.

13
Semper. Design for theater, Syndenham Crystal Palace, 1854. (Semper-Archiv
Zurich)

However, it remained a design, perhaps because of the chronic lack
of money, but also perhaps because Semper's constant fear that English
architects would not let him get ahead may have been justified in this
case. Two entries in Cole's diary seem to suggest so. On January 21
he noted: "With RR [Richard Redgrave] to Sydenham. . . . Saw O Jones
& Wyatt—the first annoyed at introduction of other Architects in
building." Again, in Paris at the end of the year, Jones raised objections
to Semper's planned architectural treatment of the British section.[291]
It indeed looks as if their relationship was not as friendly as has been
assumed; on the contrary, that Jones saw an unwanted rival in Semper
and opposed him.[292]

It seems that Semper had little contact with British architects; the
mere fact that he turned to Paris when he needed help indicates this.
From his first visit to London years before he knew Thomas L. Donaldson.[293] Thanks to Donaldson, his colored reconstructions of Greek
temples had been exhibited at the Royal Institute of British Architects
in 1851 when Donaldson gave a lecture on polychromy;[294] it was also
due to him that he received a standing invitation to the meetings of
the Institute, which gave him the opportunity to meet British colleagues
if he wished. Only one such instance is recorded—a meeting in 1853
with C. R. Cockerell, who sought his advice as an expert in acoustics

for his music room; Cockerell sent him a very friendly letter the following day, enclosing "the trifling gratuity which was agreed between us."[295] Semper of course knew all the people belonging to Cole's circle but seems to have had a personal relationship only with J. C. Robinson, the director of the museum at Marlborough House. After his arrival in London he made contact with political refugee organizations and kept it up for a while, but his interest in men whose political views and fate had been similar to his own soon changed into pure friendship.[296] Among his inner circle were the highly gifted engineer and inventor Wilhelm Siemens and the political correspondent of the *Nationalzeitung*, Lothar Bucher, each familiar with subjects that had always interested Semper.[297]

Since becoming a member of the Department, everything had taken a turn for the better. He taught a system he believed in, the number of his students grew, his income was secure with a fixed salary and occasional private commissions—only the prospect of practicing as architect in England had not yet improved.

At the time when he was busy cutting down the Mixed Textile Court program that had been worked out with Dieterle and Séchan, a letter from Richard Wagner arrived. He had been asked whether Semper would accept the post as Professor of Architecture at the Eidgenössische Hochschule soon to be established in Zurich. Through that position he would "become the highest authority in matters of architecture for all of Switzerland." Knowing that Semper was well off in London, he had not offered much hope. However, he continued, "should there be some snag in London with your position that spoils it for you, you might yet consider the Swiss offer. I am telling you all this with little hope but with the very selfish wish that you might not like it in London; because to have you here would please me no end."[298]

Wagner had hit the mark. There was indeed a "snag" in London. When, weeks later, Semper informed Cole about the offer from Zurich, he gave reasons for accepting it that show how much, in spite of the undeniable improvement of his situation, he had suffered the last two years from frustration and lack of recognition, and how unattainable a breakthrough to success in England seemed to him. "I fear," he told Cole, "1. Never to be able to master the language nor to be fully acquainted with English conditions to such an extent that I could discharge my duty as well as otherwise I would; whereas I shall regain in Switzerland my native tongue and artistic conditions and thus be more in my element. 2. My name in Switzerland is far better known than here as is evident by this offer. For that reason, it will be easier for me to find an adequate field of activity as teacher and architect."[299] This was how things looked: in England he felt restrained, suffering from not being able either to satisfy the demands made on him or to develop his artistic talent.

The hard times of the last years had made Semper discontented, suspicious, and irritable. As soon as he arrived in Zurich for an interview—the work at Sydenham delayed this until the middle of September—he was a changed man. "Semper has pleased me very much," wrote Wagner on September 18. "He is cheerful, almost gay, and takes a childlike pleasure in everything."[300] Semper negotiated with the president of the school council (*Schulrat*), Dr. Johann Konrad Kern; a few days later he returned to London, entrusting further negotiations to Wagner's friend Hermann Marschall von Biberstein.[301] Semper was apparently eagerly looking forward to being offered a chair. Marschall, who knew Semper only in the elated mood of their first meeting and was unaware of his usual changeability, thought he ought to warn him against a hasty decision. "A metropolis like London," he wrote immediately after Semper's departure, "offers men of your standing quite different resources than the modest facilities of our Switzerland."[302] When, a few weeks later, he sent him the good news that the Bundesrat had agreed to his engagement and expected his decision within one month, Semper—as usual—hesitated.[303] In such situations he always reacted in this way—trying to retain the freedom of choice as long as possible—because he feared the finality and the consequence of a decisive step. Pressed by Zurich, he at last, belatedly, accepted and agreed to bring forward the date for taking up his post from the autumn to May 1, 1855. At the last minute—grotesque as this was—he raised new difficulties, fearing complications because of his status as a political refugee. Thanks to Marschall's energetic intervention,[304] this crisis too was overcome, and the official certificate of appointment was dispatched on February 9.

Thus the die was cast—against London where the hostile attitude of his British colleagues barred his career as architect and embittered his life—and for Zurich where there seemed to be every chance for the taking. Then, a fortnight later, the longed-for, unexpected event happened. On a visit to Marlborough House Prince Albert mentioned to Cole an idea he had for a great assemblage of museums on the grounds purchased by the exhibition commissioners; he made a rough sketch on a piece of blotting paper and expressed the wish that, at his expense, Semper should work out exact plans.[305]

What prospects—perhaps he would be charged with building the museums in spite of Zurich! Full of enthusiasm, he sent Séchan the grand news of a "travail grandiose et sérieuse," which made Séchan reply that if the people in London who had a say in the matter had any sense, they would not let him go.[306] On reflection, it probably did not take Semper long to see the situation in its true light. He must have known that two years before, leading British architects— Donaldson, Cockerell, John Pennethorne—had, at the prince's initiative, submitted grand projects for the planned cultural center that were not carried out, and that the previous year a design by Cole and Redgrave for the same project had been shelved due to the Crimean War.[307] There was little chance that Prince Albert's new project, devised as a commercially viable enterprise, would be accepted.

In any case Semper could not start immediately on these plans because he had to be in Paris for the Exposition Universelle from mid-March to the beginning of June. Together with members of the exhibition committee and the Department, he worked on furnishing and arranging stands; his special responsibility was to design and execute the emblem of the British section, the so-called Naval Trophy, described in detail in one of the printed guidebooks. Semper reported after the opening that although the trophy had not turned out as well as he had wished, it nevertheless had found favor with the public.[308]

At the beginning of June he returned to London and finished the drawings for the prince—a perspective view, plan, and elevation—on which he had worked in Paris whenever time permitted. Besides the museum complex he designed a separate building, a concert hall, as requested by the prince.[309] On June 15 he showed his designs to Cole and submitted them shortly afterward to the prince, who was very satisfied and sent Semper through his aide-de-camp a gratuity of fifty guineas.[310] The plans were judged on June 28 at the Board of Trade and "much to the Prince's disappointment" rejected as too much of a commercial risk.[311] Semper, who could hardly have expected a different outcome, left London and traveled via Paris to Zurich where he arrived on July 11.[312]

Here ends the tale of Semper's exile—but not his connection with the Department of Science and Art. There is an epilogue.

Semper was a deeply discontented man. After six months in Zurich it seemed to him that "the English period [was] brilliant compared to the present."[313] Another six months, and he saw his future as an architect in Zurich so unpromising that he approached Cole, through his friend Siemens, about the chance of being reinstated. "Cole was kind," reported Siemens, "and declared his willingness to help you. He would write to you as soon as there was a prospect; but it might take three to six months."[314] The reason for this delay was that after

Semper's departure a provisional reorganization had taken place. Three of the school's students were installed as teachers, one of whom, Christopher Dresser, took over the class for botany that had also become vacant, at the same time that the other two took over Semper's classes, Architectural Drawing and Ornamental Design. At the end of the summer term 1857 these arrangements would be evaluated.[315]

As Cole could hardly have wished to fill in this way the gap caused by Semper's departure, it can be assumed that he had tried to find among English artists one fully qualified to replace Semper. The fact that he obviously had had no success then or later, if he had tried at all, reveals Semper's extraordinary, almost isolated, position in England and the uniqueness of his teaching method at the Department.[316] In any case, at the beginning of July 1857 Cole asked Semper whether he was still thinking of returning.[317] After Semper's assurance that he indeed was longing for a change, namely "for a sphere of activity as practicing architect from which I shall forever be excluded in monotonous Zurich,"[318] Cole brought up the matter at the next meeting of the Board of Trade. It was decided "to re-engage Professor Semper's services for carrying the Instruction of the Training Masters to a high point and also to advise in the arrangement of the Architectural casts" and to improve the financial terms: a yearly salary of £200 and a guaranteed minimum of £100 for "other services," by which was meant, Cole assured him, "other work connected with architecture."[319]

Semper seems to have been quite satisfied with the offer because a few days later a friend congratulated him on the appointment, probably reflecting Semper's opinion when he added, "A man like you really needs a larger field of activity than Zurich offers."[320] At the beginning of September Semper met with Cole and reported to Bertha: "He explained to me that he intends to employ me on large buildings that will have to be constructed next year in Kensington on the grounds the government has purchased. To be able to do this, to employ me on the building, I must hold an official post at the Department of Practical Art; without this position, the jealousy of the architects would not let me get on." For personal reasons he had first turned down the offer, but then he sought time until the end of the year to think about it. Cole had also promised to do everything in his power to meet further wishes he might have.[321] Obviously, it mattered a great deal to Cole to secure Semper's service.

Semper now had three months to come to a decision, three months of weighing the pros and cons, of being "again in the same agonizing uncertainty." Cole's offer was promising but, he might have asked himself, were the officially assigned tasks—reforming teacher training and acting as adviser to the Museum of Architectural Casts—really only devices for giving him the status of a civil servant that was a prerequisite for being employed, or would he in the end find that he was not to go beyond the bounds of these rather inessential activities? It was true that there was the real prospect of important building tasks, but equally true that a number of buildings had been constructed recently after the designs and under the direction of Pennethorne and Captain Francis Fowke, the Department's architect and engineer.[322] Was it not to be feared that in spite of his official position the British architects would still stand in his way and that, at best, he would play the part of an eminence grise? The apprehension was not completely unjustified, as Lord Derby's remarks show when, ten years later, he rejected commissioning Semper with the revision and execution of the late Captain Fowke's design for the Albert Hall: "it would [be]... something like a slur on the whole body of British Architects, to pass them over for the construction of a really National work, in favour of a foreign Professor, who is not even resident in England, and is not known here by any of his works."[323] On the other hand, Semper knew of Cole's extraordinary dislike of British professional architects and understood that for that reason he was Cole's man, offering as it were the unusual combination of an experienced professional architect (whom Cole badly needed) and one who nevertheless remained outside the exclusive circle of British architects.[324]

All this Semper would have taken into consideration. As the time for a final decision approached, he came to the conclusion that accepting London would be the right choice. "I shall probably leave Switzerland quite soon and return to London," he wrote on November 1 to his brother Wilhelm and a few days later also to his son Manfred; in the same vein he wrote the Fürstin Sayn-Wittgenstein, explaining the reasons for resigning his post in Zurich: "I am worn down and in order not to lower myself to the level of a junior teacher at a technical college, I seriously consider accepting an offer... which will at least take me back to a grander environment.... A competition for the Polytechnicum has been advertised here. I am expected to enter it as one of many competitors although it is frankly admitted that all this is done pro forma only and that the building has already been assigned. My experiences are such that I will not be taken in by that."[325]

At the same time he inquired, again through Siemens, whether Cole would be prepared to raise his salary to £300; but obviously he did not want to block the way by this demand and was quick to add that if circumstances did not allow this rise, Cole should let him know "what additional sum over and above the £200 could possibly be granted."[326]

Perhaps Cole declined, or perhaps the authorities in Zurich at last realized that Semper was in earnest about leaving and made last-minute definite promises regarding the design of the Polytechnicum. In any case, Semper one again reversed his decision and turned London down. From now on Zurich became, soon legally as well, Semper's new homeland.

3

The Great Exhibition of 1851 as Inspiration for Der Stil

During his years of exile, 1849–1855, Semper never gave up hope of working again as architect. Although the work at the Department of Practical Art interested him, he still longed for the day when he could build and put into practice what he had written and taught for so many years. When he finally accepted Zurich's offer, he believed that the moment had arrived; he was confident that he would reestablish his reputation as a leading German architect and that his name would emerge from oblivion. In this he was right—commissions for buildings, some of them quite substantial, indeed followed. Within ten years of his arrival in Zurich, he had designed three major buildings that were either completed or nearly finished: the Polytechnicum or Eidgenössische Technische Hochschule, an imposing building in a prominent position high above the picturesque old quarters of Zurich (1858–1864), the nearby Sternwarte (Observatory) (1861–1864); and the Town Hall at Winterthur, a skilfully planned building with the dominant classical feature of a pediment carried by four freestanding columns (1863–1869).[1] He also worked, mostly in competition with others, on large building projects that for one reason or other did not materialize: a theater in Rio de Janeiro (1858), the railway station in Zurich (1860), a casino in Baden (1866), and—the most promising and interesting of all—the Festspielhaus in Munich planned by order of Ludwig II of Bavaria for the performance of Wagner's operas.[2] Thus he was fully engaged in his profession, glad that the frustrating years of his exile were over. He may well have been unaware that it was only through his long stay in London that he had produced the work which, more than anything he ever built, secured his fame and keeps his name alive. This was his book *Der Stil*, published in two volumes in 1860 and 1863.

The Great Exhibition of 1851 was the decisive influence on Semper. As has been shown, he did not take part in its organization or in the

selection of the exhibits but, charged with the arrangement of four
stands, worked for many weeks in the exhibition hall. He made full
use of the opportunity and went around the stands daily, watching
the arrival of the exhibits from all quarters of the world, with ample
time to scrutinize them. In this way the effect of the exhibition went
much deeper than if he had visited it as a foreign tourist or sightseer.
What he saw confirmed his critical assessment of modern artistic
production.

Like many architects of his time, he was conscious of the serious
decline in artistic taste and of the lack of a unifying coherence among
the various branches of the arts. He was also alarmed by the detrimental
influence of the machine and its concomitant, speculation, on the
quality of modern industrial art. But walking through the exhibition
hall he came across displays of objects that were strikingly different
from the pretentious and tasteless machine-produced exhibits of the
great nations. He admired the assurance with which half-civilized savages—the Lapps, American Indians, Tibetans—arranged the colors
and patterns of their textiles or molded the forms of their ceramic
wares, and he frankly admitted that India, New Zealand, and many
African tribes had demonstrated their superiority in the technical arts
over anything Europe had produced. He realized that these primitive
people had achieved this high standard by instinctively following their
innate sense of color and form, a faculty that the modern nations had
lost: "None of the technical, mechanical, and economic means that
we have invented and by which we have the advantage over the past"
would help us improve our industrial art.[3] In order to equal these
people artistically, we should consciously do what they do instinctively,
namely study and respect "the properties of the material and the
requirements of the task."[4] In this way we would attain beauty of
form and color. However, we would forgo this worthwhile though
modest achievement if, heedless of the basic conditions imposed by
material and function, we strove precipitously for the highest artistic
end.

Semper found that the significance of these artifacts went even
farther. Like many writers of his time he had always been interested
in the age-old question of the origin of architecture. He rejected the
purely fictional assumption of the cave or primitive hut as the prime
model from which architecture had evolved, and he distrusted the
belief, held by many writers, that building had been man's first artistic
activity, followed by all minor branches of the arts. He became aware
that the fine products he had seen and admired were, in a way,
witnesses to societies in which man, emerging into history, gave

expression to his artistic impulse long before architecture or even building activity existed. Prehistoric man had done the same that primitive people of modern times did now: they adorned their bodies, molded clay, wove mats, fences, and carpets, made their tools, implements, and weapons from stone and metal and their fittings from pieces of timber. "The arts," he wrote later, "were far advanced in their application to adornment, weapons, implements, and vessels thousands of years before monuments were built."[5] By fashioning and adorning these objects, man instinctively applied order, rhythm, pattern, and proportion. Thus the basic aesthetic laws were first developed in the practical arts and from there carried forward, as it were, into architecture. "The industrial arts are therefore the key to understanding architectural as well as artistic form and rule in general."[6] These thoughts were the response to everything he had seen in the exhibition, the good and the bad; they grew within the next few years into a plan for a comprehensive book, which would start not with the principles and laws governing architecture but with a detailed scrutiny of those principles that had instinctively been observed by artisans of the five branches of industrial art—textiles, ceramics, carpentry, masonry, and metalwork. The immediate object of the book was to give guidance to contemporary industrial art and to assist it in regaining the quality it lacked most: style. Adopting the method of ancient artisans, Semper restricted his task to the consideration of three factors: the properties of the material used, the technical process applied, and the function the object was to perform. He called this novel approach "practical aesthetics."

Der Stil is a thought-provoking book that deals with a host of subjects. It contains a detailed classification of industrial products from a formal point of view, as well as their historical modifications, ranging from China, the ancient Middle East, Egypt, Greece, and Rome to the Middle Ages and the Renaissance. It gives an exposition of his most original ideas—about color in architecture and the important role that cladding played in architecture throughout the centuries; about *Stoffwechsel*, the transference of functionally conditioned motifs from one material to another whereby they assume symbolical significance; and about the influence of new inventions and new materials on the quality and style of products. It contains a long chapter on the architectural orders and in each of the five sections, critical remarks about modern products. His study of industrial art was so extensive that by the time he finished with the last applied art, metalwork, the book had grown into two volumes. They were to form the basis for a concluding part that was to deal with architecture. When the second volume appeared in 1863, *Der Stil* was well received; it was generally believed to be the most important book in the field. A second edition was published soon after Semper's death in 1879.

It is in a way an optimistic book, a fact that certainly contributed to its success.[7] Although it was the low standard of the industrialized objects at the Great Exhibition that made him put down on paper the conclusions he drew from this deplorable state of affairs, and although he criticized as strongly as many others the devastating influence of modern production processes, the division of labor, and speculation, he did not despair. He did not hate machines as Ruskin did; did not, like Ruskin, turn his back on modern times in disgust, or believe that salvation lay in a return to the medieval artisan's way of making things. It would be wrong, he wrote in *Der Stil*—and this sounds directed against Ruskin—"to ignore with haughty gentility the present and its inventions and offer the perfect accomplishments of the past as the one and only model."[8] At times he even pleaded for what he called "a very liberal stylistic code" that made allowance for the new conditions created by new manufacturing processes.[9] He expected taste and aesthetic sensitivity to improve, provided the new means were mastered. If that happened and "the machine learned to be subordinate to the natural properties of the material, then it will have a beneficial effect on the arts."[10] How receptive he was to new inventions and how willing to judge them without prejudice are shown by his remarkable chapters on a new material, vulcanized rubber. His description of its properties, applications, future possibilities, and stylistic characteristics is exemplary.[11] It has rightly been called "an apotheosis of synthetic material a hundred years in advance of his time."[12] Confident of inevitable progress, he exclaimed at the close of the Great Exhibition: "May the inventions, the machines, and the speculators stir up things with all their might; they will thus prepare the mixture out of which constructive science will mold the new form."[13] The book he was going to write would, when complete, serve as guide toward this new form. Little did he know when he first conceived it the pain, disappointment, vexation, and misunderstandings that would result.

The Genesis of Der Stil, 1840–1877

The pages that follow trace the origins of *Der Stil* and of the idea for a final third volume, which never appeared. The manuscript of this third volume is not among the manuscripts of the Semper-Archiv in Zurich and, as will become evident, almost certainly never existed. Still, close examination of the existing manuscripts has brought to light previously unknown events that explain to some extent the unfinished state of *Der Stil* as well as bring into focus the genesis of this work. What follows is intentionally limited to recording what has been gathered from Semper's literary estate, his correspondence, and publication agreements—it is the history of a book and does not attempt to be more than that.

The early history of *Der Stil* began in 1840 with Semper's lecture course on "Gebäudelehre," forerunner of the work with the same title commissioned four years later by Vieweg (figure 14). Over the next eleven years Semper tried to comply with his contractual obligations. The exchange of views between author and publisher regarding "Vergleichende Baulehre," about which I have written elsewhere,[1] came to a standstill in 1851 when Vieweg, on the occasion of his visit to the Great Exhibition, asked Semper to shorten and revise the preliminary manuscript he had submitted the previous year. Semper promised to undertake this immediately, and Vieweg offered to let him have back the original manuscript, which for the purpose of revision was probably "more convenient than the incorrect copy"; he was also prepared to publish, when revised, the introductory chapters as a separate installment.[2] Semper made a first attempt and then gave the disagreeable job a rest.

Vieweg waited in vain. He was reassured by Semper's promises first, that his imminent appointment to the Department of Practical Art would make it possible for him to complete the book, and then,

14
Eduard Vieweg. (*Verlagskatalog von Friedrich Vieweg & Sohn*, Braunschweig, 1911)

three years later, that his chair as professor in Zurich would bring "peace and leisure that alone will enable me to carry out the plan, conceived a long time ago, of having my 'Vergleichende Baulehre' published."[3] In his reply Vieweg again offered to return the original manuscript, which means that in 1855 they were still corresponding about the revision of the 1850 manuscript.[4] This time Semper accepted the offer and therefore was in possession of the original manuscript as well as the copy, which through Dr. Braun's good offices had been made some time ago. He looked over the manuscript, made some changes and corrections,[4] but once again did not get down to a thorough revision and shortening of the text. This was partly due to circumstances that will be dealt with below, but above all to the change in his views on architectural problems. Decisive impressions during the last years — the Nineveh reliefs in the Louvre, the Great Exhibition of 1851, and teaching at the Department — made him doubt more and more whether the scheme of eleven building types that he had originally drawn up was suitable for attaining the goal he visualized. Increasingly he believed that he had to build on a broader foundation if his work on how "forms of art develop out of their earliest stages"[5] was to be convincing and influential on contemporary architecture.

In the letter from Zurich in which he wrote of the peace and leisure that he hoped would allow the completion of "Vergleichende Baulehre," he intimated for the first time that he had been contemplating a work that exceeded the scope of this treatise. He mentioned the catalogue of metalwork compiled some time ago for Cole, which he had composed "in a way similar to a larger work I intend to write about the whole range of forms." This is the first mention of a larger, far-ranging work.

But the letter was really about different matters. Semper suggested having "Vergleichende Baulehre" brought out in installments whereby Vieweg would run no risk since he, Semper, was quite clear in his mind about the whole as well as the details and what mattered now was "to make a resolution and *begin*." He also asked Vieweg — and this was an important reason for writing the letter — to consider if "it would not be easier to fix the fee according to the number of sections and of drawings for the woodcuts and accordingly to change the agreement, which is still in force and which relates to the total work."

Vieweg agreed to bring the book out in installments, although in view of the possibility that "the author draws out . . . the work and abandons it" he thought it necessary to fix a date for the completion of the whole — a reasonable demand that, however, showed amazing confidence after years of Semper's failure to deliver the manuscript.

Nor did he object to changing the contract, provided they could agree on the amount payable for each section; he suggested about four louis d'or or forty guldens a section. Since he was shortly going to Ragaz, he proposed a meeting there or in Zurich.[6]

At this meeting Semper explained in detail his fundamentally changed views. As he later reminded Vieweg,

I told you that I had in mind making essential changes to the plan of my book; I wanted to have the technical arts precede architecture because stylistic laws and symbols that later were employed in architecture were first developed in works of the technical arts and for that reason could most clearly and visibly be shown there in their elementary form; also because the established architectural . . . forms achieved significance and meaning only by being contrasted to the related forms of movable objects, etc., that had been developed in earlier times and were therefore familiar to man; and lastly because most recently the need and demand for an artistic development of the technical arts have more than ever become apparent, as the industrial exhibitions make particularly evident.[7]

The meeting ended with the understanding that Semper would begin with this work and that Vieweg, after receiving the first installment, would give his opinion of the new plan.

Nine months later the "far-ranging" work, which Semper titled "Kunstformenlehre" (Theory of Art Forms), was so far advanced that he dispatched in a wooden box the first installment.[8] The box also contained one hundred drawings, almost all drawn directly on blocks. The extent, and up to a point the contents, of the manuscript can be deduced from sheets listing the woodcuts and drawings by section and chapter, and also from another treatise, written at about this time, which in disposition and some particulars agrees with the list.[9] According to these records, the manuscript sent to Vieweg consisted of preface, introduction, and two sections of the first part of the text. The first section of about sixty pages dealt with the "Simplest Combinations": the basic principle of ornamentation, simple and alternating rhythm, and also a lengthy discourse on adornment. The second section, about 350 pages on "Ceramics," followed an order that Semper later adapted in the second volume of *Der Stil.* Elsewhere he gave a short summary of the overall plan of "Kunstformenlehre": the first part was to consist of six sections—simplest combinations, ceramics, textiles, masonry, carpentry, and metalwork; the second part was to provide a comparative history of architecture as agreed upon with Vieweg.[10]

Semper had probably already begun the preparatory work for "Ceramics" in London, making use of his Department lectures. This would explain the comparatively short time of nine months for the completion of such an extensive work; in Zurich he would have had to work only on the drawings and the introductory chapters. It seems likely also because at the time of his meeting with Vieweg, or shortly after, he was thinking of tackling the section on textile art, the next after "Ceramics." But here he met with difficulties. Although it was a subject in which he became especially interested at the Great Exhibition, during his time at the Department he had never properly studied it, not wishing to trespass on a colleague's field of activity.[11] Therefore, two months after his arrival in Zurich he wrote to his friend Lothar Bucher, at the time Paris correspondent of the *Nationalzeitung*, who took an interest in industrial art yet was in no way an expert. The letter reveals Semper's lack of knowledge of the relevant literature, which is strange for one who was going to write a treatise on textile art. He hoped that Bucher could answer his questions: Was there an illustrated work on Indian and oriental weaving in general? On ecclesiastical robes and antique cloth in reliquaries? What was the title of the book on Indian style that Bucher had mentioned at Siemens's house? All in all, he needed notes on the technical and historical aspects of textile art and was certain that Bucher had collected something interesting about it. "I lack source material here, a drawback which almost makes me tired of Zurich."[12]

Whatever Bucher's answer was, it did not help Semper. A month later he decided to ask the Department for help. In connection with a planned edition of his metalwork catalogue he had been in touch with a former colleague and friend, John Charles Robinson. He now asked him to find out whether Cole and Redgrave would be willing to apply to the Board of Trade for a grant to Octavio Hudson, the head of the textile class, that would allow him to co-edit the section "Textile Art." Robinson's reply was disappointing:

I have consulted both Mr. Cole and Mr. Redgrave . . . but with every wish for the success of your undertaking, and I think I may say the best disposition to render you every service in their power, they seemed to think it would not be possible to cooperate in that way—in the first place Mr. Hudson is thoroughly impracticable—altho' he possesses considerable knowledge in Textile art he has no power of putting that knowledge in any tangible form, whilst on the other hand, his jealous excitable temper would never allow him to cooperate with anyone else . . . . And further, and more important, Mr Cole seemed to think it would be very difficult, if not impossible, to induce the Board of Trade to grant the pecuniary means in the manner required. . . . Quand à Moi—my services such as they are, are frankly at your disposition—I think that when you have thoroughly matured your scheme you would do well to publish it in an English dress, and in that case, I should be willing to edit your English version.[13]

So Semper was left to his own devices. He had no doubts that he could master the difficulties, but before continuing he had to know what Vieweg thought of the first installment. On June 19, 1856, he had advised the publisher that he had dispatched the manuscript and woodblocks. Weeks passed without an acknowledgment. Semper was worried; Vieweg's silence was strange. At last, at the beginning of September, a letter from Vieweg arrived. The box "hung around, God knows for how long, on freight carriages and trains" and had arrived only three weeks ago. He would have written before, but he was coming to Switzerland to take the waters at Bex and he would visit him in Zurich. "I shall bring your manuscripts, the preface, and the introduction to talk over the whole subject with you. I must confess that I cannot yet make out your new plan, which differs so much from the one we had agreed on."[14] The meeting took place on September 16 or 17.

As mentioned, Semper had already touched on the question of payment. In the meantime he had been told by his new colleagues in Zurich that the terms agreed between him and Vieweg twelve years before were inadequate; other firms, for instance Jacob Moleschott's publisher, Brockhaus, paid one hundred guldens a section.[15] Thereupon Semper had contacted the publishing house of Bruckmann in Frankfurt had arranged a meeting with its manager, Friedrich E. Suchsland. By chance or design, Suchsland arrived in Zurich on the same day as Vieweg.[16] Semper negotiated with Suchsland, of course without Vieweg's knowledge, but no definite agreement was reached. The same day, and again later in Bex, Semper discussed with Vieweg the plan of his "Kunstformenlehre." He must have been successful in meeting Vieweg's objections and reservations about the "far-reaching" changes because a new contract was drawn up that stipulated payment of four louis d'or a section plus an additional amount for the drawings. This was considerably less than the going rate, yet Semper was satisfied, or at least raised no objections. He handed over to Vieweg the manuscript on Greek slingshot missiles, "Schleudergeschosse," with the request to bring it out as soon as possible, and accepted half the advance of 500 francs. All seemed to be in order. Semper used the 250 francs for a trip from Bex to Geneva.[17] During these days he was plagued by the thought of having sold himself too cheaply at a fee that "vis-à-vis my colleagues must look almost degrading."[18] Back in Zurich, he was determined to enforce a decision—to confront Vieweg with the alternative of either paying the normal fee of one hundred guldens a section or losing him as an author.

On October 12, two days after his return and expecting Vieweg's visit, he sent a telegram to Suchsland in Frankfurt: "Regarding matter recent visit: can you undertake immediately Kunstformenlehre (two parts technical arts, architecture). Terms: 100 guldens section including drawings to be done by me? Type as my books published Vieweg. You to attend to blocks. Vieweg returns today [crossed out: tomorrow these days]. Must make decision. Please reply at once wire and letter."[19] Suchsland declared by return his willingness to undertake the work on Semper's terms and indicated that he considered the exchange of telegrams as the first binding step to a contract. This had not been Semper's intention! What mattered to him was to strengthen his position and to safeguard his retreat should Vieweg be inflexible. To correct the misunderstanding that an immediate agreement was possible, he explained to Suchsland on the same day: "I am under some obligation to Vieweg; besides, I am under contract with him though on conditions which make it impossible for me to make a living. . . . Herr Vieweg is, I believe, not very keen any more on the publishing business— rather than agreeing to give me the same fee that you are prepared to give, he will hand over to you my work, the first installment of which he already has . . . but the matter is best settled by mutual agreement."[20]

The next day Semper sent Vieweg a letter in order to make his position clear before their meeting. Had it really been his intention to come to an amicable understanding, then what he wrote lacked all sensitivity and was so clumsily worded that it could not possibly have led to this result. Because he soon afterward denied having intended to put pressure on Vieweg, it is necessary to look at the letter in detail.

Following a short first paragraph in which he explained that innate fear of speaking in his own interest and of appearing ungrateful and inconsiderate had kept him so far from raising objections to the draft for the new contract, he spoke almost exclusively of his demands for money.

You know the money worries . . . I have had for years. And now [he underlined the whole sentence] I have offers in my hand assuring me for everything I am going to write payment of 100 guldens a section including drawings which I have to provide. My colleagues receive the same, for instance Moleschott from Brockhaus. . . . If I compare this with what I shall receive from you according to the new contract, it would not even come to half of what other people offer me for the work. . . . Because the greater number of drawings in the section that you have are of small pots and ornaments, the payment of four francs may seem adequate, but in the part dealing with architecture the majority are of plans, elevations, and sections with all exact details. . . . I would have let the matter run its course, were the work not so extensive that it would keep me occupied for years. I bind myself as it were for life whereas at the same time I have offers assuring me of twice the sum. . . . For a long time, this has weighed upon me like a nightmare. I am convinced that you will put yourself in my position and be just to me.

At the end he urged Vieweg once more: "Would you be prepared to give me the same that has been assured to me by another party and that my colleagues receive, that is, 100 guldens a section that includes everything except the blocks? . . . Awaiting a reply as soon as possible, either by letter or orally, and with the assurance of my highest esteem and the request to recommend me to your ladies who were so kind toward us, I am always yours, Gottfried Semper."[21]

Vieweg was deeply hurt. Semper, his friend, by whom he had stood when he was in need, whom he never had dropped in spite of his failure to fulfill the contract, from whom he had quite recently parted on the best of terms—all this Semper disregarded, threatening him with higher offers from other publishers without even mentioning the bonds of a long friendship. He waited a week to reply and then left the same day, probably to leave Semper no time to come to Bex.[22] The breach was final. Semper did not exist for him anymore. Yet as publisher he did not release him. He took with him the manuscripts of "Kunstformenlehre" and of "Schleudergeschosse" to keep in pawn.

Semper was alarmed. He had not reckoned with this reaction but had expected that Vieweg would either agree to the higher fee or return the manuscripts. Secretly he had hoped Vieweg would choose the second alternative, for then he could forget the faults and failures concerning "Vergleichende Baulehre," the delays that Vieweg reproached him for again and again, could face the new publisher free from blame and guilt, and would suffer no more under Vieweg's "protection."[23]

What mattered now was to reach a settlement. With this in mind, he answered immediately and wrote again a week later after he had realized that Vieweg had avoided him and had left without seeing him; only then did it dawn on him how deeply he had offended Vieweg. He wanted to smooth over the bad impression of his disastrous first letter, looked for convincing reasons for his behavior so as to put right what could never be put right, defended himself, denied that he had wanted to get more out of Vieweg, appealed to his kindness—it was a pathetic, pitiful, and for Semper humiliating letter. At the end he made clear what really mattered to him—what he had forfeited through offensive insensitivity—the return of the manuscripts. "I consider it advisable . . . in both our interests, especially now since this dispute has happened, that we come to an understanding on the terms proposed by me. Once more I beg you . . . to consider that for me it is a question of my livelihood and . . . how unimportant the whole matter is for you. . . . Convinced of your kindheartedness I am sure that you will please me with a quick and hopefully favorable answer." But then he ended the letter with an almost threatening phrase that ruined any chance of winning over Vieweg: "However, should I be wrong and should there be no answer within eight to ten days' time then I must do without the continuation of the work I have begun and, with God's help, start a new one."[24]

This was the beginning of a fight for the manuscripts in which Semper tried to put the blame on Vieweg, and Vieweg to pay Semper back for his betrayal of trust. It was an unpleasant performance that went on for the next two years. Semper, coming back constantly to the delayed acknowledgment of the box of manuscript and drawings, reproached Vieweg for laziness and negligence, thus reversing the facts; maintained that his manuscripts would "be buried forever . . . under the mass of enterprises surrounding Vieweg"; even dared to blame him for not publishing "Vergleichende Baulehre" although "for seven years he had the drawings and manuscripts in hand . . . without making any attempt to start printing." Vieweg insisted on his rights; wanted to force Semper to continue working for his firm on the terms agreed between them; demanded repayment of the advances; threatened going to court—in short, tried to harm Semper as much as possible.[25] In November Semper handed over the whole affair to his solicitor,[26] but agreed, on Suchsland's and his friend Karl Ritter's advice, to let someone try to mediate. Suchsland corresponded with Vieweg, only "to have to put up with a bunch of insults."[27] Semper's son Manfred had a fruitless meeting with Vieweg in Paris.[28] Semper himself turned to Vieweg's son, hoping that he could achieve the return of the manuscript "Schleudergeschosse."[29] This time Vieweg saw the illegality of holding the manuscript, although it was another eight months before he handed it over.[30]

However, he was adamant regarding "Kunstformenlehre." When he finally agreed in August 1857 to release this manuscript too, it was on conditions that he must have known would be unacceptable to Semper. Vieweg contended that Semper was contractually bound for two works, "Vergleichende Baulehre" and "Kunstformenlehre." He would meet Semper's wish to cancel the contract for the latter, provided Semper committed himself now to the fulfillment of the other, the first contract. This should be done in such a way that installments of each work would appear alternately at strictly fixed dates, "Kunstfor-menlehre" at Bruckmann, "Vergleichende Baulehre" at Vieweg's. To safeguard adherence to the terms, he demanded securities, probably legally recoverable fines.[31] Vieweg's letter reached Semper in Paris, where he stayed for a few days on his return from London and his meeting with Cole. Outraged, he replied at once: "I shall never lower myself to become a literary slave . . . however much it were in your power to harm me and to hinder me in my work. . . . To write two works simultaneously as you imagine so that everything must be fin-ished at fixed dates is quite impossible for me." Moreover, there had never been two contracts. All they had agreed to in autumn 1855 had been a change in plan and title of "Vergleichende Baulehre," which "according to the new plan should form the last volumes of the work." From the list of contents and the introduction sent with the manuscript in the box it was quite clear that it had never been his intention to make two separate books out of "Kunstformenlehre" and "Verglei-chende Baulehre." "Once again I must strongly protest your view that we had ever talked about two different works."[32]

Thus Vieweg's proposition did not change the situation: Semper was still bound by contract to him. Suchsland made a last attempt in June 1858 to make Vieweg change his mind. He traveled to Braun-schweig, but this approach also failed. After a talk with Vieweg's brother-in-law because Vieweg was in Berlin, he came to the conclusion "that a friendly settlement is a long way off. From what Herr West-ermann told me I could clearly see that in their opinion the difference has to do with friendship rather than with business. You and Herr Vieweg, it seems to me, had once been intimate friends, the bond has slackened, and nothing is in such a case harder than for a third person to reach a fair and sensible settlement."[33]

So Vieweg had the section "Ceramics" from "Kunstformenlehre," which he could publish if he felt like it—"out of spite," Semper thought.[34] It was different with "Vergleichende Baulehre"; of that he had only the woodblocks, not the manuscript, which he had returned to Semper before the breach. It was, however, indisputable that he had the publishing rights, and Semper knew that to come to an agree-ment with Bruckmann he had to offer a new work that did not infringe on Vieweg's rights. At first he thought of writing an architectural dictionary like that by Christian Ludwig Stieglitz "but more in the style of the French work by Viollet-le-Duc," but he gave up the idea when he heard of the forthcoming new edition of Stieglitz's book. He then sought Suchsland's opinion about a work titled "Cultural-Historical and Art-Technical Studies on Architecture." "I would also consider

the technical arts, like ceramics, textiles, carpentry, masonry, metalwork, etc., but more in their relation to architecture than judged on
their own merit—because otherwise I would get too close to
'Kunstformenlehre.' " Two days later he suggested a different title,
"Theorie und Geschichte des Stils in der Baukunst und in den übrigen
technischen und bildenden Künsten in ihren Beziehungen zu der Baukunst" (Theory and History of Style in Architecture and the Other
Technical and Fine Arts in Their Relation to Architecture) and gave
a short summary of the contents of the first part: "Development of
the concept 'Style'—Theory of style—Theory of the genesis of art,
i.e., the practical side of aesthetics—Origin of the most important
basic forms and symbols in architecture and their further development
and modification . . . through national . . . and cultural ideas . . . from
their first beginnings to modern times." The contents of the second
part were "Theory of Composition. The most important tasks of the
present in their cultural-historical relation to the works of the
past . . . critical analysis of the main buildings of recent times." The
outline that had been agreed upon with Vieweg had, in his opinion,
the disadvantage that each building type would have to be traced
from its origin, which would necessitate a cumbersome repetition of
cultural and historical chronology. "I now avoid this because under
the new plan I can refer, when dealing with the tasks of the present,
to the cultural-historical roots as something known to the reader because
this factor will be treated comprehensively in the first part."[35]

This was the work—strongly oriented toward architecture—for
which Bruckmann was now preparing a contract. In January 1857
Semper received the first draft, and in April and May they were still
corresponding about details. Probably because Semper had not given
up hope for the release of the manuscript of "Kunstformenlehre," the
contract was not signed until January 15 the following year. Semper
first assigned to Bruckmann "Kunstformenlehre," provided that the
differences with Vieweg were resolved; should this prove impossible,
Semper undertook on penalty of a fine of 400 guldens not to publish
the work within five years, a clause that was to protect Bruckmann
against possible, though unlikely, competition. Second, Semper assigned
to Bruckmann the new work under a title suggested by him, again
with the exlusive right of publication. The book was to appear in two
volumes and contain a total of at least seventy sections. Semper's fee
was fixed at 7000 guldens, which came to one hundred guldens a
section as he demanded, provided he kept to the total number of
sections. The manuscript was to be delivered by the end of 1859.[36]

As we have seen, Semper had started the chapter on "Textile Art" long before the contract was signed. He must have overcome the difficulties of obtaining source material because in November 1856 a small installment of three sections was already finished.[37] During the next two years the work progressed well.

The manuscript was almost finished when in February 1859 he received the disturbing news that due to the threat of war Suchsland was going to suspend production of the book.[38] Semper was alarmed; he suspected this was only a pretext that concealed other reasons; he hinted that in spite of the war he had other offers and turned to Friedrich Bruckmann himself, whose intercession settled the incident in such a way that everything was readied for the volume to appear as soon as the crisis affecting the business had passed.[39] There was nothing Semper could do but show patience. The economic crisis lasted, and it was not until 1860 that the first volume of *Der Stil* appeared.

Soon, however, another difficulty arose, and this time Semper was responsible. After finishing the aesthetic-formal and technical-historical parts of "Textile Art," he decided to add a discourse on "The Principle of Cladding in Architecture." This was a concept he considered his own, and one decisive for a true understanding of monumental architecture; it originated from the controversy about polychromy that had so passionately engaged him as a young man and formed the basis of his entire architectural theory. No wonder that he had much to say; did not want to omit any literary or archeological piece of evidence; brought in issues that did not really belong; and—discipline as a writer not being one of his virtues—eventually found that three hundred new pages had been added to the two hundred of textile art, which meant that he had already used up half of his seventy sections, leaving only thirty-five for the second volume.

Still, he thought he could manage. In February he had declared— only to prevent Suchsland from suspending the work—that the two parts of the second volume were almost finished except that in the first part, which was to deal with the remaining four technical arts, "Ceramics" was missing, the manuscript of which he had still hoped to retrieve from Vieweg; the manuscript for the second part, the actual "Building Theory," was ready for the press.[40] Both statements were certainly not true. It can hardly be assumed that, having just finished "Textile Art," he had already written the three remaining technical arts chapters, and it is certain that the manuscript supposedly ready for the press was none other than the partly finished "Vergleichende Baulehre," returned to him for revision by Vieweg years before, and which he himself had only recently stressed as inadequate to use in the new work. The pretense is nevertheless interesting as evidence that Semper still believed that he could cram into the second volume the rest of the planned content—ceramics, tectonics (carpentry), stereotomy (masonry), and metalwork as well as the second part about architecture. He admitted that this might be difficult because by contract he should not exceed a fixed number of sections or if so, then only at his own expense: "It will indeed be difficult to give all I want to give and yet observe the fixed limit; nevertheless, I shall keep to this clause unless you prefer me to overstep the limit when the subject demands it, and then it would of course be understood that I would not be paid a lump sum for the whole but by section."[41] Obviously, he was after a change of contract, although later he again declared, "I shall not exceed the seventy sections which have, unfortunately, been laid down in the contract"[42] and drafted a prospectus announcing a work of two volumes, the second of which would consist of thirty-six or thirty-seven sections: twenty-four for the four technical arts mentioned and twelve or thirteen for architecture in general.[43] Shortly afterward, he realized that this was impossible. Why he suddenly came to this conclusion, one cannot say. In any case, he now negotiated with Suchsland about changing the contract.

This led to a supplementary contract between Semper and Bruckmann on October 7, 1859—birthdate of the third volume. The work was now to appear in three consecutive volumes: textiles in the first, ceramics, carpentry, masonry, and metalwork in the second, and architecture in the third. Bruckmann's willingness to bring out architecture in a separate volume gave Semper the freedom of action he had demanded; it would now be possible for him to treat the four remaining technical arts adequately. Yet he had not won the hoped-for financial improvement. After the manuscript of the second volume had been delivered, he would be paid 5000 francs, which with the advance of 7000 francs already paid would bring the total payment for the two volumes to 12,000 francs or 3000 guldens. "The rest," reads the contract, "which remais fixed at 4000 guldens, even if the number of sections is exceeded, will be paid four weeks after delivery of the third volume."[44] The third volume was therefore included in the original lump sum of 7000 guldens. As Semper worked out much later, around 1876,[45] the fee for the total work including the third volume, which he estimated then at thirty-five sections, was thus reduced to a rate of sixty-six guldens a section. The total was still more than Vieweg had offered him, but only if he wrote the third volume. If this did not happen, all he received was 3000 guldens for the first two volumes, or forty-two guldens a section, which was almost equivalent to the offer by Vieweg, who would have paid less by section but more for the woodcuts. The result of this calculation: the rupture with Vieweg had been unnecessary. But of course Semper counted on earning the balance of 4000 guldens by delivering the third volume.[46]

There had been some discussion about the title of the three-volume work. It was agreed that the title proposed by Semper and entered into the contract, "Theorie und Geschichte des Stils in der Baukunst," was too colorless and weak to attract a wide public. Suchsland and Bruckmann found in the word "Kunstformenlehre," coined by Semper, what they had been looking for: "It is the best title and of great importance for sales."[47] Semper protested: "I cannot possibly give my consent to adopting the title that had been intended for the Vieweg book. . . . I am certain that, because of it, Vieweg will make trouble for me. Therefore, if you insist on calling the book 'Kunstformenlehre,' I must ask you . . . to state in writing that this was done without my consent and at your own risk."[48] For their part, Suchsland and Bruckmann rejected Semper's proposed title, "Praktische Aesthetik" (Practical Aesthetics) and suggested a compromise: "Die Lehre von den Kunstformen, oder der Stil und seine praktische Anwendung in den technischen und tektonischen Künsten" (The Theory of Art Forms, or Style and Its Practical Application in the Technical and Sturctural Arts).[49] For Semper even this modified "Kunstformenlehre" was so risky a title and "practical aesthetics" a concept so important to him that he could not accept this proposal. Soon afterward the final title was agreed upon—*Der Stil in den technischen und tektonischen Künsten, oder Praktische Aesthetik* (figure 15). Suchsland's and Bruckmann's reservations proved to be unfounded: the first two words—*Der Stil*—contributed their part to the success of the book.

The first volume was already in the press, and promotion became necessary. As mentioned, Semper had drafted two prospectuses that outlined the contents. According to the first version, the book, still in two volumes, would be divided into two major parts. "The first part deals as it were with the earliest grammar (*Urgrammatik*) of style in the technical and structural arts, while the second part has as its subject the general meaning and spirit of this language of forms and our response to its modifications brought about (most powerfully and comprehensibly in architecture) through moral, religious, political, local, and climatic conditions." The first part would of necessity go into great detail and would therefore be by far the largest; the second part would deal with the phenomenon of art as a whole and "the grander that is the better it can be grasped through only a few striking char-

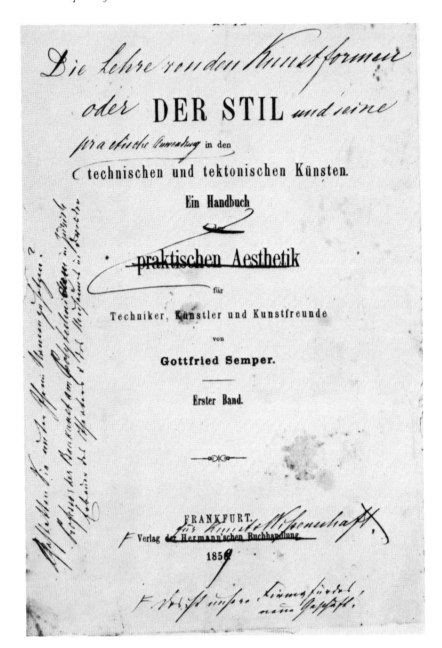

15
Der Stil. Design for title page. (Semper-Archiv Zurich)

acteristics; verbosity and detailed analysis will only confuse." In his introductory remarks Semper referred to architecture only in a general way: "Architecture will be the main subject of the book, first on its own but then also in its relationship to art in general because it is the principle of architectural rule and order . . . that in all arts makes up the style."[50] The second, more specific, prospectus sets out in detail the contents of all the sections—including, for the first time, the sixth and final section.

Revised and shortened, the second prospectus became part of the final prospectus for the three-volume edition, in which the sixth section had become the third volume. About the content it reads:

All functional, material, and structural factors that relate to the problem of style in architecture have been amply dealt with in the five preceding treatises about the technical arts. . . . To these, however, must be added as the most powerful factors of style in architecture the social structure of society and the conditions of the times, which to express artistically in a monumental way has always been the most eminent task of architecture. The comparative method applied to the study of the history of arts is the only way to achieve true knowledge and appreciation of these important moments of the monumental style.

Semper then added a sentence that set the whole work a goal which, though always visualized by him, he had never formulated so clearly:

A vast field for inventiveness will be revealed to us once we try to make artistic use of our social needs as factors of the style of our architecture in the same way as had been done in the past; whereas it would hardly ever be possible only through new materials and their use in new methods of construction to bring about a decisive and lasting change in architecture and even less so through the simple power of a genius who has dreamed up his so-called new style.

At the end of the prospectus Semper listed the contents of the third volume in greater detail and he again referred to modern architecture. Six chapters would deal with ancient art (western and eastern Asia, India, and Egypt), Greece, Rome, Christian Rome, the Middle Ages, and the Renaissance—the same division of cultures as in his treatise "The Principle of Cladding in Architecture," a similarity to which we shall return. Under the heading "Renaissance" the prospectus posed interesting topic questions, among them: "Has [the Renaissance] solved what it had set out to achieve? Has a new era already started for us or are we only at the beginning of the Renaissance? How do we recognize and with real historical sense for style make use of the social factors and everything new that the present offers? What are the most important tasks in this regard at the present time? How have they been solved up to now?" The third volume was to conclude with a chapter on "Critique of Modern Conditions" and to answer the final question: "Has the new medieval trend in architecture a future?"[51]

The correlation between theory and modern architecture appealed to Bruckmann. To ensure that the third volume would impart this up-to-date quality to the whole work, he added a last clause to the new contract: "It is understood as a matter of course that in the third part special attention will be given to the most important architectural tasks of the present and that it will contain a critical assessment of the outstanding buildings of our century." Semper signed; he did not foresee what headaches this would bring him.

However, what mattered at the moment was to get on with the second volume. This was not difficult, although for "Ceramics" he "would have to collect the material all over again."[52] He dispatched parts of the manuscript as they were finished and though it was not until 1863 that the last installment was delivered, he could be blamed for the delay only to the extent that he often kept the printer waiting many weeks for the return of the proofs (figure 16).[53]

In the fall of 1861 he was ready to embark on the third volume. At once, he met a problem that he did not know how to solve, a difficulty that he did not feel confident to overcome. Doubting, hesitating, looking for advice, he turned to Friedrich Bruckmann. The publisher's reply gives an indication of what was worrying Semper.[54] Although he wanted Bruckmann to believe that it was only a question of revising and editing an existing manuscript, the plan to conclude the whole work with a critical assessment of modern architecture proved on closer examination to create great difficulties. He who "had been an active champion in the present-day arena" not only lacked the impartiality indispensable for a task like this one, but also, as a refugee with a warrant against him, lacked the freedom to enter Germany, so that criticism based on personal inspection was impossible.

Bruckmann met Semper's reservations in a most friendly way; he tried to restore his self-confidence, the understanding reasonable publisher giving advice to the distressed author—an attitude not unlike Vieweg's years before and a strange repetition of that relationship, which subsequently was going to recur. In his opinion, only someone who had proven himself through independent, creative work was entitled to make a valid judgment. "A decisive and clear standpoint based on firm principles seems to me for any critic . . . rather a necessity and advantage than a sign of weakness." With regard to traveling in

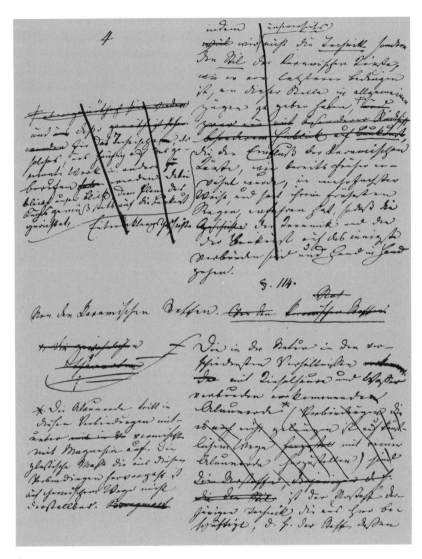

16
Der Stil. A page of the original manuscript. (Semper-Archiv Zurich)

Germany, Semper's apprehensions were unfounded. Nowadays one could travel there quite easily without a passport. Should he still feel uneasy about it, then he, Bruckmann, would be quite happy to make the journey with him "so that wherever I am known personally or by name you as my companion could pass unhindered." Furthermore, France and England presented no obstacles to travel, and Semper's opinion that these countries were of only secondary importance to Germany was certainly not true; the new buildings in Paris would be of great interest to the German public. England too should not be disregarded. May the third volume of his work, like all his writings, turn out to be sound and—Vieweg's exhortation of old—"above all be practical."[55]

If Semper had hoped that Bruckmann would release him from this pressing obligation, then his answer was disappointing: the work ahead had in no way been made easier for him. The Via Dolorosa of the next fifteen years had begun; the stations were Semper's promises, excuses, and more promises, and Bruckmann's entreaties, hopes, disappointments, and finally threats. It would be monotonous to trace the dialogue between publisher and author in detail. Nevertheless, to highlight the fate of the third volume the essential events must be summarized.

September 1864: Bruckmann to Semper. Semper had offered him two small essays and had asked him at the same time for an advance on the third volume. Bruckmann declined the essays in a courteous though impersonal manner. As for the third volume, he was willing to start printing and asked for delivery of the manuscript at Semper's earliest convenience. Payment would be made after receipt of the last installment, in accordance with the contract.

December 1864: Bruckmann's office to Semper. Renewed request for delivery of the manuscript which, according to Semper's statement during his last visit to Munich, "was complete and only needed another revision."

February 1865: Bruckmann's office to Semper. Probably in order to gain time, Semper had blamed his delay on the fact that Vieweg had retained the drawings. The office now reported that Vieweg had rejected their request for the return of the drawings; they urged Semper to advise about dispatch of further material.

December 28, 1866: Semper to Bruckmann.[56] This winter he was going to work on the third volume. He was pleased about the publication of Lübke-Burckhardt's *Geschichte der Renaissancebaukunst* because he could now make use of it. "Please preserve for me also in future your kind forbearance about the delay which incidentally . . . will be to the book's advantage." The course he had taught this year on the same subject had shown him how much was still missing or had to be changed (fifteen years earlier he had written in almost identical terms to Vieweg).[57]

November 1867: Bruckmann to Semper. Again a whole year had passed since Semper had promised the early dispatch of the manuscript. Semper would make him very happy by giving him an assurance that he would soon receive the manuscript and drawings.

December 1868: Bruckmann to Semper. Was it quite impossible for Semper to comply with his commitments? Publication had been advertised as forthcoming back in 1865; the three-year delay had a bad effect on public and publishing firm alike.

March 1869: Draft for the lecture "Über Baustyle."[58] With the intention of claiming priority for some of his principal ideas, Semper made this remark about the fate of the manuscript of "Vergleichende Baulehre": "My work, soon to appear, had already been lavishly advertised in 1848 under the title 'Vergleichende Baulehre' by my former publisher in a detailed prospectus; but the announcement was the end of it. After the failure of the uprising in Dresden, a room full of drawings and other papers, including the manuscript which was, unknown to me, among them, were sent to a paper mill because of a rash order I had left behind. I myself, in exile, was cut off from all my old connections." This remark is cited only as proof that Semper did not shrink from inventing or falsifying events when he wished to make his delays plausible.[59]

The lecture "Über Baustyle" gave him the impetus to make a start with the third volume by revising and enlarging the lecture and by incorporating part of "Vergleichende Baulehre." A short manuscript of thirty-nine pages has survived.[60] He soon gave up the attempt, being satisfied that the general notions he had propounded in the lecture had appeared in print.

October 1869: Bruckmann's office to Semper. He should not take it amiss if they asked him again and again not to delay the publication any longer. After all, it must be possible for him to find someone who could, under his supervision, finish the remaining drawings.

February 1870: Meeting between Semper and a Mr. Berlepsch, probably Bruckmann's representative. Semper reported that the manuscript was finished and "only needed a last revision to have it ready for the press"; he also expressed his wishes regarding payment and made suggestions about the probably soon-needed second edition of *Der Stil*.

February 1870: Bruckmann to Semper. He was glad to hear from Berlepsch that Semper had at last decided to continue with the work on *Der Stil*. He would be quite willing to pay the block designer, as Semper had requested, and upon each delivery of partial manuscript or drawings to make pro rata payments. He was also interested in Semper's suggestion of changing and cutting the text for the second edition and of here and there making it more popular. Preparation for this work should be undertaken as soon as the third volume was finished. For the third volume he should always make deliveries of at least five or six sections plus the drawings.

August 1870: Bruckmann to Semper. In spite of having promised Berlepsch to deliver the manuscript by the end of February, he had so far sent nothing except a few drawings for the blocks. Therefore Bruckmann was forced to look at the matter from another angle and point out that through the interruption, now stretching over many years, his firm had suffered considerable losses; he must now ask Semper to let him know within eight days "on how far we can count, on the one hand, on a dispatch of further sketches for the draftsman and, on the other hand, on delivery of the manuscript (at least of the first installment) relating to these drawings, so that we can then consider further steps."

October 28, 1870: New contract signed.[61] Put off for so long with promises, Bruckmann believed—as had Vieweg before him—that the only way to make Semper carry out the work was through contractually fixed delivery dates. According to the new contract, sections one to six had to be delivered by the end of January 1871, sections thirteen to sixteen by the end of January 1872, and the rest (the total was set from twenty-five to a maximum of thirty-five sections) "without fail to Herr Friedrich Bruckmann on September 1, 1872 ready to go to press." The fee was agreed at 2000 guldens with a bonus of 1000 guldens if the final date were met. This would again come to about one hundred guldens a section but meant a considerable reduction from the 4000 guldens stipulated in the contract of 1859 for the third volume, especially if the final date were not kept. To forestall the usual excuses, Bruckmann insisted on this clause: "For a belated delivery of the [last installments], only a serious illness of Professor Gottfried Semper can be pleaded and in that case only for the duration of the illness." Semper signed everything. In view of his conduct during the preceding years, it is hardly conceivable that Bruckmann really believed he could force Semper to work by this contract. If so, he soon learned otherwise.

March 1871: Bruckmann's office to Semper. When could they expect delivery of the installment scheduled for the end of January?

July 1871: Bruckmann to Semper. Referred to the new contract and laid down the end of August as the final date for the first installments. Should he not keep it, then Semper would put him in the unpleasant position of having to take legal action.

March 1872: Bruckmann's office to Semper. They had been so often disappointed in their hopes to see the work completed that they "had almost lost faith in it." They knew that other commitments kept him from working on the third volume but had expected him to look for a solution; they would suggest that he enlist the collaboration of other people. Would Georg Lasius be capable of this and be acceptable to him? Ideally, of course, he should write the manuscript, "but is there still any hope of this?"

April 1872: Semper to Bruckmann. He assured the publisher— exactly as he had assured Vieweg twenty-five years before—that he "seriously has in mind to undertake the work."

April 1872: Bruckmann to Semper. He had spoken in Rome to Semper's son Hans, who would be willing to assist Semper in Vienna with the work on the third volume during his four months of vacation.

July 1872: Bruckmann's office to Semper. Urge delivery.

September 1872: Bruckmann's office to Semper. Urge again.

February 1873. Bruckmann's office to Semper. In spite of a binding contract and many promises, nothing had happened. What prevented him from keeping his word? "The preliminary work had taken shape long ago, the material is there." A new catalogue was in preparation; it was impossible to put off the public any longer with promises. Would he therefore please reply by return whether the firm could state that the first installments would definitely appear in the course of this year. Should he not be able to give this assurance, they would be forced to safeguard their reputation by referring in a note to his guilt in this matter.

April 10, 1873: Semper to Bruckmann.[62] Reply to preceding letter: "Any attempt to justify myself for the delayed publication of the third volume of my 'Der Stil,' which was entirely caused by me, would be in vain [twenty-five years before to Vieweg: "Shall I try to say anything in my defense? I would come off badly over it"[63]]. Therefore, I think it quite in order to name me publicly as the man who alone is to be blamed in this matter. . . . I am working hard on the book but cannot possibly say how much of the overdue work will be finished and ready for dispatch by the end of the year." He then explained at length the reasons that had again and again kept him from continuing the work (we shall return to this important part of the letter). At the end he mentioned having learned that Bruckmann was preparing a second edition of *Der Stil* and had commissioned a young scholar to revise the text. He should at least have been notified, since it would have given him the opportunity of enlarging and correcting the text, but he still believed that it was a misunderstanding.

April 1873: Bruckmann to Semper. Reply to preceding letter. Reading Semper's letter he "could not supress a feeling of hope" since the candor with which he spoke about the reasons for the long delay proved that he was willing to complete the work. All that Semper needed to do now was to make a firm resolve, quickly sort out the material for the first and second installments, and make it ready for the press in one go. The so-called second edition had been in fact only a reprint of certain parts of the second volume and a few pages of the first, which had become necessary because otherwise they could not have sent out any complete copies.

November 29, 1873: Telegram from Bruckmann—still hopeful—to Semper, congratulating him on his seventieth birthday and referring to the third volume.

The documentation of the next few years is so sparse that one has to rely on assumptions. It seems that Semper was so upset about Bruckmann's arbitrary behavior in making changes in *Der Stil* that he decided to sue the firm or, more probably, that he used this incident as a pretext to get out of his contractual obligations. In September 1874 he sent several documents to his son-in-law Dr. Sickel with the request: "1. to ascertain the illegality of the reprint, and 2. with regard to the third volume to have the contract either modified or canceled."

Nothing is known about the events of the next eighteen months except that in January 1875 Bruckmann's agent Capellen negotiated with Semper. The tension between Bruckmann and Semper grew worse during this time until Bruckmann gave up hope of ever seeing *Der Stil* completed and eventually was willing to cede his rights to another publishing firm.

March 1876: The bookseller Ebner, of the firm of Ebner & Seubert in Stuttgart, to Semper. Ebner informed him that he planned to take over the publishing rights of *Der Stil* from Bruckmann and would like to hear what Semper thought about it. Semper replied that he was flattered "to see his obscure name stand next to that of a Lübke, Burckhardt, Kugler, Braun, Waagen, etc., etc." and that he agreed in principle to undertake the revision of the second edition. He would soon have the leisure to work more steadily on the third volume. But first the relationship with Bruckmann must be clarified so that there would be no complaints and belated claims.[64]

It is possible that Ebner's inquiry was made at Bruckmann's instigation. Bruckmann at least knew about it, for Capellen asked Semper on March 29 to come and see him "after he received Ebner's reply." But the negotiations must have fallen through because on May 23 Bruckmann, without notifying Semper, ceded all rights regarding *Der Stil* to the Leipzig firm of Veit & Co. Semper heard about it through Veit, was outraged that his intellectual property was being bartered away, and forced Bruckmann to cancel the sale.[65]

The main issue in the negotiations between Semper and Bruckmann that followed was that Bruckmann needed Semper's consent for a new edition and that Semper would give it only if Bruckmann released him from the obligation of delivering the third volume. Because Bruckmann could not find the original contract of 1858, Semper believed that his position was strong. Replying to proposals sent by Bruckmann on June 28, 1876, he declared a few days later that he was very interested in the publication of the improved reprint of the first and second volumes of *Der Stil*, "so that the work will be rehabilitated in the eyes of the public after the numerous and senseless faults pretending to be corrections, which you made in violation of the agreement, stigmatized the reprint." Yet he could never accept Bruckmann's proposals regarding the third volume, and saw only two possibilities: first, "the third volume should be given up altogether, which could easily be done in view of the fact that the subject matter dealt with in the first and second volumes is complete in itself, the more so as when revising . . . I intend to eliminate any reference to the third volume, which I never contemplated in the first place."[66] Bruckmann would be free to come to an agreement with him about the supposed loss the firm had suffered or to try his luck and sue. Or, if Bruckmann insisted on the completion of the third volume, then he would have to make other proposals; in particular, Semper would "never again be tied to fixed delivery dates."

October 1876: Semper wanted to institute civil and criminal proceedings against Bruckmann.[67]

February 1877: Attorney Dr. Riegel negotiated with Bruckmann, without reaching agreement.

June 1877: After some difficulties, Bruckmann finally succeeded in having Suchsland hand over the original contract of 1858, which he had taken with him upon leaving the firm. Bruckmann could now prove that he indeed possessed unrestricted publishing rights. Semper's legal position had collapsed. His lawyers, as well as Dr. Sickel, advised him to give up resisting Bruckmann's demands and to try only to make him abandon the third volume.

October 1877: After further negotiations and delaying actions by Semper, and renewed threats by Bruckmann to place the matter before an arbitration tribunal, Semper sent a telegram from Dresden accepting Bruckmann's terms.[68] This led to the last supplementary agreement, dated November 8, 1877.[69] In it Bruckmann declared his willingness to renounce his rights to the third volume insofar as he "will not institute proceedings for damages for the still undelivered manuscript if Herr Professor G. Semper gives his consent to the reprint of the first and second volumes."

And that was the end of the third volume.

Semper died on May 15, 1879. Afterward Bruckmann instigated a search for the manuscript of the third volume. The literary and artistic estate had been divided between the two sons. Both were convinced that the manuscript existed, and each expected it to turn up with the other's part. Hans had only "a clean bulky copy of the first two volumes of *Der Stil* and also that of 'Vergleichende Baulehre' and several fragmentary drafts." Manfred's search was just as unsuccessful.[70] It is understandable that Bruckmann, whom Semper had so often assured that the manuscript was as good as finished, was skeptical about the sons' statements.[71] However, after years passed without the manuscript being offered to him or to another publisher, he was probably satisfied that it did not exist and in December 1883 proposed that Hans make use of his father's material and write the third volume; he made him an offer and asked for partial delivery of the manuscript beginning in early 1885.[72] The preface of *Kleine Schriften* implies that Hans accepted the offer; yet the third volume remained unwritten.

When the Semper-Archiv was put in order many years later, the voluminous manuscript of "Vergleichende Baulehre" was brought to light and was thought to be that of the third volume. It certainly was not: Semper had written it in Paris in 1850, long before the far-reaching concept of *Der Stil*, so different in its whole plan, had matured. Of the survey of building types planned back in Dresden, the manuscript contained only the beginning of the first section, pre-Hellenic domestic architecture. This did not fit into the framework of *Der Stil*, the third volume of which, dealing with monumental architecture of past and present, was to have summed up the preceding review of the technical arts. The subject matter dealt with and some ideas touched upon in this manuscript could have been of only very limited use for writing the third volume; only in these terms could Semper's frequent remark that his work was only a matter of revising an existing manuscript have a semblance of justification. Such a revision has not been found in the archive but, of course, like any negative finding, this cannot be regarded as absolute proof that it does not exist.

Although up to 1873 Semper often insisted that he was hard at work, he had always given this assurance easily; had he really had something ready, however small, he would have dispatched it if only to be spared Bruckmann's urging. What prevented Semper then— one must ask with Bruckmann—"from keeping his word"? What was it that made writing the third volume such an extremely hard task for him?

We can exclude some obvious possibilities at once. It was not difficult for him to put thoughts to paper—the size of the literary estate is proof that writing came easily to him. Anxiety about finances does not seem to have played a part, either. He tried to receive advance payments and made calculations about the rates by section, but no- where in his letters to Bruckmann did he suggest that insufficient remuneration kept him from working; in this regard the tone of his letters was different from those he had once written to Vieweg. Nor can it be said that his professional obligations as teacher or architect did not leave him enough time; while he was fully engaged with the planning and construction of the Polytechnicum, he wrote the text of the first two volumes almost without a break.

The difficulties were inherent in the task itself, and he was fully aware of their nature. As mentioned above, he doubted whether he could muster the impartiality needed for the survey of contemporary architecture. The apprehension was not unjustified. Semper was a poor critic or, rather, he criticized too much, judged too little. His lecture "Über Baustyle" is full of sharp, often malicious remarks about contemporary buildings and styles. Unable to make a dispassionate, constructive judgment about trends that he totally rejected, he was afraid to offend the reader with his tone, acceptable perhaps in a lecture or pamphlet but not in an important work. This doubt, however, could have arisen regarding only the concluding two chapters, and should not have prevented him from at least making a start.

The difficulties he met there were different. He wrote about them in the letter that impressed Bruckmann by its frankness.[73] "I can assure you," he declared,

that it was not carelessness, indifference, and certainly not ill will, but motives and emotions of quite a different nature that prevented me again and again from fulfilling, once and for all, the obligations I have toward you and the public . . . motives and emotions that were always stronger than my strongest good intentions. The path of inquiry that the first two volumes pursued was almost untrodden, almost undiscovered, at the time they appeared . . . but now it is a question of entering a field that has been explored in depth in all directions and which, to mention only Germany, is resplendent with the names of Hirt, Stieglitz, Schnaase, Kugler, Bötticher, Lübke and so many more. . . . In consequence, the reader expects . . . to be led by me to new points of view that will make the long-familiar appear in a new light. That is just what frightens me and what deprives me of my former spontaneity, which I am losing anyway more and more with growing age and the greater demands I make on myself. . . . All things considered, it was . . . a fortunate fate that hung over my book insofar as the often-promised third volume did not appear years ago in the form I had already drafted in the early fifties and had partly written down. It was perhaps the right instinct that has since then forced me to put down my pen whenever I took it up again to complete at last the partly finished opus I had conceived more than twenty years ago. Much of what I had written then . . . would have been scornfully rejected by the tribunal of art historians and art critics as idle brooding and useless digging into the primeval history of things; . . . therefore, until a few yeas ago the publication of the third volume would have been premature.

Semper might have written this as a consolation for Bruckmann, just as twenty-three years earlier he had, with similar words, tried to make the delay palatable to Vieweg. Nevertheless, the inhibitions he hinted at were real. It is true that a few years before in the lecture "Über Baustyle" he had sketched a survey of architecture to the present in which he had talked about traditional symbolism in art, the social basis of styles, the close bond of ancient architecture with state and religion; had talked about democratic Greek art and Roman imperialism, about the Gothic style of the priests and the baroque of the Jesuits—but insights such as these were not enough for the third volume, which had to match the format of the first two and like them present the subject matter in detail. To do this, to bring the book up to date, and to meet the reader's high expectations aroused by the first two volumes, he would have had to study art history thoroughly and to catch up on many things "in view of the ever-widening horizons of our present-day ideas and the grandiose discoveries of our time in the fields of archeology, philology, and the history of civilization."[74] The desire to range as far afield as possible and the fear of not being able to stand up to the experts hampered his initiative.

There is, I believe, an additional explanation for Semper's strange hesitation and unwillingness to continue the work. It has to do with his decision to deal extensively with his theory of cladding in the first volume. Because this principle was rooted in textile art, where it could most easily be traced back to archetypes (*Urtypen*), there was indeed, some justification for letting the discussion follow directly that of textile art. But it was equally true that the principle appeared in the other applied arts too, as Semper constantly noted, and that only after all branches of industrial art had been examined could a convincing case be made for its effect on monumental architecture. To demonstrate the important influence of "cladding" or "coating" on the development of styles was of great importance to Semper. His whole theory centered around this concept.[75] If he could have brought himself to wait to present these ideas until the end of the whole work, he could easily have fulfilled the reader's expectations "of being led to quite new points of view" and aroused their interest; it would have needed comparatively few additions of architectural and historical significance to bring the volume to the required size. It is quite possible that Semper later realized the mistake he had made in discussing prematurely the theory of cladding—a mistake that he could not undo, that made work much more difficult for him, and that might well have been one of the reasons that he got tired of it.[76]

These, it seems to me, were the reasons that stopped Semper "from keeping his word" and why the third volume was never written. Yet, this sad publishing history has brought to light much that is of interest for the work as we have it today. To this I will now refer.

The quarrel with Vieweg, ending in a complete break, affected *Der Stil* in various ways, starting with the title. The final title was a stop-gap solution, a substitute for the better title "Kunstformenlehre," which because of Vieweg's threatening attitude could not be used; it was a kind of camouflage to hide the same or closely related text. It was devised only after the first volume had been written and printed.[77] The result was the extraordinary appearance of a book under the title *Der Stil* without a definition of this term. Nowhere did Semper explain, neither in the "Prolegomena," nor in the introduction, nor in the text, what he understood by "style."[78] Yet he had tried to explain it on several occasions, the final time in a lecture in London in 1853.[79] Partly following this English text, he repeated the definition in "Theorie des Formell-Schönen," written in 1856.[80] He based the "Prolegomena" of *Der Stil* to a large extent on this treatise: he took over whole paragraphs, followed the order of the contents, adopted the conceptual structure (symmetry, proportion, direction, and the supremacy, oddly called "authority," of one of these formative factors over the others); these and other concepts, systematically dealt with by him for the first time in "Theorie des Formell-Schönen," all reappear in the "Prolegomena."[81] In the manuscript of "Theorie des Formell-Schönen," immediately following the classification of the "authorities" was a section titled "Vom Styl" (On Style), in which he gave a lengthy explanation of style as a function of variable coefficients, as in the London lecture, concluding with the definition published in *Wissenschaft, Industrie und Kunst* in 1852 and adding a new one.[82] There is nothing of these in the "Prolegomena." Up to the last page Semper followed the manuscript of "Theorie des Formell-Schönen," but he left out these definitions. A strange decision! Is it possible that the title, chosen at the last minute, made him omit the section "Vom Styl" in the belief that such a discussion had its place in a work on aesthetics, but not in a work that dealt with the arts from a practical point of view and from which the true nature of style would finally emerge?

The quarrel with Vieweg affected the work in another way. The manuscript that Semper had submitted in 1856 had begun with ceramics, in accordance with his theory of the four elements of architecture and the dominant rank he had allotted to the hearth, which he considered the most important formal symbol.[83] To the hearth belonged the ceramic product hardened in fire. He had introduced his London course on ceramics with the statement: "Of all the different branches of industry the potter's craft is perhaps the most important one for the general history of art and practical aesthetics."[84] Later, when listing the various branches of industrial art, he always began with ceramics, even in the letter to Suchsland in which he sketched the contents of the planned work for the first time: "I would also consider the technical arts like ceramics, textiles, carpentry, masonry, metalwork, etc."[85] Only because he did not get the manuscript on ceramics back from Vieweg did he begin *Der Stil* with textile art. However, this does not mean that he had underestimated the importance of textiles or had only now recognized their influence on architecture. In the manuscript of "Vergleichende Baulehre" of 1850, and also in a London lecture read in 1853, he had emphasized the special position of textile art, which research had so far disregarded.[86] Although it made sense to start with ceramics, there was, on the other hand, much to be said for giving priority to textiles. If this was not done in "Kunstformenlehre," and if he started there with ceramics, it was for the purely incidental reason that he had not yet brought together the material needed for textile art. In this regard it was almost fortunate that the quarrel with Vieweg dragged on for so long; it gave him enough time to collect material so that when there was no longer any hope of a settlement, he was ready to begin the new work with textiles as the most important technical art. But the other side of the coin was that if there had been no disagreement, or if Vieweg had returned the manuscript right away, ceramics would have taken up the first half of the first volume, the second half would have been left for textiles, and with that the first volume would have been complete. That Semper would have added to it "The Principle of Cladding in Architecture" is improbable. Then, having completed the next three sections about the remaining technical arts, he would in the second volume have had enough space left to integrate his thoughts about cladding into the last, the architectural, section. The work would have been complete; there would have been no need for a third volume, no difficulties, no inhibitions created by the increased size.

All this would have been possible. But there are too many ifs. In reality things took quite a different course, so different that the work remained, to our loss, a torso.

II

Semper's Aesthetic Theory

1

Was Semper a Materialist?

The public received *Der Stil* as a complete major work in which Semper dealt comprehensively with industrial art as a whole and with the factors conditioning the artistic process. Because throughout the book he emphasized the decisive influence of material and function, he was, and at times still is, thought to have been a materialist. This he certainly was not. He himself stated explicitly that he "opposed modern materialism in art on principle" and that the "constructive-technical interpretation advanced in [*Der Stil*] had nothing in common with the crude materialistic notion according to which the essence of architecture was nothing more than developed construction, as it were, an illustration and illumination of statics and mechanics, simply a display of material."[1] The reason that he considered material and function to have this overriding importance lay in the task that he had set himself: to trace the way back to the archetypes and show that the primitive makers of the whole range of artifacts had instinctively followed principles identical with those that were in time established for architecture. It was a purely empirical approach; he did not intend to expound on art theory. When he did deal with art in general, however, it is obvious that he was aware of the important impact that factors other than materialistic ones had on artists and their creations.

While still in London, before he had begun *Der Stil*, Semper began a treatise, "Theorie des Formell-Schönen," in which he intended to deal with "the abstract and formal attributes" of a work of art to the exclusion of "all that is extrinsic to the phenomenon, everything that does not relate to it directly, in particular its development in history and the differences in material."[2] He identified these abstract qualities of formal beauty as symmetry, proportion, and direction. In response to the old maxim urged upon artists and architects alike to take nature as their model, he set about probing deeper into the structural laws of nature. Adopting the classification that writers on aesthetics commonly used, he examined the structures of crystals, plants, and animals, including man. The method he applied was unusual but to him quite normal: he reduced the natural object, as if it were a building, to an abstract projection of ground plan, sections, and cross sections. He observed dynamic forces that in crystalline formations coincide, thus neutralizing their effect. In higher organisms, culminating in man and works of art, they either conflict or are polarized into a unified direction. To the centers of these forces (or axes) belong the three attributes of formal beauty—symmetry, proportion, and direction. Of these three one will always be the dominant element, while the other two act only as accompanying factors. But—and this is important in the present context—he went further and identified a fourth attribute, which in its effect surpasses the other three: the quality of content or purpose. This concept might have been suggested to him by Friedrich Theodor Vischer, his colleague at the Polytechnicum.[3] But even so it is significant that Semper, who seemingly upheld materialistic principles when examining industrial art products and processes, sought out this concept although the subject of his study was not "style" but beauty as a whole. This fourth "authority," fitness of content, can, he wrote in "Theorie des Formell-Schönen," "culminate in certain phenomena of a higher order in character and expression . . . it is the cardinal point of the phenomenon, it is the phenomenon's purpose."[4]

Years before, Semper had subscribed to the belief that the idea was the foremost factor determining beauty. In an 1843 letter to Vieweg he criticized those architects who "often give the material precedence over the idea which, although it is freeborn, they put into iron fetters by asserting that the store of architectural forms is in essence conditioned by and has evolved from the material."[5] Twelve years later he still stood by these principles, the greater part of which he incorporated in the preface to "Vergleichende Baulehre." Toward the end of this manuscript he interrupted his description of Egyptian architecture with this significant note: "It cannot be repeated too often that the author has been convinced from the beginning that the material, though essential, is in no way the first and most important coefficient to affect the configuration of architectural forms. Material must conform to the idea; the idea must not evolve out of the material . . . This conviction will be the basic theme resounding throughout the book."[6]

Unfortunately, he never got farther than that. "Vergleichende Baulehre" remained unfinished, as did "Theorie des Formell-Schönen." Realizing that his contract for *Der Stil* precluded the possibility of publishing any other manuscript he had in hand, he decided to make use of the greater part of the preface and introduction to "Theorie des Formell-Schönen" and work it into the prolegomena to *Der Stil.* In this way he hoped to ensure early publication of his theories of art, apparently not minding that these purely theoretical observations would appear to have little relevance to the empiricism of *Der Stil.* Again, wishing to make public his ideas about the formative elements of adornment, he gave a lecture in 1856 on this subject in which he repeated the content of a chapter of "Theorie des Formell-Schönen" and added a summary of his aesthetic theory. The lecture was published the same year.[7] Architectural style was the theme of another lecture. Semper was convinced that architectural styles reflected the social, political, and religious conditions of their times, and he cited as an illustration the detailed accounts of ancient buildings and cultures he had given in "Vergleichende Baulehre." This lecture also was published and became the only one, shortly after his death, to be translated into English.[8]

2

Semper's Position on the Gothic

The eagerness with which Semper tried to revive Greek architecture in his first publication;[1] the single-mindedness with which he, supreme master of the canon of classical forms, pursued in his buildings a new direction; the strong conviction with which he believed in the potential force of the Renaissance—all this makes his critical attitude toward the Gothic style seem logical and natural. He frequently voiced it in his published work, above all in *Der Stil*.

He rejected a style that ignored, in his opinion, the most important architectural principle, that of "cladding"; rejected a style that considered its main element to be "the bare appearance of functional parts" and that "like the armor-clad crab makes a show of its skeleton."[2] The Gothic way of building was in essence nothing but "fully developed construction," the application of a crude materialistic principle; in this consistency it went farther than other styles,[3] so as finally "to destroy itself by its own consistency and logic."[4] He condemned the Gothic system, which by its "strict hieratic-architectural scheme" had checked the unfolding of the promising Romanesque art;[5] he condemned a system that was "complete in itself" and offered no "possibility for further development,"[6] so different from that of the Renaissance; he condemned "the hieratic-structural tyranny of the system"[7] and ridiculed a style that "had produced a compendium that thinks and invents for you."[8]

More remarks in a similar vein, taken from Semper's unpublished writings, will be cited below and will further prove his basically negative attitude toward the Gothic. Quite unexpected, therefore, was the surprising discovery, from a scrutiny of his early manuscripts, that in the beginning he took a positive interest in the style he later criticized so severely.

Semper grew up at a time when Romanticism was the leading movement in German spiritual life; the influence of this trend awakened

17
Antwerp Cathedral by Peter Neeffs, ca. 1650. (Victoria and Albert Museum, London)

interest in the medieval past of one's own country and an understanding of the beauty of medieval art. It would have been strange if this spiritual climate had left him unaffected. One hears the echo of this influence in a letter he sent home from Antwerp, after traveling on foot through Holland, at the age of twenty-four. "The cathedral," he wrote, "in its simple elegance is the most beautiful not only of those here but of all Gothic churches I know [figure 17]. The French plundered it and with that all the profusion is gone. Only a few fine paintings by Rubens and three great altars adorn the church and do not disturb (as in most churches) the impressive effect of the Gothic arches, which have more beautiful proportions than I have seen anywhere else."[9]

This was written before he went to work for Gau in Paris where, mainly through Jakob Ignaz Hittorf's discoveries, he was led to the study of ancient polychromy, at that time a topical subject that was certainly one reason for his Greek journey in 1831/1832.[10] When he returned via Rome and Munich in 1833 he used the occasion of a prolonged stay in several towns of the Danube region as well as in Bamberg and Naumburg "to enlarge my knowledge of pre-Gothic and Gothic architecture."[11]

In Altona, where he arrived at the beginning of 1834, he at once started a report about his journey, which he published as a pamphlet the same year.[12] Although his main objective was to submit evidence of the use of color on Greek temples, at times he mentioned medieval architecture, which "offered an indirect way of uncovering what had been lost to us of antiquity."[13] Admittedly, this rather general statement referred mainly to medieval polychromy which, in contrast to the Greek, was often still intact. However, there are two remarks of greater significance for Semper's attitude to Gothic architecture in the same manuscript and in the same context. Wishing to prove that polychromy was not a sign of barbaric bad taste, he pointed out that "it is found only on monuments built in periods enlightened by a particular artistic flair," such as under Pericles and Phidias in Greece, the Moors in Spain, the Normans in Sicily, the Medicis in Florence, and (ending his list) "even the Gothic architects relied much on the effect of colors to enhance the wonderful magic of their buildings."[14] Again, when discussing the value of medieval paintings as source material for an understanding of ancient motifes, he was certain that "the Goths [and in this context he certainly meant Gothic architects] knew Greek better than is generally thought."[15]

Shortly after the pamphlet appeared, in the spring of 1834, Semper was made a professor of the school of architecture at the Academy at Dresden. A few months later he started a course on a general history of art, of which an incomplete manuscript has survived.[16] By way of introduction he stated why in a survey he could not offer more than his own lengthily acquired views. During his prolonged travels it had been impossible for him to think of "scholarly studies and a methodical pursuit of the history of art." The easy way out would of course be for him to recapitulate any one of the popular compendiums. Apart from the fact that this would go against his nature, he did not consider any of the handbooks suitable because they "deal comprehensively only with part of the history of architecture and also because the medieval history of art in particular is still groping in the dark in spite of the invaluable research of my famous compatriot Herr v. Rumohr."[17] Obviously, he thought it necessary to fill this gap. In the course of the lecture, he again repeated the charge that architecture was neglected by most writers on art, Carl F. von Rumohr not excepted. Some of them were conscious of being incompetent to make valid judgments on architecture; to some, Gotthold Ephraim Lessing, for instance, architecture was deeply distasteful, while others regarded "the strict laws of architectural order as too much of a restraint. . . . At most, they admit medieval architecture not only because its laws are less strict but rather because the misty distance in which it still lies, through insufficient knowledge, allows them in the end to make of it whatever they fancy."[18] With these words he dismissed the attitude of the Romantics and recognized that further research was necessary to shed light on this obscure period and thereby bring about a fairer appraisal.

About ten years later, while looking through his manuscripts, he added a marginal note at the place where he had written about the lack of suitable handbooks: "Since this was written, great progress has been made in the study of medieval architecture: Quast, Kugler, Schnaase, Bülau, Hoffstadt."[19]

None of these authors' books, with the possible exception of Hoffstadt's, had appeared when Semper began his course on building types ("Gebäudelehre"), in which a lengthy section deals with church architecture of the Middle Ages.[20] The manuscript of this course contains an explanation and basic assessment of the Gothic style, the only comprehensive one we have from him.[21] He briefly listed the publications on which his account was based: Stieglitz's *Von alt-deutscher Baukunst*; Moller's series of the most important buildings in Germany; Boisserée's publication on the Dome in Cologne; Clemenz Martin's on the Dome in Magdeburg; Bülau's on the Dome in Regensburg; and Schnaase's quite recently published *Briefe aus den Niederlanden.*[22]

At the end of a section dealing with the influence of the Byzantine style on Western architecture, Semper referred to the Romanesque churches on the Rhine, admiring their picturesque composition which, however, in his opinion applied only to the exterior. "The interiors of these churches," he continued, "were surpassed by the Gothic cathedral, which was designed according to strict laws of perspective and in which the interior was everything while the exterior had to be subordinate."[23] The Romanesque, called by him the Byzantine style, was not pursued to the degree of perfection that was attainable. "It was interrupted in its development by the influence of the pointed arch, introduced at the beginning of the thirteenth century."[24] Research on medieval buildings had established that the pointed arch, though increasingly discovered in use in earlier centuries, had been used as "a basis for a new style" (Semper's correction of "as a matter of taste") not before the thirteenth century. "Undoubtedly," he declared, "the pointed arch is the outward sign of that Christian style that we know by the name of Gothic; but this style was also conditioned by other factors unconnected with the pointed arch."[25] Although Semper admitted that the orientalizing influence engendered by the Crusades played a role in the formation of the Gothic style, he was emphatic about the power of the style's own creative momentum. Writing about the effect the Crusades had on Western culture in, for instance, education, customs, dress, weapons, and even furnishings, he continued:

Architects too could not possibly swim against the tide. An oriental preference for light form and rich decor emerged and even single forms were copied more or less well. But . . . to copy . . . or to make a critical and scholarly study of the monuments ran counter to the spirit of the age; it was really the imagination and vigor of the system in its prime that assured the full development of a truly independent art. . . . Here we have reached a very difficult point about which much has been written but which in no way has been settled.[26]

What worried Semper was the difficulty of giving a rational explanation for the aesthetic pleasure we experience in Gothic churches. He felt that "this part of the history of architecture is shrouded in mystery. . . . These monuments remain for us in many respects grandiose enigmas; the depth of the conception can, it is true, be recognized in details, but in its totality it is only dimly felt. Thus we admire the perfect execution of the construction, which in the Gothic more than in any other style shows itself in all its beauty, clearly and openly. Construction is not only the means of embellishment, it is beauty itself."[27] Having admired the openly displayed construction, he then referred to the equilibrium of its parts: the buttresses, the pointed arch, the flying buttresses, the high roof, and the turrets—"all are structural forms that at the same time are the most beautiful adornment of the building."[28] The effect of this structural system was that the bare wall disappeared, that the horizontal members were felt to be "increasingly awkward," resisting as they did the upward surge, and that "by consistent application of the principle to admit only structural forms, the ancient architrave became incompatible with buttresses and pointed arches and "was done away with."[29]

Semper then turned once again to the consideration of what he had found so puzzling in the Gothic style: "How these architects created the moral effect of their buildings is more difficult to comprehend or at least to express in words. That they consciously had this intention is obvious; the laws that produced this effect were perfectly clear to them . . . but we no longer know these basic rules and can only guess and grope."[30] The "Bauhütten" (masons' guilds) did everything to keep such knowledge secret, and thus "we are at a loss to understand the precepts of a system that was exceptionally perfect."[31] Only by studying the monuments could we hope to come to some, though inadequate, understanding of the aesthetic laws that the Gothic builders had applied.

Carl Schnaase believed that their rules had a musical basis,[32] whereas he, Semper, thought it more probable, and in any case easier to prove, that the Gothic builders had applied optical laws. In vision and in Gothic architecture "the same interchange between strictly mechanical and technical principles and the most sophisticated sense of beauty" was at work. This was especially noticeable inside the church, where the intention was "to lift the mind toward the sublime. . . . That is why the ceilings of these churches almost vanish at their distant height" and why the pillars with their system of ribs and cross springers, grouped so differently than the columns in ancient temples, increased the diversity and produced "that magic of perspective for which everything seems to be designed. . . . Buttresses serve the arch that they support, whereas the column of the temple had no other use than to carry the entablature. The Gothic builders saw as their main task the perfect disposition of the interior; they achieved it with means we can only surmise."[33]

This then was the impression that Gothic church architecture made on Semper in 1840: struck by the grandeur of the interiors and fascinated by their inexplicable, pervasive magic and by the beauty of the openly displayed construction, he recognized the Gothic style as of equal value to styles of other periods. Even though he did not hide his predilection for Romanesque architecture[34] and though he took for granted the uniqueness of classical art, he still emphasized those characteristics of Gothic churches that meant an enrichment of aesthetic pleasure over that of the preceding period and—it sometimes seems— even over that of classical art.

Semper was critical only in one respect, and even this criticism was mitigated by the manner in which it was presented. Having praised the beauty of Gothic interiors, he continued: "For all the admiration one may have for Gothic architecture, one cannot help admitting that faults, if found, certainly do not appear in the interior. As for the exterior, the spirit that combines science and beauty is at work here too; yet in spite of the effort made to embellish the structurally necessary parts through good proportion and fine decoration, the exterior of a Gothic church always gives the impression of being unfinished or as if it still needs to be clad."[35] Yet, according to his report on a design for a Gothic Revival church, written about the same time, he did not want the construction of the exterior to be completely concealed. In the scheme that he was judging certain flying buttresses were to be covered over so that from the outside the wall would look bare. Semper disapproved of this solution, believing it to be better "if the exterior of the aisles gave some indication of the buttresses that, in fact, exist inside."[36]

Notwithstanding this criticism of Gothic exteriors, he basically appreciated the style, as evidenced by his report on the restoration of the cathedral in Meissen, submitted six months later in January 1843:[37] "Within a few decades," he remarked by way of introduction, "the general opinion has turned so much in favor of the art of our ancestors that today nobody can claim to be a person of culture and taste who does not voice a just admiration for the masterpieces of the twelfth, thirteenth, and fourteenth centuries." Nowadays, he continued, nobody would find it inappropriate to apply on contemporary buildings, instead of alien elements of Greek and Roman art, those principles by which the masters of the Middle Ages had created a truly national and original style that accorded so well with the climate, the physical conditions, the materials, and the customs of the country. Admittedly, a good part of Semper's statement was conditioned by the fact that he had been asked to judge a Gothic monument of national importance—nevertheless, it remains remarkable that in this case he preferred the principles of medieval architecture to classical forms.

In the spring of the following year, a competition was advertised for the rebuilding of the church of St. Nicholas in Hamburg. Semper sent his design in October and enclosed a memorandum, "Explanatory Remarks to the Attached Designs" (figure 18).[38] His design was unusual in two respects: the church was a centrally planned building, not a basilica, and its style was what he called Byzantine not Gothic.[39] He explained these singular features: the centrally planned space was especially suitable for a church designated for the delivery of sermons, and for its artistic forms a style derived from the earliest prototypes, in other words the Byzantine, came nearest to the true spirit of Protestantism.[40] The Byzantine church had arisen from the ruins of pagan temples as a new free edifice; a style evolving from it would therefore harmonize better with the modern classical trend than would the Gothic style with its pointed arches. The Gothic basilica, he argued, "in its innate consistency and the severity of its system, which remains true to itself even in the most imaginative adornment, is the veritable embodiment not of the early Christian but of the Catholic hierarchy, which itself is a work of art no less admirable than its cathedrals."[41]

Semper went on to write that because he condemned the Gothic basilica as incompatible with the requirements of the Protestant service, it should not be thought that he was biased against the style as such. As evidence, he would only mention that he had "several times tried to prove himself, not without success, in this style that he [found] more

18
Semper. Design for St. Nicholas, Hamburg, 1844. (Semper-Archiv Zurich)

perfect then any other art," and in fact "would build a Catholic church in no other than the Gothic style," the beautiful interiors of which had made a deep impression on him. "Nobody can experience the solemn and uplifting impression of a Gothic basilica without being deeply moved. The pillars that rise, it seems, without effort, that display not flat surfaces but only lines that draw the view upward, that incline reluctantly toward each other to form with the cross vaults a ceiling high up in the misty distance—all this lifts the spirit heavenward."[42] However, to achieve this effect, there should be no galleries to interrupt the view—and galleries are imperative for a Protestant church.

Probably to lend greater force to his arguments against a design for a church in the Gothic style, he exaggerated the dangers inherent in the style and their disadvantages. "The consistent avoidance of flat surfaces . . . the inverted artificial system of counterbalancing the lateral pressures of the vaults . . . the rich and delicate adornments . . . all these features peculiar to the Gothic style contain the elements of destruction." The constant conflict between the buttresses and the arches and vaults cause the pillars, thus pushed sideways, to press into the ground "and in consequence settlement and fractured vaults occur frequently, especially on a ground such as Hamburg's. In short, many Gothic churches built less than six hundred years ago have suddenly collapsed. Those that are still standing are maintained with great trouble and cost. Which style runs the risk of being destroyed by its own system?"[43] Semper's intention in calling forth this dreadful spectacle is obvious. Yet in case he had not succeeded in shaking what he feared was a general preference for the Gothic style, he stated at the end of "Explanations": "In spite of the reasons that the architect of these designs has given for not employing the Gothic style, he had in fact started on a design in that manner" without, he added, departing from the essential idea of the plan as now submitted. "Time was too short to finish the design and dispatch it with the other one. If wanted, and provided he was given until Christmas to complete it, it would be at their disposal."[44]

Semper had no need to worry: the architects appointed by the church commission to assess the submissions recommended his design for first place, for second place Johann Heinrich Strack's, and for third place Gilbert Scott's Gothic design. It was a great success for Semper, and one that must have given him special pleasure: it meant the definite prospect of being entrusted with the execution of a prominent building in his native city.

The designs had hardly been exhibited when a public discussion began and was carried on for many weeks in local newspapers and quickly printed brochures. Semper's design was attacked by the influential "Gothic" party, which spared no effort to help Scott's design become the winner. An anonymous brochure, comparing Scott's and Semper's designs, argued that only the type of Gothic basilica, that is, "the German style of the pointed vault," was "the sublime expression of Christian ideas," and rejected altogether the cruciform Byzantine church and the Romanesque style as "bulky, dumb, and lifeless" compared to the churches of the German style.[45] Notes that Semper made while reading the anonymous pamphlet have survived, some of them of interest to the present theme.[46]

In reply to the criticism of Romanesque church architecture and to the statement that "the greatest spiritualization of rigid masses" was to be found only in the Gothic style,[47] he remarked:

These views are personal ones, and one can easily counter them with an equally personal view. I find the lively aspect of well-composed masses of the pre-Gothic churches more impressive, at least from the exterior. The Gothic church is a purely inward building. The exterior is only there to support the interior; these supports, though self-assured, still remain supports. Both the interior and the exterior of the pre-Gothic building are more independent. Every part of the interior is apparent from the outside and is integrated into the whole.

He had made similar comments in his lecture course, but now, defending his point of view in a professional dispute, the criticism was sharper, less qualified: "A Gothic building, seen from the distance, is too much of an openwork; the masses disappear, and the details too. It looks as though it were in the process of being built, surrounded by scaffolding."[48] This attitude appears even more strongly in an annotation refuting the statement that the Romanesque style was no match for the Gothic style because of its crudeness: "As the Byzantine sculpture is finer and simpler, so is the architecture. Pointed architecture on the one hand has too much system, on the other too much mannerism."[49] In "Explanations," wishing to underline his impartiality toward the Gothic style, he had declared that in his opinion Gothic architecture was nearer perfection than any other art and had then added, "Perhaps that is the reason why it is so difficult to further develop it." Now he declared categorically, "The style in question cannot be developed; it has spent itself."[50] If one considers that nearly all architects of Semper's period, partisans of the "Gothic" as well as of the "classical" trend, stressed the finality of a style they rejected for reasons of taste because it excluded any further development, and regretted the premature interruption of a style congenial to them which they nevertheless welcomed because it gave them the possibility of continuing it, then his unequivocal declaration can be seen as the first indication of a change in his assessment of the Gothic style.

Semper's friend Theodor Bülau informed him from Hamburg about the agitation against his design.[51] Early in March 1845 the situation was alarming; it was rumored that the commission had decided to obtain an expert's opinion from outside Hamburg. Thereupon Semper gave up the idea of replying to the brochure and instead drafted a letter to the commission. He rejected the criticism voiced by the anonymous author as unjustified and proved that his design basically conformed to the influential book by Bunsen on Early Christian basilicas, the supposed disregard of which had been held against him.[52] The admittedly "unethical step" of making an unsolicited appeal to the commission on his own behalf and its possibly damaging effect caused him to desist from sending off the letter; instead he enlarged and published it as a brochure.[53]

Once again he wrote about the contrast between Romanesque and Gothic art and the rupture that the organic development of Romanesque architecture suffered through the advent of the Gothic style. The fact that the Gothic builder did not adopt the important feature of the Romanesque galleries proved that "the traditional Germanic (pre-Gothic) style for church buildings was disrupted in its further development, at the time of the Hohenstaufen, by the new elements of the pointed arch and the system of pillars and buttresses."[54] His predilection for the round arch (*Rundbogen*) made him go so far as to claim that "with [this feature] it is possible to bring the representation of architectural forms almost to the level of physiognomical finesse, in the same way as had been the case with the Greek and Roman columnar system" and that "subtle changes in form and proportion are sufficient to give the building, as they give the human face, a totally different character."[55] The opposite attitude was "the spirit of the twelfth, thirteenth, and fourteenth centuries . . . the spirit of scholasticism, the weighing up of crass opposites in a most artificial way and the balancing of conflicting forces."[56] He arrived at this conclusion: "As surely as the saga of the Nibelungen is closer to us than all the fantastic songs of the thirteenth century, so is the pre-Gothic architecture of the *Rundbogen* closer to our times than the pointed arch. This style of the round arch . . . has not outlived itself like the Gothic style and, for that reason, is more capable of further development . . . being more flexible and less exclusive."[57]

When the brochure appeared it was really too late. On March 20 the commission had resolved to postpone a final decision and to obtain an independent opinion on the three designs recommended by its own jury. Since one of these experts was the architect-in-charge of Cologne Cathedral, Ernst Friedrich Zwirner, the other the tireless champion for its completion, Sulpice Boisserée, their report of May 8, as no doubt expected and desired from the start, rewarded first prize to the Englishman, Gilbert Scott.[58]

This was a blow from which Semper did not easily recover—the offensive manner with which he and his work had been rudely brushed aside, doubly wounding because through the publication of the first jury's judgment the derogation was there for all to see. It would be understandable if this trauma, consciously or unconsciously, affected his receptiveness to the positive qualities of the Gothic style; indeed, as mentioned above, his critical remarks, above all in *Der Stil*, are so incompatible with his earlier views that explaining the shift as a purely intellectual development is hardly adequate.

During the following years Semper spoke about Gothic architecture only once—or, rather, among the fragmentary lecture manuscripts only this one has survived—but it already shows the break from his positive evaluation of a few years earlier. The theme of the 1849 lecture was "Domestic Architecture in Italy."[59] Seeking an explanation for the uniqueness of Italian architecture—individual diversity combined with representation of the characteristic—he compared it with Egyptian, Greek and Roman, and, finally, Gothic architecture, on which he had this to say:

Far less favorable with regard to characteristic and individual representation is the so-called Gothic style, which in this respect lags far behind all the preceding periods. The schematism that gradually took hold of this style through the influence of the *Bauhütten* was, of course, opposed to any finer characterization and individual representation, just as the style was the mainstay and support of the hieratic rigidity and stability of the Roman Catholic priestly ideas that dominated the world at that time.

Furthermore, individual Gothic builders were not allowed to be more flexible in the use of architectural forms. "No artist created these works, but the guild or building cooperative."[60] There was no mention in this lecture course of "oriental preference for light form and rich decor"[61] adopted under the influence of the Crusades; it became "the annihilation of mass in architecture," a consequence of the "fantastic contempt for wordly things injected into man by the monk's caste."[62]

The last words reflect an attitude that would have been almost inborn in Semper, growing up in the Protestant North: to mistrust the Catholic Church. In the early years, after his return from Greece, he occasionally expressed this antipathy, for instance, when he praised the religion of the ancients as poetry and philosophy of nature "not obscured by fanaticism"[63] or when he spoke of the "sinister Church of Rome" that was dislodged by the "pure teachings of humanism."[64] But having studied medieval art more thoroughly, he was, as we have seen, considerate enough to acknowledge the Catholic Church as a work of art as admirable as its cathedrals. This, however, was to be his last unbiased remark about the Church. Reacting to the aggressive remarks in the anonymous brochure, he likened the final phase of medieval art, the Gothic, to the "rise, expansion, and all-powerful decadence of the Roman hierarchy."[65] His defeat in the Hamburg competition meant victory for men like Boisserée, Reichensperger, Zwirner, zealots who did everything to bring new glory to the Church by reviving the Gothic style. From now on, Gothic Revival and Catholic propaganda were synonymous terms for Semper. "The Christian-Romantic or Neo-Gothic trend," he wrote, "has found in France, Germany, and England an influential patron of the art in the party of propaganda."[66] Among the historicizing trends of contemporary architecture there was, as he called it, "one species of historians, the Gothic Romantics who . . . are the only ones who know what they want . . . that is, to pursue a political-religious end";[67] they were closely connected with a party that "pursues art as a means for propagandistic ends."[68] These architects "seek in the return of the medieval, the so-called Gothic, style the future of the national architecture and their own—and regarding the latter are hardly ever mistaken."[69] The last few words may, one likes to think, allude to Gilbert Scott, his rival and England's most powerful Gothic Revival architect. Semper went so far as to attribute the growing number of publications on Romanesque and Gothic art to the "tireless zeal of the medieval propaganda" and the revival of the "Gothic nonsense" of medieval embroideries to the activity of a "small but powerful party."[70] He rejected the Gothic Revival movement because the "calculation and affectation" disturbed him and, on a different level, because in "the program drawn up by priests and archeologists . . . a principle of constraints . . . is set out in clear and definite terms."[71]

This repelled him; he also found unpalatable the appalling effect of quite a different development: the cheap mass production brought about by speculation and known to him from his stay in England. The Gothic Revival style, he declared a few years later in "Theorie

19
Houses of Parliament, London, 1840–1865. (Conway Library, Courtauld Institute, London)

des Formell-Schönen," is especially suited to carry out "jigsaw-like variations with cheaply produced structural parts and ornament. Neo-Gothic houses and churches nowadays grow like mushrooms out of the English soil, and the most expensive building on earth after St. Peter's in Rome is the English House of Parliament which, with all its decorative profusion, is also such a boring product" (figure 19).[72]

Even when dealing with the "true" Gothic of the Middle Ages, the meaningful analogy for Semper was the Catholic hierarchy, as, for instance, his factual description of the Gothic system of construction shows: "The dynamic momentum of the lateral pressure," reads one of his numerous notes on Viollet-le-Duc's *Dictionnaire d'architecture*, "and its neutralization through counterpressure were turned into a formal principle of construction whereas the vertical pressure was hidden from view as much as possible. Thus gravity was artificially forced from the vertical and natural into the horizontal direction. *The cohesion of a political Catholic conception of a state*" (italics added).[73]

In the same way that he had fought the artistic-political aims of the Catholic Church because they were based on hegemony, so he now condemned in Gothic building the dominance of the structural system and its open display, which at one time he had praised as beauty itself. He changed the positive tone of Viollet-le-Duc's dictum,

"Le construction commande la forme," by adding three significant words: "The construction dominates the form ever more tyrannically." This, in his opinion, was the basic fault of the Gothic system.[74]

"The new style," he wrote in another note on Viollet's work, "also shows in its general disposition the influence of the construction that becomes its master."[75] This irritated and hurt him visually, trained as he was in classical architecture and classical symbolism of form. His earlier receptivity to the beauty of Gothic cathedrals had vanished; now his judgment was hardly different from that of theoretical writers of the preceding century.[76] The Gothic style, he wrote at the end of the first volume of *Der Stil*, had created a problem by dividing and subdividing the ceiling into a network of vaulting ribs, a problem that was resolved technically, even though "too ruthlessly and pedantically," but not aesthetically: "A building in the Gothic style is unsatisfactory not only when seen from inside, where the lateral pressure of the vaulting ribs is not noticeable and the outer buttresses are not visible so that every uninformed mind must feel alarmed, but it also, when seen from the outside, upsets the aesthetic feeling through the over-powering purely technical system of pillars and buttresses that resist something that cannot be seen from the outside and therefore formally does not exist at all."[77]

When comparing classical with Gothic art, Semper did not hesitate to take sides. He agreed with Viollet's statement that classical architecture did not work to scale but to module, whereas the Gothic architect applied a scale, the foot, but he then made this comment: "Good for houses but bad for temples. This makes the difference between the grand and the great. The grand has no scale. Nature works as the Greeks did—it works without scale."[78] With these words he gave his final judgment on the Gothic style.

Semper and the Archeologist Bötticher

Semper and Karl Bötticher have often been compared, from the first review of the still incomplete *Der Stil* to modern commentaries on Semper's aesthetics.[1] In most cases the comparison has been prompted by Bötticher's axiomatic differentiation between core- and art-form (*Kern- und Kunstform*), and the commentators have invariably emphasized the singularity of Semper's seemingly related views.

Semper twice referred in print to Bötticher's principal ideas—in the preface to *Über die Schleudergeschosse* and, a few years later, in the first volume of *Der Stil*. Additional comments are now known, extracted from the collection of manuscripts in the Semper-Archiv. They make it possible to give a clearer picture of the Semper-Bötticher relationship than has been possible so far.

The first congress of German architects took place in Leipzig in September 1842.[2] Semper attended and was elected a committee member. An almost complete copy of the first volume of Bötticher's *Die Tektonik der Hellenen*, at that time still in the press, was displayed there. Semper must at least have leafed through the book, which was published a few months later.[3] Yet nothing in his writings of the next decade indicates a reaction to Bötticher's ideas. In fact, as will be shown below, it can almost be taken for certain that Semper had not yet read the book. Although in his Dresden lectures and in "Vergleichende Baulehre," written later in Paris, he never got as far as Greek architecture, he nevertheless often referred to it and advocated views which, controversial as they were, would have caused him to comment on Bötticher's views had he known them at the time. To give a few examples, there would have been occasions when he stated that the decorative motifs of Greek architecture pointed to the influence of Asiatic monuments,[4] or that "the basic motif of the hut and its consequences are unimportant and irrelevant for the Greek temple" because Greek art began only with the stone temple,[5] or that "all or most ornamental forms of Greek art already appear" in the decoration of the Egyptian house.[6] In *Die vier Elemente*, the theme of which was Greek architecture,[7] there were many occasions for referring to Bötticher[8] in the same way that he did to Hope's and Fergusson's writings.[9] A remark he made when he developed his theory of cladding (*Bekleidungstheorie*) for the first time is convincing proof that he did not know Bötticher's work at the time of "Vergleichende Baulehre": he wrote there of the "influence that the carpet in its capacity as protecting wall had ... on the evolution of certain architectural forms" and discovered "to his surprise that he could not find any authority to refer to for support" of his assertion that "the carpet-wall plays an important role in the history of art."[10] Yet Bötticher had written in the preface and elsewhere in *Die Tektonik* of space-enclosing walls that were like curtains of carpets[11] and — whatever was the general verdict at the time on Bötticher's book — he certainly was an authority and in this context more relevant than Thomas Hope, whom Semper cited at this point.

As chance would have it, we know to the day when Semper studied *Die Tektonik*, certainly for the first time: in the Reading Room of the British Museum he filled out an application slip for "Bötticher, Carl G. W., Die Tektonik der Hellenen 2 volumes 4° Potsdam 1844–52" on December 13, 1852; the edition published that year comprised the complete work including illustrations.[12] Excerpts and notes now in the Semper-Archiv[13] prove that he carefully studied the preface, introduction, and text of Volume I.

What he read must have given him a shock: views that he had considered to be his most original ones had been voiced by someone else in a book published almost ten years before. At the very beginning, in the preface, he came across Bötticher's eulogy of the hearth from which "the whole layout of the house originated," comparable to the "hearth of the patrimonial god at Delphi";[14] in another place he read that it was necessary to arrrive "at a primary moment ... that would contain every germ and element that advance the development of every subsequent stage proceeding from it";[15] that woven carpets "served, at all times and everywhere, in their capacity as space-creating surfaces, be it as cover, enclosure, or floor";[16] that the Arabs "up to today treat the house as if it were a tent hung with colorful carpets," and even the decorative patterns on the plastered walls of Pompeiian buildings "unmistakably still imply this idea";[17] and finally that the wall "is unrelated to the ceiling ... [and] has its origin in the concept of enclosure and space exclusion."[18] All this, and much more, agreed in a disturbing way with many ideas Semper had expressed in "Vergleichende Baulehre," in preparation for publication, in the pamphlet *Die vier Elemente*, which had appeared recently, and in a new, still incomplete preface.[19]

Disappointed that someone had anticipated what he considered to be his intellectual property, and painfully aware that he had been negligent in his literary research, he exploded in an unjustified and uninhibited attack against Bötticher. A few days after beginning to read *Die Tektonik*, he called him "the vicious little mystagogue from Berlin, the founder of a new era in architecture, the Pythagoras of the nineteenth century revealing the secrets of tectonics, and the rediscoverer of the 'Analoga,' before whom and his trismegistos[20] Schinkel the world had groped in the dark and had no idea of Greek architecture or of architecture in general."[21]

In spite of this outburst—whose deletion from a series of letters published three years later was probably due to the editor, Dr. Friedrich Eggers[22]—Semper realized after a more thorough study of *Die Tektonik* that it was a work that challenged him to make his own position clear: the numerous excerpts and notes prove it. In the first note, under the heading "On Bötticher's Tektonik," he extracted this sentence by Bötticher: "The concept of each part can be thought of as being realized by two elements: the core-form and the art-form. The core-form of each part is the mechanically necessary and statically functional structure; the art-form, on the other hand, is only the characterization by which the mechanical-statical function is made apparent."[23] In principle, Semper did not object to this formulation. His comments were: "The author separates the core-form from the art-form in the details, why not also with regard to the temple as a whole?" and "The parts of an architectural work of art can be explained as material parts of a construction not only by their real or symbolic significance; they also have a traditional and historical significance"[24]—a remark that indicates a point of view different from Bötticher's and one to which we shall return below. He let pass without comment Bötticher's statement on the same page that the art-form "is only a covering and a symbolic attribute of the part—*decoratio, κοσμος*" and objected only to Bötticher's expression that the core-form was "conceived." It "was not conceived but arises out of necessity," was his comment.[25]

However, when Bötticher again referred in the introduction to the attributive character of the art-form, Semper's criticism began. After copying Bötticher's definitions of tectonics and symmetry and making some observations on what Bötticher had to say about the principle of the Hellenic grammar of forms (*Formensprache*),[26] he reached a passage in which Bötticher contrasted a work of nature and a tectonic structure. Bötticher explained that unlike the work of nature in which the life force causes the embryonic form to unfold, tectonics makes its forms out of dead material and is unable to express this process "in any other way than in semblance to the natural unfolding, which here seems as if applied and added to it from the outside."[27] Semper remarked that in this instance he could not agree with the author. "I admit that decorative symbols have no real static function, but it is wrong to conclude that they are applied and added from the outside"[28] (whereby he disregards, as did many other commentators, Bötticher's two little words "as if").

He probably had this quotation from Bötticher's book in mind a year later, when in the first draft for *Die Schleudergeschosse* he described the Greeks as the only people who achieved "giving their architectural structures and tectonic products an organic life so to say. . . . Greek temples and furnishings are not constructed and skillfully joined, they have grown; they are not structures adorned by having floral and animal forms attached to them; their forms are like those that organic forces call forth when striving against mass and weight."[29] Semper repeated this passage, somewhat reworded, twice in print—first, three years later in *Die Schleudergeschosse*, where he referred to "so-called structural systems (*Strukturschemen*)" and to Bötticher by name,[30] and then more explicitly in *Der Stil*. Having explained that the Greek temple was a synthesis between the Egyptian system of stone construction and the Asiatic principle of incrustation, he concluded, "Therefore, the Greek style did not differentiate between core- and art-form, a distinction that unmistakingly reveals a hierodulic-egyptianized thought"; for having propounded this erroneous notion he sarcastically blamed "Professor Carl Bötticher, with the greatest respect for his learning, taste, and acumen."[31] Semper promised to "motivate" the difference between his and Bötticher's point of view on another occasion which, however, he failed to do.[32] But at least he set out his own ideas in detail in *Der Stil*.

Semper's theory of the relationship of core- to art-form started from a certain construction peculiar to the people of Western Asia— "the process of cladding a wooden core with metal plates,"[33] which, according to him, "was among the oldest processes used in the technical arts."[34] Because experience had taught that the metallic cover gave sufficient supporting strength,[35] there developed at an early stage of Assyrian art a tubular metal style in which "the wooden core transferred its functions to the cover and then vanished."[36] The type of hollow tube, as Semper called it, was mainly employed in Assyrian columnar structures and was, in his opinion, retained even after a metamorphosis into a style using stone had taken place, with the result that "the art-form arose simultaneously out of both the covering and the structure; in this way the opposites were resolved."[37] With all people of antiquity, except the Egyptians, "construction withdrew more and more from the core," became peripheral, and became identified with decoration;[38] "the emancipation of monumental form from matter was not accomplished" until the Greek style.[39]

It was a rather artificial schema, which based its interpretation of Greek architecture on the assumption that it had derived from hollow metal statues and metal-clad "planks and posts."[40] One might think that it was Semper's reaction to Bötticher's dualism of core- and art-form that made him devise this structure. It is true that he had mentioned the importance of the hollow-body structure before he had read *Die Tektonik*,[41] but only in *Der Stil* did he set forth the peculiar thought that with the disappearance of the core the dualism of core- and art-form also disappeared, and that finally in Greek art the two elements merged into each other.[42] Indeed, it is not impossible that it was Bötticher who had stimulated this interpretation. Having spoken in his second Excursus of the symbolic language of tectonics, of analogous forms and their transformation into stone, Bötticher continued: "[In Hellenic[43] tectonics] the intention is not to characterize the stone as dead stone but, on the contrary, to let the dead substance of the stone fade away . . . . As soon as the stone is covered by a form analogous to its idea [i.e., an art-form], the concept of the stone has disappeared and that of the analogue takes its place."[44]

Whatever Semper's assessment of Bötticher's principal thesis, its author was certainly not as "one-sided and doctrinaire" as Semper once called him.[45] It is true that Bötticher differentiated between the constructive and the decorative element, but at the same time he stressed their dependence on each other, constantly relating the core- to the art-form on which the unique organic character of Hellenic tectonics was based.[46] The art-form, he declared in the preface, "arises at the same moment that the mechanical scheme of the part [i.e., the core-form] is conceived; the two are thought of as a unity and are born simultaneously."[47] Elsewhere he emphasized even more strongly the connection between both elements: as the tectonic part is in thought fitted with all symbols at the moment of conception, "so it comes to life fully finished from the moment the hand is put on the block from which it is going to be formed."[48] Because both elements—the structural part and the decorative symbol—are so closely related that one cannot be altered without affecting the other "each must be a primary element born simultaneously with the whole."[49] He emphasized repeatedly that the close corelation between core- and art-form made it impossible for decoration to be applied arbitrarily to structural parts. "It is in the nature of things," he wrote, "that this simple law will restrain any subjective and arbitrary desire to cover the core-form haphazardly with symbols"—"The essence and the idea of a structural part prohibit arbitrary decoration and do not allow one to deal with the decorative elements as one pleases."[50] He expressed this similarly elsewhere: "The different symbols and decorative attributes of a structural part . . . are circumscribed by laws; they are never arbitrary trimmings."[51] It was absurd to consider them "pure adornment"[52] and not realize what they really were, namely, "a covering suggestive of a function performed by the core to which it closely clings."[53] Thus Bötticher's system was less schematic, less rigidly classified, than it seemed at first sight.

In fact, Semper took a similar view. Many of his factual, non-polemical observations hardly differ from Bötticher's. He too was of the opinion that the decorative parts of Greek architecture were closely connected with the construction and that their purpose was to express symbolically the mechanical functions of the structural parts—giving support, carrying a load, countering pressure. "Greek ornaments," he declared in an English lecture, "are emanations of the constructive forms and, in [sic] the same time, they are symbols of the dynamical functions of the parts to which they belong."[54] Bötticher could have formulated this in almost identical terms; he also would have endorsed the manner in which Semper demonstrated with a single part—the cyma—that the structural interplay of forces were expressed symbolically: "[The cyma] is the uppermost crowning member of a structural and dynamically functional part; it gives expression to both the concept of crowning and the measure of the existing conflict."[55] Semper spoke, like Bötticher, about the "analogies and symbols" derived from nature, about the "structural significance of these symbols"[56] and the "structural-functional meaning of the ornament";[57] he called the Doric capital a "structural symbol of monumental severity"[58] and emphasized that the Greeks "aimed in the first place at symbolic expression of the structure."[59] He too recognized that giving form and structuring material were two separate yet interrelated factors. He came close to Bötticher's point of view when he tried to counter an objection made against his theory of cladding: the fact that the Greeks, when describing their monuments, always referred to the structure but never to the covering did not in his opinion contradict his statement about the negation of matter because "in order to forget matter it is necessary at the form-

giving stage to take all its properties into fullest account."[60] This re-
sembled Bötticher's statement that the criterion for the potential creativity of a nation depended on "how thoroughly it had apprehended
matter for tectonic purposes and had mastered it."[61] Semper, on his
part, seemed to have forgotten his criticism of the dualistic nature of
core- and art-form when he wrote that the analogues for the function
of "binding" (important for both ceramic and architecture) "were *attached* to the work"[62] or stated as a general explanation, "Hellenic
tectonics . . . *envelop* bare form with an explanatory symbolism" (italics
added).[63]

It seems probable from these citations alone that Semper's discussion
about the symbolic-structural function of the art-form had been influenced by *Die Tektonik*. This is confirmed by numerous excerpts he
made of passages that bear on this theme. He copied the heading
"Symbolism of Load and Support in Conflict" and translated into
English long excerpts about the Doric cyma, one of the most important
tectonic symbols.[64] He made use of this translation in one of his London
lectures, adding further interpretations of the symbolic-structural character of the cyma that so clearly stemmed from Bötticher that an
acknowledgment of the debt he owed him would have been appropriate; in fact, the whole lecture was based on Bötticher.[65] This was
equally noticeable in a second draft of the same lecture, where he
spoke of the "symbolic investments [he meant "application"] to the
bare structure, with the aid of which we give it greater significance,
artistic expression, and beauty" and titled this part of the lecture,
undoubtedly derived from Bötticher, "On Structural Symbols."[66]

After copying more excerpts (again in English) about a second Greek
structural ornament, the echinus,[67] Semper reached the section of *Die
Tektonik* where the tectonic principles established so far through close
examination of certain structural parts in architecture were now applied
by Bötticher to movable and, in particular, ceramic objects.[68] The
"Excursus on Implements," as Semper headed the notes, was clearly
of special interest to him: he repeatedly returned to these sixteen
pages and made three sets of excerpts, each time in still greater
detail.[69] From now on, one frequently finds in his writings echoes of
what he had read in this section. He adopted from this part of *Die
Tektonik* the fundamental difference between implement and monument, which consisted in the mobility of the one and the stability of
the other, two qualities that had to be given formal expression.[70]
Semper stressed this difference, which also affected the selection of
symbols, for the first time in "Die Theorie des Formell-Schönen" and
thereafter several times in *Der Stil*.[71] Bötticher's influence is especially

noticeable in manuscripts dealing with ceramics, written at various times—for an English lecture on ceramic vessels and their parts,[72] for a section of "Theorie des Formell-Schönen,"[73] and for an extensive section in *Der Stil.*[74] Although he did not transcribe his notes word by word, it is obvious that they were close at hand when he was writing these discourses.[75] Bötticher's comments on "implements" must have impressed him, the more so because they became known to him at a time when his ideas about the relation between industrial art and architecture began to crystallize.

In summary, a comparison of Semper's interpretation of Greek architecture with Bötticher's shows that although Semper sharply criticized the dualism of core- and art-form, when analyzing specific architectural forms he came fairly close to Bötticher's point of view.

Moreover, in spite of all his criticism, Semper did not consider this particular concept of core- and art-form as the essential issue that separated him from Bötticher. In 1867 he was the examiner of a thesis whose author, G. F. Peyer, followed Bötticher closely and largely uncritically when dealing with Greek architecture. Semper made marginal corrections.[76] However, he let pass without comment Peyer's statement that the Greeks created perfect tectonic forms "with which to envelop the core of the work."[77] Yet he must have read this passage because he made a critical note on the immediately following and related sentence on Egyptian and Assyrian art. In another place he read the formulation "the exterior form of architectural parts that envelops its core"[78] and further on about "the creation of architectural forms and their decorative adornment that clothes the structural mechanism of the building"[79] without in any way objecting to these views, which were certainly adopted from Bötticher, although here too he made marginal notes on the preceding and following pages.

While the gap between Semper and Bötticher thus was bridgeable, their approaches to Greek architecture were so completely different that the principles derived from them were diametrically opposed.

Bötticher's position was clear and unambiguous: Hellenic tectonics resulted directly from the capacity, or, as Bötticher expressed it, the "potency of the Hellenic race of expressing any concept in an artistic way"[80] and had arisen only because "the Hellenes . . . possessed from the beginning a higher intellectual potency,"[81] which enabled them "to represent the innermost character of stone architecture";[82] it thus becomes evident that "the architectural style of the Hellenes was original, had only been made possible through their potency, and had never been transmitted by primitive tribes from outside."[83] He constantly and unyieldingly repeated this last argument: the race of the

Hellenic nation was so unique, its identity so original, "that it did not need foreign help and for this reason the adoption of alien and barbarous forms . . . was simply impossible."[84] The analogies used by the Greeks were not borrowed from the art of other races but were original Hellenic concepts; the two essential elements of Hellenic architecture, the Doric and the Ionic orders, were "two independent styles."[85] Because Hellenic architecture was "originally invented for stone-building" it contained nothing that suggested primitive timber construction;[86] "the traditional view that stone architecture imitated timber building is untenable."[87] The symbols "had originally been created for stone building; they had not been taken over from an earlier fictitious building made from wood."[88] Finally, he pronounced: "All concepts of this art, from its first beginning to its highest development, are Hellenic in their origin."[89]

Semper must have rejected all of this, which contradicted his basic beliefs. From the beginning of his work on the comparative history of architecture, his aim had been to search for the primary origin, being convinced that in the field of the arts, as in every other field of social activity, nothing arose in isolation and nothing that had ever been created ceased to have an effect. The recent Assyrian discoveries confirmed his belief in the evolutionary significance and lasting influence of primitive archetypes. In contrast to Bötticher, he stressed the "barbarous" influences on Greek architecture, those influences that interested him most.[90] Having mentioned in *Der Stil* "the important excavations and discoveries on deserted fields where the ancient kingdoms of the Assyrians, Medes, and Babylonians once flourished," he continued, "The most important result of these latest triumphs in the field of art history is the collapse of an outdated scholarly theory that greatly impeded the understanding of ancient art; according to this theory Hellenic art is thought to have been an autochthonous product of Greek soil, whereas it is the splendid flower, the ultimate destiny, and the final result of an ancient formative principle, the roots of which spread as it were through the soil of all countries . . . having a firm and deep grip."[91] In a draft to this passage he added, "With shortsighted zeal, a fanatic and fallacious Hellenomania took the classical spade and systematically cut off the widespread roots and fibers that provided the lofty plant of Hellenic civilization with the basic conditions for its existence and gave it support."[92] Similarly, and with specific reference to Bötticher, he attacked the "speculative philosophy of art [that] dreams of an ideal Doric scheme that has not evolved historically" and talks of a "legendary miraculous birth."[93]

He also rejected the conventional notion of a contrast between the barbaric and the Hellenic character, which, in his opinion, originally did not exist and "only began at the moment when the flower that the culture of ancient people had tended for a long time blossomed forth on the soil of Hellas. . . . The elements of Hellenic art too are barbaric."[94] He made an equally categorical statement in the latter part of the first volume of *Der Stil*: "The formal element of a system like the Hellenic had, of course, to rest on traditions . . . it could never have arisen from pure speculation without them, and these traditions were Asiatic."[95] In a lecture at Marlborough House he declared (and it would have shocked some listeners): "The Greeks were a collection of tribes not much distant in civilization from the conditions of the American Indians, while Assyria and Egypt were already the seat of highly developed forms of society."[96] When Peyer maintained in his thesis that "Greek architecture . . . was autochthonous and had not been conditioned by alien influences from outside," Semper wrote in the margin, "An assertion by Bötticher; at least, the author ought to show that he knows the opposite views."[97]

Semper's different attitude is also evident in another field. As mentioned, Bötticher dealt at length with crafts, stressing for instance the importance of the carpet and the tent canvas; but for him the significance of these objects—implements, furnishings, and fixtures—consisted only in providing the Greeks with a new range of analogies with which to express structural forces, no different in that respect from natural objects. The crafts as such were of no interest to him. They only served "plain needs," he wrote,[98] in contrast to tectonics, and followed "obsolete conventional traditions that mechanically carried on the customs of a trade."[99]

Semper shared the common view that "applied" and "high" art differed in value but, historically oriented as he was, he recognized the unique task that fell to the applied arts in the evolutionary process. The very concept of *Der Stil* arose from his conviction, set out in an English lecture, "that the history of architecture begins with the history of practical art[s] and that the laws of beauty and style in architecture have their paragons in those which concern Industrial art."[100] He made his attitude very clear in a commentary (marked "my own") on Bötticher's discourse on implements, "Symbolism of Free--Standing Supports Shaped like Trunks or Stalks."[101] "The history of implements," Semper noted, "is of greatest importance and ought to be dealt with before architecture. Oldest kind of such support: wood in metal casing. This became a custom that was traditionally retained even in the latest phase of development."[102]

The men also differed in their views on the significance of material as a formative factor. The material employed, its properties, and its negative or positive effect on form and shape were of decisive importance for Semper. To Bötticher it mattered only that the function was clearly expressed, and it was therefore of no consequence to him whether the part "was made out of silk, wool, hemp, raffia, skins, or any other stuff"[103] or "out of stone, wood, or metal."[104] Of course, this did not mean that he considered material irrelevant when evaluating an architectural style. On the contrary, as many quotations have shown, he strongly opposed the view that certain features in the Greek temple suggested its derivation from a primitive wooden construction; stone was the original material for Hellenic architecture and the Greek temple was "an independent organic building conceived in stone."[105] Semper thought untenable a theory according to which a prerequisite for the understanding of the Greek temple, in both overall structure and details, was the assumption of its having been conceived in stone. In his opinion material was subject to the same evolutionary process as any other artistic phenomenon. When change from one material to another took place, some motifs, though modified, were also transferred, a process that had started at the very beginning and still continued.[106]

In a lengthy commentary to *Die Tektonik* Semper questioned whether Bötticher's assertion that "the Greeks had been lithotechnicians [stone-builders] from the beginning" was justified. His answer was: "History and the accounts written by the Ancients, not only that of Vitruvius, contradict it. . . . What imagination could have been so powerful as to have invented arbitrary symbols like triglyphs, viae, guttae had they not been analogies taken from a previously known technical process? Were the stone statues and stone artifacts not also perceived to be in perfect agreement with that material and to have a style of their own, and yet only repetitions of older statues made of metal, cast bronze, and even wood?"[107] Later in *Der Stil* he once more condemned the theory in words that were clearly directed against Bötticher: "Examinations of the remains of ancient monuments on Egypt, Asia Minor, Italy, and Greece suffice to invalidate the too-clever fairy tale of the allegedly absolute and specificly Hellenic monumental tectonics that had been 'formed out' of the very essence of stone."[108] Where Peyer asserted that "the temple was the exclusive product of a primordial stone building" Semper noted in the margin, "Once more Bötticher's one-sided point of view."[109]

There was another basic difference between Bötticher and Semper: the point of view from which each man evaluated Greek architecture in comparison to the other great stylistic periods. To Bötticher Hellenic art was static; Hellenic tectonics represented an absolute climax unaffected by outside influences; it was a unique phenomenon that could never be repeated. Semper, on the other hand—in spite of a deep and sincere admiration—was constantly aware of the fact that Greek art belonged to the eternal stream of evolving human civilization, was born and formed by it. Bötticher, as Semper believed, may have been doctrinaire, but at least he was consistent: nothing that other people had created before Greek art had contributed to its glory, everything that followed thereafter—Rome, the Middle Ages—was a decline. Semper, brought up like Bötticher in the classical tradition, also believed in the crowning and unrepeatable achievement of Greek architecture, but his faith was not easily compatible with his aim of objectively comprehending the historical process that embraced many cultures and many periods. This is why, on the one hand, he singled out the uniqueness of Greek art, which "will live on when all other styles, once they have spent themselves, will exist only as historical phenomena"[110] and, following Bötticher, stressed the "general and absolute truth" of its principles[111]—and why, on the other hand, he declared that "architecture had achieved in the Greek columnar building a perfect stage, but had not yet reached its highest goal";[112] that in spatial arrangement the Egyptians surpassed not only the barbaric nations but the Greeks too;[113] that the Roman system of wall and column had a logical lucidity not achieved even in the Doric temple;[114] that the Greeks' quest for ideal beauty "hemmed the development of what is called characteristic expression";[115] that in his Zurich lecture course he warned the students not to sacrifice direction to symmetry, "the only mistake the Greeks could be reproached for";[116] and finally that, without reservation, he gave a prominent place to the Renaissance, praising its "splendor and abundance of ideas, which put even ancient art in the shade," concluding a later section with the bold statement that the "imposing superiority of Renaissance art places it above everything that preceded it, including the highest art of the Greeks."[117]

Die Tektonik influenced Semper in still another way. "Tectonics" and "analogy" did not originally belong in his terminology; these words appeared in his writings only after he became acquainted with Bötticher's book. From then on the idea of "tectonics" played an especially important role in his aesthetic system. Toward the end of his years in London, he worked on "a larger work . . . about the whole range of forms,"[118] "Theorie des Formell-Schönen." In a first synopsis for it, he posed the question: "What is tectonics? What is its relation to the other arts?"[119] The definition that he then gave in the introduction was comprehensive: "Tectonics is an art, the model and ideal of which is nature in her eternal sway over universally valid rules and laws . . . it is a truly cosmic art. . . . Therefore the history of tectonics forms an important chapter in the history of mankind."[120] In an outline of the subjects to be dealt with in the book he noted that "tectonics as a cosmic art forms a triad [together] with music and dance" and that "its impact on the other two fine arts [painting and sculpture] is strong."[121]

The main text of the same manuscript again began with a definition: "Tectonics deals with the product of human artistic skill, not with its utilitarian aspect but solely with that part that reveals a conscious attempt by the artisan to express cosmic laws and cosmic order when molding the material."[122] The heading to this part of the text is "Part I. On the Technical Arts," and this, as follows from an additional note,[123] "is the main part of the book that deals with tectonics." This means that tectonics, as defined by Semper, comprised all technical arts. He knew that this comprehensive definition was unusual and when, in the same manuscript, he listed the four technical arts and named tectonics as the third, he added, "in the narrower sense of the word."[124] Some time later, when revising the text, he eliminated the word "tectonics" wherever he had used it in the wider sense and replaced it with words like "fine arts"[125] or simply "arts" or, for instance, changed the beginning of the above definition to "This *book* deals with the product of artistic skill."[126] He used a great deal of "Theorie des Formell-Schönen" in *Der Stil*, yet the term "tectonics" in the wider sense is not to be found there.[127] Was it under the influence of Bötticher's book that he emphasized—in "Theorie des Formell-Schönen" and only there—the great importance that he attached to this concept? Was its deletion caused by the wish not to invite a comparison of *Der Stil* with *Die Tektonik?* Conceivably this could have been the reason, but of course it cannot be proven. In any case, it is remarkable that in his writings before he had read Bötticher's book, he never used the word "tectonics."[128] At that time, he defined the process of building as "joining material into an organized form";[129] named as one of the basic technical skills—next to ceramics, metalwork, and masonry—"the timberwork around the roof";[130] wrote of the "significance of the roof as an architectural element" and referred in this connection to "the woodworker's technique"[131]—in short, he was specific because he lacked the significant general term. He found it in Bötticher's *Die Tektonik*, where it was defined as "any activity having to do with building and furnishing."[132] Semper's first reaction had been to widen the notion "tectonics" into a category comprising all the technical arts, only to narrow it later and confine it to denote nothing more than the third of the four technical arts—carpentry and its relation to architecture.

Die Tektonik der Hellenen is a difficult book written in a complicated and tedious style. It is quite possible that Semper did not appreciate the unquestionable merit of this "epoch-making work," as a somewhat over-enthusiastic contemporary called it.[133] Yet there cannot be any doubt that the book was significant for him—the criticism that it provoked, the reaction it aroused, and not least the importance it attached to the analysis of art symbols in fields that interested Semper most were all a stimulus to the development and consolidation of his own ideas.

Semper's Position on Contemporary Architecture

During the years that were decisive for Semper's development—the second and third decades of the new century—architecture had reached the last phase of classicism. Buildings had arisen designed by architects who valued the classical principle of simplicity, accepted the limitation to a few basic forms, and exercised great restraint in architectural composition and all decorative adornment. Toward the beginning of the third decade, the forms of this style were widely used and generally accepted. For Semper, who was younger than the architects who had developed classicism, it expressed an artistic attitude with which he did not identify and which he wanted to overcome.

His reaction was unambiguous and sharp. The buildings of recent times were "old and disagreeable,"[1] and "meagerness, dryness, severity, and lack of character" their hallmark.[2] The latest example of modern architecture, Valadier's design for the Piazza del Popolo, finished only a few years prior to his stay in Rome, was for him "the very type of modern lack of character," in comparison to which he found even an overloaded baroque palace pleasing.[3] He could have said the same of Weinbrenner and his followers (figure 20). The special quality that distinguishes the buildings of Weinbrenner and his school repelled him. Where others admired purity of forms he saw thoughtless observance of aesthetic precepts and severe schematism. "The school of architecture in southern Germany (Karlsruhe)," he wrote, "which cultivates so-called purity can serve as an instructive example" typical of the "dreary impoverishment of the art forms helped on . . . by so-called connoisseurs and art patrons."[4] The Schinkel school did not escape his criticism either: "A certain school in Germany . . . that cannot free itself from the domineering power of a late master's genius[5] has become victim of this aesthetic schematism in spite of a desire for freedom and the right to choose that occasionally succeeds in single

20
Friedrich Weinbrenner. Design for marketplace, Karlsruhe, 1804. (Badisches Generallandesarchiv, Karlsruhe)

episodes, and in spite of the undoubted talent of many of its adherents."[6] Today one complained generally "and surely rightly about the facelessness, emptiness, and impracticality of recent buildings,"[7] a statement he repeated in his first lecture in Dresden.[8]

He held the French architect J. N. L. Durand responsible for this state of affairs—correctly so, because Durand's teaching methods greatly influenced the architecture of this period, especially in Germany.[9] The aggressive, sarcastic tone with which he ran Durand down shows how he hated the trend that he represented. "Schachbrettkanzler," he called him; according to an early draft of *Vorläufige Bemerkungen*, this was his translation of "Chancellor of the Exchequer."[10] To follow the system developed by Durand, all one had to do was to take a large white sheet of paper, draw horizontal and vertical lines on it like a chessboard, and thus form an infinite number of squares on which large projects "would arrange themselves in proper proportion and symmetry like a beautiful embroidery pattern for ladies" (figure 21). According to the express assurance of the inventor, "the first-year student of the Polytechnique could advance within four weeks to the status of a fully trained architect." An assortment of elevations shown on the chessboard "provides in any possible combination a suitable facade with arches, niches, porticoes, frontispieces and attics, cupolas and semi-cupolas. With the ancients, who unfortunately did

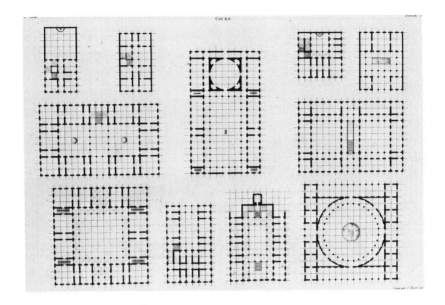

21
J. N. L. Durand. *Précis des leçons d'architecture* (1809) 1, pl. 16. (Photo British Library)

not know this grand invention, everything lay in a disorderly mess whereas . . . we moderns understand how to accommodate the most heterogenous elements and, by simply counting the squares, to bring everything within the best rules of mathematical symmetry. What does it matter if purpose, use, and place go against the system? Symmetry and uniformity are the motto!" Everything "is overcome by iron force and subjected to rule and symmetry . . . whole towns like Mannheim and Karlsruhe are marked out and built according to these squares. What unity, what sublime idea!"[11]

This was how he looked upon Durand's system—a precept for the schematism he opposed. "In Germany," he declared in his Dresden lecture course, "architecture as an art has been confined to a beautiful facade, planted there without any attempt at integration." Little notice was taken of what he called the "lyricism of spatial proportions," by which he meant loosening the massive body of the building and giving the ground plan a more varied form.[12] "No other century," he exclaimed, "is so rich in artists and so poor in art," and he asked, "What is the cause for this disparity?"[13] Blaming architects for the "helpless state of modern art" would be unjust; one should "rather try and trace the deeper causes that hinder the rebirth of architecture."[14] From then on he kept asking himself: What was the cause for the decline of architecture and what were the special circumstances that nowadays made it so hard for architects to create buildings of equal quality to those of the past?

He saw the cause above all in the changed interrelationship of the fine arts. In the past, at the apogee of Greek art, "all the fine arts worked closely together and . . . were knit . . . into a harmonious, well-proportioned whole. . . . How differently were the arts interlocked in those far-distant golden times!"[15] Greek monuments had served as "an arena," where, led by architects, the arts worked "hand in hand in fine harmony."[16] So it also was in more recent times with the Renaissance; but "to the extent that true feeling for art was eclipsed, the fatal separation of the arts began . . . poor architecture was deserted"[17] and "became a branch set apart."[18]

Because "one could not or would not give up the unfortunate separation of the three arts, the dynamic of the work was dissipated for lack of unity."[19] He was convinced "that any separation of the arts, any abstraction . . . had only harmed the arts and was both the consequence and the cause of the decline and fall of true art."[20]

Most of these remarks have been taken from the manuscripts of his first publication on ancient polychromy, but later he also often returned to the subject. The realization that both phenomena—great artistic achievement and the unity of the arts—were closely interrelated might have come to him through Carl Rumohr's writings; in any case, he must have thought "household of the arts" (*Haushalt der Künste*) such a precise expression for the phenomenon that he repeatedly referred to this term coined by Rumohr: in his inaugural Dresden lecture,[21] twice in "Theorie des Formell-Schönen,"[22] in the prospectus for *Der Stil*,[23] and finally at the beginning of the "Prolegomena" to *Der Stil*.[24]

What he had learned from the Great Exhibition and his work at the Department of Practical Art confirmed his view that a recovery of art could be achieved only through all branches of the arts working together and this, he now thought, included above all the industrial arts, the so-called "minor arts" (*Kleinkünste*) because "their decline (which cannot be denied) makes the recovery of the higher arts, which are based on them, quite impossible."[25] For this reason, he wrote in a draft of the preface of *Der Stil*, that "when working on *Der Stil* the author paid special attention to these interrelations between the arts that have been thrown into confusion by the conditions of our time and by its obsession with speculation."[26]

There was still another reason for this artistic confusion. It was associated with the abundance that in the first decade of the century had become more and more apparent—abundance of means and abundance of knowledge. The means—the materials and processes of production—had increased so rapidly through numerous new inventions that the artistic quality of industrial art products had suffered considerably. Semper realized that the damage done could not be blamed so much on the new inventions, which in themselves were useful and welcome, nor on the resulting new means of production, but on the inability to master these inventions and processes and make them our servants. He wrote of it in the brochure *Wissenschaft, Industrie und Kunst* and in *Der Stil.*[27]

What directly and unfavorably affected the creativity of the architect, however, was the abundance of knowledge—the profusion of historical material, the wealth of information about past cultures and foreign architectural styles through constantly expanding detailed research. In short, it was the effect of historicism and its inherent dangers that Semper recognized and that he believed to be a fundamental cause for the decline of the architecture of his time.

The first draft of *Wissenschaft, Industrie und Kunst* contains this passage: "Just as the abundance of technical means is an embarrassment to us, even more so are we perplexed by the immense mass of historical knowledge, which increases daily. Every trend of taste is familiar to us, from the times of the Assyrian and Egyptian styles to the age of Louis XVI and beyond. We can do everything, we know everything except ourselves."[28] He had made the same observation in his letter to the church commission in defense of his project for St. Nicholas in Hamburg. "It is quite natural," he wrote, "that we, the late-born sons of this age, find it difficult to remain artistically masters of the profuse material and yet maintain our spontaneity in a time of great versatility."[29] Later, in London during the time of the Great Exhibition, he pointed to the overpowering and confusing impressions that the vast variety of exhibits aroused in the visitor: "The enormous diversity and cosmopolitan trend of our age has the same dangerous effect on sensible, clear thought and on purposeful direction of will and deed."[30] This diversity was fatal to the architect and his artistic aspiration.[31]

He often came back to this theme. One has the feeling that the words he used to explain the cause of the inadequate state of contemporary architecture may have referred to his own bitter experience, which had taught him how much the "abundance of knowledge" could impede creativity. Did he not also mean his own "lack of spontaneity, inexperience, and indecision" when he complained that nowadays the architect was expected to cope with the disjointed subjects taught, "left entirely on his own to unite the unsystematically assembled material into a whole while looking in vain to the handbooks . . . for advice?"[32] Under these circumstances it was hard for the architect "to retain the spontaneity needed for creating a true . . . work of art" and "to maintain among these diverse artistic trends and tendencies . . . one's own definite point of view, without which the persuasiveness that alone invests the critical assessment with true inspiration and strength is lacking."[33] Altogether, the present wealth of writings and the poverty of works "leads one to believe in a connection between the two phenomena and to wonder which of the two is the cause and which the effect."[34]

The mass of publications of every kind allowed architects to choose freely among the architectural styles of past cultures for their models. At first Semper saw this historicism only as an attempt to turn away from the demands of the present and to escape into the past; this was evident from the senseless copying of historical masterworks. Contemptuously he called the copies "historical treatises in stone and chalk" and "eerie phantasmagorias";[35] he despaired of "the prospect for a productive artistic life . . . as long as we hunt after every old shred"[36] and derided those who "pin their hope on a commission of a Valhalla à la Parthenon, a basilica à la Monreale, a boudoir à la Pompeii, a palace à la Pitti, a Byzantine church, or even a bazaar in Turkish taste."[37] Leo von Klenze's displeasure at these remarks, which he rightly interpreted as aimed at him, led to a correspondence between the two men, of which unfortunately only Klenze's letters have survived.[38] We can deduce that in reply to Klenze's first letter, and certainly in connection with the wounding remarks about historicized buildings, Semper had spoken of the "eclectic trend of contemporary architecture."[39] Klenze assured him that he felt the shortcomings of this movement as painfully and deeply as anyone but that he was convinced that perfection in architecture could not be achieved by the work of individual artists but by that of centuries and that until then "one must admit, though with grief and anger, that what *is must* be!" and that "in architecture there can be only one thing worse: trying to produce a new architecture out of abstraction and theory."[40] This might have raised doubts in Semper about the justification for his sweeping criticism. Besides Klenze's tolerance his teacher Gau's attitude may have made him reflect. At about the time of Klenze's letter, Semper prepared a lecture on Egyptian art, for which he no doubt used Gau's important work on the antiquities in Nubia.[41] In the introduction he read: "We have reached a state of perfection that no longer allows us to exclude all styles for the benefit of one; we cannot say that it is solely the Greek style, Roman architecture, or the Italian taste that we need, but we have to study, to know and, above all, to adopt with skill to our needs what is good in any nation."[42]

Some of this tolerance was noticeable in Semper's lecture course "Lehre der Gebäude" when he came to talk about German architecture of the beginning of the century: represented by Klenze's and Schinkel's buildings, this architecture "could be called eclectic as it took not only ancient art as its model but did justice to other trends too." After referring to the church buildings of Hübsch, Gärtner, and Ohlmüller, he continued: "Reproducing diverse styles of different periods is characteristic of our times, which proves, as far as art goes, the dire poverty of our own ideas and our dependence on those of others; yet it may be possible to develop from this diversity an all-embracing independent style that would be especially suitable to fit the purpose of every building."[43] In the same year, 1840, he tried to advise a former student now in Paris on the course of his studies and explained to him the advantages and disadvantages of the comparative method: "The good periods of art were in every essential so closely related to each other that by comparing them the intelligent and sensitive artist acquires a sure feeling for what is better; this will guard him from bias as well as from caprice and bad taste. You should regard classical art as the mother of our art, her late-born daughter who has world history as tutor and the present as nurse. Our art must and should be more versatile, it cannot affect the quiet naiveté . . . of a child of nature, but should master the abundance of subject matter with self-confidence."[44]

It had become clear to him that sensible acceptance and adaptation of traditional types were in accordance with the spirit of the historically oriented present and indispensable for the evolution of modern architecture. One had to admit, he declared in his report on the restoration of the cathedral in Meissen, "that the versatility of our education must have a decisive influence on our architecture because the exact knowledge of the styles of all centuries and all nations could not be deliberately forgotten and to exclude it would neither conform to the spirit of the time nor be at all appreciated."[45] He sided even more decisively with eclecticism in his pamphlet *Über den Bau evangelischer Kirchen*, written a few years later: "No century can be erased from world history . . . none, not even the most decadent, has passed without leaving an indelible impression on our condition." Contemporary art "must therefore give some indication . . . of the connection between the present and all past centuries and must, with self-assurance and without prejudice, achieve full mastery of the abundant material."[46] In the

"Explanations" for his project for St. Nicholas in Hamburg he declared that he had approached his task from the historical point of view "because we late-born, well-read people who have to know everything that has existed previously could not and should not deny past impressions."[47]

Believing in the beneficial effect of traditional values, he turned against those architects who thought they could manage without taking into account the historical sequence of architectural forms. This basically mistaken attitude was, in his opinion, detrimental to the works of two groups—the historical-eclectic and the materialist-constructive, as he called them. Although both started from diametrically opposed points of view, they had, nevertheless "similarities and points of contact in their errors . . . the [Historians] by becoming engrossed in a past or alien world that is no longer understood and can be made to fit our present conditions only with difficulty; the [Materialists] by constructing the given task only out of the task itself and out of the relevant and often unusual materials. They will always remain isolated in their work and, even given great ability and favorable opportunity for building, will never exert a lasting influence on the direction of architecture."[48] On the contrary, it was the architect's duty to let "the task evolve freely out of its elements into an independent work yet at the same time [to show] the necessary and clearly felt connection . . . with related ideas" and other works adjacent in space or time.[49] "Architecture," he declared, "has over the centuries created its own store of forms from which it borrows the types for new creations; by using these types, architecture remains legible and comprehensible for everyone."[50]

This comprehensibility—for Semper the indispensable requirement for an effective contemporary architecture—was, as he once wrote, "largely . . . dependent on historical traditions."[51] He compared "the architect who spurns these conventional forms [to] an author who constrains his own language by adopting an antiquated, foreign, or self-invented order of words and mode of expression. He will be understood only with difficulty and . . . will not make his fortune, whereas he would have lost nothing in originality had he used simplified but intelligible terms."[52] While he upheld the preservation and application of traditional building types by this argument, his attitude had nothing in common with the tendency he criticized in the historical-eclectic school of allowing ancient masterworks an excessive influence. In a draft to the part of *Der Stil* in which this subject matter still echoed, he stressed the difference clearly: one should not discard the conventional types and invent new ones "but rather try and express new ideas with the old types. This, and slavishly using old schemata that for centuries have belonged to history, are two different things."[53]

So Semper was in the best sense of the word a traditionalist. Of course, like all his contemporaries he was painfully aware of the fact that in contrast to the great civilizations of the past, the modern era had no clearly defined style of its own; yet he did not share the view of those who placed their hope of achieving the longed-for new style on patiently developing whatever style that they happened to favor. One could almost say that he regarded the development of style as a biological evolutionary process, in any case as a process that by far exceeded the lifespan of an individual. There were architects who, being impatient and wishing to escape the reproach of unoriginality, believed that they could create a contemporary style by their own efforts, guided only by the "material and the purpose of the building" and in disregard of traditional forms. He asked these architects to bear in mind "how imperceptible and slow had been the transition from one artistic trend to the next in times that to us appear so creative," and that therefore "the advance and evolution of a new architectural trend cannot possibly be perceived in the present and that only later centuries have the right to pass judgment on our times."[54] The prospectus for *Der Stil* contained the same warning: "A decisive and lasting change in architecture will hardly ever be brought about by new materials and their use in new methods of construction, and even less through the simple power of a genius who has dreamed up his so-called new style."[55]

His sarcasm, always ready to sting, was directed against those who still attempted to invent "a brand-new style."[56] He introduced his Zurich lecture course with the statement that "the traditions of architecture are very old and for this reason it is downright nonsense when nowadays architects want to invent new architectural styles. This would be an enterprise like wanting to invent a new language."[57] Another time he compared the problem of inventing a new style with that of perpetual motion, meaning that even posing the question was absurd.[58] Altogether, it was "arrogant to strive for immortal fame as the creator of a new style"; this "has led many a person at best to fall into ridicule but at worst to gain the sad fame . . . of having advanced the state of anarchy that exists in the field of art at the present time."[59] This led him on to condemn the destruction of old Paris carried out by the "usurper Louis Napoleon" and his prefect, the boastful new opera house (figure 22), the no less reprehensible Palais de Justice, and, on German soil, the "Maximilianstil" created "at a king's most gracious command."[60] As he criticized these buildings, he knew that

22
Charles Garnier. Paris Opéra, 1870. Lithograph by Philippe Benoist, ca. 1872.
(Musée Carnavalet, Paris. Photo Bulloz)

they signified something more than just unpleasant examples of a
passing anarchic state in architecture; together with many other indications they pointed to a deep-rooted crisis threatening the whole
of modern civilization.

In the well-known introductory sentences to *Der Stil* he compared
the nebulas in the nocturnal starry sky—forms that gave rise to doubt
whether they were old systems scattered throughout the universe or
cosmic dust being formed around a nucleus—with the "symptoms of
decay in the arts and the mysterious phoenix-like birth to new artistic
life out of the destruction of the old."[61] He had already used this
metaphor at the beginning of "Theorie des Formell-Schönen" but
there he had added an analysis of the art historical evolutionary process.

He identified three phases: first, the transition into an amorphous
state; second, the preparation for a new formation; and finally, the
sudden crystallization into a new formation. The first phase was that
of the violent destruction of art systems, which then often crumbled
into several systems; the second phase, the fermentation before the
rise of a new system, was so imperceptible that it was difficult to
detect the borderline between the two phases; and the appearance of
the third phase, "the third moment in the process of becoming," was
still an unexplored mystery.

It seems, however, that the "metamorphosis of the motif as prepared by man's tellurian creative instinct into art formation did not come about through a slow process of evolution but in a single act of giving birth. We cannot help but assume," he continued surprisingly, "that the Egyptian temple palace, the Assyrian royal residence, the Indian rock temple and the Doric building crowned by a pediment were, so to say, suddenly created like Pallas Athena as a complete type and fully equipped: creations of a genius in whom society was individualized and who was able to give artistic form and architectural expression to an idea that had been alive in society."[62] This statement is surprising not only because it seems to contradict his basic attitude that attached great importance to the rise and gradual development of art types within an historical context, but also because it conflicts with his previously clearly expressed opinion that neither "the power of the genius" nor "the frail individual" could become creators of a new architecture.[63]

However, that it is not really a contradiction is proven by his statement at the end of the preface: he tried to decide whether we were, according to the state of affairs in modern art, in the first or second phase of the amorphous state; he excluded the first alternative, the collapse into the amorphous state, as too hopeless for the architect (a strange reason), but accepted the second "whether well founded or erroneous" (a kind of working hypothesis) as long as one did not presume to become the inventor of a new style, and then closed with these words: "No modern Anthemius of Tralles or Isidor of Miletus will be ingenious enough to create a new style unless a new concept of universal historical importance has first become overwhelmingly evident as artistic idea."[64] "A new concept of universal historical importance"—he had already laid this down as a basic condition for the rise of a new architecture in *Die vier Elemente* and had repeated it later in his lecture "Über Baustyle."[65] Through this concept alone could the third phase be reached, the sudden crystallization into a new formation, and even then only at a propitious moment, rare in history; at that moment the genius would arise who would be able "to give artistic form and architectural expression to the idea that for a long time had been present in society, striving to become manifest."[66]

What Semper put forward here was a long-term prediction about events that lay beyond the duration of his and the following generations. In the present and the foreseeable future, however, progress would remain imperceptible; the individual architect, active in the present, would have no influence on those near-cosmic events.

Semper's theoretical writings contributed a great deal to the pursuit of the less distant aim. His main work, *Der Stil*, contained the practical instruction, while the manuscript of "Theorie des Formell-Schönen" (and in shorter form the "Prolegomena") outlined the theoretical foundation comprising the three basic qualities of formal beauty— symmetry, proportion, and direction.

These qualities also determined the formal laws of adornment, a subject he dealt with extensively in "Theorie des Formell-Schönen" by way of introduction to the technical arts.[67] At one point he interrupted his classification of adornment to speculate about the probable development of contemporary art: "If I may venture a prognosis of our future: a peculiar *evolutionary* trend, possibly arising out of our fast-moving present, will be of a mainly *dynamic* character; the principle of *movement* and also that of *direction (Richtung)*, which so far we lack altogether, will be reflected in this trend, not only in the products of the specific subject dealt with here but even in the great artistic creations."[68] Semper did not repeat this remarkable and for him unusually optimistic notion, neither in the lecture on adornment nor in *Der Stil*, and even within contemporary architectural literature it seems to be unique.

5

Semper's Position on the Primitive Hut

The wooden hut appeared in Semper's writings three times: as Vitruvius's "primitive hut" (*Urhütte*), as the first dwelling of prehistoric people, and as the symbol of sacredness.[1]

According to a well-known thesis, going back to a passage in Vitruvius and often repeated by writers on the classical theory of architecture, an archetypal wooden hut had been the direct model of the Greek stone temple. Semper rejected this thesis. In one of his first lectures in Dresden he declared that "The question whether the human races . . . lived first in caves and from there derived the motifs of their later buildings or whether they built leaf-covered huts and tents" was a futile controversy that he was not going to discuss at all "because these different means of protection could at the most have had an influence on the construction of the later buildings but not on their basic forms."[2] In a chapter of "Vergleichende Baulehre" he ridiculed "scholars who tired themselves out in making ingenious deductions to prove that Chinese architecture had derived from the tent" just as "it had been a favorite theme of many learned dissertations to deduce Greek architecture from the hut."[3] Certain writers had taken great trouble to trace the different architectural styles to their origin whereby, after the nomadic tent, "the famous Vitruvian hut, supposedly the model of the Greek temple," had played a prominent part, but the more general and less doubtful influence of the carpet-wall had not been taken into consideration.[4] These, he thought, were "strange and fruitless speculations" filling numerous folio volumes "that, since Vitruvius, had been written about the derivation of the Greek temple from a wooden structure."[5] He, on the other hand, was of the opinion that "conclusions drawn from assumptions that the hut was a basic motif were . . . unimportant and irrelevant for the Greek temple."[6] On another occasion, he declared with the same reservation as in the

Dresden lecture that the hut "was important only for the general composition . . . but unimportant for the detailed shaping of the art form."[7]

When Semper became aware of the significance that implements had for monumental art through his work on *Der Stil*, in particular the section on "Tectonics" [carpentry], his rejection of the Vitruvian theory of the wooden hut was complete. "This important circumstance," he proclaimed, ". . . does away once and for all with the pointless dispute about the Vitruvian wooden hut as the supposed model and crude motif for the temple, that is, for its general form as well as for its architectural parts."[8] He expressed himself just as unambiguously in a footnote that he added, in the original manuscript of the section "Stereotomy" [masonry], to his critical remarks about "the over-clever fiction" of an absolute and specifically Hellenic stone architecture: "The seventh main chapter about the formal aspect of tectonics contains my views on the value of this fiction. If the content of this chapter has any validity at all, the opinionated attitude of scholars who have chosen the Vitruvian hut as their bone of contention must indeed seem futile in every respect."[9]

With all this, he seemed to kick at an open door because by then hardly anyone still upheld the thesis of a direct metamorphosis of the wooden hut into the Doric temple. In Germany Aloys Hirt was probably the last who accepted it without reservation; in England, Thomas Hope. Both men belonged to the older generation.[10]

However, another question was eagerly discussed at this time — whether wood or stone had been the primary building material, whether architectural laws had derived from wood or stone building. In one camp were those who were convinced that the Greek temple had been conceived in and exclusively developed from stone, with Karl Bötticher as their most eminent champion. In the other camp were those who regarded the autochthonous birth, as it were, of monumental architecture as impossible and who submitted as proof of the historical development from wood to stone building the numerous vestiges on the stone temple of the typical forms of wooden construction. Semper shared this widely held view with many architects and writers.[11]

Most confined themselves to submitting evidence with examples taken from the Greek temple, in particular the Doric. Semper, however, did not think of the evolution as an exclusively Greek phenomenon. His work on "Lehre der Gebäude," which took up most of his time in Dresden — first only as a subject for a lecture course, later as the basis for a larger work commissioned by Vieweg — broadened his view.

He, too, recognized in the Greek orders "a timber architecture adapted to a style that was right for stone" and also thought that "the oldest temples had been built in wood" and that "even in later times when the walls of the cella were made of stone, the old way of construction with regard to columns and architraves" was faithfully followed.[12] But he found the same to have been the case with Assyrian architecture. He did not doubt that "the trunk of the palm tree . . . had certainly been used first as a column for the support of the airy halls . . . and was only later reproduced in stone according to its essential characteristics,"[13] and he was convinced that Persian architecture had developed in the same way: "The whole structure of the columns proves that they were direct reproductions of wooden columns."[14]

Yet it was the Chinese who, in his opinion, had kept most tenaciously to the timber style; at the time that their civilization became ossified, they had reached "the stage of the simple-hut construction" so that "in Chinese buildings we can recognize the timber architecture of primeval times."[15] Even more remarkable were his comments about Indian temple architecture. Semper rejected as a "chimera"[16] the common view according to which Indian architecture was typical for a style evolved from stone, that is, from cave buildings. The cave temples were, in his opinion, late structures made at a time when the architectural forms had already gone through a long development: "Surely these works hewn out of stone were not the first ones. Unmistakable signs indicate that they were reproductions of older timber buildings." Later in the same manuscript he wrote, "Obviously, these architectural elements were not originally products of the chisel, which only reproduced them in stone."[17] Even in Egypt he saw "the clearest signs of an original timber construction having been imitated" and though he admitted that Egyptian architecture, in its large monuments, was above all stone architecture, it had "all the same originated from wood or rather reed structures. . . . It retained the characteristic traits of its origin even in its final development into the perfect stone style."[18]

Thus the transformation of parts of an original timber construction into those of a monumental stone building was a normal development common to all people of the past, the Romans alone excepted. He called them "the inventors of true stone construction,"[19] who introduced the joints of an ashlar walling as a decorative element and thus achieved "a turning point in the history of architecture";[20] with the grandiose Roman style—the "world domination expressed in stone"—"architecture had started on a completely new course."[21]

The realization that traces of a primitive timber construction could be found in the monumental buildings of most peoples caused Semper to give the dwelling a special place in his "Lehre der Gebäude." Domestic architecture formed the first section in his scheme of eleven building types. Believing this type to be the basis of all architecture, he dealt with it so thoroughly that when he came to write down the result of his studies for publication, he never got beyond it, and even so he only managed the part that dealt with the ancient cultures of the Far and Near East.[22] At first, in his lecture course of 1840, he still thought it necessary to point out that although dwellings as the "simplest and earliest buildings" belonged by right to the first class of building types, it remained doubtful "whether these, when considered as objects of architecture, meaning as pure art, really were the first buildings in which the artistic sense and skill of the people had shown itself."[23] Later, however, he had no such reservations. His constant search for the primary elements of architecture led him to see the dwelling in a new light. When trying to justify the privileged position of domestic architecture in the last lecture he gave in Dresden, he spoke of man's original creative instinct to build and of "the indisputable fact that if not architecture then certainly building, that is, joining materials into an organized form, was first applied to dwellings in the widest sense of the word."[24]

Now, if it is correct that the building activity of a people began with domestic architecture, then it derived ultimately from the dwelling in the form of a hut. Semper differentiated between two forms of primitive dwellings: one, a "firm enclosure of an open place"[25] erected for the protection of the hearth and for defense, a form that he called "court building" (*Hofbau*), whose essential motif was the wall; and, the other, the hut whose basic form was the roof either directly attached to the substructure or resting on supports.[26] In Dresden he had taught that "the form of the hut . . . was adhered to even after the temple building had been further developed."[27] Ten years later he offered a similar formulation: "The victories in earliest times of tribes of hut dwellers explain why the cult of most ancient peoples was linked to forms that were reminiscent of the pitched roof of the primitive hut."[28] Another time he pointed out that because the carpenter's ancient craft had first been developed by work on the roof, the form given to some parts "retained a certain symbolic significance even when no timber was used anymore."[29]

Obviously, Semper had in mind real huts, not ideal or fictitious structures; he examined the influence of these huts in the past on the rise and modification of architectural forms. He did not accept the normative function of the fictitious model of the hut, which had been commended by many writers on the classical theory of architecture, for instance Laugier, as a guideline for contemporary architecture. The hut "is *not* the material model and pattern for the temple," he declared in *Der Stil*, and he saw to it that this "not" was the only word in the entire text that was printed in bold face.[30]

These huts that had served as dwellings at the beginning of history had, of course, long since vanished, except perhaps two: certain ancient clay models and, according to Semper, the Chinese house. As evidence that simple huts were the form of early dwellings, he referred to some "curious baked clay models of huts" (figure 23) found in graves near Albano and published by François Mazois; he mentioned them frequently, the first time in a footnote to his translation of Mazois's *Le Palais de Scaurus* on which he worked during his stay in Paris.[31] The Chinese house — in his opinion, as mentioned, a "frozen image" of a primeval timber building — represented as well that primitive phase that had never gone beyond material needs: "The roof is an umbrella against rain, the columns are supports, the supports are upright, planed, and painted trees."[32]

These were the only direct witnesses, as it were, of the ancient world; for other examples of primitive forms of hut he had to turn to ethnology in the belief that, judging from the low level of civilization of primitive tribes of the day, one was justified in taking their type of dwellings as an analogue for the primeval hut of the ancient world.[33] This was why he chose "a picture of an Indian's hut in Trinidad (elevation and plan) with the clearly recognizable four elements, which are, still in the primitive manner, unconnected with each other" for the vignette at the end of the preface to the "Vergleichende Baulehre." "Here is the roof supported by columns of bamboo; its structural parts are tied together with ropes of coconut fiber; it is covered with palm leaves; the terrace has bamboo railings; the walls consist of mats."[34] This was certainly the same hut that he called the "model of a Caribbean hut exhibited in the colonial section of the Great Exhibition of 1851" in a later lecture, and showed, together with a Chinese house, as "an instructive illustration of the system based on the four constructive elements of architecture."[35] In another lecture and later in *Der Stil*, he returned once more to the Caribbean hut in which "all elements of ancient architecture appear in their most original and unadulterated form: the hearth as center, the mound surounded by a framework of poles as terrace, the roof carried by columns, and mats as space enclosure or wall."[36]

The Caribbean hut was an example of the material stage of primitive domestic building (figure 24). Only the Chinese among the great civilizations had stopped at this stage and had failed to develop the

23
Hut urn from the Alban Hills. (The University Museum, University of Pennsylvania)

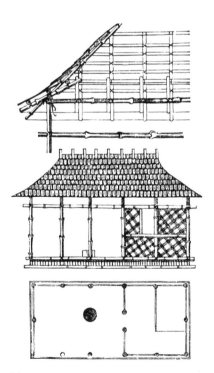

24
Caribbean hut. (*Der Stil*, 2, p. 276)

principles latent in the original timber construction; the social and political structure of the empire prevented it. "In the Chinese manner of building," Semper wrote; ". . . one recognizes . . . the faithful adherence to the primitive state. Constrained by building regulations enforced by unintelligent 'building officials,' their creative genius was never free to develop the elementary idea; this idea remained barren and was not allowed to evolve from the material state to higher symbolism and to a work of free art."[37] The people who had reached this highest stage and to whom Semper was referring, were of course the Greeks, who, he declared in a London lecture, "considered these elementary constructions as quasi-natural objects and treated them in a symbolic manner as they did with vegetable and animal forms."[38] When "art entered into the construction" basic structural forms were symbolized and ennobled. This symbolization, which affected the elementary parts of the hut—"the substructure, the fence, the roof"—began in early times.[39] Within all the styles of the ancient past—the Egyptian, Chaldean, Assyrian, and even in the Greek orders—vestiges of timber architecture could be found, but "all these traces were only symbolic . . . being derived from a timber construction, they express symbolically certain more general aesthetic notions."[40]

Significant as this symbolic-functional interpretation was, another aspect of the primitive hut made an even stronger impact on Semper: it had been the symbol of sacredness from early times. In the lecture "Über Baustyle" he declared that it was "an important observation that the domestic hearth of the nomads with its primitive protective roof structure remained at all times the sacred symbol of civilization; civilization found in the altar and the cella of the temple its highest religious manifestation."[41] On another occasion, he called the "gabled roof the universal symbol of the deity"[42] and taught that "the primitive hut retained . . . its sacred significance from old traditions and became the supreme task of architecture in the form of the temple."[43] On the symbolic level "sacred hut" and "house of God" were identical for Semper.[44]

In the historical-technical part of the section "Tectonics" in *Der Stil*, which had as its theme the properties and use of timber for buildings and furniture from Roman antiquity to the Renaissance, Semper wrote once again of the "leaf hut, with its protective roof supported by tree trunks, covered with straw or reeds, and enclosed by wickerwork." This description would suit both the hut of Romulus on the forum in Rome and a similar hut on the Areopagus in Athens, both referred to by Vitruvius.[45] This leaf hut, Semper explained, was regarded by the Graeco-Italians as "the mystical-poetic and at the same time artistic motif . . . and the hieratic analogue or symbol of the sacred arbor (σκηνή) might well have been a relatively late, poetical creation [developed] by the Athenian dramatists, which could nevertheless have influenced the architecture of that time."[46] Therefore, what Semper wrote about here was a concept of the ancients that was not his own, though he recognized its importance. In any case, it had nothing to do with "the pedestrian Vitruvian theory," as he put it, according to which the "marble temple was . . . nothing more than a petrified primitive hut," a theory which, as previously shown, he rejected. There were authors who, while opposing Vitruvius's fiction, eagerly supported the view that the temple was directly conceived in stone independently of any outside influences; yet even they "must come back to what they call the hieratic allegory or symbol of the sacred arbor (σκηνή)."[47] This statement was directed against Bötticher, who, in spite of having propounded most effectively the thesis of the "stone" conception of the Greek temple, had spoken of the hieratic tent or σκηνή embodied in the temple, the tent, which, he had to admit, was "the ideal analogue for the mechanism of a freely structured stone building."[48]

To recapitulate: in the introductory paragraph to the section "Tectonics," Semper declared that the hut "was not the material model" for the temple; that he rejected Vitruvius's thesis of the "petrified primeval hut"; but, on the other hand, that he thought that the mystical-poetical leaf-covered hut might have had some influence, the more so as even those who upheld the sovereignty of Greek stone architecture could not do without the notion of the sacred tent. He concluded his explanation by writing that he was confident that he would not be misunderstood after all that he had said when he now presented the Caribbean hut as "conforming to the Vitruvian hut in all its elements."[49] The misunderstanding he wanted to guard against was this: if he had given an illustration of the Vitruvian hut at this point without an explanation beforehand, it easily would have been assumed that he believed in the direct and material translation of the hut's system into that of the temple, whereas in fact he "had taken from ethnology a very real specimen of a timber structure," just that traditional type of a dwelling that contained the four basic elements of architecture and that had in early times become the symbol of sacredness.

This seems to me to be the meaning of this oft-quoted paragraph that sheds light on Semper's attitude on the theme "hut."[50] That he thought this symbolism to be the hut's essential aspect follows from a remark he made in a different context. When, at the end of *Die vier Elemente*, he wrote about the ancient Hellenic sacrificial cult he explained that in early times the altar used to be erected on a mountain summit and that next to it stood a chapel without columns but with a gabled roof. "Out of this mud hut," he concluded, "and not from the Chinese column-supported roof, arose, with foreign elements added to it, the Greek temple."[51]

6

Semper's Position on Iron as a Building Material[1]

At different times Semper commented upon iron as a building material, initially immediately after his return from Greece. At first he intended to give only an account of his journey, then he planned a comprehensive work about the reconstruction of ancient temples, and in the end he was satisfied with a preliminary report where, in spite of the prosaic title *Preliminary Remarks on Polychrome Architecture and Sculpture of the Ancients*, he managed to find a place for his radical ideas on archeology, politics, religion, and architecture.

Among these was his radical comment on iron, well known and often quoted: "Let the material be true to itself . . . brick should appear as brick, wood as wood, iron as iron, each according to its own statical laws."[2] These seem to be prophetic words, almost a hundred years in advance of their time. But were they really? The year was 1834.

To which buildings did the words refer? Perhaps to Schinkel's predilection for the decorative use of iron or to smaller iron bridges? With the exception of the dome of Mainz Cathedral by Georg Moller (1828), iron had not yet been used on a large scale in Germany. Even in Paris, where Semper had studied under Gau, iron at that time played a minor part: when he left Paris, the iron and glass building of the Galerie d'Orléans had not been finished and that of the Jardin des Plantes not yet started. Apart from the Pont des Arts, only the cupola of the Halle au Blé could possibly have made him reflect on the properties of iron as building material. This was hardly enough to explain his radical remark. It may help to look more closely at its context.

Semper's point of departure was the intellectual reorientation that his century was undergoing, evidenced, he thought, by the increasing interest in the state but also by simplified domestic arrangements. As an example of this simplification and restraint and of the comfort and grace demanded of the new home, he pointed to England where the leisurely ease of domestic furnishings were of the highest standard, where industry tirelessly tried to satisfy the most trivial needs of the household, and where the study of natural sciences had led to most important discoveries. Immediately following these observations came the statement that "brick, timber, especially iron, metal, and zinc have replaced stone blocks and marble," and that to imitate the latter would be wrong. Then came the sentence quoted above.[3] This means that Semper's demand for material, including iron, to be true to itself related to the English domestic house and English interiors. He referred again to England a few lines below, where he condemned the fashionable nonsense of the neo-rococo (a decorative style that had become the fashion in London at about this time);[4] because, in this connection, he added after the word *einfach* the translation "simple" (in quotation marks), it seems that he had before him an English publication or a report on English conditions.[5] What that could have been has so far not been established—perhaps Thomas Hope's book *Household Furniture*.[6] He certainly did not know English architecture from his own observation; only five years later did he go to London on a study tour.

However that may be and from wherever the influence came, what he then added as an explanation makes it evident that when he wrote of iron he did not mean the building material. Iron, he declared, could be covered like stone and wood with "an inoffensive ornamental embroidery"; its "weight and capacity of resistance demanded light, delicate, and openwork forms"; the ancients too had employed wood, iron, and bronze according to the static laws appropriate to each material, of which one could get a good idea from the mural in Pompeii. In short, for Semper iron was not much more than a material well suited for decorative purposes. It seems that we, subconsciously influenced by our knowledge of the development of iron architecture, read too much into Semper's statement. It might have signified a progressive point of view, but certainly not an epoch-making vision.

Subsequent comments by Semper confirm this interpretation. It was a basic attitude to which he adhered. When fifteen years later, exiled to Paris, he inspected the recently completed Jardins d'Hiver, he wrote a highly critical report that he summed up with these words: "So much is certain that . . . architecture . . . must not have anything to do with this quasi-invisible material when it is a question of mass effects. . . . As gratings for an enclosure, as delicate lacework, architecture could and should employ and show metal in the form of rods, but not as girders carrying a great weight, as support for the building, or as the keynote of a motif."[7] Again, almost fifteen years later, at the end of section "Metalwork" in *Der Stil* he warned against iron construction in monumental buildings and exclaimed, "Let us look for the true sphere for applying wrought iron, not in monumental architecture but in minor parts, in the interior, and on fittings."[8]

In his opinion, iron caused difficulties when used as a formative element in architecture because structurally it needed little volume to fulfill its function effectively. He stressed this disadvantage in 1842 in a report on a project for a parish church by one architect Heuchler,[9] who had designed a Gothic-style church using stone for the walls and buttresses but iron for the supports of the interior—slim iron columns and pointed iron arches. (If it had been built, it would, as far as I know, have been the first church in Germany built from iron.) Even more unusual was Heuchler's idea of making the tower in an open framework of light iron[10]—a sort of Eiffel Tower in miniature. This aroused Semper's criticism: "The attempt of Herr Heuchler to introduce iron into monumental architecture seems to have failed with regard to the tower." In his opinion, the failure in this as in all other unfortunate attempts to give iron a major part in "serious" architecture seemed to be due to the fact that "because of its particular lack of volume iron almost vanished from sight at a short distance" unless one gave it a thickness that, considering its strength, would be unjustified. "This would lead to a contradiction—to sacrifice either beauty or function; to combine both would be impossible."[11]

Equally, his criticism of the Jardins d'Hiver (figure 25) was directed not against its construction from metal rods and metal wires (which the purpose of the building demanded) but against the lack of mass of the "enormous glass box [which] absorbs everything" and "leaves too small a share to architecture."[12] In *Der Stil* he mocked: "A poor soil for art! A proper wrought- or cast-iron style is out of the question; for that the ideal is invisible architecture. The thinner the metal web, the better it is."[13] He then hinted at the reasons for his negative attitude. There existed, he explained, a difference between absolute proportions of stability and those relating to the mechanical actions of the material. If the material was stone, the two converged; if it was iron, they conflicted. Representation of absolute stability had been a basic principle of ancient aesthetics. According to a general aesthetic law, the mind feels at ease when perceiving architectural structures only "if they do not display anything that could give rise to the thought, let alone doubt, about their permanence. . . . Nobody, at the sight of something upright . . . thinks of its stability provided the proportion of height to base is correct." In short, Semper had the same feeling of mistrust and unease toward construction in iron as the classically

25
Théodore Charpentier. Jardins d'Hiver, Paris, 1847. (Photo British Library, from
L'Illustration, 1848)

trained architect of the preceding centuries had had toward the Gothic style.[14]

There is another more profound reason for his critical attitude, which has to do with his "theory of cladding." According to it, the primordial motif (*Urmotiv*) of architecture was the cladding of the material: this, not the core, was the essential element; the mechanical function of the core was symbolically expressed in the cladding. In rudimentary form, the theory already existed in *Vorläufige Bemerkungen*; there, polychromy and stucco played an outstanding part in Semper's interpretation of ancient architecture. When after extended studies, above all during his stay in Paris and London, Semper had developed his theory further, he became aware of the importance of metal as an original cladding material; the more he studied this material, its history and technical properties (and this happened increasingly with his position as head of the metal class at the Department for Practical Art), the more important seemed to him its influence on the development of basic art forms. He realized that ancient people had developed "a momentous principle of construction" — the hollow-body or tubular system. He repeatedly wrote about it in *Der Stil*: in his opinion, there was nothing of greater importance in the entire history of style than this system that had been latent in primitive metal-clad posts and boards; he even went so far as to maintain that nature produced all organic formations according to the tubular system. Now, a tubular structure was especially suitable for metal; the larger circumference of the hollow tube would give metal a more substantial appearance so that in this form it would, like stone, appear absolutely stabile, yet because of its high degree of resistance would not have a larger sectional area than was needed.[15]

When writing this, Semper must also have had in mind modern iron structures. In his article on the Jardins d'Hiver, he indicated a possible and aesthetically acceptable development of iron construction: it had been proven, he said, that hollow metal prisms possessed a higher degree of resistance than solid rods of the same sectional area. We ought to follow the example of the Romans and make ceilings out of metal. For "fine art" architecture, metal should be used only in the form of sheet metal, and with this he included hollow-cast columns.[16] He was more positive later in *Der Stil*: after he read the page proof of the paragraph in which he had explained the advantage of using tubes instead of solid rods in tectonics, he inserted at the last minute, as it were, this sentence: "In recent times, the principles of the tubular system have been taken up again in bridge building and even in domestic architecture. Although the sense and spirit in which this has been done have so far been purely technical, there can be some hope in it for the future of art; our way of construction would once more be in accordance with monumental forms."[17]

Despite this more positive tone, his dislike for iron construction remained. Only a few pages earlier, he had declared categorically that only stone was the true material for monumental art[18] and had ridiculed the fortunately (as he thought) failed attempts in "iron" Gothic: he was not averse to hearing praises of the iron trusses of railway stations as symbols of the provisional nature of these buildings, but he begged to be spared the admiration for iron libraries, banqueting halls, and buildings of that kind—a dig at Labrouste's reading room of Ste. Geneviève (1844–1850; figure 26).[19] A few years earlier, before the room was finished, Semper had already criticized it: he missed there the seclusion that made the reader feel "gemütlich" and thought that it was no different from all other attempts to use iron in architecture, which had only led to a kind of bare railway style that precluded any friendly or festive atmosphere[20]—a reaction similar to that at the beginning of our century when modern interiors were rejected for their clinical coldness.

Semper commented positively on only two iron buildings. One was the interior of Heuchler's project for a church, which in his opinion could "be quite effective"—a judgment that one suspects might have been due to consideration for a colleague.[21] In the case of the second building, the Crystal Palace, his appreciation was certainly sincere. The festive, lyrical atmosphere of the glass-covered space, the harmonious fusion of nature and technics, daily delighted him anew. But he was generous with his praise for the structure itself.[22] "It is hardly possible," he noted, "to conceive a different let alone a better solution— the best criterion of an inspired conception," and he praised "the inventive masters of technical science who by new means have completed a glorious work—this enormous and airy and yet strong building, a wonderful triumph!" He mused: "If the slender columns had become the bearers of the primitive *velum*, which would have completely harmonized with the suspended draperies and figured carpets, . . . then we should have seen in this marvelous building the original type of the most primitive form of architecture unwittingly realized"—for the author of *Die vier Elemente* the highest possible praise.[23] Of course, he also noticed the many shortcomings, for instance, the "absurdity" (*Unding*) of its boundless length and the impossibility to take it in from the outside in one glance as one's aesthetic sensibility demanded (figure 27).

26
Henri Labrouste. Reading room, Bibliothèque Ste. Geneviève, Paris, 1850. (Conway Library, Courtauld Institute, London. Photo James Austin)

27
Crystal Palace, London, 1851. Exterior. (Semper-Archiv Zurich)

However, in view of his overall critical attitude to iron buildings, the suggestion that the Crystal Palace could be the start of a new development was surprising. In time, he thought, this "shapeless and gigantic" conception could mature into well-defined forms; if for this endlessly long building, this tower of Babel in reverse, the true focal point could be found, then this initial attempt could lead to a true building of the future.[24] The sensation that the Crystal Palace created at the time might have been the cause for this remarkably positive assessment; yet the fact that Semper had watched the building rise, that he knew the architect and had been given an assignment there (the first since his flight from Dresden), which required his daily attendance and allowed him to make daily tours through the exhibition stalls—all this led to such intimate knowledge of the building that at the end of the Great Exhibition he bid this palace of glass and iron a loving and nostalgic farewell (figure 8).[25]

It changed nothing in his basically negative attitude. Lothar Bucher, with whom he often discussed the exhibition and its historical-cultural significance, was likewise of the opinion that it would not have been possible to fulfill the given task better than Paxton had done and that the much debated and much disputed beauty of the Crystal Palace was due solely to him; but to imagine that a new style or an architectural revolution would date from this building was just a poorly thought-out notion.[26] This sentence sounds as if it expressed exactly Semper's feelings; it might even have echoed his opinion. But there were professional men, well qualified to know what they were talking about, who were of the opinion that with this building a new architecture had indeed begun. Since space does not permit relating in detail the lively debate on iron style then taking place, the contributions of only two outspoken advocates of iron style shall be referred to in conclusion, so as not to give the impression that Semper formed his attitude in a vacuum.

One was Anton Hallmann. Semper must have met him during Hallmann's stay in Dresden, which lasted for more than a year; he possessed Hallmann's *Kunstbestrebungen der Gegenwart* (Present Trends in Art), published in 1842, the same year as Semper's report on Heuchler's church. In connection with his project for the Berlin Cathedral and the iron construction of its galleries, Hallmann made some general observations about this material. Surprisingly, he wrote of the aesthetic conflict that had arisen with the introduction of iron as of something that belonged to the past, and even went so far as to maintain that iron was the chief material of the century now that one had become familiar with this type of construction once thought to be a neckbreaking affair. He was convinced that as long as the proportions of the parts were correct and the nature of the material clearly apparent, any interior constructed in this way would be called beautiful and dignified.[27]

More profound was Karl Bötticher's prediction of the future development of art. His speech at the Schinkelfeier of 1846 was full of ingenious thoughts of which I shall select only those that are relevant here. The previous year Eduard Metzger, Semper's friend and colleague, had talked, somewhat vaguely, of the "future of forms of art" and about the powerful influence that iron construction would have on covering space; by this he was mainly thinking of its possibilities for the Gothic system.[28] For Bötticher, the future looked fundamentally different. According to him, new architectural systems arose through the invention and the effect of new principles of static forces that made a new system of covering space possible. Historically, there had been only two such systems, the Greek and the Gothic. Trying to develop them in an eclectic manner would mean gilding the lily. Both systems had been and would never return to their previous form; both had thoroughly exhausted the potential of stone. Was there, he asked, a different static force that would bring about a new system of covering that would be his generation's own system? He saw it in the absolute strength of iron, which would transform the static principle of the arch to a completely new and unknown system. These new static forces would be represented symbolically in art forms as had happened with the art of the Hellenes. Static principle and material were the basis of all art forms. The principle of force, properly applied, would lead to a third style that would rank with the Greek and Gothic styles.[29]

Semper replied to this argument in *Der Stil*: he would have nothing to do with the "crude materialistic notion according to which the essence of architecture was nothing more than developed construction, as it were, an illustration and illumination of statics and mechanics," and warned, "The dangerous idea that out of iron construction, applied to monumental buildings, a new style was bound to arise had led many a talented . . . architect astray."[30] He taught his own students in Zurich that "The proper monumental material is ashlar,"[31] just as he had criticized the fact twenty years earlier that "we get iron from England . . . while we have the best ashlar stone on our doorsteps."[32]

Semper was convinced that a new material alone could not bring about a new architectural style; nevertheless, he guessed that functional buildings in which iron was by then widely used would play their part in future architectural development and that as an architect he would have to define his attitude to the problem. Like so much else, he deferred the discussion of this difficult problem to the third volume of *Der Stil*—and therewith forever. In a manuscript that contains a list of contents for a work on formal beauty that he planned to write, he noted of its third part: Among the many buildings there are some where "until now only a functional and structural system has been applied; of these the most outstanding examples will be selected and dealt with as extensively as possible in view of the present trend; after that the attempt will be made to show how this system could be made to profit art."[33] It is a pity that he could not, or would not, find time to show how functional buildings and "serious" architecture could be reconciled.

III

Five Manuscripts

translated by Wolfgang Herrmann

Semper's literary estate was considerable. It contained manuscripts, in several versions, of all the books and articles published in his lifetime, of the annual courses he had given as professor of architecture in Dresden and Zurich, of the many public lectures he gave at Marlborough House, written in English (incidentally, a language he never quite mastered). It included the voluminous manuscript of over five hundred pages of "Vergleichende Baulehre," the work on which he was engaged for so many years, and an equally extensive manuscript, again in several drafts, of "Theorie des Formell-Schönen"; prefaces and introductions of both these treatises are translated in this section. There are also manuscripts relating to buildings he had been commissioned to execute by order of the Emperor Franz Joseph of Austria in 1869: the so-called Kaiser Forum in Vienna, a grand project integrating the Imperial Palace or Hofburg into a cultural center, similar to the Dresden Forum with which, almost forty years before, he had started his career.[1] Of particular interest are the detailed programs for the statuary embellishment of the executed buildings, the Burgtheater and the two museum buildings. The ingenious allegorical significance of this decor engaged Semper's intensive and sustained interest.[2] Other documents of this period concern the building of the second Hoftheater at Dresden (1870–1878) after the first burned down in 1865. Semper directed the execution of his new design from Vienna, his permanent residence after 1871.[3]

Studying this great collection of manuscripts, one becomes aware of Semper's fertile mind. He was interested in a wide range of subjects: everything that concerned architecture was, of course, important to him, but so were art and artistic problems in general; he had an almost scholarly knowledge of matters connected with archeology and philology, was conversant with modern scientific achievements, and was fascinated by mathematical problems. Thus, exploring these manuscripts will always be a rewarding pursuit. Five of them have been chosen to make up this section.

Except for the introductory source notes, the footnotes are Semper's notes; numbered notes and bracketed passages are the editor's additions or comments. Every two or three folio numbers are given in brackets at the end of the last full paragraph on a folio.

1

Influence of Historical Research on Trends in Contemporary Architecture*

[Historical Development of Science]

Science ended the first stage of its development by an unquestioning acceptance of things; it then passed on to criticism and became fragmented into hundreds of doctrines; finally, it endeavored to grasp and formulate a generalized idea that alone gave value and direction to specialized research and resolved the conflicts that criticism had brought to light, which then was no longer divisive, but unified.

During its youthful, heroic age Science mastered what it had so far acquired by its creative imagination, ordered what was not known by analogy to what was known, and constructed its own well-ordered artificial world of perception. The Greeks reached this stage, for instance, in the natural sciences. But as the spirit of Plato and Aristotle continued a phantasmagoric existence conjured up by monkish spells, as the antique form thereupon became the palladium of ignorance, and as the great Bacon adopted skepticism—from then on Science dissipated its energy more and more in speculation and experiments; it burrowed into the earth to look for treasures, was glad if it found earthworms, and produced a chaos of erudition without coherence or principles. Out of this chaos the men of the seventeenth and eighteenth centuries, the Newtons, the Laplaces, the Cuviers, and the Humboldts,[1] created a new form of Science generated by a universal world view [Weltidee].

Other doctrines passed before our eyes, as it were, through the first stages of their development; some still grope unsteadily within the

---

*Preface to "Comparative Building Theory" ("Vergleichende Baulehre," 1850): MS 55, fols. 1–13.

second. For instance, since Lavoisier everything in chemistry is directed toward specialized research and every apprentice at a pharmacy adds spice to his exam with a newly discovered alkaloid.

It can be predicted with certainty that this Daedalus will become regulated within a more advanced, still undiscovered system.

[*Abundance of Specialized Architectural Literature. Durand, Rondelet, German Architects.*]

This also seems to be the case in the science of building, where every pensionnaire returning from his journeys unfailingly endows the Academy with a specialized contribution. [fols. 1–2]

The store of erudition consisting of a measureless and daily growing mass of writing and collection has been more than we can cope with; we have lost direction and are at the end of our tether.

In order to get out of this predicament, the vastly increased material has been divided into different subjects, each of which has begun to take form as a separate doctrine.

Many of these doctrines have been the work of nonarchitects, in particular the doctrine that deals with the historical or philosophical aspect of architecture.

The authors of other writings are men of practice; although they know their subject matter thoroughly, they often lack the ability to adopt a wider point of view.

Thus we have a mass of books on aesthetics and the history of architecture, on theories of design, construction, and materials, on building by-laws, on estimating, etc., not to mention the numerous auxiliary branches of Science. In addition, there are a great number of special works on specific subjects: domestic and religious architecture, civil and military engineering, instructions on timber and brick building, and so forth; all are works that contain rich stores of knowledge and experience and, at times, intellect and talent.

But only a few writers have tried to show the interrelation of these doctrines, and these few have kept to the grooves of the trend especially familiar to them. They are thus distracted from the goal they have set themselves—the reunification of arbitrarily separated doctrines into a general theory of building.

The French architect Durand came closest, at least superficially, to this goal. But having been charged with drilling students of the Polytechnique to become architects in the shortest possible time and lacking practical experience, he often got lost in lifeless schematism; in this he was possibly also influenced by the then fashionable trend [neoclassicism]. His representations of monuments are incorrect and his reconstructions arbitrary. But in spite of all these shortcomings, his handbooks are still the most valuable for beginning architects.* [fols. 3–4][2]

The work of Rondelet, on the other hand, is purely practical; in spite of progress since made in the field, his handbook—dealing with all doctrines relating to design and execution, with the science of materials, with construction, administration, and the technical side of architecture in general—is still the most complete so far. Yet how the elements whose mastery he taught, when joined by more intellectual elements, together bring forth an organic art form—this, the true theory of building, lay beyond his field of inquiry.

We Germans can boast even less of having demonstrated with any success as a general principle that the combined effect of all actual or potential intellectual and material factors results in architectural works of art; on the other hand we are blessed with a host of books on specialized subjects.

The history of architecture was for the first time, and the most successfully, dealt with by us. The same is true of aesthetics. The scientific-technical part of the science of building is also represented in our country by numerous and often excellent writings, although we lack the practical experience, sustained by costly experiments, of the French, English, and Americans.

The abundance of unrelated teaching material that our architects are expected to master, resulting in self-consciousness, inexperience, and irresolution, is in my opinion one reason why our works lack originality and why they are not equal to the progress achieved during this century.

[Classification of Modern Architectural Trends: Historians, Aestheticians, Materialists]

Lacking spontaneity, our architects have followed three different directions; they can be called the historical-eclectic, the aesthetic, and the materialistic directions. [fols. 4–5]

The Historians. The historical-eclectic school, the one to which most architects belong, came about through the ease with which monuments of all times can now be studied and through the great diversity of taste created thereby.

*Durand, *Traité d' architecture*, II Vol. ditto *Parallèles*, etc.

The school finds it more convenient to reproduce existing works unchanged or, at least, to fashion works after whatever the given task requires, in an arbitrary and unnatural manner; it finds this more convenient than the reverse method of letting the task evolve freely out of its requirements into an independent work, yet at the same time showing the necessary and clearly felt connection not only with related ideas gradually brought forth in time but also with adjacent works as spatial and temporal conditions require.

The Aestheticians. If the theory of taste were a perfect science, if it were not so deficient and, for lack of clear concepts, so full of undefined and probably erroneous notions, especially when it deals with architecture, it could fill the gap and join the separate yet intellectually related doctrines into a coherent building theory.

But philosophy, when applied to art, is in the same position as is mathematics when approaching problems of physics where many immeasurable but interrelated forces and quantities are involved. The most gifted artists hardly take note of aesthetics in its present state; only the so-called art experts favor its rules and formulas—partly arbitrary, wrong, or at least unproven, partly too general and uncertain—by which they assess the value of a work; they have no standard of their own and believe they can apprehend the secret of architecture in a dozen precepts, whereas the infinitely varied architectural forms assume their characteristic quality and individual beauty only through exceptions to the rules or, rather, deviations from the system.

In no way could it be said that schematism is the most noticeable fault of present-day achievements, whereas it was predominant toward the end of the sixteenth century on account of the rediscovery of the Vitruvian books and the firm and confident bearing of the great Italian masters during the glorious era of the fifteenth and sixteenth centuries. Once before, at least in Germany, it had been apparent in the geometrical forms of the so-called Old Germanic or Gothic style. [fols. 6–7]

However, a certain school in Germany, which cannot free itself from the domineering influence of a late master's genius [Schinkel], cannot be wholly acquitted of aesthetic schematism in spite of the good number of undoubtedly talented adherents who wish to pursue in a free manner of their own choice what, in occasional episodes, proves to be a success. All the same, the works coming from this school still reveal some faith and conviction, whereas the historical trend proper indulges in romantic or classical notions.

The Materialists. Our present artistic attitude has been influenced even more powerfully by those sciences that teach mastery over the building material. The subject has been treated with exhaustive thoroughness, and the material has often been given precedence over the idea; by professing that the store of architectural forms was exclusively conditioned by and evolved out of the material, one has placed the idea in iron fetters.

Regarding construction as the essence of architecture, the Materialists stray almost as far from the goal [of a unified building theory] as those who think of architecture as a kind of sculptured or painted decoration to be applied to houses.

Material must always be subservient to the idea and should never direct it. This is how nature works; it is the example nature has set. Although this *Urmeisterin* [primordial matriarch] chooses and uses her material in conformity with this law, she nevertheless imprints shape and character on her formations according to the ideas that are embodied in them; but because the most suitable material is chosen for their embodiment, her formations gain beauty and expression through the emergence of the material as a natural symbol. [fols. 7–8]

This gives us the measure of the part that technics plays in architecture; it shapes the forms of architecture according to natural laws as conditioned, on the one hand, by the changing purpose of the thing to be formed and, on the other, by the properties of the material to be used.

Those architects who attribute a decisive influence to material for the genesis of architectural forms belong to the third, the materialistic school. In a sense they are the extreme opposite of the Eclectics (Historians), but both have, as is common with extreme positions, similarities and points of contact in their errors. Both arbitrarily abandon the traditional standpoint: the [Historians] by becoming engrossed in a past or alien world that is no longer understood and can be made to fit our present conditions only with difficulty; the [Materialists] by constructing the given task only out of the task itself and out of the relevant and often unusual materials.

They will always remain isolated in their work and, even given great ability and favorable opportunity for building, will never exert a lasting influence on the direction of architecture.

Although architecture produces original formations and is not an imitative art like painting and sculpture, it has over the centuries created its own store of forms from which it borrows the types for new creations; by using these types, architecture remains legible and comprehensible for everyone. The architect who spurns these conventional forms is like an author who constrains his own language by adopting an antiquated, foreign, or self-invented order of words and mode of expressions. He will be understood only with difficulty and, at least as an author, will not make his fortune, whereas he would have lost nothing in originality had he used simplified but intelligible terms.

[Semper deleted the next two sentences: The reproach is being made, more or less justifiably, that our times lack originality. This has induced many architects to follow the route hinted at without having yet become prophets and even less messiahs of a new art. If one bears in mind how imperceptible and slow had been the transition from one artistic trend to the next even during creative periods, one would realize that the rise of a new architecture could not possibly be perceived in the present and that only the spirit of the age, and not frail individuals, will be able to deliver it from the womb of the past.

[*Essence of True Theory of Building*]

Architecture creates original formations, which are not contingent on fully finished natural forms but which have evolved historically according to natural laws and to the human mind's inclination toward order; to a certain extent the formations have been fixed, though this does not prevent their further improvement and development. [fols. 9–10]

These formations are called organic if they spring from a correctly conceived basic idea and if they make evident the rule of law and inherent necessity, the two qualities that make nature appear admirable and perfect in everything she creates.

The power of a genius may subconsciously achieve such nature-like creation. But the task of an intelligent architect should be to seek and pursue the rise and development of basic ideas and to reduce to its simplest expression the law that lies hidden within the artistic covering.

In this search, the architect will encounter so many difficulties and complications that he will be able in a few cases only to hear the mysterious passage of man's thought throughout the centuries. But he cannot fail to have some success if, guided by this, he explores the domain of architecture and selects from the infinite variety what is most outstanding, groups what is related into families, and reduces what is derivative and complex to its original and simple state.

In the end he will realize that in the same way that nature, for all her abundance, is thrifty in her motifs, in the same way that she modifies the few basic forms a thousandfold according to the evolutionary stage reached by living beings as well as according to varied living conditions—making some parts short, some long, some fully developed while others are only hinted at—in the same way architecture, too, is based on certain standard forms which, contingent on an original idea, through constant reappearance make possible infinite variations that are conditioned by particular needs and closely defined circumstances.

It will certainly be important to trace these standard forms and the idea inherent in them. Not only will the overall view and the understanding of what exists be made easier, but it will also be possible to derive an architectural theory of design and inventiveness that shows how nature works and avoids equally both monotony and fancy notions.*

Once a standard form has been established as the simplest expression of the idea, it will come to life, modified according to the conditions of the site, the period and its customs, the climate, the material to be used, the idiosyncrasies of the client as well as of the artist, and many more incidental circumstances.

To make the basic idea visible within the great variety of formations and to create a whole that has individual character but, at the same time, is in full harmony with itself and the environment—therein lies the great secret of architecture. [fols. 11–12]

If the author, guided by these ideas, uses this time of involuntary leisure to journey through the domain of architecture, he does so without presuming to present a theory of building in the sense outlined here. This task would be beyond his faculties and means. But he hopes to have stimulated the reader and to have produced a useful handbook for disciples of art by weaving into the subject matter (arranged according to a schema set out on the next page) everything he thought, observed, and collected in his former position as teacher and practicing architect. [fol. 13]

Gottfried Semper, Paris, May 4, 1850

---

*By the shell we know the nature of the kernel, in the same way that comparative natural history can build up the animal from the bone structure. Works of architecture are the shells of nations and of individuals, expressing in a clear and intelligible way these organisms long since dead.

2

The Basic Elements of Architecture*

[The Dwelling the First Form of Man's Building Activity]

First Chapter. Introduction.

Any discourse should first go back to the simple origin of the subject under review, trace its gradual development, and explain exceptions and variations by comparing them with the original state. For this reason, it hardly needs justification that the present study, which tries to arrange into groups, families, and classes all that architecture has created, opens with the dwelling or private house as the original and simplest type.

Yet there may be some reason to doubt whether architecture as such really started with the building of dwellings. Art history shows that nations with a more pronounced artistic inclination singled out public buildings, especially temples, by embellishing them; whereas the life of the individual and consequently the private house took on artistic refinement only when religious and political decline had set in, and with it a retreat from public life and a compensating pleasure in a life of splendor and luxury.

Therefore—I hear people assert—the buildings of public worship ought to be dealt with first; they are supposed to be the first and only cause for the rise of *true*, national, and *fine* art, and without piety this could not have happened.

No doubt true art without piety does not exist: piety causes man to take delight in the living beings that the Maker has created; it drives him, enraptured, to express himself creatively and like a deity in his own work.

*Introduction to "Comparative Building Theory" ("Vergleichende Baulehre," 1850): MS 58, fols. 15–30.

But this artistic piety is pantheistic and turns everything it embraces into temples of an all-pervading deity. Although it finds its fullest embodiment only in the sacred temple building, it has been present in man right from the beginning: it was expressed in the first garland and in the first attempts at ornamentation.

The nations we first meet in history were religiously and politically well organized. Yet before they reached this comparatively high degree of civilization they had had to travel a long road—which might have been only an attempt on their part to regain a height they had lost in even earlier times. [fols. 15–16]

For instance, it is improbable that the frugal private life of the Greeks was the one they had led from the beginning, just as it would be wrong to conclude from the severe simplicity of the Doric style that even plainer forms had preceded it. On the contrary, unless we are greatly mistaken, the heroic and the political-historical times were preceded by a period of comfortable living and private luxury.

In those times, according to legend (and confirmed by fairly safe indications), great care was taken with the palaces and domestic houses, whereas public life gave art no opportunity; moreover, temples, as we understand them, did not exist.

The temple has evolved from the funeral cult; tombs being the houses of the dead, the temple is the refined and idealized form of the same motif that underlies the development of human dwellings.

For that reason, the sequence chosen here is justified, the more so since it cannot be denied that, even if not architecture, then certainly building—in other words, joining material into a well-planned form— was first at work on dwellings and tombs.

Because of the great number of relevant subjects, this section will be longer than all the remaining sections put together; it is also the most important one because it introduces in their original forms those elements whose development will be the subject of the sections that follow.

The beginning being so important, it is necessary both to make more general preliminary remarks and to go into many details, even though much may seem to lie outside the plan and framework of this book.

The thoroughness here will allow the remaining sections to be much shorter and to rely on references back to this section.

Because of the comprehensive plan of this work it is not possible to do more than touch upon the important geographical, moral, political, and religious interrelations between nations and the changes that have occurred over the centuries. The author's intention is to put the reader into a frame of mind that will make the works of these nations understandable to him. [fols. 16–18]

[The Hearth and Its Symbolic Significance]

Second Chapter. The Hearth. *

Before men thought of erecting tents, fences, or huts, they gathered around the open flame, which kept them warm and dry and where they prepared their simple meals. The hearth is the germ, the embryo, of all social institutions. The first sign of gathering, of settlement and rest after long wanderings and the hardship of the chase, is still the set of the fire and the lighting of the crackling flame. From early times on, the hearth became a place of worship; very old and long-lasting religious ideas and forms were associated with it. It was a moral symbol: it joined men together into families, tribes, and nations, and it contributed to the rise of social institutions at least as much as want and simple need. The house altar was the first object to be singled out for adornment; throughout all periods of human society it formed the sacred focus around which the other separate elements were crystallized into a whole.

The hearth has kept its age-old significance up to the present. In every room the center of family life today is still the fireplace.

Sharing the meals at the domestic hearth was a mark of being a member of the community. In Greek and Latin the words "koine" and "caena" took on the meaning of social associations; the German "Genossenschaft" [association] is derived from "geniessen" [to savor food].

But the significance of the hearth was even greater in antiquity: it was the sacred place for solemn worship. The ancestors' grave was close to the hearth. This is still the custom with the Indians of Colombia. Some, for instance the Salives, place the tombs of their chiefs in the center of their huts; other tribes dry the corpses over the fire and suspend them from the beams of the roof.†

Who can doubt that the Egyptian practice of embalming the dead and of displaying the mummies at festive meals, and the Roman lectisternia with their waxen ancestral portraits, originated from equally

---

*Vitruvius 2, p. 1.
†Millin, *Voyage en Colombie*. Hüllmann, *Urgeschichte des Staats*. [Karl Dietrich Hüllmann, *Urgeschichte des Staats* (Königsberg, 1817), especially pp. 113ff, 120. The book on Colombia has not been identified so far.]

coarse ancestral customs? It was therefore the ancestors who had first satisfied the urge to relate one's own devout emotions to a real object. Altar and hearth became kindred notions and the mask of the deceased the first idol.

When tribes intermarried and concluded alliances, the chiefs of the families that were related by marriage came together at the hearth of the patriarch who had arranged the meeting. On these occasions the two families would jointly venerate their ancestors and offer them libations—the origin of polytheism.

Thus the hearth, identified with the ancestral tomb, became the core and center of the temples in the form of the sacrificial altar.

The palace of the chief became the memnonium, that is, the royal court, and the tomb became the temple and seat of government. [fols. 18–20]

[*Protection of the Hearth. The Four Elements of Architecture: Hearth, Roof, Mound, and Fence. The Two Basic Forms of Dwelling.*]

Third Chapter. First Elements of the Domestic House.

Protection of the hearth. There is no need to prove in detail that the protection of the hearth against the rigors of the weather as well as against attacks by wild animals and hostile men was the primary reason for setting apart some space from the surrounding world.

What made this separation necessary differed, however, according to different circumstances.

In regions with a mild climate and in the plain, where people could live in the open air for most of the time, a light tentlike cover against the weather was needed.

While this sort of protection against the weather was easily achieved, making the settlement secure against the vehemence of the elements was more difficult. Mounds had to be built to protect the hearth against inundation by the nearby river.

But enemies too had to be kept away from the hearth; the much-coveted fields in the plain attracted the envy and rapacity of man, while the herds were exposed to attacks by wild animals.

Enclosures, fences, and walls were needed to protect the hearth, and mounds were needed to make it safe from flooding and also to espy the enemy from afar.

Thus, four elements of primitive building arose out of the most immediate needs: the roof, the mound, the enclosure and, as spiritual center of the whole, the social hearth.

In rocky regions the many caves offered a natural though rough protection against the climate. Natural grottoes could easily provide everything else that was needed for a safe dwelling. One can therefore assume that when men began to live together in very early times, grottoes were used. Yet one may rightly doubt that these tribes, content with having some protection, and living in such cavernous but small region that they never became numerous or powerful, could greatly influence the development of mankind. The shapeless form of the grottoes surrounding these people from the first day of their lives must have had a lasting effect on them, which would have made them grow up into men engrossed in fantastic visions rather than devoted to the well-ordered world of architecture.

Therefore, we believe we are fully justified in not admitting the grotto as a motif of consequence to architecture and in disregarding it completely when inquiring into the origin of architecture; we shall try to substantiate this course when the occasion presents itself. [fols. 21–22]

Living conditions of another kind also induced men to join and live together in dwellings. The hunting inhabitants of mountainous, wooded regions felt themselves amply protected against the elements as well as against enemies by the nature of their country, their poverty, and their self-assured strength. The thinly scattered population held the fields and produce of the land as common property and let everyone freely use it. They needed neither walls nor dikes. Only the climate was a powerful enemy; a solid, warm roof was needed for protection against it. Originally this roof rose directly from the ground; only later, when combined with the protective wall, did it take on the form of a house.

There are many indications that the earliest inhabitants of Latium did not know the Etruscan-Greek way of building that the Romans, their descendants, were to adopt. The earliest form of their dwellings are known to have been simple roofed-in huts, some of which were still standing in late Roman times. Further evidence is provided by strange clay urns in the form of huts, found under a volcanic layer near Albano. The volcanic activity in Latium reaches back far beyond historical records and even beyond traditions and legend. How ancient the people of this country must have been! The vignette at the end of this chapter shows a picture of these clay models after Mazois [cf. figure 23].

Life in these huts was comfortable and friendly, the opposite of life outside with its toil and combat. The hut became a small secluded world on its own; the family, including the cattle, were part of it. A roof protected it all.

These huts stood next to each other, but loosely grouped, in the primordial landscape.

We can thus distinguish between two basically different ways in which human dwellings arose. First, the courtyard with its surrounding walls and, within, some open sheds of minor importance, and second, the hut, the freestanding house in its narrower sense.

In the first arrangement the enclosure, which later became the wall, dominated all other elements of the building, whereas in the second, the roof was the predominant element. [fols. 23–24]

[Development of Social Organizations: Hierarchy and Autocracy]

Fourth Chapter. Continuation.

In the preceding chapter we have shown how the first domestic settlements evolved out of the earliest stage of social life, the family. For this process we assumed only motives of a material nature, arising from the need for shelter.

These settlements could retain their simplicity when the first states, through agreements between chiefs, were organized into federations, which modeled their civil institutions after similar constitutions based on rule by kinship.

These first federal constitutions developed everywhere into hierarchic or autocratic constitutions. The most ancient history recounts numerous cases that prove this, although the circumstances that brought about these changes are seldom indicated.

A priesthood might formally retain the old federal constitution, except that priests belonging to a favored family now dominated the federation. They were privileged to attend to the chief religious services and, in consequence, took on the permanent supreme direction of all affairs of state, a prerogative emanating from the priesthood's ancestral hearth. Examples of hierarchic rule were the Amphictonic League (the union of the original Hellenic tribes around the common hearth at Delphi), the covenant of the Twelve Tribes of Israel around the arc of the Levites, and the Egyptian league of the Twelve Kingdoms; the latter, however, was not grafted onto the original federal alliance of free tribes but followed after an intermediate stage during which the tribes became dominated by autocratic rule from which the hierarchic federal state then arose.*

*Herod[otus] 2, pp. 99, 147, 151, 159.

Except where an autocracy had paved the way for a state dominated by priests, the hierarchic constitution was not much different in form from the original federal constitution; therefore, the basic features of domestic institutions were hardly affected by it.

The autocratic constitution might in a few cases have been introduced through agreements between members of a tribe. But in most cases it was the result of wanderings and expeditions into foreign lands, which overpopulation or other reasons had forced the members of a federation to undertake. [fols 27–28]

The bond created by these common ventures was to a certain extent the opposite of the original and natural bond between families of the same tribe. Men joined together not from kinship but from love of adventure; youth, courage, and strength, perhaps also poverty and debts, made them eager or willing to take part in daring and dangerous expeditions. They were led by a commander either freely chosen or elevated to that position by force of circumstances, family prestige, or personal capability. Thus, out of these expeditions arose the arbitrarily ruled military state.

Unlike the primeval form of society based on ownership of property and individual independence, the military state followed socialist ideas; it demanded that the individual merge into the whole, the ideal expression of which was the state as personified in its ruler.

All Asiatic states, from their earliest history to the most recent times, had a socialist base. Property ownership was replaced by military feudalism, of which the supreme head, as the visible representative of an ideal notion, the state, ruled over all the material and moral means of the state. He had power over life and death. All possessions derived from him and all reverted to him as soon as he demanded them or when the owner died.

In his report on the excavations at Chorsabad Monsieur Botta has shown by a striking example that these principles are still valid in the Orient: "Dans les pays des musulmans il n'a pas de propriété veritable, mais un simple droit de possessions, payé chaque année par un redevance à un être idéale nommé imâm, représentant de la communauté musulmane et représenté lui même par le gouvernement. Celui-ci, n'étant en quelque sorte qu'un tuteur, dispose du sol dans l'intérêt de la société qu'il personifie, mais il ne peut l'aliéner pas une vente à perpétuité."[1]

Only powerful and well-organized societies could succeed in making the route through the desert safe for trade. They alone had forced labor and slaves at their disposal; they alone could in this way master the elements, claim the muddy soil from the river, and sow on it that which would bring them unheard-of riches and enable them to build sky-high monuments and towns stretching across the land.

Wealth and ease, however, cut the lifeline of a state whose whole existence depended on war. Peace was bound to lead to stagnation and a pause in social development that would last for many centuries until revolutions occurred, brought about not from within but by outside forces.

What then followed was not an improved and more progressive form of the preceding phase; it was another example of the same kind, which devours its father and, once its destiny is fulfilled, itself falls prey to its successor.

The oldest Asiatic people whose monuments still stand or are known to us through literary sources were joined into states in a similar way. We shall deal first with their monuments, those amazing witnesses to their power and wealth; not only because they are the oldest but also because their influence on the people living on the northern shore of the Mediterranean, on those highly organized countries where civil liberty brought with it the free unfolding of the arts, has recently been recognized.

Our first task, therefore, will be to show what influence the warlike socialist conditions of society had on the formation of domestic establishments. [fols. 28–30]

3

Structural Elements of Assyrian-Chaldean Architecture*

The social conditions and the general nature of the land inhabited by the Assyrian-Chaldean people had some influence, as we have shown in the preceding pages, on the development of architectural forms.

But the characteristic features were to a great extent also conditioned by the available materials. Important questions then arise and must be considered regarding these materials and the way the people of Mesopotamia used them.

Chinese architecture is in this regard of great art historical interest. When we reach that section, we shall have the opportunity to show that the two basic elements of the building—the roof with the supporting columns, and the vertical enclosure later to become the wall of the living room—were completely independent of each other without any structural interaction. It seems that in Assyrian-Chaldean architecture too an organic interplay between the two elements had not yet taken place. They both existed independently of each other: while one element, the roof column, was dominated throughout its full architectural development by one primary material, so were the motif and norm for the development of the other element, the vertical space-enclosure, determined by a different primary material.

In our inquiry we shall therefore keep both elements separate and shall write first about the vertical space-enclosure and thereafter about the roof and its support.

Vertical Space-Enclosure. [Assyrian Wall Decoration.]

The primary material establishing the norm for the vertical enclosure was not the stone wall but a material that, though less durable, for a

*Chapter 10 of "Comparative Building Theory" ("Vergleichende Baulehre," 1850): MS 58, fols. 94–120.

long time influenced the development of architecture as strongly as stone, metal, and timber. I mean the hurdle, the mat, and the carpet.

There are writers who devote much time to searching with minute thoroughness into the origins of art; they believe that they can thus trace and explain all the different ways of building.*

The nomadic tent plays a rather important role in their arguments; they see in this structure the origin of the Tatar-Chinese way of building. But while they detect with great acumen the catenary curve of the tent in the curved lines of the Chinese roof or indulge in other equally erroneous assertions, they overlook the important influence that the carpet in its capacity as protecting wall had on the evolution of certain architectural forms and even on those of the fine arts, on painting and sculpture, so that to my surprise I look in vain for an authority to refer to as support for my assertion that the carpet-wall plays an important role in the history of art. [fols. 94–96]

Strictly speaking, my thesis is not directed against a contrary one, but only follows from an indisputable fact that, in my opinion, has so far not been taken sufficiently into account.

It is well known that any wild tribe is familiar with the fence or a primitive hurdle as a means of enclosing space. Weaving the fence led to weaving movable walls of bast, reed, or willow twigs and later to weaving carpets of thinner animal or vegetable fiber. The budding artistic instinct of early man asserted itself first in this primitive industry. Only the potter's art might with some justification claim to be as ancient as the craft of carpet weaving.

The first attempts at decoration and the first crude imitations of natural objects in outline and colors were made on the simple utensils and woven mats of primitive man.

Using wickerwork for setting apart one's property and for floor mats and protection against heat and cold far preceded making even the roughest masonry. Wickerwork was the original motif of the wall. It retained this primary significance, actually or ideally, when the light hurdles and mattings were later transformed into brick or stone walls. The essence of the wall was wickerwork.

Hanging carpets remained the true walls; they were the visible boundaries of a room. The often solid walls behind them were necessary for reasons that had nothing to do with the creation of space; they were needed for protection, for supporting a load, for their permanence, etc.

---

*Hope pursues these chimeras with British doggedness in his *Historical Essay on Architecture*.

Wherever the need for these secondary functions did not arise, carpets remained the only means for separating space. Even where solid walls became necessary, they were only the invisible structure hidden behind the true representatives of the wall, the colorful carpets that the walls served to hold and support.

It was therefore the covering of the wall that was primarily and essentially of spatial and architectural significance; the wall itself was secondary. [fols. 97–98]

The covering of the wall retained this meaning even when *other materials* than carpets were used either because these materials lasted longer or because they were cheaper, easier to clean, or more magnificent, as for instance when carpets were replaced by stucco, paneling, alabaster, or metal plates.

For a long time the character of the new covering followed that of the prototype. The artists who created the painted or sculptured decoration on wood, stucco, stone, or metal, following a tradition that they were hardly conscious of, imitated the colorful embroideries of the age-old carpet-walls. The whole system of oriental polychromy and consequently also the art of painting and of bas-reliefs arose from the looms and vats* of the industrious Assyrians or from the discoveries of prehistoric people who preceded them.

In any case, the Assyrians should be regarded as the most faithful guardians of this primordial motif. In the oldest annals of mankind, Assyrian carpets were highly praised for their splendid colors and the skill with which fantastic pictures were woven into them. Written descriptions of mystical animals, dragons, lions, unicorns, bulls, tigers, etc., agree fully with the images on the walls of Niniveh, Nimrud, and Persepolis, not only in the kind of animals depicted but also in the manner of representation. The family likeness between Assyrian sculpture and carpetwork is indisputable. Sculpture clearly kept within the originally imposed limits and also to those prescribed by the developed form of the motif after it had been transferred into an alien material [figure 28].

The style of these sculptures indeed shows a trend toward naturalism, restricted not by theocratic precepts as in Egypt but by the peculiar features of a technique foreign to sculpture.

---

*It seems certain that the Assyrians used mainly vegetable matter for wall painting; for this reason, it is not possible to determine the composition of the colors. Only the few metallic paints that they used could withstand the climate and humidity and are thus preserved.

28
Northwest palace, Nimrud. A winged deity. (British Museum, London, no.
124561. Photo © Werner Forman Archive)

These features include the predilection for ornamental accessories, the scrupulous accuracy with which details were depicted,* sharp threadlike contours, stiff postures, glaring coloring, lack of any emotional expression, and strict parallelism in the composition. The bas-relief must have been especially suited to this style, but in the murals too the same technique is noticeable. According to Layard, the wall paintings have strong black outlines while the ground is blue or yellow. [fols. 98–100]

Borders with long inscriptions around the paintings are indications of the same origin. Even the character of the cuneiform may have derived from embroidery. Would it be possible to think of a more convenient way of writing with thread and needle?†

While carpet manufacturers nowadays attempt to reproduce the works of the great painters by skillful weaving, it was the reverse at the dawn of art when the works of painters were reproductions of motifs that had their origins in carpet embroidery.

This strange example of a complete reversal in the original relationship between industrial and artistic activities is not an isolated instance; it gives rise to interesting reflections, which the space and plan of this work do not permit us to pursue here.

The carpet certainly also determined the forms of other objects, for instance door curtains, window screens, and portable shelters. There are indications that leave no doubts in this regard. The beautiful bronze lions, masterpieces of Assyrian sculpture that were found at Chorsabad pegged into the ground to the right and left of the gates they guarded, were certainly meant to have curtains attached to them.

Moreover, it follows from the simple finishing of the floors of the festive rooms at Chorsabad and Nimrud that they too had been covered with carpets; this practice preceded the later luxury of mosaic floors, which therefore was determined by the same motif that had such an important influence on wall coverings.

The art of mosaics was a daughter of carpet weaving; for a long time it retained the imprint of its origin.

One further conclusion can be drawn from what has been said, which is of great importance not only for an understanding of the Assyrian style but for the correct assessment of ancient architecture as a whole:

Walls never appeared in their structural nakedness; they were always covered on the inside as well as on the outside—inside in the manner

---

*It is precisely the oldest monument, the northwest palace of Nimrud, in which the dresses and jewels of the figures are shown in the greatest detail.

†Every washerwoman marks the laundry in cuneiform script.

mentioned above, outside with stucco or a similar coating that was weather resistant and malleable. On festive occasions the display of carpets would have recalled the original motif in its proper form, as still happens in our day in the Orient and in southern European countries. [fols. 100–102]

This also explains and justifies the use of raw bricks, which was common practice among the Assyrians, Medes and Persians, Chinese and Indians, and finally among the Egyptians. Colored stucco was not invented because the raw bricks needed a coating, but quite the reverse: since the color, form, and even weather resistance did not matter with a wall that was hidden under the customary strong and decorative coating, the material chosen for the wall needed only to meet basic requirements of structure and low cost.

Often a plaster of lime mortar was used for this coating, an ancient technique that the Assyrians already knew well at the height of their power, and the Egyptians about six thousand years before Christ.

The original significance of the coating was apparent too when glazed bricks painted in enamel were used and colorful decorations with friezes of animals and other images adorned the plain surfaces of the minimally structured walls; in this way the carpet style, so alien to the actual construction, was retained.

[Semper added the following four paragraphs as a note next to the text: I do not totally exclude the possibility that construction with tiles could make a kind of mosaic carpet-decoration. But fragments of painted and glazed tiles from these early periods seem to exclude the late Roman and medieval use of colored tiles for mosaic pictures.

I have, on the contrary, made the following observations of the fragments of glazed tiles from Chorsabad and Babylon in the Louvre in Paris: (a) they were fired imperfectly and at low temperature; (b) there are two kinds of glazing or enamel (one is more opaque than the other); (c) with the exception of some inscriptions, friezes, borders, and continuous rows of decoration, all other ornaments (painted or enameled) were made regardless of the rectangular shape of the bricks and seem to have been freely drawn. Even the ornamental friezes take into account only the horizontal grooves so that rosettes or palmettes happen to be at times in the center of the brick, at other times across a groove or between two grooves, each variation quite haphazard; (d) only the upper surface of the brick was glazed or enameled but frequently the color flowed beyond the edge of the outer surfaces. All this leads to the following conclusions. First, the Assyrian and Babylonian tiled walls were not made like a mosaic out of enameled bricks, but, second, the paint was applied to the bricks when they

29

Susa Palace. Colored and glazed tiles. (Louvre, Paris. Documentation Photograph-
ique de la Réunion des Musées Nationaux)

already formed a surface; third, this surface was laid horizontally at
the time the painting was done; and, fourth, during the operation the
bricks were not joined by mortar [figure 29].

This leads to the reasonable assumption that for the intended wall
decoration the bricks were arranged on the ground according to the
width and height of the wall before firing and that the whole surface
was painted over, after which the bricks were fired and finally attached
to the rough bricks of the wall in proper order as an incrustation.

This proves that brick building, though very old in Assyria, nevertheless had no structural significance. Its ornamentation had not evolved
from construction but had been adopted from that belonging to another
material.]

There will be an occasion in the course of this section to show that
the old tradition of coating the walls and all other parts of a construction
remained universally valid throughout all periods up to Roman times,

even when the walls were made of expensive material such as marble and granite; it will also be seen that polychromy was closely connected with this practice and that only at a late stage of architectural development was the construction of the wall used as a decorative element. Originally this was the case only with the foundations of walls and of terraces.

Terrace Walls

Stone and Brick Building

It is high time to refer to this subject so as not to be open to justified objections to the forgoing observations. Therefore, I repeat that my remarks have applied only to walls that served certain requirements of the domestic dwelling, and that other stonework, especially terraces and waterworks, had a different origin and consequently developed a different style. Stone blocks as ornamental elements can, indeed, be found at the oldest monuments; but they occur only on foundations for walls and terraces. [fols. 102–104]

The need for these terraces and waterworks must have arisen very early, in fact at a time when the dwelling still consisted of a simple tent. Work on these walls taught the art of masonry, which gradually spread to house building; in its upper parts, the house probably never lost the character of a light construction on a solid substructure.

The country lacked timber and in parts even ashlar, whereas the firm clay soil, as soon as it was broken up, offered material ready for use in building. Its easy availability must have been an incentive to undertake great building projects. Although kiln-dried bricks were known and used from early times, unburnt sun-dried bricks remained the most commonly used building material.

With the exception of terraces and floors, all masonry in the monuments at Niniveh was of burnt bricks made from the same clay that was used for joining them. The outer cladding, as mentioned above, consisted of alabaster slabs, mortar, and burnt bricks.

Construction was somewhat different in Babylon. Mortar and bitumen were used as a binding material, and for a better joint layers of reeds mixed with bitumen were from time to time placed between the courses. It seems that the firing of bricks was more unusual here; on the other hand, ashlar was hardly ever used because transport was very expensive.

The walls of unburnt bricks had to be unusually thick so that they could resist the weight of the mass piled up on them. This explains the disparate proportion between walls and rooms that we notice from the ground plans of the monuments at Niniveh. It is obvious from the thickness of the walls that they were meant to carry a high superstructure. [fols. 104–106]

Vaulting

The interesting question of whether the Assyrians were familiar with the art of vaulting has now definitely been answered in the affirmative. Traces of vaulting and even a completely vaulted room have been discovered at Babylon, and the story by Diodorus of the vaulted tunnel under the Euphrates no longer sounds improbable.

But how vaulting became generally accepted is difficult to determine. It has already been mentioned that the main gates of fortresses and castles are invariably depicted with a semicircular vault whereas the smaller doors and all windows are square-headed. It would be important to find out whether the strange structures seen in many wall paintings were really meant to represent vaulted houses. I admit that I do not know what to think of them and leave it to others to find a solution.* Should they really represent vaulted niches (in later times, it is true, a favorite form in the Orient) this would prove that in very early times people already knew how to solve the most difficult methods of vaulting.

It seems that vaulting was introduced into Egypt only during the Eighteenth Dynasty, a time when this nation was in frequent contact, either peaceful or hostile, with the Assyrians. This has led to the assumption that the Egyptians adopted the art of vaulting from the Assyrians. [fols. 107–108]

Timber Construction

However long the art of vaulting might have been known to the Assyrians, it never asserted itself over the customary and hallowed system of a horizontal cover made of wooden beams; vaulting had no lasting influence on the development of architectural forms.

It is well documented that timber was widely used in Babylonian and Assyrian architecture, although only poplars and palm trees grew

---

*Could they not rather represent huts made from wickerwork, a kind of light construction that the Romans, especially, used when they besieged towns?

on the land. This peculiar fact struck foreigners, especially the Greeks, as a characteristic feature.*

This is about all that we know with certainty, and we are quite in the dark about the way timber was used for constructing roofs.

Did the founders of Niniveh know the column as an architectural element or did they never use it in their houses with their strange ground plans? In my opinion, the latter is unlikely because wall paintings depict buildings that certainly have columns; moreover, the Medes, Bactrians, and Persians, the heirs to the Assyrian-Chaldean civilization, used columns in abundance. From the slender form of the stone columns of Ecbatana, Pasargade, and Persepolis it can be deduced that their models, the wooden Assyrian columns, were essentially like them and that, in accordance with the timber style, they were covered with rings, notches, beads, moldings, and grooves, and in addition were elegantly finished in color and gold. This agrees with the above-mentioned passage by Strabo in which he wrote of trunks of palm trees with reeds nailed onto them.†

Therefore, it cannot be doubted that the Assyrians knew and used columns; but one can hardly do more than guess at the manner in which these columns were applied in the awkward spatial conditions known to us from the ground plans of buildings at Nineveh. [fols. 109–110]

Layard, who discovered and wrote a book about the monuments of Nineveh, is positive that there were no traces of columns in any

---

*Shortly before the assault on Babylon, Xenophon encouraged his companions by assuring them that Vulcan would fight on their side because the gates and columned halls made of cedarwood would be easy prey to their firebrands. Other references to the timber architecture of the Assyrians have been mentioned before. A very interesting relief from Chorsabad depicts a large bay, filled with many ships, where floating timber is being pulled out of the water and carried ashore. Timber trade, above all with India, was so important for commerce in general that a ruler who favored it was given full credit for it and his achievement commemorated in pictures.

†The ornament that resembles the volute of the Ionic capital and that horrifies our aestheticians by its strange (for us) application to the capitals of the columns at Persepolis often appears in the wooden furniture of the Assyrians, mainly in tables and chairs. This confirms the reasonable assumption that the column, like these tables, was regarded as a turned and carved piece of woodwork and that a strong analogy existed between all the wooden implements and the column with its entablature, which was likewise made from wood. The vignette at the end of this chapter represents a garden pavilion with a complete columnar order [not reproduced]. On several capitals there is the same volute, now in a horizontal position. Can anyone doubt that there is a close relationship between the Ionic and this Assyrian volute? That gabled roofs were common in Assyria is clear from the representations on the walls of Niniveh.

of the Assyrian houses he examined. Yet the traces are clearly there, in precisely these buildings. Stone socles in the form of sphinxes are found in the southwest palace at Nimrud with circular saddles on their backs—could they have had any other purpose than to be a base for a column-like support. The position of the two pairs of sphinxes, linked together and placed symmetrically in the passages between the rooms, seems to indicate this purpose as much as does their form.

However, even if this assumption proves correct, the use of columns in these rooms would be an isolated case. They probably were used only as supports for door lintels. Because the rooms show no trace of wooden columns their ceilings could have had no inner support. This would explain their narrow plan; the widest rooms at Kuyunjik were only forty-five feet wide, and those at Nimrud only thirty-five feet wide with a length of one hundred sixty feet and more, which about tallies with the load-bearing capacity of a palm tree. This assumption would confirm Strabo's attribution of the narrowness of Assyrian houses to the length of the available timber.

Besides, I would not confine my search for traces of columns to these narrow inner rooms; I would look for them in the grounds of the square courts around which these rooms are arranged. These courts are so similar to square multicolumned rooms at Persepolis (which we shall describe below) that it is reasonable to see them as models for the Persian rooms.

As becomes clear from the plans published by Layard and Botta, these areas were not completely cleared; only one trench along the walls was dug and the excavated soil was left in the center of the court. The discoverers were interested only in excavating the slabs with the bas-reliefs that covered the length of the walls. Thus the most important architectural question raised by these strange ruins remains unsolved. My assumption that these courts were the multicolumned main hall of the palace finds its only support in the analogous example of the multicolumned rooms at Persepolis. [fols. 110–112]

Layard assumes that the narrow rooms were lit from above through an opening in the center of the wooden ceiling. He deduced this from an opening in the center of the floor through which a wastepipe drained away the rainwater. I do not believe that such a provision existed in the ceiling of the rooms. I think it more likely to have been provided over the court, which could have served the same purpose and have had the same provision as the Roman atrium.

Several reasons make it plausible that the long narrow rooms with their disproportionately thick walls were basement rooms, or rather cellars, with perhaps many stories above them and no source of light at all or one from side openings above. Their very preservation, due only to a great mass of debris covering the floor, speaks for the assumption of a multistoried building. This debris could only have come from the sudden collapse of the upper stories.

According to a passage in Diodorus, mentioned above, there were richly decorated corridors (συριγγες) in the substructure of the terraces. His description fits these rooms remarkably well. They really are pipes—long narrow passages that could receive only poor or artificial light*—yet, nevertheless they were magnificently decorated. The thickness of the walls supports the assumption that they were the ruins of a similar terrace building. It should not be overlooked that the thick walls would have kept the rooms cool like a grotto, a feature still very much appreciated in these countries.† The elongation of the rooms made them particularly suitable for ceremonial processions.‡

Once again the evidence vindicates the often-suspect Ctesius, who was Diodorus's main source.

To judge from some traces, timber must have been widely used in these rooms. Charcoal and half-burnt pieces of wood were found everywhere, probably having fallen from the wooden ceiling. Its paneling was divided into squares decorated with flowers, animal figures, and arabesques. Some were inlaid with ebony of which some beautiful pieces have survived. A surround of graceful borders was richly adorned with gold and silver. [fols. 112–114]

One would look in vain for proper timber architecture in these rooms. As mentioned, that kind of construction was used in the multicolumned courts as well as in light pavilions erected on top of the terraces; many of these can be seen in the wall paintings at Khorsabad and Nimrud.

*I venture to voice the assumption that the upper stories rose in tiers. This explains the peculiar fact that the inner walls are often thicker than the outer ones. I believe that these structures are the foundations for towers with recesses similar to the one illustrated above [not reproduced].

†The houses in Bagdad and Mosul have subterranean rooms that are deliberately dimly lit because it is in these rooms that the inhabitants spend their time during the heat of the day.

‡In India the rajahs still favor the elongated form of audience chambers. Bishop Heber was received by the Rajah of Baroda in a room the description of which is interesting because of its similarity with the Assyrian rooms. See Heber, *Travels* [*Narrative of a Journey through . . . India*, London, 1828].

The Exterior. [Town Planning.]

Practically nothing has been preserved of the exterior decoration, which therefore contributes little to completing the general image we have formed of this extraordinary building complex. For this we have to rely on the descriptions by ancient writers, on analogies, and on deductions.

We know from Herodotus that the houses often had four stories; terrace buildings are so much like multistoried houses that his statement is quite credible. It must, however, be assumed that only some parts of the house reached that height while others remained low.

The ancients tell wonderful tales of the outer walls with their sculptured and painted decoration. Herodotus claimed never to have seen anything more luxurious.

A good part of these tales is taken up by the description of the bronze gates and the costly metal ornamentation that contributed much to the splendor of the building. There was, however, little architectural structuring; the edges of the terraces were crenellated, resplendent in shining metal and colors, as were the terraced ledges and flight of steps of the pyramid with the temple of Belus [Belos–Baal] on top. The immobile mass of walls was interrupted by some parts rising higher, like towers, and others projecting forward. The decoration of windows and doors consisted of simple frames and moldings; the doorways were often vaulted. [fols. 115–116]

Above the terraces and the apexes of the pyramids appeared light pavilions, the uppermost signs of the actual house (οικος). On top of the Belus pyramid, the οικος became the temple of the god. The roofs of the houses rose above the surrounding groves and gardens.

To complete the image of an oriental residence one has to imagine the costly furnishings of gold-plated couches and chairs,* divans, candelabras, all kinds of vases, carpets, and the fragrance of incense.

Although this picture cannot possibly be as vivid as reality, it nevertheless helps to reconstruct a style that had its roots in the soil of the land and in the social conditions of the people—a style that had its own range of forms and unique motifs.

The sensible arrangement, the calm majesty of the pyramidally towering mass, the contrast of ease and elegance with the solemnity of the colorful murals resembling carpets covering the walls—all this made the style the true expression of an oriental dynasty.

---

*We admire the richness and originality of all the objects depicted on the bas reliefs at Niniveh. The taste is at its purest in the oldest palace.

It is certain that in the beginning similar grand farming complexes were dispersed over the land and that it took a long time before they were joined up into towns. Legends about the foundations of Niniveh and Babylon definitely indicate this. Exploitation of indigenous people and the difficulty of tilling the ground for the first time led to social conditions whereby the majority became the slaves of the few so that, besides the great families and their tenants, only foreign traders who were highly respected could lay claim to the rights of free citizens. Slaves and serfs lived in the forecourts of the rich, while for the foreigners magnificent caravansaries were built where with rare self-sacrifice suffered by the population every possible want was catered for.* [fols. 116–118]

Out of these elements, the will of the monarch suddenly created towns that only noblemen were permitted to inhabit.

The overall conception of these towns was a repetition of the same motif that formed the basis of the dynastic courts. The same concentration, strength, and spacious planning distinguished the towns. The royal palace was for the town what the high terrace was for the palace. Public buildings, courts of justice, etc., are not mentioned. All governmental life was concentrated in the palace of the great king. Around this center as around the sun congregated the courts of the noblemen, which in turn formed the centers for their satellites.

There were large areas of tilled land and of pastures, covered with the tents of nomads whom the busy life of the capital had attracted. They camped between the outer walls and the inhabited part of the town. Wide main streets crossed the town;† between them was a jumbled network of passages and narrow streets, courtyards, and shops.

High walls, crenellated like fortifications, with small windows and richly decorated doorways, charming arbors, and pretty pavilions on the roof of the terraces contributed to the colorful spectacle of oriental street life.

Marketplaces are not mentioned; trade was carried on in the wide courtyards of the bazaars and in the caravansaries where any luxurious fancy could be indulged.

The building of canals was an important item in the national budget; they helped to secure public welfare; they determined not only the

*Herodot[us] 1.
†According to Xenophon, the main streets must have been unusually wide. One hundred horsemen could pass through abreast, and there was still enough room left to cordon off the people.

whole aspect of the town and the regularity of its layout, they also created variety and made the town more lively and pleasant.

In the course of centuries, the pyramidal formation of the town around the acropolis of the palace and around the temple on top of the pyramid might be disturbed, new quarters might transform the unity of the organism into two entities, complications and entangle-ments might arise as in Babylon—all this, however, left the basic principle untouched: the focus of the whole always remained the residence of whoever ruled over the town at that time. [fols. 119–120]

4

The Attributes of Formal Beauty*

[Definition of Tectonics]

Tectonics is an art that takes nature as a model—not nature's concrete phenomena but the uniformity [Gesetzlichkeit] and the rules by which she exists and creates. Because of these qualities nature seems to us who exist in her to be the quintessence of perfection and reason. The sphere of tectonics is the world of phenomena; what it creates exists in space and manifests itself through shape and color.

Tectonics is a truly cosmic art; the Greek word κοσμος, which has no equivalent in any living language, signifies cosmic order and adornment alike. To be in harmony with the law of nature makes the adornment of an art object; where man adorns, all he does more or less consciously is to make the law of nature evident in the object he adorns.

The cosmic instinct manifests itself at the earliest stage of civilization when primitive man adorns his body, and as culture advances it becomes evident in industrial works, in pottery and implements, and finally in the protection given to the hearth and the dwelling. This instinct gives man's products an inevitability so that in a certain sense they seem to be creations as natural as if nature had produced them through the skillful hands of intelligent and independent beings.

Therefore the history of tectonics plays an important role in the history of mankind and general physiology. The fossilized potsherds, these oldest witnesses of human civilization, and the decayed and buried monuments of prehistoric times reveal to us the physical and mental capabilities and state of knowledge of the earliest generations,

---

*Introduction to "Theory of Formal Beauty" ("Theorie des Formell-Schönen," ca. 1856/1859): MS 179, fols. 1–46.

just as the solid parts of animals and plants, fossilized through the effect of millennia, tell us of those organisms of which they are the remains.

[Relationship of Tectonics to the Other Fine Arts]

As a cosmic art, tectonics forms a triad with music and dance inasmuch as they are not imitative arts either; furthermore, all three have the same cosmic conception of their task and a similar idealistic way of expression, although each one performs in quite different ways.

In music, too, law determines form and embellishment while adornment underlines the harmonious working together of the various elements. But whereas tectonics aims at creating space by means of motionless and heavy masses of material, music's most vivid expression comes from the fleeting realm of sounds caused by movement; music pursues what is acoustically perceptible, shaping and molding it according to laws analogous to those valid in tectonics. [fols. 1–2]

From the different means used by both arts a basic difference in representation necessarily follows.

Although the ear is capable of receiving different sounds simultaneously, characteristically it receives and gathers sequential sounds and turns them into a cohesive whole, which as a linguistic symbol calls forth a thought, or as music moves deeply, or as a song has both effects. In contrast, the eye is the organ that can absorb the greatest number of impressions simultaneously, at least when perceiving art objects, but it is less capable of turning consecutive impressions into a cohesive whole because when the eye moves quickly the impressions merge, or when slowly they get blurred.

Moreover, a sequence of visual impressions can rarely be determined by the artist; it depends on the viewer's unpredictable way of perception. In contrast, the special character of music consists of arranging the sequence of sounds and of controling the rhythmical and melodious tones as they change, at times gradually, at other times suddenly; it is through this power that music captures the hearer's whole attention and exerts a magic effect on his mind.

Because of this difference, the two arts, by common cosmic character otherwise closely related, are in actual practice poles apart: the ideal of tectonics is static, that of music dynamic.

But just as statics implies dynamics, so potential movement asserts itself within tectonics; conversely, by more or less following d'Alembert's principle, musical movement can be traced back to static equilibrium.

The Greeks were aware of this intimate relationship between the two arts, and from this premise they certainly developed the sublime principles of their theories comprising both arts. They created synonymous terms for certain qualities of formal beauty in both arts, such as harmony, symmetry, analogy, eurythm, and rhythm, and it is not clear to which of the two arts these terms originally belonged. We too ordinarily refer to the tone of a color, to high and low sounds, and to rest and movement in architecture. These are not just symbolic expressions or simple analogies but really signify identical qualities, except that each art achieves its end by different means.

In principle is it not immaterial whether an overall image affects the senses by consecutive and isolated impressions, in waves as it were, while the observer himself is at rest, or whether a work of art is set up so that the observer experiences its total content by moving around it and in this way gathers isolated impressions one after the other, which together present the mind an overall image? It is totally wrong to imagine that an art object is perceived in a single unit of time, an assumption that has harmed mainly architecture (but will soon harm sculpture as well). It will be the future's difficult task to redefine the points of contact that the dogmas of a one-sided theory have separated.

In this treatise, the present author has set himself the task of trying to resolve this difficult problem: to deal with tectonics from the static-dynamic point of view. [fols. 2–4]

Parallel with the three cosmic arts (of which dance, as veiled music with twirling and swaying figures symbolizing celestial harmony, will be left aside) are two further groups. The first group consists of sculpture, song, and "meloplastic."[1] They are the microcosmic arts, which find their ideal not in the general uniformity of nature but in concrete natural objects, particularly in man. They recognize in the human being the quintessence of highest potential of the universal principle and represent him as the purest manifestation of natural laws, freed from all that is incidental and transient.

These three microcosmic arts form the transition between the cosmic triad and the third group, which consists of painting, poetry, and drama. These are the three historical arts insofar as they present man as actively and passively in conflict and entanglement with the world and, by isolating historical episodes, demonstrate the general idea and uniformity of world history in its well-ordered cosmic formation.

This third group participates in the activities of the two other groups; we may call it the cosmic-microcosmic group. Having at its disposal a wealth of adaptable technical means and not trying to apprehend reality but only reflecting it in illusionary images of colors and tones, this triad is the most independent, the most unrestrained, of all the groups. Nevertheless, it is tied to the cosmic triad by inner and outer bonds—painting to architecture, poetry to music, drama to the rhythm of dance. Even more closely tied to the cosmic triad is the intermediate group of sculpture, song, and 'meloplastic.'

Referring only to our foremost concern here—the relationship of architecture with sculpture and painting—we learn from art history that the origin of both sculpture and painting goes back to pre-architectural industrial techniques, that in the polychrome relief both arts long formed a closely knit unit, that after architecture had been created they progressed by relating to and depending on architecture, and, finally, that in the times of the Greeks they reached their full development and at the same time parted, each proceeding in two fundamentally different directions. Although thereafter the three fine arts were active independently as individual arts in their own spheres, painting hardly went beyond the limits that were valid for sculpture until Christian era. It was only the Christian conception of the world that raised painting to the status of an historical art (the term understood in the sense the aestheticians give it) and allowed even sculpture to enter this field.

As an historical art, painting still remained linked to architecture for some time, and even now, after its complete emancipation, it needs the architectural frame for the necessary surround, so to say, as a proscenium for the painted drama or comedy. [fols. 4–6]

In the same way, the most independent piece of sculpture, the statue, needs the accompaniment of architecture; it is comparable to a song that is weak without musical accompaniment. The sculptured relief is bound to architecture to a still greater degree.

What has been said so far concerns the external relations of the three fine arts to each other. But tectonics penetrates still deeper into the sphere of the sculptor and painter: both have to consult tectonic laws of symmetry, proportion, etc., for the simplest compositions, for arranging groups, lines, and mass, and even for coloring.

All this has to do with the relationship of architecture to the fine arts—what Rumohr called the "household of the arts," an expression that aptly signifies the organizing and at the same time subordinate role that architecture played in the genesis of the independent arts of sculpture and painting.

Thus tectonics, by penetrating into the very essence of the other two fine arts, has every right to attract both arts into its own sphere even when they are completely independent.

This relationship affects the extreme edge of the sphere of tectonics, where the entrance is marked by the simple products on which tectonics first manifested itself—I mean adornment, weapons, carpets and clothing, pottery, implements—in short, the practical arts or so-called industrial art. [fols. 6–8]

[*Origin of Architecture in Industrial Art*]

According to an often proclaimed axiom, the decorative arts (an expression that is meant to signify painting and sculpture in the service of industry) owe their origin to architecture and must therefore remain dependent on it; this in a sense may be justified insofar as it is especially difficult in architecture to evade a law that is valid in decorative and technical arts and plainly evident in architecture—the law of composition; it may also be justified because an hierarchical influence of architecture on industrial art asserted itself in certain artistic periods when architectural forms and even structural elements, which derived from stone or wood building, were transferred to earthen vessels and metal implements. Nevertheless, the history of civilization contradicts and reverses this principle; it shows that the development of practical and industrial arts had reached a high level before architecture as an independent art had even been thought of.

Luxury dwelt in huts, tents, and crude mounds; the arts were far advanced in their application to adornment, weapons, implements, and vessels many thousands of years before monuments were built. As late as the time of Homer, even the Greeks combined an unbelievable luxury with the most primitive household furnishings; what distinguished the ruler's palace was only the decoration of the bare walls and posts with industrial products like carpet-walls, metal incrustations, figures of embossed metal, precious implements, vessels of clay and metal, trophies, shields, weapons, and additional adornments of festoons of real flowers and real sacrificial spoils.

The same palaces that were decked with chased gold, silver, and tin had no floors, chimneys, or windows.

A counterpart to this image of a Homeric palace is the strange mixture of simple living conditions and luxury that still amazes travelers today when visiting the tents and homes of Arab sheiks.

While conditions in Greece were still patriarchal, we meet an ancient monumental art on the plains of the Euphrates and the Nile; here too we notice the same principle of adorning the structure with movable objects, though already in a more or less advanced manner.

As we shall see later, many tectonic forms can be traced back to these origins; the industrial arts are therefore the key to understanding architectural as well as artistic form and rule in general. [fols. 8–10]

These are the works in which the stylistic laws and architectural *symbols* had been first developed, in which they can be best witnessed in their primitive state and most easily comprehended. There are some architectural parts that are essentially analogous to certain movable furnishings but are, unlike them, static and monumental; this contrast can be emphasized by omitting from the architectural parts symbols that are typical of movement and would mark them as movable. It would be possible to establish a scale ranging from extreme mobility to extreme stability from which one could choose the greater or lesser degree of monumentality and severity appropriate for the style the building should have. Such extremes are, for instance, the light leg of a piece of furniture or the shaft of a candelabra, clearly characterized as movable by form and symbolic adornment, and on the other hand the Doric column, which looks monumental not only because of its proportions but also because there is nothing to suggest that it could exist as an independent and isolated object.

This alone justifies the plan to be followed in this book: to start with pre-architectural industrial art and to consider house furniture before the house.

Another significant reason causes me to adopt this plan—the importance that industrial art and the crafts have always had but that the general public has only recently been made aware of through the great industrial exhibitions; these have also made it evident that a book on the theory of art must devote an important section to this artistic activity, which is much too neglected by our aestheticians who, feeling superior, look down on it from the point of view of fine art.

[*Plan of "Theorie des Formell-Schönen"*]

For these reasons, the first part of this treatise will deal with the technical arts, though mainly in their relationship to architecture. The second part will attempt to show how the different monumental styles were formed through, as it were, solidification of the art industrial elements around an intellectual core and a center to which they all relate; it will also be shown how each of these styles was to become a symbolic expression and repository of a particular form of society. Of course, these societies must already have found their definite form and inner vitality, must have become sufficiently strong to engage in monumental art.

Just as in the terrestrial story of creation simple and massive organisms preceded complex and finer beings, and just as thereafter the contradictions of old and outdated principles of life were resolved at a higher conceptual level, so the history of architecture leads us gradually from the colossal primordial formations and their fossil remains to the more complex and finer representations of secondary and tertiary social organisms.

The end of the second part will discuss the question of how far it is possible and admissible to integrate all art manifestations—plastic, tonic, and mimic—into one grand all-embracing artistic whole that would express the highest stage reached by man in his moral and political development. [fols. 10–12]

Art processes and principles established as correct in the preceding two parts will be tested in the third part by applying them to the present. I shall take the revival of the fine arts in Italy as the doorway to the modern age; again, this will let me introduce the subject matter with art historical observations. It will be seen that the building material that can be used artistically is plentiful, that it has been transformed or newly created by modern social progress, and that at present it is used only in functional structures; of these the most outstanding examples will be selected and their functional and structural schemes discussed (as is appropriate for our time, this discussion will be as detailed as possible); then the attempt will be made to solve the question of art.

At its worst, which means if this attempt should fail, the method will at least offer the opportunity of classifying and testing what has been learned so far, namely the historically traditional and practically constructive elements of contemporary architecture.

These are the main features of the plan to be followed in this treatise. The author also means to examine the formal laws and logic noticeable in the creation of artistic works wherever they appear for the first time; his aim is to comprehend the laws of beauty in general and artistic beauty in particular by a purely empirical method. Yet he finds at once that he has to contravene this method and that he cannot spare the reader an exposition of his ideas concerning the attributes of formal beauty although he will make it as short as possible. He believes this to be necessary partly because his views differ in important points from those held by art philosophers, and partly to save tiresome disgressions from his subject matter by explaining beforehand certain frequently used terms in the sense in which he wishes the reader to understand them. But he will take care to let the reader observe that the theorems anticipated here develop empirically in the course of the treatise.*

[*Aesthetic Theories: Pythagoras, Vitruvius, Zeising, Semper*]

On the Attributes of Formal Beauty

It is said that Pythagoras, who in 520 B.C. proclaimed to the world, "The earth is one of the planets and moves around the sun," brought home from his journeys through Phoenicia, Egypt, and Chaldaea several discoveries of which the most useful and the most admirable was the theory of analogies.

This theory was said to be the key to the "*harmonic proportions*" in architecture and music as well as in all other plastic and tonic arts; the Doric temples were also believed to have been built according to the Pythagorean analogies.

Pythagoras left nothing in writing, and nothing can be gained from the works of ancient writers about his analogies, which were probably kept secret. Had Greek writers and architects proclaimed them in their treatises on architecture, none of which has survived, Vitruvius would have known them, which certainly was not the case. In Chapter 2 of Book I, headed "Ex quibus rebus architectura constet," he uses a number of terms each with a Greek equivalent that he might have taken from some Greek treatise on aesthetics, but his own etymological explanations are so uncertain and ambiguous, and the text moreover so corrupt, that efforts to reconstruct the theory to which these few fragments belong have been in vain. [fols. 12–14]

In another place Vitruvius writes of symmetry and its derivation from proportion, which the Greeks called "analogia." This reference is important because it contains the sentence that no temple could be built and look noble unless it corresponded to the exact proportions of a well-built human body. Vitruvius enumerates man's proportions in detail, writing that great painters and sculptors had observed them and become famous; however, he adds nothing about the application

---

*The general notion of formal beauty is made up of three parts—sensual, proportional, and moral-intellectual beauty. In what follows, only the *second* will be considered, although anything that concerns character and style will automatically lead to the third manifestation of beauty. I refer in this connection to von Rumohr's excellent essay, "Zur Theorie und Geschichte neuerer Kunstbetrachtungen" [On the Theory and History of Recent Artistic Trends], in the first part of his *Italienische Forschungen* [Italian Researches].

of these proportions to architecture and soon loses his way in observations about the system of Greek measurements.

The principle of proportion has often since been the subject of aesthetic conjecture. It has been treated exhaustively by [Adolf] Zeising in his book *Neue Lehre von den Proportionen des menschlichen Körpers* [A New Theory of the Proportions of the Human Body], Leipzig, 1854, as well as in his *Ästhetischen Forschungen* [Aesthetic Researches], Frankfurt a.M., 1855.

Gothic architecture had its canon, too; but we know nothing definite about it, probably again because those who were in possession of the rules had to commit themselves to secrecy. The fundamental difference between the canons of the Greek and the Gothic style seems to be that the Greeks took human proportions as their model, the Gothic builders took them as their scale.

The Italian architects of the fifteenth and sixteenth centuries also had their rules of proportions, based partly on the study of Vitruvius and the Roman monuments, partly on the analogy of the human body as suggested by Vitruvius.

In more recent times, architects have relinquished almost every rule or have confined themselves to following the exact proportions of past monuments with slight and often unsuccessful deviations.

Modern aesthetics untiringly tries to solve the secret of formal beauty and hopes to "raise the veil of Isis if not all of a sudden then at least by slowly lifting it and explaining."[2]

Among these recent attempts, the work of the aesthetician Zeising is of interest to the professional artist because he arrives at a definite rule. He traces the Vitruvian norm of the human body back to the axiom that at proportional divisions the ratio of the smaller section to the larger section equals that of the larger section to the whole. This division into two parts is, in my opinion, valid only in certain cases and for phenomena where the law of proportionality is still undeveloped; for complete systems the law of three-part division is valid. This can be deduced from the human body, a subject to which I shall return later [pages 236–238]. [fols. 14–16]

[Semper then cites Zeising (*Ästhetische Forschungen*, p. 124). Referring to paragraphs 161 and 163 (pp. 174ff), he summarizes some of Zeising's remarks on pure beauty and concludes, "Instead of refuting this theory in detail I may be allowed to set against it my own and to leave the reader to decide between the two." He then continues:]

[The Phenomenon's Relation to the General, Direction of Configuration, and Direction of Movement]

A phenomenon can be given the attributes of formal beauty only if as an individual object it isolates and separates itself from the general; in most cases this separation is not absolute but conditional, and this conditionality is reflected in the phenomenon. The phenomenon can exist in its individuality only insofar as it depends on the universe or is bound to it in some way, and in the same way this dependence or being bound must be mirrored in the phenomenon. The parts of the configuration [*Gestaltung*] must be arranged in such a way that the relation to the general is expressed as clearly as possible so as to give the impression of rest, permanence, and perfection; otherwise the phenomenon will fall apart and signify the transition into the shapeless universe, a condition which can be beautiful only under special circumstances and in connection with other impressions.

But because our perceptivity is limited we can observe the relation of the individual phenomenon to the universe only in the primary transitional steps leading from the particular to the general. Examples: relation of the moon to the earth, the earth to the sun, the relation of man, animal, monument to the center of the earth; the relation of leaves to twigs, through them to branches, through them to the stem, and through the stem to the center of the earth. The last example already belongs to those in which the law [of formal beauty] becomes complex and difficult for us to understand.

While in this way the phenomenon is bound to the ground from which it evolves, at the same time it follows its own individual direction of configuration [*Gestaltungsrichtung*]; in this direction, too, the multiple elements of the phenomenon that are to be unified [*die zu einigenden Vielheiten der Erscheinung*] must arrange and form themselves in such a way that their working together reflects their necessary relation to the new factor of unity. This new factor can be thought of as a center of energy situated on a line that shall be called the axis of configuration [*Gestaltungsaxe*]. Examples: Development of animal organisms in the direction of the spina dorsalis, upright development of man against gravity, as also the tree; development of branches at certain angles diverging radially from the stem, of twigs from branches, of leaves from twigs. Crystallization of crystals in the direction of the molecular force of attraction.

Finally, many phenomena need unification of their elements in a third direction that can be called the direction of movement or of volition [*Bewegungs- oder Willensrichtung*]. Two possibilities then arise:

either the phenomenon moves or the point that the phenomenon is facing moves toward the phenomenon which, incidentally, comes to virtually the same thing. Thus in man the direction of movement, which is horizontal, lies at right angles to the axis of his vertical development; the same is the case with many monuments and furnishings, which have a front and a back relative to the person who turns toward them or is going to use them. In one case the person moves toward his goal, the monument; in the other case the furnishings confront the person for whose use they are meant and who is for them the unifying element. In other phenomena the direction of movement and the axis of configuration coincide; this is the case with most animals and figuratively also with plants that grow toward the zenith and at the same time seek, as it were, the center of configuration [*Gestaltungsmittelpunkt*], which counteracts the center of gravity.

[*The Three Qualities of Formal Beauty: Symmetry, Proportionality, Direction. Fitness of Content the Fourth Quality.*]

From these different relationships arise these three qualities of formal beauty: (1) macrocosmic unit or order (symmetry); (2) microcosmic unit or order (proportionality); (3) unit or order of direction (direction).

These three formal qualities of beauty are analogous to the three spatial dimensions; as little as one can imagine a fourth dimension, it is just as impossible to add a fourth quality *homogenous* with the three mentioned above. Moreover, there is also this universally valid law: *the symmetrical axis is always horizontal and intersects the direction of movement at right angles.* Example: the snake, whose axis of direction coincides with its axis of proportion; its symmetrical axis is normal in relation to the other two and is horizontal. The human figure has three orders of beauty in normal relationship to each other—it is symmetrical, it is proportioned, and it has unity of direction [*Richtungseinheit*] according to the direction of the three rectangular spatial coordinates.

Nevertheless, there is a fourth center of relations, not homogenous with the other three; their reflections in the phenomenon bear the same relation to the fourth center as the multiple elements of the phenomenon [the three formal qualities of beauty] bear to each of their own centers. This fourth element of unity is the cardinal point of the phenomenon: it is the phenomenon's purpose. [fols. 18–20]

That quality of beauty that arises from the interaction and orderly arrangement of the parts of the phenomenon around this fourth center is *fitness of content* [*Inhaltsangemessenheit*], which in certain phenomena of a higher order can culminate in *character* and *expression*. Fitness of content adds to formal beauty the attribute of goodness, in other words it is what the Greeks called "callogathia."

Formal beauty—unity in variety and rest in movement—arises therefore from the harmonious interaction of these different factors, making the whole appear as unity of purpose [*Zweckeinheit*].

[*Groupings of the Qualities of Formal Beauty, Exemplified in Plant and Animal Formations*]

In this process of interaction various groupings can occur depending on whether certain axes of direction coincide or remain separate and whether the centers along these axes form one whole or are separate.

The simplest combinations occur when the various factors all come together in one point, as is the case with certain natural objects that are formed from the more or less undisturbed molecular force of attraction. With these objects, the macrocosmic center is embedded in the phenomenon itself and forms one whole with the microcosmic center and with the center of direction. Symmetry and proportion are identical here, and direction is altogether radial—in other words, it does not exist. Their character, or rather type, is perfect regularity, arranged either in a peripheral, radial, or radial-peripheral manner. All regular formations of crystals belong to this kind of phenomena; in a sense they are true worlds within worlds because they isolate themselves completely from the universe, are self-sufficient, and by their form express the possibility of existing without the outer world. Like the universe they are indifferent and without a volition of their own since they do not relate to anything outside of them. Among these phenomena, the sphere best expresses this type. Here regularity turns into the most perfect uniformity; this form is more or less distinctly represented by the celestial bodies, although, strictly speaking, like falling waterdrops they already have a special macrocosmic axis of direction.

The firmament also appears to us as a sphere. It symbolizes uniformity in the most consistent and complete manner because it is only in the form of a sphere that we can imagine the point. Like the polyhedron with an infinite number of sides, the sphere expresses the idea of infinite variety, and like the circular wheel the idea of all-round movement. For this reason the sphere became the symbol of the universe.

The embryonic forms of the vegetable and animal world—the vegetable cell and the egg—also come near to the form of the sphere, which means that here too the microcosmic life is still indifferent, is not related to the macrocosm.

Out of this indifferent germ the plant evolves, assuming in this process a far wider range of relations. [fols. 21–22]

In plants, a straight line between the microcosmic and the macrocosmic relational centers [*Beziehungscentrums*] represents the relational axis [*Beziehungsaxe*] common to both; the two centers, however, counteract each other, the one being positive the other negative, unlike crystals that follow one direction only. The momentum of growth forces the plant to soar up radially against gravity toward an infinitely distant point of the firmament. The plant has no other *direction* than this *life direction* [*Lebensrichtung*] against gravity.

If we imagine a simple stem without branches, for instance an asparagus, then it appears symmetrical to us in its horizontal section and, within this plane, totally symmetrical in the peripheral, radial, or peripheral radial grouping of its parts.

Looked at as a whole, the symmetry of plants is planimetric in contrast to that of crystals, which is stereometric and determinative in all directions.

Along the life direction, the growing plant complies with the law of proportionality so that on this axis the dual activity, that is the attraction to the earth and the counteracting life principle toward the zenith, is reflected in the arrangement of the parts. (See below: "On Authorities.")

More complex conditions arise in the single parts of plants when considered individually from a formal point of view.

The stem pushes the branches out radially and thereby follows the law of uniform distribution of mass, or symmetry in its wider sense, relative to the vertical axis of the stem. If we imagine first a branch growing out of the stem at right angles, then branching out and finally forming twigs and leaves, then the law of symmetry must be apparent in the branch and its parts so that symmetry is complied with in relation to both the main stem and the center of the earth. The symmetry of horizontal parts is not planimetric because of this dual relation but is linear, that is, horizontal. The symmetrical axis of a leaf is horizontal, intersecting the stalk at right angles. In the same way, many leaves arrange themselves differently according to the kind of plant, yet always symmetrically around the twig according to the law of horizontal and linear equilibrium. Trees that branch out horizontally, for instance fir trees, acacias, and beeches, show this symmetrical arrangement. This law becomes more complex when a different principle of radiation is characteristic for the plant, when for instance the branches shoot up like a broom in acute angles to the stem, as with the poplar and cypress. Here again, the symmetrical order comes close to the planimetric symmetry of the main stem without, however, being strictly symmetrical. Symmetry, striving under such complex interrelated circumstances, impels form-creating nature to perpetual changes in the botanical world: here we divine, more than perceive, the law of symmetry as it more or less winds its way through proportionality; this in part creates the romantic magic that the world of plants evokes, arousing our artistic sensibility.

Although in the animal kingdom nature is infinitely freer and richer in her creations, the qualities of formal beauty are also more apparent and comprehensible than in plants. [fols. 22–24]

With animal forms, the life axis is identical with the axis of direction; both are as a rule horizontal (as for instance in the previously mentioned examples: the snake, quadrupeds, fish, and birds in flight). Therefore the proportionality of animal organisms is independent of gravity, wherein it differs from the proportionality of plants and men, which certainly is not independent of gravity. (See below: "On Authorities".)

As to symmetry, with animals it is directly dependent on gravity, which means that the symmetrical axis must intersect the horizontal axis of direction at right angles.

Unlike plant forms, the symmetry of animal forms is always linear. With highly developed animals sections passed through any of the three main axes of spatial dimension or projected onto them, are never completely regular. The only exceptions would be zoophytes and some of the most primitive organisms, which all grow upward like a plant.

[The Human Figure]

The human figure is the noblest, freest, and grandest of all; it reveals its attributes of beauty most clearly.

With man as with plants, the macrocosmic and the microcosmic relational centers are positioned on the same vertical line and counteract each other; the direction of movement, on the other hand, is quite independent of the life direction (whereas animal direction of movement is not); in its macrocosmic relation it is also independent of gravity (whereas plants must strive against gravity.) Of all natural phenomena, the human form is the only one in which all three relational axes are distinct from each other, thereby conforming to the three coordinates of bodies, the extensions of length, width, and depth. Its symmetrical axis is also linear. Thus the human figure has the grandest proportionality upward, the clearest symmetry toward right and left, and the noblest contour toward back and front.

Many products of human artistic skill are basically akin to the human form insofar that their three relational axes are also completely separate (i.e., the axis of proportionality upward, the axis of symmetry horizontally and linearly, the axis of direction equally linearly and intersecting the axis of symmetry at right angles). This is the case with monuments (one of the few exceptions are for instance the pyramids; their multidimensional direction *characterizes* them in a profound way as tombs of famous rulers of the world). [fols. 24–26]

This alone explains the importance of the human figure for architecture and makes it understandable that at all times architects had in mind, consciously or unconsciously, the proportionality of man as a measurable model.

It has been said above that fitness of content is the supreme unit of which the three units of symmetry, proportionality, and direction constitute the three analogous elements, and that the human form and the basically analogous art form have three distinctly different axes of formation. From this it follows that the ultimate unity, namely fitness of content, reaches its fullest and most significant development only in man and his products.

Where two of these units coincide, as in plants and animals, fitness of content will be less clearly marked and less richly structured than in formations in which each unit exists by itself; this will be shown presently in greater detail.

Where all three elements coincide, as with crystals and water globules [*Wasserkugel*], which are ruled only by stereometric symmetry, fitness of content forms one unit with symmetry and is undeveloped.

To repeat once more: fitness of content means stereometric symmetry with crystals, type and character with animals and plants, expression with man and works of art.

On Authorities[3]

Authority is an expression used in several places by Vitruvius, which he adopted, like many other technical terms, from a lost Greek work. It is impossible to find or invent an equivalent that would express the satisfying impression given by parts that unite and work together toward a total effect.

This effect is achieved in a work of art when certain parts stand out from the rest and are, within their sphere, so-called leaders of the chorus and visible representatives of the unifying principle appropriate to the set of elements to which they belong. The remaining parts relate to the dominant part only by supporting, modulating, and accompanying the note that the authority intones as a keynote.

According to this definition and the theory of unity developed above, there are four different authorities: (1) the macrocosmic authority; (2) the microcosmic authority; (3) the authority of direction; (4) the authority of content.

Within their spheres, these four authorities are each the reflections and representatives, as it were, of their particular element of unity which, as we saw, is an ideal point situated outside the phenomenon and therefore not perceptible. [fols. 26–28]

Here attention should be drawn to a law deeply rooted in nature, namely that an authority supporting a unified idea is apparent only where the plurality to be unified consists of more than two parts. Where the whole consists of two parts and one dominates the other, the authority of one part will always assert itself at the expense of the tranquillity, unity, and equilibrium of the whole. Where the parts are grouped as a *triad* and one assumes authority over the other two groups, the unity of the whole will be evident in the most perfect way.

On Macrocosmic Authority

This manifests itself in two ways: (1) as symmetrical authority; (2) as the keynote of proportionality.

As to the first, it must be remembered that with natural objects as well as with art objects, symmetry is either stereometric, planimetric, or linear. Crystals and the sphere show the ideal stereometric symmetry of perfect regularity without any dominant authority. Although the polyhedrons right down to the tetrahedron are also multidimensionally symmetrical, they lack symmetrical authority. This authority becomes apparent only in the ellipsoid and oval, the hexahedron or dual tetrahedron linked to a base, the prism, the pyramid, etc.

Snow crystals, flowers, plants, and trees show planimetric symmetry. In these formations, authority is often marked by a concentration of parts close to the center around which they rotate and from which they radiate. Contrasting colors help to emphasize authority.

Linear symmetry is present in the leaves and branches of plants, animal formations, man, and most works of art, especially in monuments. It conforms to the law of equilibrium and consists in the horizontal and even distribution of the plurality of elements around a vertical axis at right angles to the direction of movement. Authority asserts itself through the emphasis given to a complex of parts surrounding the vertical axis; these parts stand out from the rest by their mass, richer structure and ornamental decoration, by strong color contrast, by being taller or raised higher, or through the combined effect of some of these means; in this way, they attract special attention and present at a glance the quintessence of the symmetrical whole, while the remaining parts only resound in unison and accompany the emphasized part, which for them can be said to represent the gravitational center of the earth around which all else rotates. [fols. 29–30]

By careful selection of this kind of symmetrical authority, architecture[4] is often successful in being able to disregard strict symmetry, which in many cases is incompatible with the higher demands of content and character.

But macrocosmic authority asserts itself in still another way: in phenomena where life direction (or microcosmic evolutional direction) coincides with macrocosmic relational direction [*Beziehungsrichtung*], the result is that both directions counteract each other as, for instance, in trees, men, or towering buildings that rise in tiers with supporting columns and walls. In these formations, macrocosmic authority appears as the *keynote* or *base* of proportionality. Further discussion of this subject is possible only after all that is necessary has been said about microcosmic authority.

On Microcosmic Authority

This authority never appears independently, never on its own, but always in connection with the other two homogenous authorities: (1) the *macrocosmic authority*, and (2) the *authority of direction*.

In connection with macrocosmic authority, it appears in individual and radially arranged features of the phenomenon that have either grown directly from the depth of the earth or branched out from the main stem. To consider only the most essential aspect here, that is, the vertically arranged individual features of the phenomenon—they show, as mentioned several times, the polarizing effect of two opposing forces of direction on one and the same axis of formation. Both activities or forces are in conflict, and this conflict manifests itself, or at least ought to manifest itself, in the phenomenon so that as a result the equilibrium becomes evident at the same time.

[Proportionality According to Division into Two or Three Parts]

First, the *base* of proportionality asserts itself as the reflection of the tellurian element of unity [*Einheitselement*] near the foot of the vertical phenomenon.

Then, the *dominant part* of proportionality stands out as a reflection of the individual element of unity near the crown of this vertical phenomenon.

Mediating between base and dominant part is an intermediate structural part; it shares their attributes with them, being attracted by both of them and causing the opposites to resolve in unity.

The *base* reflects the tellurian unified element either through inert mass, simple structure, and correspondingly dark coloring, or through column-like complexity, load-bearing capacity, and resilience. [fols. 30–32]

The *dominant part* reflects the opposite element of unity through rich structuring and adornment, concentration of all that is characteristic, and through splendid and bright coloring. In volume and especially in height it is the smaller of the two; by being near the crown of the phenomenon it is characterized as something that is carried.

The *intermediate part* has the dual character of supporting and of being supported. In its bearing and coloring it is a mixture or at least reflection of the character and color of both the base and the dominant part. *In everything it forms the proportional mean between the two extremes* so that the *base* is to the *mediating* part as this is to the *dominant part.*

All this does not agree with Zeising's previously mentioned theory of bisectional proportionality [page 227], according to which the smaller part is to the greater as the greater part is to the whole. In certain cases this law may suffice to lend formal beauty to a whole which, following Zeising, had been divided into two unequal parts, but it certainly is not universally valid. In particular, it does not suffice for the case that concerns us here, namely for individual features of a vertical phenomenon where the effect of two polarizing directions becomes evident on the axis of configuration. It does not suffice because the division into two can at best show only the conflict between the two polarizing elements of the unit; the mediation between the two, however, is not indicated at all.

It also seems farfetched to me to consider simultaneously the whole as part of the whole so that the greater part is to the whole as the smaller is to the greater part. No one who had not been told of this law would recognize it merely be perceiving the phenomenon that had been divided into two parts in this way; even less would he realize its sense and importance. Actually, the arbitrary division into two parts is potentially a division into three parts and thus implies recognition of the correctness and validity of such a three-part division. It may, incidentally, be not amiss to point out that my *own* mean proportionality should be understood more figuratively than literally, not as if the axis of every well-proportioned upright art or natural object would have to be divided in a strictly mathematical manner so that the middle part represented exactly the proportional mean of the upper and lower parts. There are many ways of ensuring that this proportion is visually satisfying. [fols. 32–34]

The law of two-part division may hold when applied to the rich and diversified structure of the human form, taking the navel as the dividing point. All the same, the law of three-part division is no less distinct in the same human figure. If one takes, as seems to be quite natural, the lowest part up to the middle of the hip joint as *base* and the head from the crown to the collarbone as the *dominant part*, then the distance between collarbone and hip joint will fairly accurately be the proportional mean of the two other parts. The same law of three-part division occurs again in subdivisions of the human figure, for instance in the arms. The upper arm is to the forearm as the forearm is to the hand reckoned from the wrist to the end of the middle finger. The same applies to the legs and the head reckoned from the collarbone, etc.

The Egyptians divided their standing figures into nineteen parts, their sitting figures into fifteen, as is proven by a painting from a tomb at Thebes discovered by Belzoni. In both cases, three parts are apportioned to the head down to the collarbone, and on the standing figures ca. 10.4 parts to the legs, so that 5.6 parts remain for the length of the torso—a division that corresponds almost exactly to the proportions of a division into three which, indeed, the actual human figure shows.

The Greeks did not make their masterworks conform strictly and rigidly to either the two-part or the three-part division of the human figure; instead they followed nature and let both divisions intermingle so that by contrast each was enlivened and strengthened by the other.

One could criticize the division into three for being too vague since there is no "golden section" according to which a length can be divided into three definite proportional parts so that the part in the middle is to the lower as the upper part is to the one in the middle. It is argued that to solve the equation one needs to know a second given apart from the total length, for instance the height of either of the three parts. But this alleged vagueness and freedom from restraint makes the law that much more valid and practical.

Furthermore, if the parts of a whole are in proportional relation to each other then they are also in proportional relation to the whole, which in any case can only be understood as consisting of these parts;

therefore, one does not need to establish with Zeising the proportionality, that is, the correspondence, between the whole and its parts.

Matters are quite different where microcosmic authority appears in conjunction with the authority of direction; as mentioned [page 235], this is the second possible combination. [fols. 34–36]

[Authority of Direction Exemplified in Aquatic Animals]

It is easy to recognize that this combination occurs and becomes apparent in most animal formations that move horizontally on the earth, in water, or through the air. Horizontal proportionality, which is more or less independent of gravity, appears in perhaps its simplest form in aquatic animals (fish and similar creatures). We shall therefore confine our inquiry to this example of horizontal proportionality since it would be impossible to discuss the subject fully here; a suggestion must suffice.

Proportionality and configuration in swimming animate bodies are in some way the opposite of what we have already noticed in *vertically* directed microcosms. The aim that the swimming creature has in sight in the direction of its movement, be it prey or any other desired object, is the point of attraction. This is a force analogous to that which the macrocosmic center, the gravitational center of the earth, exerts on the tree or any other vertically and upwardly directed configuration. In both cases, two elements of unity are situated on one and the same straight line, which is the individual line of configuration; however, with this difference, that in the first case—the swimming bodies—both elements of unity are linked and exert their influence jointly, as it were, whereas in the second case—the trees, etc.—the elements are separate and polarized in their effect.

Thus, in the first case no real conflict of forces takes place, and the law of division into three parts—base, dominant part, and proportional mean—does not apply. Authority here is a "dual" one, namely the *head* of the fish represents and reflects both the microcosmic elemental unit of individual existence and at the same time its elemental unit of movement.

So far, the fish's proportion is indeterminately two-part—a head with a tailpiece that continues indeterminately spool-like toward the back.

But there are additional formal features that will lend to the still inadequate phenomenon the imprint of unity and of completion within itself. The fish—and also the bird in the air and creatures moving in a horizontal direction on the ground—must in its course cut through a resisting medium, water; at the same time that it swims the effect of the third element of unity, the tellurian center of gravity, asserts itself. Moreover, the mass of the body with its force of inertia comes into conflict with the direction of the horizontally developed organism! The form must yield to and reflect all these macrocosmic influences. This indeed happens, as imaginary sectional planes passed through the axis of direction at right angles make evident: these sections increase in size from front to back, according to a law that cannot be gone into here, and continue to increase up to a point on the axis of direction where they reach their maximum size; according to another law, beyond this point the sectional planes decrease in size because the velocity of the resisting medium, while still acting against this slimmer part of the fish's body, no longer hinders its movement but assists it. [fols. 36–38]

Further necessary conditions are that one point within the largest sectional plane be the center of gravity of the whole system and that the spatial capacity of the system be at a maximum; the last condition depends, as already suggested, on the least possible resistance by the medium and this in turn depends on the shape of the body.*

Inevitably, the description of these complicated forces and their influence on the formation of individuals similar to the fish has been obscure. But at least it shows that with these formations a third authority needs to be present apart from the two linked in the head; this third authority is the largest sectional plane passed at right angles through the gravity of the system. The part of the body beyond this plane continues in decreasing elongation to the end of the fishtail; this part is always longer than the front part to which the head is joined, either directly as with fish or by a more or less elongated neck as with birds.

If Zeising's principle were valid anywhere, it would be with regard to the fish's proportion where, along its length, the law of division into two is very obvious.

*I have made a special study of the dynamic principles that determine the shape of aquatic bodies and have arrived at an equation which I call the Ichtyode. This equation comprises, I believe, the general scheme according to which these bodies are formed. [Semper then gives the mathematical equation, explains that, depending on the varying values assigned, the curve of a whole range of aquatic bodies can be constructed, and concludes:] The Greeks knew the laws that determine the forms of flying objects as proven by their slingshot bullets. I append a drawing of two such lead bullets that I brought home with me from Athens [not reproduced]. Their shape resembles those longish, slippery plum pits that are a missile popular with boys, who hold them between their fingers and flick them off. The air has the same effect; by squeezing behind the slingshot bullets it speeds them on their flight.

If one imagines a fish cut through at right angles to its length, then the form of any sectional plane would be symmetrical in width, but in height it would conform to the principle of vertical configuration, although here the macrocosmic influences would be more complicated than in the examples just considered.

[Fitness of Content as Authority of a Higher Order]

It remains to deal with the authority of a higher order: the reflection of the highest and ultimate element of unity, the *unit of purpose* [*Zweckeinheit*].

Since the plurality that must conform to the principle of purpose consists of the three authorities of the lower order [macrocosmic, microcosmic, and directional], the unit of purpose must be reflected in one of them; in this way an authority of a higher order will arise.

So it happens that in certain natural or artistic phenomena the macrocosmic authority reflects the unit of purpose while the microcosmic and directional authorities only accompany it. Examples: many plants, the already-mentioned pyramids, obelisks, and other funeral monuments.

With other formations, the microcosmic authority dominates and is the reflector of the unit of purpose. This is especially so with more highly developed plants. This individualistic form of the unit of purpose also appears in certain architectural phenomena. Example: the temple with a dome and spires, where the aesthetic effect depends solely on proportional beauty while symmetry cannot unfold because there is not sufficient width or, in the case of the wider domed building, is resolved in eurythmy; direction is of no or hardly any importance. [fols. 38–40]

The directional authority is dominant and the main reflector of the unit of purpose in some animal species like the snake, the pike, and the swift stag. This is also the case with industrial objects and works of art. Example: the fast sailing ship, the winged war chariot, the tobacco pipe of the roving prairie hunter.

Here again, it is in the human face that the unit of purpose is reflected in the most noble and expressive way because two authorities, the microcosmic and the directional, jointly reflect it.

The way in which the authority of purpose appears in the Greek temple is analogous to the way it appears in man: the *crowning pediment* is the proportionally dominant part and, at the same time, the reflector of the approaching sacrificial procession of the Hellenes.

I must leave to those more competent than I the examination of how far these aesthetic principles, applied to formal beauty, are also valid for the acoustic arts and whether music, which is so closely related to architecture, is governed by similar principles. It only remains to be pointed out that in chromatic phenomena, color harmony is based on analogous principles. In colors too there is symmetry; their arrangement too is proportioned with keynote, dominant, and mean; a directional authority also reigns; and character of color dominates these three factors and arranges them *hieratically* according to circumstances. In the course of the treatise, there will be an opportunity to return to this subject.

On Style

[*Style Defined as a Function*]

The concepts that have been discussed in the preceding pages—*symmetry, proportionality, direction, and fitness of purpose*—are all *collective*, meaning that they fuse a plurality into a unit; furthermore, they are absolutely formal, that is to say they adhere to the abstract and formal attributes of the finished phenomenon; they exclude as foreign all that is extrinsic to the phenomenon, everything that does not relate to it directly, in particular its development in history and the differences in material.

However, there is also a stylistic conception of what is beautiful in art—this considers the object not as a collectivity but as a unit, as the uniform *result* or *function* of several variable values that unite in certain combinations and form the coefficients of a general equation; by giving these variables the values appropriate to the particular case, one will arrive at the solution of the problem:

$$U = C(x,y,z,t,v,w. \ldots)$$

As soon as one or some of these coefficients change, the result U must also be different and must in its general appearance show a distinct character that distinguishes it from other closely or distantly related results. Where this is not the case and where the result does not show modifications that correspond to the changed elements making up a function, there it is false and lacking in quality; this quality will presently be defined in more detail [pages 243ff]. [fols. 40–42]

[*Coefficients of a Work of Art*]

What are these variable coefficients, these elements of the general formula whose result we deem to be a work of art?

Their number is indeterminable; we shall touch upon only some of the most important ones.

They can be divided into two distinct classes: first, those elements that are contained, as it were, in the work itself and that comply with certain compelling natural and physical laws that are the same under all circumstances and at all times; second, those elements that have an influence on the genesis of the work of art from the outside.

To the first class belongs above all the *purpose* of the object, the artistic treatment of which constitutes the task at hand. It may be a purely practical purpose aimed at usefulness or it may tend more toward an ideal purpose, which in most if not all cases can be traced back to a real purpose understood in a higher sense.

Also belonging to this class is the material available to the artist that will enable him to execute the object that, depending on the circumstances, fits the purpose or makes it manifest.

Third, the utensils with which the work is to be done and the various processes for treating the material belong to this class; they strongly influence the function and artistic effect of the phenomenon by bringing out the formal aspects of the material. For instance, metal can be beaten, forged, cast, or filed. Each of these four processes is basically different in its formative effect.

The extrinsic coefficients of the artistic form of representation are more varied.

To be taken into account first are local and personal influences and factors, such as climate, topography, national education, political-religious and social institutions, historical memories and traditions, local environment (for instance, whether a house is situated in a valley or on a hill, whether it is a country or a town house), the person or group who commission the work and who wish to have it meet their specific needs, or whether the work is intended to be sold on the open market and, therefore, without personal or local connections, is made so as to adapt to any surroundings. Among numerous other influences there are also incidental circumstances that have an effect on the work in hand.

Finally, the artist's hand, his individual taste and artistic attitude as essential factors in the creation of a work of art, are among the extrinsic influences.

By considering formal beauty as an emanation of all these factors, that is as a "coming into being," we comprehend aesthetics from a purely empirical viewpoint. This interpretation will appeal to the artist as the most useful to him; it is also the one that accords with the program of this book.

We take the work as a result and as such expect it to have style. [fols. 43–44]

[Rumohr's and Semper's Definitions of Style]

The word "style" originally signified a stylus, an instrument with which one impressed letters on wax tablets; later the term was used to convey the quality of the manner of writing in general. We have adopted the word together with its meaning.

In Italy at the time of Petrarch, "style" was taken to mean a crayon for drawing or an instrument for artists; since we owe much of our artistic vocabulary to the Italians, we took over from them the application of the word to certain qualities of artistic representation whereby, however, an ever-increasing vagueness and confusion crept in.

It was Rumohr who, in *Italienische Forschungen* (vol. I, pp. 15ff), was the first to trace the notion of style to its true empirical root; but he took into account only the "crude material" when he *regarded style as a habitual submission to the inner exigencies of the material out of which the sculptor actually forms his figures and with which the painter makes them visible.*

I believe that the "crude material" is only one of several factors the inner exigencies of which the artist has to submit to and which it is his task to emphasize. I see in the word "style" the quintessence of those qualities of a work of art that come to the fore when the artist *knows and observes the limitations imposed on his task by the particular character of all contributary coefficients and, at the same time, takes into account and gives artistic emphasis to everything that, within these limitations, these contributary coefficients offer, provided this will serve the purpose of the task.*

Style therefore means *giving emphasis and artistic significance to the basic theme and to all intrinsic and extrinsic coefficients that modify the embodiment of the theme in a work of art.*

According to this definition, absence of style signifies the shortcomings of a work caused by the artist's disregard of the underlying theme and his ineptitude in exploiting aesthetically the means available for perfecting the work.

I hope to give proof that this notion of what is called style is sufficiently specific and complete in itself to be of practical use. The definition also permits wide application and warrants age-old expressions that have passed irrevocably into everyday language, notions that spring from the doubtless right, popular feeling for the correlations between seemingly heterogeneous conceptions.

Thus it is equally correct to say: Chinese style, style of the Age of Louis XIV, style of Raphael, ecclesiastic style, rural style, timber style, metal style, heavy style, light style, grand style, etc. [fols. 44–46]

5

A Critical Analysis and Prognosis of Present-Day Artistic Production*

[Decay and Birth of Art Systems]

The nocturnal sky shows glimmering nebulas among the glittering miracles of stars. It is not clear whether they are age-old systems robbed of their centers, which are being scattered throughout the universe, or whether they are cosmic dust being formed around a nucleus, or whether both hypotheses may apply.

Comparable with these phenomena are certain mysterious fog patches on the horizon of art history, signs of the disintegration of monumental art and of the reversion of its elements into a general and indifferent state of being; next to them, under favorable circumstances, are new art formations that, slowly emerging from the chaos of wrecked worlds of art, suddenly crystallize at the moment of coming to life around a new center to which everything relates.

There are three phases of these phenomena, which tax our powers of observation: (1) the transition from the formed into the amorphous state; (2) the phase of preparing for a new formation; (3) the moment of sudden crystallization into a new formation.

Although the first phase is disagreeable to observe, it is highly important for the theory of art. Art history dissects and analyzes phenomena from times when civilization had run its course and only its lifeless outer form was still there or had regressed into its elementary state. From the monuments it is possible to trace historically the various stages of this phase.

With higher organisms, the process of natural decay usually proceeds slowly and gradually. Systems based on the powerful creative instinct

*Preface to "Theory of Formal Beauty" ("Theorie des Formell-Schönen," ca. 1856/1859): MS 178, fols. 1–28.

of man's early and more tellurian stage of development can be shattered and destroyed only by the force of external collisions. They cannot crumble or slowly die off since by nature they are rigid and lifeless. After their destruction they break up into identical but separate systems and as severed parts often continue an existence analogous to the one they led before. In this they are comparable to the parts of certain lower organisms that, when separated from the main body, form new units and continue on their own. [fols. 1–2]

The transition from the phase of decay into the next phase, that of fermentation of the elements in preparation for the birth of a new system of monumental art, is so imperceptible that the borderline between the two phases cannot be detected in any relevant art historical phenomenon. But the closer the moment of giving birth to a new system approaches, the more perceptible becomes the stirring of a society that, though still following a purely tellurian and unconscious urge to form and shape, strives after a new identity. In this way society prepares the *motif of the art object*, without which the new formation could not arise nor have any significance.

The start of the third phase, the moment of becoming, is still an unexplored mystery like the moment of the creation of the world and its creatures.

The horizon of history does not extend back far enough to allow us to observe the process by which the oldest systems of national arts have arisen.

Ethnology, which presents a transverse section, as it were, of the history of civilization, cannot demonstrate by a single example the process by which a monumental art crystallized out of ethnic primordial matter [*Urstoff*] without an admixture of fragments from earlier and foreign art formations.

The oldest systems of monumental art known from ancient remains appear to us as rebirths, as higher forms of earlier ideas that had already been expressed artistically. But the monuments of these rebirths are also shrouded in mystery.

It seems, however, that the metamorphosis of the motif as prepared by man's tellurian creative instinct into art formation did not come about through a slow process of evolution but in a single act of giving birth.

We cannot help but assume that the Egyptian temple palace, the Assyrian royal residence, the Indian rock temple, and the Doric building crowned by a pediment were, so to say, suddenly created, like Pallas Athena as a complete type and fully equipped: creations of a genius who was able to give artistic form and architectural expression to an idea that had been alive in society and had been struggling for manifestation.

According to this hypothesis, men like Menes, Nimrod, Semiramis, Manu, Daedalus, and Pythagoras were in no way mythical figures, nor symbols for early periods of civilization. They were either real historical persons, lawmakers of art, or were upholders of the popularly held idea that the transition from a pre-architectural to an architectural form of society was a moment of an independent act of creation and not simply a phase in the tellurian process of mankind's evolution.

Consequently, the set of laws governing all ancient people was seen as an organic constitutional act initiated by an individual. An aggregate form of constitution like the English one was unknown in antiquity. [fols. 2–4]

When, during the decay of the Roman empire and civilization, Christianity laid the seeds for a new social structure that was going to rise from the ruins of the old, Constantine the Great took hold of the new and by then powerful impulse and raised Christianity to become the religion of the state; at the same time, he adopted not only the basilica as the visible form of the Church, but also erected in front of the tablinum of his neo-Roman imperial palace an altar to *his* Christian god, which with its lofty atrium testudinatum became the prototype of all Christian domes.

The imperial concept that had persuaded Constantine to adopt the new faith was thus embodied architecturally: Christ moved into his new abode as house god of the worldly power, the imperator mundi. Constantine was the Nimrod of the Byzantine Babel.

In the West, the Roman bishops reorganized the ancient Roman basilica, the tribunal with its covered stoa in front, into one representing their Egyptian-cenobitic [monastic] hierarchy and into a shrine of pilgrimage. The works created in this style during the first centuries of the Western Church were the most imposing and stylistically the purest. Soon afterward, decline set in that lasted almost without interruption until the end of the first millennium after Christ.

A new creative impulse was then astir, which only after two centuries found its expression in the new formation of the Gothic basilica, and this suddenly as if by magic; its formation was as much due to personal and even accidental influences as had been the case in the rise of preceding types; in no way should this new style be taken as the *inevitable result* of that newly awakened wonderful artistic life that distinguished the first two centuries of the second millennium; the Gothic basilica too was at its best in its early creations, then quickly destroyed itself through its own consistency.

These examples of the decay of the arts and the mysterious phoenix-like birth of new artistic motifs arising out of the process of destruction are the more significant concerning the state of our art, since we are probably in the midst of a similar crisis—so far as we who are in the middle of it and therefore without a clear overall view can judge.

But people certainly sincerely believe that we are in such a crisis; even the most active and most disciplined faction among those who still ascribe vitality to the old style erase four centuries of art history and thereby decidedly support this theory.[1]

There are, indeed, signs that seem to confirm this assumption. However, it is uncertain whether they are symptoms of a decline brought about by deep-rooted social causes or whether they point to normally healthy conditions temporarily brought into confusion and affecting only those faculties of man that make him recognize and represent what is beautiful, whereby sooner or later the normal state will also assert itself in this sphere to the good and glory of mankind.

In this connection, the presently prevailing, almost exclusively scientific method of education should be briefly mentioned. [fols. 4–6]

[Criticism of Present-Day Art Education]

All our national education is directed by science, which today is tending more and more toward the practical. This well-conceived but too homogenous and one-sided plan does not take into sufficient account the need to train the sense and receptiveness for impressions of an artistic nature. There is a danger that the national appreciation of art will wither away and that the gift of intuitive reflection so necessary to the artist will become rare.

The result of this one-sided intellectual method of education manifests itself in the mass of the people; they totally lack receptiveness to formal beauty not because they have no opportunity to enjoy beauty but because from the start education deters them from contemplating it; as a consequence, sensitivity for art is stunted.

Even when one comes across educated people who still enjoy beauty in art, their pleasure turns out to be more in the nature of a mental act and pleasant intellectual exercise than an intuitive perception of the artistic idea made visible. They find it philosophically stimulating in a way to transfer beauty back from the visual world to the idea, to analyze it, and to lay bare its conceptual core.

Formerly, knowing and doing were in step with each other. The art student's creative impulse was roused and tested as early as possible. He soon encountered things he had to know and which he was eager to learn in order to be able to proceed further. In this way he collected a store of scientific knowledge, perhaps not in an especially critical and methodical way but in a way that he grasped thoroughly and at once made use of artistically.

That was the kind of education received by those who were to become masters in the arts, which was not very different from that of the people generally. Nowadays, a great part of the art student's best years are taken up with learning the rudiments of science before he is admitted to the first exercises in art. Moreover, there is no direct connection between the general preparatory science lessons and the specific art the student is going to practice later; he is just given a general store of knowledge to be used in whatever way he likes. The waste of time becomes even worse through the necessity of further intense studies in order to keep up with the general scientific education so that there are not many hours left in the day for practical artistic work. [fols. 6–8]

[Abundance of New Inventions. Their Harmful Influence on Taste and Industrial Art.]

But the intellectual activity on which art is based suffers not only from this unfortunate combination of circumstances. Science is not only the present-day educator, it also dominates practical life. As the sphere of their achievements expands daily, natural sciences and related doctrines constantly enrich everyday life with newly discovered useful materials, with amazing new sources of energy, with new processes and technical means, new tools and machines.

What a long time it took for the masters of the last great period of painting to learn to use oil for bonding pigments, in replacement of older processes that they had found too restricted in their application! What a long time had to pass before the Western world rediscovered the secret of an opaque enamel, which the Persians and Saracens had known for centuries, of applying zinc oxide to faience! This was a disgrace for the science of the Western world at that time. But at least Van Eyck and Luca della Robbia knew how to use what they had invented and how to utilize its artistic possibilities and they could do this because artists looked for and found what they needed only when they needed it.

In this way, gradual progress in science went hand in hand with the master's craft and with an understanding of what was found and of why and how it had to be applied.

Nowadays, inventions precede real need and are withdrawn before their technical, let alone artistic, possibilities can be recognized and fully used, being replaced by new and only occasionally superior inventions.

Inventions are not means to guard against poverty, as formerly, or for help in times of need; today, man's needs and wants have become the sales outlet for inventions.

The present has no time to come to terms with the profusion of things forced upon it, let alone to master them artistically. The situation resembles the Chinese being forced to eat with knife and fork.

Because of inventions, industry and speculation are more active than ever and form a link between practical knowledge and consumption. [fols. 8–10]

With the means provided by science, industry easily accomplishes the most difficult and troublesome tasks: porphyry and granite can be cut like chalk; ivory can be molded into any form (a process, incidentally, that was already known at the time of Phidias and that made sense then because it was needed for executing the enormous ivory statues); Kautschuk [Caoutschouc or India rubber] and gutta-percha are vulcanized and used for making deceptive imitations of carvings in wood, metal, or stone, which by far exceed the natural limitations of the material they purport to represent;[2] metal is no longer cast or beaten but a metal coating is deposited galvanoplastically with the help of recently unknown natural energies. On the heels of the daguerreotype follows photography, which makes the former obsolete. The machine sews, knits, carves, paints, intrudes deeply into the sphere of art, and puts human skill to shame.

Who could deny that in general great benefits are bestowed on mankind by rapidly progressing science and by industry, which tries to keep up with it; these benefits will no doubt extend to every field. For the time being, however, a glance at the industry of half-barbaric people like those of India or a look back at the products of our ancestors will convince us that with all our science we have not achieved much in matters of taste and so far have made little artistic use of the available means; in fact, we will detect symptoms of regression when we compare our past achievements with what we produce today in this field.

We try in vain to master our material, with least success in the artistic field. It is just handed to us to do with as we please without its style having been developed through centuries-long popular use.

In former times, the founders of a thriving art received their material kneaded beforehand, as it were, by the bee-like instinct of the people, and they then shaped and formed the simple motif, investing it with higher significance; thus, their creations bore the stamp of both compelling necessity and intellectual freedom and became the generally understood expression of a true civilization that would live on in history as long as trace and record of it remained.

Now, however, in the midst of the rich inheritance from the past we feel at a complete loss and are like the sailor who drifts on unknown waters without charts, plumb, or compass. With all the mass of books on art and on technical instructions, of which we shall speak later, we still lack a practical *heuristic* that maps out the cliffs and sandbanks to be avoided and points out the right course to be taken.

[Negative Influence of Speculation, Mass Production, and Division of Labor on the Artist's Position. Disintegration of Existing Art Systems]

Another fact impedes the development of a national artistic taste: just as speculation appropriates its technical means from the natural sciences, so it tries to make the fine arts subservient to its own ends. However, the division of labor, a device understandably necessary for coping with the vast scale of enterprise, was contrived by speculation in a way that is highly detrimental to artistic success. Separation of the so-called ornamental from the formal-technical aspect of art is carried out in too mechanical a way, so that the lack of feeling and understanding for the true relations between the different creative activities of man is, from the outset, very obvious. [fols. 10–12]

Many gifted artists are permanently employed by English and French firms. They are then dependent, on the one hand, on the employer who does not think they have equal rights as half-superfluous taste advisers and form embellishers and rarely pays them adequately and, on the other hand, on the fashion of the day, which alone ensures the sales on which in the end the purpose and survival of the enterprise, in other words everything, depend.

Thus, the head of the enterprise has no contact with art and is even opposed to it, classifying it as a specialized activity comparable to kneading the clay or firing it, which tasks also are in the charge of employees. The difference, however, is that the manufacturer gives these employees a free hand, knowing the inadequacy of his technical knowledge, whereas everyone believes that he understands something about taste and without hesitation tampers with and distorts the artist's directions whenever they do not appeal to his personal taste or whenever some foreman has expressed misgivings about their technical feasibility. To this must be added the low position of industrial artists, first, vis-à-vis the *academic hierarchy*; second, vis-à-vis the *firm*, which is jealously intent on laying claim to the honor of any success and never or very rarely credits the artist from whom the work really stems and who has spent intellectual labor on it; and third, vis-à-vis the *public* who, lacking education, shares the prejudices of the Academy and takes little notice of the so-called decorative arts.

Those who are devoted to the fine arts—the architects, painters, and sculptors—could have a more favorable influence on the advancement of taste and art education among the people if they were called upon to participate. From time to time this has, indeed, been the case as, for instance, when Wedgwood's famous pottery was modeled after Flaxman's drawings. The porcelain factory at Sèvres also employed artists who did not let fashion and sales considerations interfere with their work.

However, this influence from the height of academic art often lacks practical foundation; an artist may be skilled and inventive in making designs and models, but he is neither a metalworker nor a potter, carpet weaver, or goldsmith. Often, therefore, the products do not live up to the ambitious expectations and contribute little to the betterment of industry. Although the work has been done according to the directions given by the artist, the finished product does not come anywhere near his intention mainly because he demanded the impossible from the material, which the craftsman had to strain in order to meet his demands. [fols. 12–14]

Until now, we have written only about the technical arts, which incidentally can be separated from architecture as little as architecture can be separated from painting and sculpture. Not only do the different arts work together within architecture, but any single product can be looked at from an architectural point of view. Apart, however, from the architectural aspect of all arts, architecture is affected by conditions characteristic of our times, hinted at above, to a far greater extent than are the other arts. Speculation has laid hands on architecture as it has on industry.

Everything that is needed for the house and in the home—structural, decorative, fixed or movable objects—are good and cheap and plentiful. Even complete houses can be bought ready made.

The domestic and even the church architecture of England and the United States has adjusted itself completely to these conditions, resulting usually in a spurious and emaciated Gothic building. This style is suited, especially in its modern version, for jigsaw-like variations with cheaply produced structural parts and ornament. Neo-Gothic houses and churches nowadays grow like mushrooms out of English soil, and the most expensive building on earth after St. Peter's in Rome is the English House of Parliament, which with all its decorative profusion is also such a boring product.

The course resolutely pursued by our industry, and thus by art in general, is obvious: *everything is made for the market* and is therefore of a general type that fits easily into any environment. It must not have character or local color (in the widest sense).

This has been the state of affairs. But even here modern industry has misjudged its position: its approach to the market is inappropriate, outdated, and not always valid; it lacks the tact that distinguishes oriental industry which, though also working for the market, knows how to present the features typical of marketwares in the most advantageous way.

A similar state of affairs exists in the so-called fine arts, painting and sculpture; they are supposed to have a purpose of their own, but the only one they display after they have become an object of speculation is that of pleasing and attracting buyers.

But what about our magnificent monuments with their frescos, painted glass, statues, pediments, and friezes!

They do not belong to us. Out of their elements nothing new has arisen that we could possibly call our own. They have not become part of our own flesh and blood. Although they are presently being collected with great care, they have not yet disintegrated sufficiently, let alone has anything new been created.

This process of disintegrating existing art systems has been taken on, it seems, by industry, speculation, and practical science. [fols. 14–16]

[Abundance of Art Doctrines and Architectural Literature]

While the indirect influence of natural science and related theories thus proves to be an effective cause for the formation and deformation of modern artistic conditions, at the same time these and other branches of modern science increasingly deal directly with art. The material assembled by science and research in a daily growing number of writings and costly publications concerning every possible style of every country almost drowns us, so that it becomes difficult to find one's way through this abundance and to maintain one's direction.

In order to make things easier, the overabundant material has been divided into different subjects each forming a complete theory. We have a mass of books on aesthetics and the history of art, not to mention the many on complementary art subjects. In addition, there are an immense number of works on specific subjects, especially architecture. We Germans have an inexhaustible production of such special architectural books, for instance on domestic and rural architecture, on church architecture, on civil and military engineering, on instructions for timber architecture, on construction in brick, in ashlar, and so forth; all these works contain rich stores of knowledge and, at times, also intellect and talent.

Since this attempt at splitting up the material into the greatest possible number of theories was based on a principle that separated more than it compared and unified, it did not eliminate the harmful and bewildering influence that infinite variety has on the faculty of perceiving and creating beauty, nor did it give contemporary art a greater uniformity of direction.

The mass of unconnected doctrines that our architects are expected to master and the resulting self-conscious irresolution and inexperience is, in my opinion, one of the most decisive causes for the bewildering state of modern art.

In this situation our architects have followed three different directions, each of which conforms to one of the three main ways in which science is applied to art. They may be called: (a) the Materialists, under the influence of natural sciences and related theories; (b) the Historians, under the influence of the history of art and archeological research; (c) the Schematists, under the influence of speculative philosophy and aesthetics. One could add as a fourth category one species of historians, the *Gothic Romantics*, who deserve special consideration because they are the only ones who know what they want; they come closer to the first category in that they have in mind a so-called practical-scientific, that is, a political-religious end. [fols. 17–18]

[*Trends in Contemporary Architecture*]

The Materialists

Our present artistic attitude has been most powerfully influenced by those doctrines that teach mastery over the material intended to be used for architectural and structural tasks. In line with the practical trend of our time and supported by the great experiences gained in engineering, above all in the building of railways, these doctrines were very successful. But often the material was given precedence over the idea; by accepting the principle that the store of architectural forms was exclusively conditioned by and evolved out of the material, one has, as it were, placed the idea in iron fetters.

Material must always be subservient to the idea; it must never be the only decisive factor for the embodiment of the idea. Making the idea manifest must not conflict with the material that conditions it, yet it is in no way absolutely necessary that the physical appearance of the material *as such* is an additional coefficient of the art phenomenon. We shall show that the principle of revealing the material was not applied before the Roman period.

Although nature, this primordial matriarch [*Urmeisterin*] whose laws we architects keep constantly before us as the ultimate ideal, choses and uses her material in conformity to her laws, she nevertheless imprints shape and character on her formations according to the ideas that are embodied in them; these formations gain in beauty and expression because the most suitable material was chosen for their physical representation and because the inflexible unity [*Gesetzlichkeit*] of the building, conditioned by the properties of the material, was made apparent as a kind of natural symbol.

Among the Materialists must also be counted those who favor the so-called naturalistic style of ornament; they often display gross ignorance of the structural principles applicable to the adornment of a core schema.

Richard Redgrave supplementary report on design in reports by the juries [for] the Great Exhibition of 1852 [*sic*].[3] [fols. 19–20]

The Historians

The historical school consists in the main of two disciplines fighting each other, the Romantic and the Classical. Both find it more convenient to reproduce existing works unchanged or, at least, to fashion works after whatever the given task requires in an arbitrary and unnatural manner; they find this more convenient than the reverse method of letting the task evolve freely out of its requirements into an independent work that still takes into account the traditional forms that have stood the test of time as expressions of certain formative principles valid for all times and in all circumstances; a work that takes into account also the necessary connection between what is conceptually related and what time has gradually brought forth, and the task with its local, temporal, and other particular conditions.

To the Romantics also belong the Christian Romantics who nowadays incline toward the Gothic style; of these we shall have more to say below [page 257].

The Historians are in a sense the extreme opposite of those architects who attribute to the material too decisive an influence on the rise of architectural forms, although both also have their points of contact and similarity. Both abandon the traditional standpoint; the [Historians] by becoming engrossed in a past or alien world, the [Materialists] by constructing the given task only out of the task itself and out of often intractable and heterogenous materials. Neither will exert a lasting influence on the direction and configuration [*Gestaltung*] of the architecture of the future, even given great ability and favorable opportunity for building.

Although architecture has its own store of forms and is not an imitative art like sculpture and painting, yet it has over the centuries created its own grammar of forms from which it borrows the types for new creations; by using these types, architecture remains legible and comprehensible for everyone.

Whoever spurns these conventional and practicable forms is like an author who constrains his own living, vernacular language and adopts an antiquated, foreign, or self-invented order of words and mode of expression. Even if these were logically well founded, he would be understood only with difficulty and, at least as an author, would make no fortune whereas he would have lost nothing in originality had he used simplified but popular terms.

The Aestheticians

If, in its third aspect, the philosophy of art were competent to prove the practical validity of aesthetics,* as it has more or less succeeded in defining and precisely circumscribing the concept of formal beauty and in analyzing its manifestation, it could unite the fragmented but intellectually linked doctrines into a coherent building theory.

But philosophy, when applied to art, is in the same position as is mathematics when approaching certain problems of physics in which many immeasurable but interrelated forces and quantities are involved.

Even if the aesthetician were successful in tackling this difficulty, in the end he would have solved only his *own* problem, which, the new philosophy of art asserts, is not identical with that of art.† [fols. 20–22]

---

*Rumohr's *Forschungen* is a first and so far unsurpassed attempt in this direction, a work that, it seems, is little appreciated by modern aestheticians and whose true value is in general not recognized by artists either.

†The purpose and aim of the artist's activity is the world of appearance, whereas to the aesthetician the beginning and the end is the idea; he sees this as the germ and the seed of everything that is, as the creative force to which everything, even beauty, owes its existence, etc. Zeising, introduction to *Ästhet. Forschungen.* Has philosophy not also the right and the liberty to look and discuss the idea as an object, as a coefficient of the work?

Among artists, the philosophy of art has so far found only a few adherents; to an even lesser degree has it reached the masses. Through patrons of the arts it had quite a notable indirect influence on the direction of the arts; however, what they learned from the arts was schematic art criticism, whereas the infinite variations of art forms attain their characteristic quality and individual beauty only through deviations from the rule, or, rather, from the schema.

In no way could it be said that schematism is the most noticeable fault of the present, whereas it was predominant toward the end of the sixteenth century on account of the rediscovery of the Vitruvian books and the overpowering talent of the great Italian masters during the glorious era of the fifteenth and sixteenth centuries.

It had been conspicuous once before, toward the end of the short-lived Old Germanic or Gothic style (at least in Germany), as a strictly geometric form.

A certain school in Germany, which cannot free itself from the domineering influence of its founder and late master [Schinkel], has not remained immune to this aesthetic schematism in spite of the good number of undoubtedly talented adherents who wish to pursue in a free manner of their own choice.

It remains to say a few words about the Gothic Romantics.

The Gothic Romantics

About forty years ago the outspoken prejudice against so-called Gothic art suddenly gave way to a favorable response, which had been created and spread mainly by the poets of the Romantic school. Yet for a long time the movement remained ineffective and led at best to some wretched garden ruins and chapels in the modern Gothic style. At the same time, it greatly stimulated interest in the preservation of the fast-decaying ancient Gothic monuments, an interest generously supported, sooner or later, by rulers and governments. This restoration work became the training ground for many young artists and skilled craftsmen, who have had the opportunity since then of applying their mastery of this style to new buildings. Moreover, in parts of England the style has remained traditional though interpreted in a schematic manner.

This synopsis of the history of the neo-Gothic style shows it to be in essence an antiquarian, restorative, and scholarly trend—in other words, a negation of the present. The number of architects and laymen who support it is considerable; most of them are men of routine for whom the compendiarium artis produced by the Gothic style is a convenient ready reckoner to be used when building. [fols. 23–24]

Some of the Materialists also support this style because the construction is consistent, though not long lasting, and because the material is the main coefficient of the object. That this style was suitable for industrial mass production of building parts has already been mentioned [page 252].

But it is also supported by highly talented artists who were more or less converted to it after having been trained in quite the opposite trend, wherein they had made a name for themselves. This is mainly the case in France, where a period of the Gothic style that could still be further developed was adopted by these artists. It is not the case in England and Germany.[4]

These prominent and intelligent adherents of the Gothic style are closely connected with a powerful political-religious party whose members trade in Catholic and crypto-Catholic propaganda; it is the same party that introduced the depraved style of the Jesuits who used the then-prevailing love for ostentation as a means for their ends. The faction is particularly active in France; they know the influence that French fashion has on the rest of Europe but forget how precarious and fickle this Parisian base is. France treats Western Europe like a pagan country which has to be reconquered for Christendom by using the same means which had been used previously to achieve the same goal. (See [August] Reichensperger's *Fingerzeige [auf dem Gebiete der Kirchlichen Kunst*, Leipzig, 1854].)

[Doubts about the Phase in Which Modern Art Finds Itself]

This picture of the state of modern art, though incomplete and only stressing the most obvious, suffices, I think, to show that we are at present in the middle of a fog patch on the horizon of art history; doubts may exist only as to whether this state of modern art points to the first or second of the above-mentioned phases of the amorphous state; that is, whether it heralds the passage into the amorphous state or a stage in which the chaos, striving for formation, is preparing to crystallize into a new art form. The first hypothesis denies hope and support to the ambitions of aspiring artists who adhere to it. The strength of an Atlas could not suffice to hold it up, and to confine oneself to help pull down what is rotten is not the task of the architect who finds pleasure only in building.

The second assumption, on the other hand, whether well founded or erroneous, is really productive as long as the artist who accepts it guards against the presumption of being able to invent the new architectural style of the future. No modern Anthemius of Tralles or Isidor of Miletus will be ingenious enough to create a new style unless a new concept of universal historical importance had first become overwhelmingly evident as an artistic idea. [fols. 24–26]

[Aim and Task of a Theory of Building]

Once the artist has realized his own modest position, he can without arrogance choose as his objective in the work in hand the process of *becoming* or, quite generally, the *becoming of art*, and set himself the following task:

> *To comprehend in detail the law-like character* [Gesetzlichkeit] *that becomes apparent in art phenomena during the process of becoming, to deduce generally valid principles from what one has found, and in accordance with them to establish the basic features of an empirical theory of building.*

A theory of building based on these principles will therefore be different from the theory of architecture. Reviewing the field of history, it will not apprehend and *explain as facts* the monuments of different countries and different times, but will *resolve* them as different values of a variable function of given variable coefficients; it will do this in order to reveal the law and inner necessity that reigns throughout the world of art forms as throughout nature.

The theory of building will lead to the realization that in the same way that nature, for all her abundance, is thrifty in her motifs, in the same way that she modifies the few basic forms or principles a thousandfold according to the evolutionary stage reached by living beings as well as according to varied living conditions—making some parts short, some long, some fully developed while others are only hinted at—in the same way architecture too is based on a few standard forms and principles, which through constant reappearance make possible infinite variations that are conditioned by the particular need of each case as well as by many other circumstances.

The principle of comprehending the work in the state of evolving could also be demonstrated in a purely technical sense. In this theory of building, technics will, indeed, be an essential aspect needing consideration, but only insofar as it conditions the law governing the process of art coming into being.

The suggested way through the field of tectonics will meet with the greatest of difficulties and will, at best, result in lacunae, blank stretches, and errors; but the abundance of the material will make it necessary to follow a set plan and put it into some order, to group what is related into families, and to reduce what is derivative and complex to its original and simple state—a regulating and comparative procedure that will at least make it easier to obtain an overall view of the vast field of tectonics, which alone will yield some practical benefit. [fols. 27–28]

List of Abbreviations

Short titles of books by Semper. For manuscripts, see the Bibliography.

Baustyle   *Über Baustyle* (On Architectural Styles)

E.K.   *Über den Bau evangelischer Kirchen* (On
                            Church Building)

4 El.   *Die vier Elemente der Baukunst* (The Four
                            Elements of Architecture)

K.S.   *Kleine Schriften von Gottfried Semper* (Selected
                            Writings of Gottfried Semper)

Schleudergeschosse   *Über die bleiernen Schleudergeschosse der Alten*
                            (On Lead Slingshot Missiles of the Ancients)

Schmuck   *Über die formelle Gesetzmässigkeit des Schmuckes*
                            (On the Formal Uniformity of Adornment)

(Der) Stil   *Der Stil in den technischen und tektonischen
                            Künsten* (Style in the Technical and
                            Structural Arts)

V.B.   *Vorläufige Bermerkungen über bemalte
                            Architektur* (Preliminary Remarks on
                            Polychrome Architecture)

WIK   *Wissenschaft, Industrie und Kunst* (Science,
                            Industry and Art)

Other Abbreviations

Cole Diary

Cole Diaries, Library, Victoria and Albert Museum, London

MS

MS numbers are those of the catalogue of Semper's writings in Herrmann (1981), pp. 70–151

SA Zurich

Semper-Archiv, Institut für Geschichte und Theorie der Architektur, ETH Zurich

Tektonik

Karl Bötticher, *Die Tektonik der Hellenen* (1852)

Vieweg Brief

sixteen letters between Semper and Vieweg, reprinted in Herrmann (1976), pp. 218–237.

Unless otherwise stated, all correspondence is in the Semper-Archiv.

Notes

Foreword

1. George F. Chadwick, *The Works of Sir Joseph Paxton* (London, 1961), pp. 74, 76.

2. Adolf Max Vogt, "Gottfried Semper und Joseph Paxton," in *Gottfried Semper und die Mitte des 19. Jahrhunderts* (Basel and Stuttgart, 1976), p. 180.

3. See ibid., p. 183.

1. The Beginnings: Semper in Dresden, 1834–1849

1. For a full account of the steps that led to Semper's appointment, and Gau's decisive recommendation, see Kobuch.

2. Gau to Semper, 22 February 1835. Unless otherwise stated, all letters and manuscripts quoted are in the Semper-Archiv (SA) at the Eidgenössische Technische Hochschule, Zurich.

3. This can be deduced from Semper's letter to his mother of 22 April 1835 in which he mentions "the new theater designed long ago" ("das lange schon gezeichnete neue Theater").

4. The sequence of events given here is based on Semper's own account in a first draft for the introduction to his book on the Hoftheater (MS 43, fol. 1). In the printed text (*Hoftheater* [1849], p. 4), he understandably played down Berlin's active role and implied that the initiative came from the authorities in Dresden. Since so far only the published version is known, the German text of the draft is reproduced here: "Geschichtliches, günstiges Urtheil des Grafen Brühl über die im Jahre 1835 ohne Auftrag von mir gefertigten Pläne zu einem Theater. Er bestellt Kopien davon für den damaligen Kronprinzen, jetzigen König von Preussen. Schinkel empfiehlt sie dem Herrn v. Lüttichau, der auf dessen Empfehlung meinen Plänen vor anderen, von ihm bestellten, den Vorzug giebt und mir den Auftrag ertheilt, sie zu modificieren und ausgeführtere Pläne und Anschläge einzureichen."

5. Gau to Semper, 19 August 1834, reply to a letter from Semper in which he made this remark (Altona, Museum Donner; ill. in Institut für Denkmalpflege, no. 264).

6. MS 25, fol. 53. Similarly some years later in MS 55, fol. 12: "To make the basic idea visible within the great variety of formations and to create a whole that has individual character but, at the same time, is in full harmony with itself and the environment—therein lies the great secret of architecture."

7. *Stil* 1, p. 44.

8. Semper, *Hoftheater*, p. 10.

9. On the history and artistic significance of the forum project, see Milde (1981), pp. 143–160; Laudel; Fröhlich (1974), pp. 40ff; Institut für Denkmalpflege, pp. 150ff.

10. Milde (1981), pp. 166ff.

11. Institut für Denkmalpflege, pp. 282f; Rosenau, pp. 238ff.

12. Polenz.

13. Milde (1979), pp. 224–229; Institut für Denkmalpflege, pp. 158f.

2. In Exile: Semper in Paris and London, 1849–1855

1. Doering-Manteuffel, p. 81: "As a determined republican, Semper, together with the fiery Gutzkow, passionately fought and rejected Wagner's demand that the hereditary presidency of the new republic of Saxony should remain with the House of Wettin."

2. To a Mr. Bayer, undated, probably from Paris. Similarly to Bertha, 21 June 1849: "My action was . . . the inexorable consequence of my often . . . proclaimed conviction and of the defeat of all hopes . . . for a united and free fatherland."

3. To his brother Karl Semper, 15 May 1849. Months later, in a petition sent from abroad, he understandably minimized his part in the uprising.

4. Montbé, pp. 34f; von Waldersee, p. 25; Beust, p. 70; Pecht 1, pp. 181f; Schubert, p. 71; Quitzsch (1962), p. 10, (1981), pp. 18ff.

5. Wagner (1964), p. 463.

6. Montbé, pp. 34f.

7. Counselor H. W. Schulz to Semper, 8 August 1849. August Röckel's evidence in the trial cited by Newman 2, p. 64. The Technical Legion belonged to the local militia as an officially recognized volunteer corps formed in 1848 by staff and students of the polytechnic college.

8. To Karl, undated (probably 28 March 1848). When the Danes had gained control, Semper, writing from Paris (11 September 1850), gave Karl strategic advice for a guerrilla war.

9. In a letter to Karl (15 May 1849), Semper mentions written negotiations with the English ambassador that could compromise him, and a requisition receipt signed by him that could become especially dangerous.

10. Details of flight in letter to Bertha, 17 May 1849; and Pecht 1, pp. 182f. On warrant for his arrest: Quitzsch (1981), pp. 19f; and *Neue Preussische Zeitung (Kreuz-Zeitung)*, 19 May 1849.

11. J. L. Finck to Wilhelm or Karl, 29 May 1849.

12. Huber 2, pp. 874f.

13. To Bertha, undated, from Paris.

14. To Karl, 28 May 1849.

15. To Karl, 30 May 1849, from Karlsruhe.

16. To Karl, 30 May 1849.

17. To Bernhard Krüger, 4 June 1849. The letters were mainly concerned with his manuscript "Gebäudelehre"; see below, pp. 15ff. On Krüger see Plagemann, p. 135; Löffler, p. 390.

18. To Karl, 10 June 1849. To Karl, still from Karlsruhe, 30 May 1849: "Idleness has become unbearable; I long for occupation and work."

19. Newman 2, p. 62 n. 6. Semper also reassured Bertha later, when civil war in France seemed imminent, that he would stay away from the movement (17 May 1850).

20. On "Letters of an Outlaw" see *Vieweg Brief* no. 5 (15 June 1849). Dr. Friedrich Krause to Semper, 30 October 1849: "I was very sorry to see that in your letter you repeatedly used the word 'outlaw' about yourself and seem to be deeply hurt by it." Semper to Bertha in 1849: "You won't believe how an outlaw feels at times" (10 June); "So, I am quite forsaken and condemned. . . . One avoids me like the plague. . . . Oh, the fugitive is very unhappy—even his comrades turn away from him and what is one's right is turned into error, and error into guilt" (21 June); "Nobody wants to have anything to do with me" (16 November).

21. To Bertha, 10 June 1849.

22. To Karl, 30 May 1849: "I can find work best in Paris." To Bertha, 21 June 1849: "With the help of my friends in France, in particular through Feuchère, I am looking for work in that country. . . . My old friends Desplechin, Dieterle, and Feuchère have not disowned me."

23. To Bertha: 17 May 1849, from Frankfurt; undated, from Paris; and on 21 June 1849: "The world is only a large prison for me. I am almost longing for a solitary prison cell."

24. To his sister Elise, 18 March 1850.

25. To Krüger, 9 June 1849.

26. To Karl, 28 May 1849.

27. To Bertha, 21 June 1849.

28. Bertha to Semper, 17 July 1849.

29. The petition exists in two drafts in the SA Zurich.

30. To Karl, 28 May 1849.

31. To Bertha, 1 August 1849: "If you have not sent the letter to the king, then keep it back. The step is quite useless, as is the petition you intended to make." Months later (18 March 1850), in a letter to Elise, he referred to the matter again. He would not ask the Ministry of Justice to lift the ban so that he could travel to Altona. People would only exploit such a request and write slanderous articles "as they had done before when, guided by a (probably wrong) sense of propriety, I wrote a letter to the king of Saxony and another one to the director of the theater. Neither of the two letters contained anything about a plea for clemency. I only asked the king's permission to submit my defense in writing and to have my dismissal postponed until after the verdict." He was so convinced of having acted honorably that on 4 February 1850 he had sent "copies of all letters I had written from exile to persons of high and highest standing" to an acquaintance in Dresden and asked him to use these letters as the basis for a reply to the defamatory article that had appeared the previous year in the *Kreuz-Zeitung.*

32. Bertha to Semper, 8 August 1849.

33. To Krüger, 26 June 1849.

34. Gau to Semper, 11 and 12 July 1849. For the full texts of Quandt's letter to Gau and Semper's draft reply to Quandt, see Fröhlich, pp. 68f.

35. To Karl or Wilhelm, undated (probably 11 July 1849).

36. H. W. Schulz to Semper, 8 August 1849. Schulz mentions the charges brought against Semper in Dresden. The king had been well aware of how even before the uprising "you had talked in public about king and monarchy. . . . You also created a lot of talk by your performance in the post house where you incited the youngsters of the Technical Legion to fight, by your conduct at von Friden's house and at Hofrat Wolf's, and lastly by meeting the English ambassador. The officers in particular speak of the fact that on several occasions you openly expressed your republican views at Dauch's."

37. To his mother, undated (probably 7 August 1849).

38. To Bertha, 16 November 1849.

39. To his mother, 1 January 1850; to Vieweg, 24 February 1850 (*Vieweg Brief* no. 6).

40. To Bertha, 17 May 1850.

41. For the history of this work from 1843 to 1855 see Herrmann (1976), pp. 202ff. For what happened to it afterward see below: "The Genesis of *Der Stil*, 1840–1877."

42. Vieweg to Semper, 18 January 1844, 6 September 1845, 21 December 1847, 18 January 1848.

43. *Vieweg Brief* no. 5 (15 June 1849).

44. Vieweg to Semper, undated fragment (probably 20 August 1849).

45. Vieweg to Semper, 21 August 1849.

46. MS 46. In Dresden Semper had been interested in the description of a Roman house by Merovic, the founder of the Merovingian dynasty. In a letter of 9 August 1844 Vieweg offered to obtain the French edition for Semper. Semper described the palace in a lecture he gave in Dresden, referring to Mazois (MS 35, fols. 41, 44).

47. On 21 August 1849 Vieweg urged: "You must make every effort to make progress with your work because I must have the greater part of the manuscript complete with illustrations, at least for every section, before I can start printing. Under the section 'dwelling' please keep in mind the practical requirements and in particular include all town- and country houses of modern nations. . . . Every one of them— England, Holland, Italy, Norway, Switzerland, Holstein, etc.—offers something characteristic."

48. MS 52. The entire manuscript consists of 90 pages including the preface.

49. MS 52, fol. 7.

50. MS 52, fol. 17.

51. Vieweg to Semper, 13 July 1844: "I am sending you herewith a copy of your beautiful letter of 26 September last in which you expressed in such a perfect way the leading ideas of the literary project discussed between us."

52. The preface is dated "Sèvres, 20 July 1849."

53. MS 52, fols. 43–90.

54. Mende (27 June 1849) could not give him any hope.

55. To Jochmus, undated (August 1849), and to his mother, 7 August 1849.

56. To Karl, July 1849.

57. G. H. Geill to Semper, 26 September 1849; to Krause, 19 October 1849; to Bertha, 16 November 1849. For this journey see Semper, "Reise nach Belgien"

(1849), pp. 501ff. Before leaving for Belgium Semper had offered to work for Johann Andreas Romberg, in whose journal this article, Semper's first contribution to it, appeared. Subsequently Semper sent many papers to Romberg who, however, rejected most of them as too long and too scholarly.

58. Krause to Semper, 3 and 19 October 1849.

59. Later Semper dedicated *Die vier Elemente der Baukunst* to his "noble friend Herr Director Friedrich Krause," but then had doubts whether this might harm Krause; his friend, however, assured Bertha that he was "proud that Semper thought him worthy of that honor" (Bertha to Semper, 18 February 1851).

60. Krause to Semper, 11 December 1849.

61. To his mother, 1 January 1850.

62. On the "sample drawing" see Herrmann (1976), p. 207 n. 19. A carpet and sideboard by Jackson & Graham are listed in the *Official Descriptive and Illustrated Catalogue of the Great Exhibition . . . 1851*, Class 19, no. 390, and Class 26, no. 261.

63. Semper to Krause, undated (February 1850).

64. William Lindley to Semper, 2 April 1850. For Lindley see Schumacher, passim.

65. Wagner to Sulzer, 22 February 1850; repr. in Wagner (1914) 2, p. 411. On Sulzer and Wagner's letter see Knoepfli, pp. 260, 264.

66. Semper to Krause, 19 October 1849.

67. Stürler to Semper, 10 May 1850. Rudolf von Stürler studied with Gau from 1827 to 1830. With the letter he sent Semper a copy of his book, *Schweizer Holzkonstruktion* (1844).

68. To Elise, 24 February and 18 March 1850.

69. Köchly to Semper, 17 July 1850 (Germanisches Museum, Nuremberg).

70. Wagner (1964), p. 506 (February 1850).

71. Semper received two letters of introduction to M. Delambre, member of the commission for the Great Exhibition, one from Armand Bertin, editor-in-chief of the *Journal des Débats*, the other from the chief of the Department of Agriculture: "Mr. Semper architecte a l'intention de concourir pour la construction des bâtiments devant servir à l'exposition des produits de l'industrie de Londres. Il désire prendre connaissance du plan adopté à Paris pour la même destination." Cf. Hobhouse, p. 16.

72. 9 December 1849. See Herrmann (1976), p. 207 n. 17. It was probably a stage design for Rossini's opera *Mose in Egitto*. The Musée de l'Opéra in Paris has no relevant designs.

73. To his mother, 1 January 1850.

74. To Bertha, 9 December 1849.

75. To his mother, 1 January 1850.

76. The correspondence took place in August–September 1850. Two letters from the countess, drafts of two letters from Semper with detailed proposals, and a sketch for the planned decoration have survived. In the first letter Semper wrote: "J'ai l'honneur de vous renvoyer les deux plans de décoration de la pièce [which Semper had submitted before] avec une espèce de croquis que j'ai fait pour essayer une manière d'éviter les colonnes verticales, qui forment le principal inconvénient du système d'ornamentation des pans coupés premièrement adopté. Ce seroit de ne pas faire des colonnes, mais des encadrements de bois qui entoureroient des panneaux

peints, avec treillis, cachés en partie par des véla [vélarium?], qui permetront de supposer des colonnes cachés derrière eux."

77. To his mother, 7 August 1849.

78. To Bertha, 21 March 1850. He also asked for the dispatch of "the drawings for the Dresden Synagogue . . . above all details of the benches, the Holy of Holies, the almemor [*sic*; pulpit], also of the candelabras and chandeliers."

79. Fröhlich, pp. 74f, ill. no. 99-1-4; Institut für Denkmalpflege, pp. 292f.

80. To Krüger, 2 May 1850.

81. Hautecoeur 7, pp. 62f, 149f; Rosenau, p. 240.

82. To Bertha, undated (June 1849); to a brother, undated (11 July 1849).

83. To his mother, 7 August 1849.

84. To Bertha, 16 November 1849.

85. To Bertha, 18 June 1850.

86. To Bertha, 16 November 1849.

87. To Bertha, 21 March 1850.

88. To Karl, 9 January 1850.

89. To Bertha, 24 January 1850.

90. "Das assyrische Museum im Louvre zu Paris," *Allgemeine Bauzeitung* (Ephemeriden), March 1848, pp. 265–278.

91. To Krüger, 30 August 1849; to Romberg, undated (September 1849); see also *Stil* 1, p. 353. The director was Charles Blanc. When Blanc, while on a study trip through Germany, intended to visit Dresden, Semper gave him letters of introduction to Privy Councillor Schulz and Bertha and wrote to her, "Through him and other influential acquaintances I soon hope to be able to secure a position, be it as teacher or architect or writer" (21 September 1849). Blanc also held out the prospect of subscribing, on behalf of the government, several hundred copies of "Vergleichende Baulehre" when translated into French.

92. *Vieweg Brief* no. 6 (24 February 1850).

93. Vieweg to Semper, 18 March 1850.

94. MSS 55–68. The preface is dated Paris, 4 May 1850. See translation of some parts at the end of this book. Semper's letter announcing the dispatch of the manuscript is dated 13 May 1849.

95. *Vieweg Brief* no. 6 (24 February 1850).

96. To Elise, 18 March 1850. On 13 August 1850 Semper signed a note for 2500 thalers that his mother had lent him at three percent interest, to be paid back "as soon as circumstances permit."

97. To a brother, undated (July 1849); to his mother, 7 August 1849.

98. To Heine, 25 April 1850: "Had you not left so quickly, I might have decided to come with you. But I did not have the money and needed at least four weeks to get it. Now I am caught in my engagement [the contract with Vieweg] and also wait for your answer. . . . Be frank with me when you reply. I have learned to listen. Tell me honestly whether it is not too late for me to come, or would I only become your competitor?"

99. To Elise, 18 March 1850.

100. To Bertha, 21 March 1850.

101. Heine advised a partnership with K. Gildemeister, an architect who had settled in New York. On 2 July 1850 Gildemeister sent Semper a detailed report about the prospects for a career there, and for the commercial projects Semper had mentioned. He also made suggestions about a possible partnership. For Gildemeister see Hautecoeur 7, p. 307, and Pevsner (1976), pp. 245f.

102. To Bertha, 17 May 1850.

103. Louis Pusinelli to Semper, 1 September 1850. Since he wrote in German, he may have been a relative of Dr. Anton Pusinelli, Wagner's friend and creditor.

104. To Pusinelli, undated (end of July).

105. Kreuter to Semper, 28 July 1850.

106. He stayed at the Hotel d'Allemagne et du Commerce near Leicester Square. Shortly before his departure, he told the Comtesse de Villeneuve that he would return to Paris the following week, which means that he never intended to remain long in London. The first thing he did was to go to a printer and order visiting cards. He had vaguely thought of going from London by boat to Altona to say goodby to his family. "But everybody advised against it, and the way the governorship acts against those who displease the German governments did not encourage me to undertake this daring step" (to Karl, 11 September 1850, from Paris).

107. Semper described the following events in a letter to Karl, 30 September 1850, from London.

108. August Emil Braun (1809–1856). From 1830 to 1832 studied archeology in Göttingen, Munich, and Dresden, in 1833 art history in Berlin; from 1833 in Rome, from 1835 permanent secretary of the Archaeological Institute (*Neue Deutsche Biographie*, Berlin, 1955, pp. 548f). Dr. Braun was an archeologist of repute "but was also active in many other fields" (Geiger, p. 190). In 1855 he supervised the construction of a model of the Colosseum that was exhibited in the Crystal Palace at Sydenham (*The Builder*, 1855, p. 357). After his death Semper was asked to continue an annotated edition of Vitruvius for which he had been under contract. There exist some critical notes to Vitruvius, Book 1, Chapter 1, that Semper wrote for this edition; it seems that it was never published (MSS 104, 105; *K.S.*, pp. 191ff.; Hugo Scheube to Semper, 21 October, 28 November 1856, 9 May 1857).

109. Braun to Semper, 22 September 1850.

110. Two fragmentary and undated drafts to this letter exist. In one Semper replies in more detail to Braun's observations: "You speak of ancient necropolises. Would Englishmen not think the medieval cemetery in a cloister, from which the Campo Santo derived, was the natural and more festive motif? . . . . How far has the matter developed and when will these cemeteries be executed? . . . To work as an interior designer would hardly agree with my plans. . . . I have lost everything and must try to build a future for my wife and six children. In this I can succeed only if I find a secure, even if dependent and inferior, position or am employed as the manager for a larger enterprise. As a designer of interiors, furniture, or ornaments . . . I would earn little; besides, this work would make me more dissatisfied than if I were to hoe or plow the land."

111. On Chadwick's life and work see R. A. Lewis's biography. The descriptions of the sanitary conditions and Chadwick's reform are to a great extent based on this authoritative work. It is not known who vom Hof was. Occasionally he is mentioned in Semper's correspondence in connection with the cemetery project, but more often as being slow in paying back a debt.

112. Lewis, pp. 238f.

113. Public Record Office, Board of Health Minutes MH 5/3.

114. Ibid.

115. Ibid. At the end of September, shortly before Semper's arrival, Braun asked the board for a license, exclusive in London, "for the deposit and preparation of monumental decorations adapted to the use of the cemeteries of the Board." Cf. postscript, dated 1 October, to Semper's letter to Carl of 30 September 1850: "Dr. Braun tries to combine certain public projects with the achievement of a private plan in which he intends to let me participate. He thinks of an 'office,' which would take care of everything needed for a funeral. It is only loosely connected with my affair, in which I deal directly with the government."

116. There are two copies of the "Memoranda of draft instructions for consideration for designs in respect to the construction of a church for the celebration of Divine Service at the National Cemetery." One, a fair copy, quoted in the text, is in the Library of London University, Chadwick Papers, Misc. 141; the other, made by Semper from a slightly different manuscript, is in the SA Zurich. Lewis, p. 240, puts the date of the memorandum at the end of 1849, connecting it with another official report drawn up at that time. But because this report hardly mentions any building, it is more likely that the memorandum was drafted after the Interment Bill had been passed, i.e., only a few weeks before Semper's arrival.

117. To Karl, 30 September 1850.

118. Chadwick Papers, Misc. 141.

119. To Karl, 30 September and postscript of 1 October 1850. That Semper indeed had reason to hope for a position is proven by a remark Lord Seymour made four years later in a speech in Parliament in which he opposed the extension of the experimental period for which the Board of Health had been set up. Referring to the study trip to Paris at the end of August 1850, he declared: "The next thing we hear of the Board was, that they wished to appoint, among others, Mr.—now Sir Joseph—Paxton, a gentleman at that time the great oracle of the town on all questions of taste, who was to be delegated to look after the decorative department of the churchyards; while another gentleman was to be appointed churchyard architect; and a third, Dr. Brown [*sic*] was to see about the planning and laying out of the burial grounds" (*Hansard's Parliamentary Debates*, London, 135 [1855], pp. 986; Lewis, pp. 365f). As the minister responsible for the Board of Health from March 1850 on, Lord Seymour knew at firsthand about the intended engagement of an architect.

120. Braun to Semper, 23 November 1850. Braun's visit to Bunsen is mentioned in Bunsen (1868–1871) 3, p. 96. To Karl, 30 November 1850: "I went to Bunsen to hand in my visiting card. A few weeks later, I wrote to him without getting a reply."

121. Séchan to Semper, 8, 13, 22 October 1850. "J'ai vu Dieterle et comme je le supposais bien il ne peut vous faire de compositions de ces divers objets. d'abord il me dit qu'il ne saurait les faire sans vos conseils, et ensuite vous savez qu'il a à faire pour moi des compositions pour le louvre" (13 October).

122. Séchan to Semper, 13 October 1850; illustration of Napoleon's funeral car in Guy, p. 25.

123. Séchan to Semper, December 1850.

124. To Braun, undated (probably 17 December 1850).

125. Braun to Semper, 1 January 1851.

126. To Braun, December 1850.

127. To Karl, 30 November; to Braun, December 1850.

128. To Karl, 30 November 1850.

129. Chadwick to Semper, 26 November 1850.

130. Chadwick to Semper, 23 November 1850.

131. Paxton to his wife, 26 November 1850 (Chatsworth Archive, Paxton 640).

132. To Karl, 30 November 1850: "Through him [Chadwick] I got to know the architect [*sic*] Paxton, the builder of the exhibition buildings. Probably I shall come to some arrangement with this gentleman by which I will at least ensure my daily needs." On Chadwick's efforts to find some work for Semper with Paxton, see Lankheit, pp. 33f.

133. To Braun, December 1850.

134. To Karl, 30 November 1850; to same, 12 October 1850: "I have an office in the City at the architect Falkener, 61 Gracechurch Street."

135. Braun to Semper, 23 November 1850, 1 and 29 January 1851.

136. To Braun, December 1850.

137. Braun to Semper, 1 and 29 January 1851. George Scharf (1820–1895) later became first secretary of the National Portrait Gallery; see Ames, p. 150.

138. Braun to Semper, 19 February 1851. Elkington, Mason & Co. had held the English and French patent rights for the galvanoplastic process since 1840 (Haltern, p. 191). Lothar Bucher wrote on 16 July 1855 in the *Nationalzeitung* (Berlin): "On the whole, the free creations of this factory have deteriorated since 1851, perhaps because our compatriot Braun, now in Rome, has withdrawn from it." See also *WIK*, p. 49.

139. Braun to Semper, 19 February 1851: "I deliberately do not mention the cemetery office here so as to exclude anything that is too far off and still vague. Should we be appointed, you will become a partner there too; this alone will provide you with a sufficient income. But even in case the Board of Health lets us down, I believe that with your help from the artistic side I can make a successful attack on the taste of the English public." Braun saw the possibility of further collaboration with Semper in the forthcoming industrial exhibition: "I have often wondered whether you could not persuade Vieweg to publish a critical report of the Great Exhibition. We could do this together; I could relieve you of a good deal of writing" (29 January 1851).

140. Rachel Chadwick to Semper, 1 and 2 December 1850.

141. London, Victoria and Albert Museum, Cole Diaries. On Henry Cole see Bell; Bøe; Minihan, chap. 4, pp. 96–137; Survey of London 38, pp. 78ff; Bonython.

142. Chadwick to Semper, 26 November 1850: "Mrs. Chadwick has commenced a translation of your paper on Polychrome decoration."

143. To Bertha, 19 January 1851.

144. *Vieweg Brief* no. 9 (19 January 1851); Herrmann (1976), p. 209 and n. 29.

145. *Vieweg Brief* no. 6 (24 February 1850).

146. *Vieweg Brief* no. 9 (19 January 1851).

147. That Semper originally intended to bring out the publication in England is proven by early drafts for the concluding paragraph of the first chapter, which read that in view of the timely theme, "the author of this Essay wishes to bring the result of his examinations to the attention of the English public" (MS 81a, fols. 35f).

148. Vieweg to Bertha, 9 March 1851.

149. Braun to Semper, 29 January and 19 February 1851.

150. An article, "On the Study of Polychromy and Its Revival," appeared in the July issue of the *Museum of Classical Antiquity*, edited by Edward Falkener, whose office Semper shared.

151. To Cole, 25 February 1851, repr. in Herrmann (1978), p. 126.

152. Chadwick to Semper, 4 March 1851. After having been told by Chadwick that as far as he knew Semper had no immediate prospects for a job, Paxton was prepared to offer him a post as assistant "in a spirit of kindness and consideration of your former position and present misfortunes." Semper asked Paxton for an interview in which, as he told Chadwick (7 March), he intended to suggest to Paxton combining his post of assistant with the planned school of architectural students. Chadwick thought the idea unworkable: "Without having conversed with Mr. Paxton, I conceive that it would not meet with his views" (9 March). Later Julia Becher wrote to Semper, "I regret evermore that you did not accept Paxton's offer" (23 June 1851). See Lankheit, p. 33.

153. To Bertha, undated (reply to her letter of 18 February 1851).

154. An attempt to place a notice in the *Kölnische Zeitung* through Dr. Julius Faucher proved unsuccessful since soon afterward Faucher ceased to be correspondent of the paper. On 2 March Semper sent a draft of a longer notice for Swiss newspapers to Friedrich Becher in Basel. A search through several German and Swiss newspapers has failed to uncover publication of the announcement. This elegantly printed prospectus probably dates from this time: "M. Gotfried Semper, late Director of the School of Architecture . . . at Dresden . . . is desirous of giving lessons in Architectural Drawing . . . to pupils who intend to practice Architecture professionally. He is also desirous of giving aid to Noblemen or Gentlemen who may either desire to study Architecture and the principles of construction as a branch of the Fine Arts, or wish to obtain such an insight into them as to enable them to judge of their application for the improvement of real property." I am grateful to Martin Fröhlich for referring me to this jewel of a Victorian announcement.

155. The program is preserved in two drafts for a letter (dated 24 December 1850); the quotations have been taken from both drafts. A report by Semper about his teaching activity at Dresden (cited by Hans Semper, p. 10) shows how closely this program followed the method adopted by him at Dresden. See Pevsner (1940), p. 252.

156. Cole to Semper, 26 February 1851.

157. Chadwick to Semper, 9 March 1851.

158. Krause to Semper, 10 March 1851.

159. Informing Cole in October 1854 of the offer of a professorship he had received from Zurich, he wrote, "being convinced that in this matter you will be as kindly disposed toward me as you were at the time . . . when thanks to you I was given work in the exhibition building." On 4 March Chadwick still knew nothing about the offer. Semper mentions on 7 March 'petits travaux' in connection with the forthcoming exhibition, but this sounds more like a reference to some private orders. Soon afterward, however, he must have been commissioned by Canada and Sweden since on 20 March his friend Friedrich Stammann of Hamburg suggested inserting a notice in a newspaper referring to these appointments. It appeared a few days later (Lankheit, p. 34). A similar notice in French is dated 1 April 1851.

160. It is sometimes assumed that Semper owed his position to Prince Albert. That was certainly not the case. Not only is it unlikely that the prince concerned himself with these details, but it is clear from the correspondence, as will be shown below, that at this time Semper was unknown to him; the first personal contact took place much later, in February 1855.

161. To Bouvert, 3 July 1851.

162. This is clear from a letter that Semper wrote in 1852 to someone connected with the Canadian stand: he had been reproached for not having applied to the Royal Commission, which gave awards to those who had worked on the exhibition the year before, but, he continues, "je n'ai pas eu l'idée de me présenter comme aspirant, ayant reçu mes gratifications de la part de mes committées."

163. Scherer, p. 75, the Canadian stand on p. 236. For detailed descriptions and illustrations of the four stands that Semper arranged, see Lankheit, pp. 34f., Institut für Denkmalpflege, pp. 131 f and ill. no. 288.

164. Report on plaster cast collection at Zurich (ca. 1860).

165. These remarks have been taken from a collection of notes (MS 95), fragmentary drafts for a critical review of the exhibition planned by Semper in the form of a letter to Lothar Bucher.

166. Cf. Ettlinger (1964), p. 60.

167. On 12 April 1851 Friedrich Wetzler contacted on Semper's behalf the editor of the *Leipziger Illustrirte Zeitung*, but without success.

168. On 3 May Semper had been asked to write an article about the exhibition for the German edition of the *Illustrated London News*. The assumption that the article had appeared (Herrmann [1978], p. 54n. 173) was confirmed when a rare copy of the German edition turned up in the exhibition *Gottfried Semper zum 100. Todestag* (Institut für Denkmalpflege), no. 286. Issue no. 3 (17 May) of the German supplement contained an unsigned article, "Die grosse Ausstellung" (see May, pp. 53ff). That Semper had been the author is made certain by MS 94 in which there is among other papers a draft in Semper's hand for the first part of this article. Another draft in the same MS is almost identical to an article in the *Edinburgh Review* 44 (1851), pp. 576f, which is preceded by an editorial comment that leaves no doubt about Semper's authorship. It has to be assumed that the article, which the *Edinburgh Review* reproduced in an English translation, was originally published in a German journal; so far it has not been possible to trace it (for more detail see the commentary to MS 94 in Herrmann [1981], p. 101. See Marx's and Engel's sarcastic remarks about the German edition of the *Illustrated London News* in *Marx-Engels Werke* 27 (Berlin, 1965), pp. 258, 260.

169. To Karl, 5 May 1851.

170. Chadwick to Paxton, 17 April 1851 (Chadwick Papers *sub* Paxton); partly repr. in Chadwick, pp. 204ff. Already on 23 October 1850 there was this entry in the minutes: "That Mr. Semper be consulted with reference to the best mode of exhibiting the contrast between the Monumental arrangements now prevailing in the Cemeteries, and such arrangements as might be adopted under a better system" (Public Record Office, Board of Health Minutes MH5/3).

171. Board of Health Minutes MH5/4.

172. Henry Austin to Semper, 14 May 1851.

173. Board of Health Minutes MH5/5.

174. By this Early English is probably meant.

175. "Instructions for the preparation of the Cemetery in draft" (Chadwick Papers, Misc. 144).

176. Braun to Semper, 1 January 1851: "I do not advise you to agree to change your project into Gothic. I shall write to Chadwick about it."

177. Board of Health Minutes MH5/5.

178. To Karl, 5 May 1851: "I have assignments from several journalists . . . and also at least one pupil. So things are getting better and I hope to gain a foothold unless something unforseen happens."

179. Julia Becher to Semper, 15 June 1851.

180. Semper to Julia Becher, undated (July 1851).

181. Julia Becher to her brother, 29 July 1851.

182. Karoline Hausinger to Semper, 26 August 1851.

183. To a German friend, 9 September 1851; probably the same friend to whom he sent the program for the school for architects (note 155).

184. To Bertha, 9 September 1851.

185. Bouvert to Semper, 9 July and 2 August 1851.

186. Dieterle and Séchan to Semper, 27 July 1851.

187. *Vieweg Brief* no. 8 (2 October 1850).

188. To Bertha, 19 January 1851; the same day to Vieweg.

189. To Bertha, undated (reply to her letter of 18 February 1851).

190. H. Belidor in New York to Karl Semper, 11 February 1851.

191. Undated draft of a letter to Dieterle and Séchan.

192. Dieterle to Semper, 30 August 1851.

193. *Zeitschrift für Bauwesen* 1 (November/December 1851), p. 385.

194. Ibid. The society has already obtained permission to use part of the exhibition building; for now, those interested should advise Semper of the objects they wish to exhibit so that an estimate of the space needed can be made. For Horeau see Pevsner (1976), pp. 241ff; Werner, p. 18.

195. Bertha to Semper, 2 September 1851; Semper to Bertha, and Manfred to Semper, both letters 9 September 1851; *Vieweg Brief* no. 11 (17 October 1851).

196. *Vieweg Brief* no. 11 (17 October 1851): "The articles were meant for a daily paper but I have been advised to bring them out as a pamphlet."

197. MS 88. Because he was preparing it for a translation, he did not write in gothic letters as he was wont to do.

198. *WIK*, p. 1. It has sometimes been assumed, most recently by Ames, p. 94, and Müller, p. 114, that the suggestion had come from Prince Albert. The tenor of Bertha's letter of 4 October (see below) about he possibility of Hanfstängl's recommending Semper to the queen and the prince shows that this was not the case. Probably it was Chadwick who suggested it; he was well informed about the reform of industrial art teaching methods planned by Cole and others, and must have thought it vital to Semper's interests that his experience with these problems should become known.

199. Vieweg to Semper, 12 November and 21 December 1851. Vieweg made use of the opportunity and urged Semper to fulfill his promise so that "the first section

of 'Vergleichende Baulehre' could soon be published." He should send him as soon as possible the final manuscript of the introduction to the chapter on the dwelling house because only then would he be able to prepare the woodblocks.

200. MS 97. See Herrmann (1976), n. 32. The translation was never published.

201. Bertha to Semper, 4 October 1851.

202. Stammann to Wilhelm Semper, who sent the letter to his brother 9 March 1851.

203. Semper advised the board about hollow-brick construction (SA *sub* Austin, 6 January 1851, 12 May 1852) and made an extract from William Chambers's description of Chinese buildings for Chadwick. Chadwick obtained an introduction for Semper to a Mr. Radley, "who will show you over St. Georges Hall Liverpool" and a recommendation as a "friend of Mr. Chadwick" to the engineering firm of J. Whitworth (SA *sub* Rawlinson, 3 December 1851). When Semper fell ill, Rachel Chadwick sent him a sum of money, pretending to have overlooked paying him for a drawing he had made some time ago for the improvement of the fountain in Kensington Gardens. She had sent in the design to the appropriate department which, however, had turned it down. He received a commission from the Canadian consul, with whom he had been on friendly terms since the exhibition; judging from the fee of £30 it must have been a substantial order, probably a design for a piece of furniture. Recommended by Braun, he made a design of an inkpot for a Birmingham metalware factory.

204. Hilary Bonham-Carter to Semper, 11 January (1852).

205. Cf. Pevsner (1967), p. 258.

206. Moritz Selig to Semper, 7 January 1852.

207. Semper to Astor, 22 January 1852, fragmentary draft; Hilary Bonham-Carter to Semper, 11 February (1852).

208. See note 150 above.

209. *Journal of Design* 6 (1851), pp. 112. A reference to the Canadian stand, "arranged by Mr. Semper, the architect of the Dresden Theatre, who is called the 'Barry' of Germany," appeared in the April issue (1851, p. 59).

210. Cole to Semper, 10 and 17 February; Cole Diary, 8 February: "R Redgrave came to talk over simple drawing Copies."

211. MS 47–49; repr. in *K.S.*, pp. 58ff; the whole letter repr. in Herrmann (1978), pp. 126f.

212. On the complex of buildings at South Kensington see Survey of London 38; chap. 4 deals with the negotiations for the purchase of the estate.

213. In two notes that Cole sent a few days later, he mentions only the article, not the application. 10 February: "I have seen one of the Editors of the Anthenaeum and he does not give much hopes of printing your paper but he has not decided." 24 February; "I am happy to tell you that the Athenaeum will print your paper." This may refer to the last four chapters of *WIK* or to the manuscript of Semper's essay "Über das Erechteum" (MS 99), which at that time Falkener had urgently asked for. This essay did not appear in the *Museum of Classical Antiquity*, nor was any article by Semper published by the Athenaeum.

214. On Minton see Atterbury.

215. In "Notes of a Journey to Vienna and back in November and December 1851 in Company with Herbert Minton" (London, Victoria and Albert Museum, Library, MS 101 A72).

216. To Cole, 9 April 1852; repr. in Herrmann (1978), pp. 128ff. The Minton archives in Stoke-on-Trent include references that imply that Semper occasionally made designs for Minton, including two fountains and a "plain Semper vase." The latter is included in a Minton shape book and can be dated between 1852 and 1854 by its shape number. I am deeply grateful to Paul Atterbury for giving me this information, which he came across while carrying out research for a forthcoming encyclopedia, to be published by the Antique Collectors Club.

217. Braun to Semper, 24 April 1852: "I hasten to reply to your kind letter of 14 April and assure you that I shall try to be helpful in every possible way."

218. *Vieweg Brief* no. 16 (20 May 1852).

219. Braun to Semper, 24 April 1852.

220. Fragmentary undated draft.

221. *Vieweg Brief* no. 16 (20 May 1852).

222. To Cole, 10 June 1852; repr. in Herrmann (1978), pp. 130f.

223. To Bertha, undated (in reply to her letter of 3 August 1852).

224. *Vieweg Brief* no. 16 (20 May 1852).

225. Braun to Semper, 4 May 1852.

226. Among Semper's letters in the Landesbibliothek Dresden are fifty application slips for books for the period from 30 April to 19 August 1852.

227. There are two drafts to this letter, of which one is repr. in Herrmann (1978), pp. 130f.

228. Cole to Semper, 22 June 1852.

229. To Bertha, undated (August 1852).

230. To Séchan, undated (probably after 27 June 1852).

231. To Bertha, undated (August 1852).

232. On 29 July 1852 Charles A. Somerset offered "to copy again the whole manuscript or as much as is necessary" and acknowledged on 7 August the receipt of £3.10 "for copying Ms of Catalogue."

233. To Bertha, undated (August 1852).

234. On the metalwork catalogue see Mundt (1974), pp. 100ff, and Wingler, pp. 72ff. When Semper left the Department, Cole let him have the catalogue; immediately after moving to Zurich, Semper prepared it for publication, but soon seems to have given up this work (see correspondence with J. C. Robinson, 1855, 1856). In November 1867 he offered the manuscript to the Kunstgewerbemuseum in Vienna (Rudolf Eitelberger to Semper, 25 November 1867).

235. Cole Diary, 19 August 1852: "In the Evg. reading Semper's Metalwork."

236. Cole Diary, 21 June 1852: "Saw Chadwick about Semper." 2 July: "Settled Class book on Metals for Semper. H. [J. W. Henley, president of the Board of Trade] did not object to his being a foreigner—if he were fit—not his being a political refugee—not if he had 'hoofs and horns.'"

237. To Bertha, 17 August 1852.

238. Cole Diary, 8 September 1852: "at Bd of Trade—3 hours with Mr. Henley settled professorships of Metal and Printed Fabrics." 10 September: "Semper & Hudson approved the condition of their appointment."

239. The document is dated 11 September 1852.

240. To Bertha, 13 September 1852.

241. To Bertha, undated (August 1852). 5 Gloucester Terrace was pulled down a few years ago to make room for a new building. The rest of the street remains undisturbed. It belongs to a district that had become fashionable at the time when Semper and his family moved into the newly built house.

242. The official reports contain essential information. Those that include Semper's period are *First Report of the Department of Practical Art* (London, 1853), cited as "Report 1," and the first reports of the *Department of Science and Art*, (London, 1854 and 1855), cited as "Report Science 1" and "Report Science 2."

243. Report 1, p. 22. See Bell, pp. 148, 185, 193.

244. Cole Diary, 29 March 1852: "Walked home with O Jones & discussed professorship with him."

245. Digby Wyatt, *Metal-Work and Its Artistic Design* (London, 1852); Pevsner (1950).

246. Report 1, pp. 20ff, 380ff.

247. Public Record Office, Ed. 28/1, No. 214: Minutes of the meeting on 23 July 1853: Cole proposed "to terminate [J. C. Richardson's] appointment to coincide with reopening of School in Autumn." Ibid., No. 82 on 8 September 1852: Cole proposed: "Having found two gentlemen willing and competent to conduct respectively classes for practising Art in Textile Fabrics . . . & Paper Staining and in Metal working . . . I propose that arrangements be made to form one class for instruction in Art for Woven & Printed Fabrics under the Superintendance of Mr. Octavius Hudson, and another for Metal-Working under the superintendance of Professor Semper." To make use of the expert knowledge of the two teachers before the beginning of the term in October, Cole asked Hudson to visit cotton and lace manufacturers and Semper the Royal Collection of Arms at Windsor Castle and to make suggestions for an armory department at the museum. Semper handed in his report on 27 September. Several drafts, MSS 107–110; Report 1, p. 364; *K.S.*, pp. 76ff.

248. Report 1, pp. 22, 27. Before Cole had proposed the establishment of special classes, he had made sure "by inquiry among Manufacturers, that they consider the experiment desirable" (Public Record Office, Ed. 28/1, No. 82). On the copy of a report by the Board of Trade, he made this marginal note: "In the meantime the establishment of these classes must be regarded as experimental" (London, Victoria and Albert Museum, Library, Cole Misc. X, fol. 35).

249. MS 114; in edited form Report 1, pp. 372ff. It is obviously similar to the program of the school for architects that he had planned back in 1851.

250. Report 1, p. 373.

251. Report Science 2, pp. 147f: The class for architecture "is the only [one] which enables me to apply that system of instruction which I practised for many years at the Royal Academy at Dresden, combining theory and aesthetics with immediate practice, and making the last the basis of the system. . . . Although my practice at present is comparatively but little, it would nevertheless afford an opportunity of pursuing the same system of teaching art here."

252. See Ettlinger (1939), pp. 254ff; Redgrave, pp. 100f.

253. Report 1, p. 29.

254. Redgrave, p. 101; Cole to Semper, (24) October 1852.

255. *Illustrated London News* 21 (1852), p. 463. After the funeral the car was placed in the crypt of St. Paul's where it remained until recently when the present duke

had it moved to his country seat, Stratfield Saye House, to form part of an instructive permanent exhibition of the "Iron Duke's" life. Unfortunately, the narrowness of the room makes it impossible to photograph the car in its entire length. The caption on the official lithograph published at the time reads: "Funeral-Car of the Duke of Wellington designed from the general idea suggested by the Superintendents of the Department of Practical Art by the Art Superintendent Mr. Redgrave RA. The constructive and ornamental details by Professor Semper, the details relating to woven fabrics and heraldry by Octavius Hudson, Professor. By Authority publ. Nov. 17 1852 by Day & Son . . . and Ackerman & Co."

256. Report Science 1, p. 210: "This opportunity [of introducing students into practice] presented itself, when I was entrusted with the execution of the metal works of the funeral car." In a footnote to *Stil* (1, p. 318) he mentions Wellington's funeral car, but all that he maintains is that he executed it, not that he designed it.

257. Ettlinger (1939), p. 257 n. 4.

258. Reising, p. 61, draws the same conclusion.

259. Report Science 1, p. 210. Tennant to Redgrave, 20 November 1852; Redgrave to Semper, 7 and 11 December 1852; 5 February 1853: "Meanwhile will you present my best thanks to Prof. Semper for his intent and trouble about this matter. I hope to be able to call at Marlborough House on Monday & repeat them in person."

260. Lord Mylde(?) to Cole, 12 October 1852.

261. Illustration of the sketches in Herrmann (1978), p. 76.

262. Report Science 1, p. 211: "I have had several private commissions besides those mentioned, which have been executed in presence of my students and partly with their assistance."

263. Public Record Office, Ed. 28/1, No. 239, 10 September 1853: "Design for Certificate by Professor Semper. Mr. Semper to receive £20 for drawing on the wood and the Engraving executed to Cost £40."

264. Fröhlich, p. 78, ill. no. 128-1-3; Institut für Denkmalpflege, nos. 501, 502, 503, 505.

265. On 26 May 1853 he wrote to the editor of *The Builder* asking for further information about the competition. Martin Fröhlich drew my attention to the great number of designs for the pottery school in Zurich and Dresden, which argues against the assumption that they were made for a competition. However, at times detailed planning was requested; the invitation for a town hall in Leeds, for instance, specified "a complete set of Plans, Sections, Elevations and explanatory Drawings" (*The Builder*, 24 July 1852).

266. J. B. Collinson, Captain R.E., to Semper, 17 December 1853, 5 and 13 January 1854, 17 and 23 February 1854, 10 June 1854.

267. Contract of appointment (see above, p. 64), clause 3: "You will be required to give demonstrations to your Class and occasional public lectures." Report Science 1, p. 220; Report Science 2, p. 148.

268. Manuscripts of the following lectures are in the Semper-Archiv:
1. "On the Relation of the Different Branches of Industrial Art to Each Other and to Architecture." Read on 20 May 1853. MSS 117-121; repr. *K.S.*, pp. 344-350.
2. [Draft for a system of a comparative theory of style.] Read probably on 11 November 1853. MSS 122-128; repr. *K.S.*, pp. 259-291.
3. [Development of wall and stone construction.] Read on 18 November 1853. MSS 129-132; repr. *K.S.*, pp. 383-394, 90-94.

4.–6. Three lectures on ceramics:

4. [Classification of vessels.] Read on 25 November 1853. MS 133; repr. *K.S.*, pp. 18–34.

5. [The parts of a vessel.] Read on 2 December 1853. MS 134; repr. *K.S.*, pp. 35–42.

6. "Influence of the Materials and Their Treatments upon the Development of Ceramic Types and Style." Read on 9 December 1853. MS 135; repr. *K.S.*, pp. 43–57.

7. [Fragment of lecture on roofs.] Read probably 16 December 1853. MSS 136–137; the second manuscript is titled "On the Modes of Resistance of the Materials." Not published in *K.S.*

8. [On the genesis of style in architecture.] Read probably 23 December 1853. MSS 138–140; repr. *K.S.*, pp. 369–382.

9. [On architectural symbols.] Read 1854. MSS 141–143; repr. *K.S.*, pp. 292–303.

10., 11. [On the connection between architectural systems and civilization.] Two Friday lectures of which the second is dated 6 December 1854, which makes the date of the first one 29 November 1854. MSS 144–147; partly repr. *K.S.*, pp. 351–368. Only the titles of lectures 1, 6, and 7 (MS 137) are Semper's; the others are translations of the German titles given by Semper's sons when editing *K.S.* Cf. Pevsner (1972), pp. 260 ff.

269. MS 118. Report Science, 1, p. 220: "May 20th. On the relation of the different branches of industrial art to each other and to architecture."

270. MS 117, fol. 1.

271. Redgrave to Cole, 25 September 1852: "I think Mr. Hudson & Professor Semper should prepare a set of Dogmas, Canons or Axioms—the principles of Designs applied to their various sections—to be publicly exhibited in their class room— something in the shape of Owen Jones propositions—These should be considered and approved" (London, Victoria and Albert Museum, Library, Cole Correspondence, Box 14).

272. The program of Jones's lecture course is in London, Victoria and Albert Museum, Library, Cole Misc. VII, fol. 149: "Department of Practical Art. Lectures on the Articles in the Museum of the Department by Mr. Owen Jones . . . Marlborough House June 5th . . . London 1852." The "set of dogmas" published in Report Science 1, p. 22, begins with Jones's first proposition.

273. Contract of appointment (see above, p. 64), clause 5. Mundt (1971), p. 324, has already stressed the contrast between Semper's point of view and that of the Department.

274. Cole Diary, 20 May 1853: "Stayed for Semper's lecture: his first: thoughtful & suggestive."

275. MS 117, fol. 4. Similarly in a later lecture: "The history of architecture and of art in general is based upon that of practical art, and the laws of beauty and Style in architecture have their Analogs and parallels, and it may be added their origins and keys in the principles of Style in practical art, and the separation which now exists between both of them, has shown itself as one of the principal reasons of their decay" (MS 123, fol. 13).

276. Report Science 2, p. 147. That this new arrangement went against conventional ways of thinking is shown by an objection raised by the Board of Trade on another occasion: "[it is] a decided departure from the object of the Schools of Design, which were established for the instruction of persons, not in the construction, but in the ornamenting of buildings" (Cole 1, p. 299).

277. Report Science 2, p. 148.

278. *Schleudergeschosse*, p. 6.

279. To Krause, 14 January 1854.

280. Benjamin Witsche to Semper, 9 February 1854.

281. Cole Diary, 21 January 1854; MS 116, fol. 1.

282. Thomas Belshaw to Semper, 6 February; James Fuller to Semper, 26 March; Grove to Semper, 5 and 25 April 1854. Work on the commercial courts was behind schedule; none was ready at the opening (*Art Journal* 6 [1854], p. 181).

283. Grove to Semper, 16 May 1854.

284. To Séchan, 23 July 1854.

285. Beatty (for Paxton) to Semper, 3 August 1854.

286. The correspondence between Semper and Séchan contains much information about the planned decoration. A thorough study of the material (estimates, bills, correspondence) would no doubt result in a more detailed picture of Semper's court than the necessarily short description given here. Of the two designs in the collection of the Denkmalpflege Dresden, the elevation is probably of an early scheme (Institut für Denkmalpflege, nos. 292, 293).

287. Contract between I.L. Coulton and Semper, dated 12 October 1854; Coulton submitted his account on 11 December 1854; Dieterle and Séchan sent Semper their account on 28 February 1855.

288. *Quarterly Review* 96 (1855), p. 307. In a preliminary review of the exhibition at Sydenham the commercial courts and their architects, among them Semper, are mentioned (*Art Journal* 6 [1854], p. 144).

289. To Séchan, 23 July and 11 August 1854: "J'ai écrit à Jules [Dieterle] sur le dos d'un plan du grand transept que j'en join. Poussez le qu'il fasse un croquis d'orchestre théatral."

290. Fröhlich p. 81, ill. no. 134-1-1. On the design see Biermann, pp. 59f and ill. 38; also Herrmann (1978), p. 85, ill. 14.

291. Cole Diary, 8 November 1854: "Paris: At building long discussion with Owen abt Sempers plan: He objected to any architectural treatment of the Nave portion." Semper to Bertha, from Paris, undated: "The English architects have snapped up everything and the great column will not be executed."

292. Pevsner (1972), p. 254 n. 6: "Semper, while in London, must have been specially friendly with Owen Jones."

293. To Donaldson, undated draft of a letter (November 1848): "la bienveillance personelle que vous m'avez bien voulu accorder pendant mon séjour malheureusement trop court, à Londres dans l'an 1839."

294. *The Builder* 10 (1852), pp. 53f; Zanten, p. 210.

295. C. R. Cockerell to Semper, 11 March 1853.

296. He was elected a committee member of the refugee organization founded by Gottfried Kinkel and Oskar Graf von Reichenbach (Quitzsch [1962], p. 12). Later on, he does not seem to have been active in the cause. His correspondence mentions only an invitation to an evening meeting of all German Democrats (Rudolf Schramm to Semper, March 1851), the remittance of money handed over to him for a relief organization (E. Meyer to Semper, June 1852), and his admission in July 1852 to the German Society for Charity and Harmony (R. Schwiges to Semper, July 1853).

297. In a letter to his brother Werner (28 October 1854), Siemens refers to Semper as his friend and neighbor (Siemens-Archiv Munich). On Siemens see Pole; on Bucher and his interest in Semper's ideas see Herrmann (1976), n. 42 with biographical references.

298. Wagner to Semper, 4 August 1854, repr. in Manfred Semper, p. X.

299. To Cole, undated draft in German (early October 1854).

300. Fehr, p. 307.

301. On Hermann Marschall von Biberstein and more details about the negotiations see Knoepfli, pp. 265ff.

302. Marschall to Semper, 18 September 1854.

303. Marschall to Semper, 5 October 1854: "You will be director and first professor of the department for architecture. In spite of all my efforts I could not procure a higher salary than 5000 francs but, as an exception, a position for life."

304. Marschall to Semper, 31 December 1854 and 23 January 1855.

305. London, Victoria and Albert Museum, Library, Cole Misc. XIII, fol. 188: "Prince Albert suggested that a Company should be formed to erect buildings on the quadrangle piece of ground near Brompton Church. . . . The buildings should be somewhat on the plan of the Palais Royal. Shops with a Colonnade and flats above. The buildings should form a Colonnade in the interior of the quadrangle and in the centre of it there should be a large covered building suitable for the performance of Music. H.R.H. sketched a ground plan & Elevation on blotting paper & desired that Mr. Semper should be requested to make a set of drawings: for which he would be prepared to pay" (the blotting paper with sketch is on fol. 189). The letter is reprinted in Cole, p. 322; the passage concerning the concert hall is omitted. This was the first time Semper had worked for Prince Albert. The statement in Survey of London 38, p. 98, that he had, by order of the prince, made a design for the museum building two years earlier is wrong due to the incorrect transcription of the date on Semper's letter of 9 June 1855 as 1853.

306. Séchan to Semper, 11 March 1855: "J'ai lu votre lettre à toute ma famille et nous avions été bien heureuse d'apprendre qu'il y avait pour vous l'espoir . . . d'un travail grandiose et sérieuse. Si les gens qui disposent á Londres des choses d'architecture avaient quelque sens ils ne vous laisseront partir de chez eux."

307. On this in greater detail see Survey of London, 38, pp. 81–85.

308. *Guide dans le Palais de l'Industrie et des Beaux Arts* (Paris, 1855), p. 62. To Bertha, 16 May 1855.

309. The remark in his letter to Cole of 9 June 1855 (repr. in Herrmann [1978], p. 133) that he had not yet made a model but only a perspective view of the interior refers to the concert hall. But subsequently he must have made a cardboard model because when he was considered for appointment to the post as architect in charge of building the Albert Hall ten years later, it was stated in support of the proposition that "he made drawings of a Hall for HRH many years ago, with a sort of card model" (Col. Grey to Fisher, 11 January 1866, Commissioners of the Exhibition of 1851, Archive, XXI, 45). Even at that time the drawings could not be found. Cole possessed the model; in March 1871 he wrote to Semper: "I propose to exhibit the Model of a Hall you made in 1855 for the Prince Consort." It still existed in 1888, but has since disappeared (Cole, p. 322).

310. Col. Phipps by order of the Prince, 21 June 1855. Col. Grey to Lord Derby, 12 January 1866: "Professor Semper of whom the Prince Consort had a very high opinion" (Commissioners of the Exhibition of 1851, Archive, XXI, 45 [bis].

311. A. Bowring to Semper, 21 June 1855: "Sir Martin Peto and Mr. Cubitt are to meet in my room here on Monday morning [27 June] 11°clock to look at your plans." Redgrave to Cole, 30 June 1855: "Peto and Cubitt after 2 hours going carefully over Sempers plan decided that the scheme could not be carried out to pay—very much I believe to the Princes disappointment" London, (Victoria and Albert Museum, Library, Cole Correspondence, Box 14).

312. "Ticket of Swiss postal administration for Hr Semper from Bâle to Zurich 1 seat in mail-coach."

313. To his mother, 27 December 1855.

314. Siemens to Semper, 26 June and 12 August 1856.

315. Public Record Office, Ed. 28/4, No. 110: "the following arrangements are to be made as experimental for the Autumn and Spring sessions only, to be modified or confirmed hereafter as experience may show to be desirable"; then follows a list of new appointments. (See also *Third Report of the Department of Art and Science*, 1856, p. 34.)

316. Pevsner (1940), p. 256. On the history of the "Department of Science and Art" after Semper's departure see Minihan.

317. Cole to Semper, 4 July 1857.

318. To Cole, undated (reply to ibid.).

319. Public Record Office, Ed. 28/7, No. 254. On the occasion of the newly built auditorium the Department drew up a list of prominent speakers on which Semper's name appeared next to those of Ruskin, Digby Wyatt, Owen Jones, and Thackeray.

320. Friedrich E. Suchsland to Semper, 14 August 1857.

321. To Bertha, 11 September 1857.

322. Survey of London 38, pp. 86, 99ff.

323. Lord Derby to Col. Grey, 17 January 1866 (Commissioners of the Exhibition of 1851, Archive, XXI, No 50; see Survey of London 38, p. 183).

324. Survey of London 38, pp. 87, 145.

325. Semper to Carolyne Sayn-Wittgenstein, 8 December 1857. The letter is reproduced in Sayn-Wittgenstein, pp. 299ff, but with important passages omitted. The original is in SA Zurich.

326. Siemens to Semper, 6 December 1857; Semper to Cole, undated draft (in German).

3. The Great Exhibition of 1851 as Inspiration for Der Stil

1. Fröhlich, pp. 224ff, 294ff, 150ff.

2. Habel.

3. *Stil* 1, p. 193.

4. *Stil* 1, p. 124.

5. MS 175, fol. 9; see also MS 117, fol. 4.

6. MS 179, fol. 10; see also MS 117, fol. 4.

7. Vischer 3, p. 338.

8. *Stil* 1, p. 192.

9. *Stil* 1, p. 44.

10. *Stil* 1, p. 104.

11. *Stil* 1, pp. 112–119.

12. Kühne, p. 113.

13. *WIK*, p. 35.

4. The Genesis of Der Stil, 1840–1877

1. Cf. Herrmann (1976), pp. 202ff.

2. Vieweg to Semper, 12 November 1851: "As already offered orally, I will gladly send you your original manuscript through Williams & Norgate should you think it easier to revise the original than the incorrect copy."

3. To Vieweg, 20 May 1852, from London (*Vieweg Brief* no. 16), and 25 July 1855, from Zurich.

4. There cannot be any doubt that he made the corrections only after the return of the original manuscript. In 1850 he had sent it from Paris to Vieweg, in whose hands it remained for the next five years. That it then had none of these corrections is proven by the copy made of it in 1851 (MSS 71–73; see Herrmann [1976], n. 27.) The corrections Semper made are chiefly stylistic but at times also concern the content.

5. MS 97, fol. 1. This MS is a new introduction written in 1851/1852.

6. Vieweg to Semper, 22 August 1855.

7. MS 182a. Fragment of a letter in Semper's hand without date and without naming the adressee, but most likely the draft for the letter to Vieweg of 19 June 1856 (see note 8).

8. On 8 September 1856 Vieweg confirmed receipt of the manuscript and of Semper's letter of 19 June enclosed with it.

9. The list of woodcuts and drawings: MS 182. The other treatise is called "Theorie des Formell-Schönen"; it exists in several drafts (MS 168–181). The best and longest manuscript, though breaking off in the middle of the section on ceramics, is the fair copy MSS 178–180, which Semper revised several times (see English translation at the end of this book). It is doubtful how far, if at all, it is possible to infer the content of the preface and introduction of "Kunstformenlehre" from MSS 178–180.

10. To Friedrich E. Suchsland, 29 October 1856.

11. For the same reason he did not give a lecture in London that dealt specifically with textile art. A section given the title "Bekleidungskunst" ("Art of Cladding") by the editors of the *Kleine Schriften* (p. 285) belongs to an earlier draft that Semper omitted in a later and probably final version.

12. To Lothar Bucher, 28 August 1855. See Herrmann (1976), n. 42, and Semper's remarks in *Stil* 1, p. 92.

13. J. C. Robinson to Semper, 23 September 1855.

14. Vieweg to Semper, 8 September 1856.

15. Cf. Keller (1916), p. 428.

16. To Suchsland, 21 October 1856: "[Vieweg's] arrival in Zurich which coincided with yours. . . . I am much annoyed that at that time when you were here we did not come right away to an agreement."

17. Semper related these events some time later in a letter to his lawyer, Dr. Erhard (January 1857; by mistake he wrote December).

18. Semper to Suchsland, 12 October 1856.

19. The draft to this telegram, written by him in pencil, is in SA Zurich.

20. To Suchsland, 12 October 1856.

21. To Vieweg, 13 October 1856.

22. To Vieweg, undated: "In reply to your letter of 20 October, I wish to say first of all how sorry I am that, as I can see from your letter, my remarks have hurt you so much."

23. To Suchsland, 21 October 1856: "Besides, he affects a tone as if he is my protector which I do not like." To Suchsland, 27 October 1856: "It is really not the money alone that for me spoils any further dealings with Herr Vieweg but also his role as protector which he adopts toward me."

24. To Vieweg, undated (ca. 27 October 1856).

25. For Semper's accusations see his letters to Suchsland of 21, 27, 29 October 1856, and to Dr. Erhard of 15 January 1857. How untenable they are is evident from Vieweg's understanding and helpful letter to Bertha of 9 March 1851. For Vieweg's unbending attitude see above all Semper's letter to Dr. Erhard and Suchsland of 4 January 1857 and Vieweg's letter to Suchsland of 23 July 1858.

26. To Suchsland, 23 November 1856: Because of Vieweg's dilatory tactics "I have decided to hand the matter over to a lawyer who straight away peremptorily demanded all the works that Vieweg had withheld."

27. Suchsland to Semper, 22 February 1858.

28. To Vieweg, 14 September 1857: "my son probably misunderstood you because from his report I could not make out anything about your discussion with him."

29. To Heinrich Vieweg, 8 December 1856.

30. Suchsland to Semper, 14 August 1857: "Many thanks for sending the MS of 'Schleudergeschosse' which I have already given to the printer." Vieweg behaved in the same way toward Gottfried Keller: he took in pawn a manuscript of "Galatea Novellen" that Keller had offered him and only returned it one year later; see Keller (1938), pp. 97ff.

31. Vieweg to Suchsland, 23 July 1858.

32. To Vieweg, September 1857, in reply to a letter from Vieweg of 22 August 1857, which is lost. For Semper's meeting with Cole see above, p. 81.

33. Suchsland to Semper, 24 June 1858.

34. To Suchsland, undated (January 1857): "The only possibility is that out of spite he would print that part which he has in his hands . . . but . . . I would see to it that this single part of the whole project (on ceramics) remains isolated and will not conflict with ours." The manuscript of the section on ceramics is not in the archive of Friedrich Vieweg & Sohn, Braunschweig (from where the firm recently moved to Wiesbaden). It was probably destroyed many years ago when the incomplete manuscript was of no use to the firm.

35. To Suchsland, 27 and 29 October 1856.

36. The contract signed by Semper in Zurich and by Suchsland on behalf of Friedrich Bruckmann in Frankfurt is in the archive of F. Bruckmann KG, Munich.

37. To Suchsland, 23 November 1856.

38. To Suchsland, 25 February 1859. The news was even more disturbing coming so soon after his wife had died on February 13.

39. Suchsland to Semper, 5 April 1859.

40. To Suchsland, 25 February 1859.

41. To Suchsland, undated (April 1859).

42. To Suchsland, 14 June 1859.

43. MS 195.

44. Copy of contract (attested by notary 9 February 1877) in archive of F. Bruckmann KG, Munich.

45. MS 276.

46. In the preliminary negotiations with Suchsland, Semper had tried to obtain some financial advantage for himself. To judge by later correspondence, no concessions were made to him either about the amount of money contracted for or about the method of payment.

47. Suchsland to Semper, 11 April 1858.

48. To Suchsland, 22 April 1858.

49. MS 194; ill. in Herrmann (1978), p. 109).

50. MS 195; dated 1 September 1859.

51. MS 202; the new prospectus exists in several drafts.

52. To Suchsland, 25 February 1859.

53. In November 1860, because of some disagreement that led to legal proceedings, Suchsland had left the firm. From then on Friedrich Bruckmann took over the correspondence with Semper. In his first letter, 22 January 1861, he assured Semper that he would publish his "wonderful work as quickly as possible in a form worthy of its content." Yet he did not respond to Semper's request that printing be started before he had finished the section on metalwork. Bruckmann asked him not to take it amiss if he "withheld a further part payment because I sincerely believe that in this way the publication of this volume will be speeded up." Semper finished the chapter on metalwork during the next months, and Bruckmann wrote on 25 October 1861: "Having received the completed manuscript of the second volume, it is with great pleasure that I send you enclosed Frcs 5000"

54. Bruckmann to Semper, 7 November 1861.

55. Bruckmann to Semper, 7 November 1861.

56. Munich, Staatsbibliothek (*sub* "Neue Autographen").

57. *Vieweg Brief* nos. 4 and 6 (3 December 1848 and 24 February 1850).

58. MS 281.

59. MS 281, fol. 4r and v. One must be equally skeptical about Semper's assertion of having burned his manuscript, as someone told Constantin Lipsius.

60. MS 283.

61. Archive F. Bruckmann KG, Munich.

62. Archive F. Bruckmann KG, Munich.

63. *Vieweg Brief* no. 4 (3 December 1848).

64. Semper to Ebner, 20 March 1876.

65. The assignment of his rights to Ebner, signed by Bruckmann on the contract of 28 October 1870, was thereupon crossed out.

66. Strictly speaking, it was correct to say that a third volume had not originally been envisaged, but, of course, a final chapter dealing with architecture had been planned from the beginning.

67. Legal opinion of Semper's lawyer in Munich, Dr. Riegel, dated 9 November 1876.

68. Note by Manfred Semper on back of Bruckmann's threatening letter.

69. Archive F. Bruckmann KG, Munich.

70. Bruckmann to Manfred, 25 September 1879.

71. Bruckmann to Manfred, 4 October 1879.

72. Bruckmann to Hans Semper, 19 December 1883.

73. Semper to Bruckmann, 10 April 1873. See above, pp. 109f.

74. Semper to Bruckmann, 10 April 1873.

75. *Stil* 1, pp. 226, 229. In the draft for the prospectus of 1859 he emphasized that the concept of the principle of cladding and its influence on architectural styles he "could truly call his own" (MS 195 fol. 12). On his theory of cladding see Quitzsch (1962), pp. 65–82; Eggert, pp. 125ff.

76. Originally, Semper had not intended to link the theory of cladding to textile art. In an early synopsis of *Stil* (MS 184) he listed the various materials used for covering walls by imitating carpets and then noted, next to "origin of ashlar": "here perhaps only intimate; yet, make it clear that the concept of covering [*Bekleidung*] wall entails more than textile fabric" (fol. 2).

77. The type was certainly set before the decision to add a third volume had been made. When Semper wrote the section "Textile Art" the intention was to divide the whole work into two parts, of which the second was to deal with architecture. This part was repeatedly referred to in part one, and when the third volume was allocated to architecture, the necessary corrections were overlooked. References to the second part—incidentally quite informative about the problems to be dealt with there—remain: *Stil* 1, pp. 212, 230, 233, 243, 313, 321f, 339f, 358, 405, 431, 443, 480, 506; 2, pp. 151, 281, 395. However, in the section "Stereotomy" reference is made to the third volume: pp. 371, 463.

78. The nearest he comes to a definition is in vol. 1, p. VII, where he refers to the "aesthetic necessity" and "a codex of laws," evident in the earliest artifacts.

79. MS 122, fol. 15; *K.S.*, p. 267.

80. MS 179, fols. 42ff; see note 9 above.

81. *Stil* 1, pp. XXXI–XLII, and MS 179, fols. 23–41.

82. MS 179, fols. 42–46; *WIK*, p. 15. The lecture on adornment, "Über die formelle Gesetzmässigkeit des Schmuckes," which contained a summary of his theory of beauty, also finished with a definition of "style" taken over from "Theorie des Formell-Schönen" (*Schmuck*, pp. 28ff). For the English translation of these definitions of style see below, pp. 241 and 243.

83. *4 El.*, p. 55; MS 124, fol. 18; *K.S.*, p. 286. Vogt, p. 183.

84. MS 133. Semper actually wrote: "for the general history of art & for *artistical science* [italics added]"; in *K.S.*, p. 18, this phrase has been translated back into German as "einzelne Kunstfächer" (various branches of art). I believe that Semper meant to express in English the idea, so important for him, of "practical aesthetics."

85. To Suchsland, 27 October 1856.

86. MS 59, fol. 11; MS 124, fols. 19f; *K.S.*, p. 287.

1. Was Semper a Materialist?

1. *Stil* 2, p. 249; *Stil* 1, p. 7.

2. MS 179, fol. 42.

3. Vischer 1, pp. 72, 151.

4. MS 179, fol. 20f.

5. 26 September 1843 (*Vieweg Brief* no. 1); see also MS 178, fol. 19.

6. MS 68, fol. 55.

7. *Über die formelle Gesetzmässigkeit des Schmuckes* (1856).

8. *Über Baustyle* (1869). Translated by John Root and Fritz Wagner, *Inland Architect* (December 1889, January–March 1890).

2. Semper's Position on the Gothic

1. *Vorläufige Bemerkungen über bemalte Architectur und Plastik bei den Alten.* (1834).

2. *Stil* 1, p. 320. See Stockmeyer, p. 52.

3. *Stil* 1, pp. 7, 509.

4. *Stil* 2, p. 320, and MS 178, fol. 5.

5. *Stil* 2, p. 527.

6. *Stil* 1, p. xviiin.

7. *Stil* 2, p. 326.

8. *WIK*, p. 50. MS 178, fol. 24: "a convenient ready reckoner."

9. 27 July 1829. Cf. Schnaase's detailed description of Antwerp Cathedral, which made the same deep impression on him as on Semper (Schnaase [1834], pp. 188–218). When Semper saw Amiens Cathedral years later, his assessment was equally positive "Reise nach Belgien" [1849], pp. 501ff).

10. Hammer, p. 113; also Fenger, pp. 6ff. On polychromy see the recent article by Zanten; also Middleton (1980), pp. 101f.

11. To his sister, 26 December 1833. See Kobuch, p. 112, no. 7.

12. *V.B.*

13. MS 2, fol. 36; *V.B.*, pp. 39f.

14. MS 2, fol. 11; cf. *V.B.*, p. 20, where in a note, added shortly before publication, he writes of the colorful decor of Gothic churches and the tinted sunbeams passing through the stained glass windows.

15. MS 2, fol. 37.

16. MS 19.

17. MS 19, fols. 5f. On Rumohr's studies about German medieval architecture see Robson-Scott, pp. 241f.

18. MS 19, fols. 19f.

19. MS 19, fol. 6. Quast (1842), Kugler (1842), Schnaase (1843), Popp and Bülau (1834), Hoffstadt (1840).

20. MS 25, fols. 180–240: a student's notebook, revised by Semper; dated 1840–1841.

21. MS 25, fols. 194–214. There is a short description of the Gothic vaulting system in MS 257, fols. 62f.

22. MS 25, pp. 205ff. Stieglitz (1820; the last number of vol. 2 was published in 1839); Boisserée (1823–1832); Clemens, Mellin, and Rosenthal (1837); Schnaase (1834). Semper obviously did not know the articles by Franz Mertens on the French origin of Gothic architecture, published from 1835 onward (see Börsch-Supan, pp. 167ff, 636ff).

23. MS 25, fol. 195.

24. MS 25, fol. 196.

25. MS 25, fols. 196f.

26. MS 25, fol. 199. In an earlier manuscript (MS 20, fols. 24f) and in a different context, Semper had already mentioned that "in the Middle Ages the romantic blending of oriental elements with nordic needs and taste caused a wonderful surge of poetry and architecture and consequently of all the fine arts."

27. MS 25, fols. 200f.

28. MS 25, fol. 201.

29. MS 25, fols. 201ff.

30. MS 25, fols. 203f.

31. MS 25, fol. 205.

32. Schnaase (1834), pp. 479f.

33. MS 25, fols. 209ff.

34. MS 25, fol. 213: "Masses have rarely been grouped as picturesquely as those of Byzantine churches." See Dolgner, p. 83.

35. MS 25, fol. 212. Seventy-five years before, Laugier had expressed similar views (*Observations sur l'architecture* [Paris, 1765], p. 298).

36. MS 7, fol. 5. The report is dated 28 August 1842. See below, p. 176.

37. 22 January 1843; published in 1904 in *Zentralblatt der Bauverwaltung*. Cited in full in Bibliography.

38. MSS 8, 9; dated "Dresd, 25th Oct. 1844" (fol 23).

39. Ill. in Fröhlich, pp. 48 and 49.

40. MS 8, fols. 3f, 8.

41. MS 9, fol. 6.

42. MS 8, fols. 9f, 11.

43. MS 8, fols. 10f.

44. MS 8, fol. 12. The Gothic design ill. in Institut für Denkmalpflege, p. 289.

45. *Andeutungen über die Aufgabe der evangelischen Kirchenbaukunst* [Hamburg, 1845], pp. 9f, 15. Only Scott's and Semper's designs are mentioned by name. The author was F. Stöter. On the controversy see Pevsner (1972), pp. 255ff. Many years later, at the time of the consecration of the new church, Stöter again took part in a discussion about Scott's and Semper's designs (*Recensionen und Mittheilungen über bildende Kunst* [Vienna, 1864] 3, pp. 9ff, 67ff).

46. MS 13. Semper's article "Noch etwas über den St. Nikolai-Kirchenbau" (1845) is a reply to a different article, which preceded the *Andeutungen*, or at least Semper's knowledge of it.

47. *Andeutungen*, p. 14.

48. MS 13, fol. 5.

49. MS 13, fol. 4, in answer to *Andeutungen*, p. 9.

50. MS 8, fol. 10, and MS 13, fol. 3, in answer to *Andeutungen*, p. 8; cf. *Stil* 1, p. xviiin.

51. Bülau to Semper, 1 March and 20 May 1845.

52. MS 14, fols. 4f; Bunsen (1842).

53. *Über den Bau evangelischer Kirchen* (1845).

54. *E.K.*, p. 12; cf. *Stil* 2, p. 527.

55. *E.K.*, p. 25.

56. MS 14, fols. 19f. A shorter version in *E.K.*, p. 27. See Frankl, pp. 488, 591f.

57. *E.K.*, p. 27.

58. On the history of the competition see Faulwasser, pp. 70ff, and Germann (1972), p. 103.

59. MS 34. The final lecture of this course is dated 23 April 1849; it was probably the last lecture he gave before his flight from Dresden.

60. MS 34, fols. 13f.

61. MS 25, fol. 199.

62. MS 35, fol. 60: lecture course "Lehre der Gebäude" of 1848/1849.

63. MS 6, fol. 29.

64. MS 3, fol. 8; the paragraph containing this remark was eliminated before *V.B.* went to press (cf. p. ix).

65. MS 13, fol. 4.

66. MS 170, fol. 26; cf. "Baustyle," p. 30.

67. MS 178, fol. 18; also MS 168, fol. 3.

68. MS 169, fol. 1; see *Stil* 1, p. xvi. In MS 175, fol. 37, he cites, in addition to the ship and the chariot, "the Roman-Catholic propaganda-seeking [*sic*] basilica" as an example for the "authority" of direction.

69. *Baustyle*, p. 9.

70. *Stil* 1, pp. 507n, 201.

71. *Stil* 1, p. xvii.

72. MS 178, fol. 15; MS 88, fol. 34. "The Parliament Building in London has been made distasteful through the mechanical process of production." The mistake was made "to arrange the rooms in such a way that the magnificent rooms are in the interior, the small and lower ones in the parts facing the outside; this produced façades of petty proportions—the architecture is rich but monotonous" (*WIK*, p. 19; MS 257, fol. 139).

73. MS 254, fol. 13.

74. MS 254, fol. 9; Viollet-le-Duc 1, p. 146.

75. MS 254, fol. 5; *Stil* 2, 527: "The Gothic style subjugated . . . the minor arts, too." Similarly in *Stil* 2, pp. 326f.

76. For documentation see Herrmann (1962), pp. 236 ff.

77. *Stil* 1, p. 508; see also the critical remarks quoted at the beginning of this chapter.

78. MS 254, fol. 16 (refers to Viollet-le-Duc 1, p. 147). Similarly in MS 179, fol. 15; also *Stil* 1, pp. 320f. Cf. Stockmeyer, p. 49.

3. Semper and the Archeologist Bötticher

1. Lützow, pp. 85f; Redtenbacher, nos. 43–47; Gurlitt, pp. 626f; Prinzhorn, pp. 27f; Tietze, pp. 110, 392; Ettlinger (1937), pp. 84, 93ff; Stockmeyer, pp. 50f; Quitzsch (1962), pp. 75, 79; Bauer 1, pp. 150, 163; Eggert, pp. 137f. For an excellent account of Bötticher's work and its importance see Börsch-Supan, pp. 556ff, 20f.

2. *Allgemeine Bauzeitung* (Vienna, 1842) 7, pp. 378, 388.

3. Vol. 1 was published in 1843, book 4 of vol. 2 in 1849, books 2 and 3 of vol. 2 in 1851, and the complete edition in two volumes in 1852.

4. MS 58, fol. 30.

5. MS 67, fol. 245.

6. MS 68, fol. 57.

7. MS 78, fol. 40: "before returning to Greek architecture, which is the subject of this pamphlet."

8. For instance, on fol. 97, where he discussed the relation of Doric to Ionic art.

9. MS 78, fols. 54, 94.

10. MS 59, fols. 10f; similarly in MS 58, fol. 96, and almost identically in *4 El.*, p. 56.

11. *Tektonik* 1, pp. XIX, XVIII, 166, and Excursus 6, p. 81.

12. Sächsische Landesbibliothek, Dresden, t. 3584. Semper forgot to enter the year, but since all his other application slips are dated 1852, there can be little doubt that this was also the year for this request.

13. MS 150. There are no notes to the Excurses or to books 2, 3, or 4, but in *Stil* 2, p. 467, he refers to book 2.

14. *Tektonik* 1, p. XXI.

15. *Tektonik* 1, p. 112.

16. *Tektonik*, Excursus 6, p. 81; see also note 11 above.

17. *Tektonik* 1, p. 146.

18. *Tektonik* 1, p. 143.

19. MS 97, of 1851/1852 (cf. Herrmann [1976], n. 32). Hearth: MS 52, fol. 33; MS 58, fols. 18f; *4 El.*, p. 55. Tracing back to original motif: MS 31, fol. 3; MS 33, fol. 4, MS 55, fols. 11f. Carpet-wall: MS 58, fols. 95f; MS 59, fol. 11; *4 El.*, pp. 56ff; MS 97, fols. 22f.

20. The meaning is that of coryphaeus or leader.

21. MS 101, fol. 16. From a letter to Johann Karl Bähr, dated 25 December 1852.

22. The letters (MS 101) were published under the title "Briefe aus der Schweiz. Die neben den Propyläen aufgefundenen Inschrifttafeln" in *Deutsches Kunstblatt* 6 (1855) nos. 38, 42–46. The relevant letter appears in its expurgated version on pp. 388ff.

23. *Tektonik* 1, p. XV.

24. MS 150a, fol. 1.

25. MS 150a, fol. 1.

26. MS 150a, fol. 2, referring to *Tektonik* 1, pp. 3, 5.

27. *Tektonik* 1, pp. 7f.

28. MS 150a, fols. 2f.

29. MS 156, fol. 5; see also MS 129, fol. 15.

30. *Schleudergeschosse*, p. 5.

31. *Stil* 1, p. 444.

32. *Stil* 1, p. 390n.

33. *Stil* 1, p. 389.

34. *Stil* 1, p. 304.

35. *Stil* 1, p. 417.

36. *Stil* 1, p. 390.

37. *Stil* 1, p. 417.

38. *Stil* 1, p. 424.

39. *Stil* 2, p. 393; also *Stil* 1, pp. 444, 445. On the notion of the emancipation of matter see Stockmeyer, pp. 45ff, and Quitzsch (1962), p. 72.

40. *Stil* 1, p. 304.

41. Semper, "Wintergarten" (1849), p. 522.

42. *Stil* 1, p. 422.

43. For Semper the words "Greek" and "Hellene"/"hellenic" are synonyms, thereby conforming to the terminology of German archeological and philological literature of his time. Bötticher, as the title of his book indicates, preferred the term "hellenic". I have therefore retained this term when quoting or paraphrasing whenever it occurs in the original. In my own text I use the common term "Greek."

44. *Tektonik*, Excursus 2, p. 29. This passage is cited and commented upon by Bauer, p. 151. Bötticher's explanation of the hollow-body structure (*Tektonik* 1, p. 129) is similar to that given by Semper in *Stil* 2, p. 393; Bötticher also refers, as did Semper before him ("Wintergarten," p. 522), to the statics of a hollow iron column.

45. MS 169, fol. 2.

46. See above, p. 141.

47. *Tektonik* 1, p. xv.

48. *Tektonik*, Excursus 2, p. 34.

49. *Tektonik* 1, p. 35.

50. *Tektonik* 1, pp. 11, 13; also pp. 16, 23, 85, 101.

51. *Tektonik* 1, p. 23.

52. *Tektonik* 1, p. 37.

53. *Tektonik* 1, p. 17.

54. MS 129, fol. 14. Text as written in English by Semper.

55. MS 180, fol. 79.

56. MS 180, fol. 97.

57. MS 180, fol. 98.

58. *Stil* 2, p. 464.

59. MS 180, fol. 156; also *Stil* 1, p. 386.

60. *Stil* 1, p. 448. Draft to this passage: MS 208, fol. 16.

61. *Tektonik* 1, p. 17.

62. MS 180, fol. 155.

63. *Schmuck*, p. 16.

64. MS 150b, fol. 1; *Tektonik* 1, pp. 28f.

65. MS 141, fols. 14f. In this respect, Semper was not very particular: his lectures in Dresden contain numerous comments, seemingly his own, which in fact had been taken over verbatim from Rumohr and Heeren: MS 19, fols. 24ff, 33ff; MS 20, fols. 50–139.

66. MS 142, fols. 1, 9.

67. MS 150b, fols. 2, 3.

68. *Tektonik* 1, pp. 42–58. On p. 3 Bötticher divides "the total tectonic activity into two spheres—that of architectonics and . . . that of tectonics of implements."

69. MSS 150b, fol. 5; 150c, fols. 1–3, 5–7; 150d, fols. 11–16.

70. *Tektonik* 1, p. 42.

71. MS 175, fol. 10; MS 179, fol. 10n. 13; *Stil* 1, p. 382; *Stil* 2, pp. 210, 240, 427. Only once before, in his "Gebäudelehre" (MS 58, fol. 110), had he briefly referred to the analogy between the wooden Assyrian column and the wooden implement, without, however, explaining the basic difference between the two types of works.

72. MS 134.

73. MS 180, fols. 151–173. The only time that Semper acknowledged the importance of Bötticher's observations on ceramics occurs in the same manuscript (fol. 112): "Karl Bötticher's *Tektonik der Hellenen* (Vol. I, p. 42) contains many excellent remarks on ceramics."

74. *Stil* 2, pp. 78–118.

75. Especially MS 150d, fols, 11–16.

76. MS 275, fols. 2, 5. When Peyer contrasts the Parthenon with the Erechtheum, Semper remarks: "All taken from Bötticher."

77. MS 275, fol. 71.

78. MS 275, fol. 45.

79. MS 275, fol. 43.

80. *Tektonik* 1, p. 6.

81. *Tektonik* 1, p. 98, also p. 111n.

82. *Tektonik* 1, p. 118.

83. *Tektonik* 1, p. 96.

84. *Tektonik* 1, p. 23.

85. *Tektonik* 1, p. 103.

86. *Tektonik* 1, pp. 102f.

87. *Tektonik*, Excursus 2, p. 27.

88. *Tektonik* 1, p. 85, also p. 117.

89. *Tektonik* 1, p. 24.

90. On the historical unity of oriental and Greek art as conceived by Semper, see Ettlinger (1937), pp. 74ff, 85.

91. *Stil* 1, p. 218.

92. MS 208, fol. 19.

93. *Stil* 2, p. 405.

94. *Stil* 1, p. 219.

95. *Stil* 1, p. 444.

96. MS 130, fol. 1; another version, MS 129, fol. 13.

97. MS 275, fol. 2.

98. *Tektonik* 1, p. 3.

99. *Tektonik* 1, p. 101.

100. MS 122, fol. 9; MS 179, fol. 9: "the development of practical and industrial arts had reached a high level before architecture as an independent art had even been thought of." Ibid., fol. 10: "The industrial arts are therefore the key to understanding architectural as well as artistic form and rule in general."

101. *Tektonik* 1, p. 38. Bötticher had inserted this section in the middle of the introduction without giving any reason for it.

102. MS 150b, fol. 4.

103. *Tektonik*, Excursus 2, p. 37.

104. *Tektonik*, Excursus 6, p. 91; in contrast cf. MS 179, fol. 43.

105. *Tektonik*, Excursus 6, p. 104.

106. This is known as Semper's *Stoffwechseltheorie* (theory of change in materials). On this concept see Stockmeyer, pp. 39ff; Quitzsch (1962), pp. 65f; Bletter, p. 151. For the incompatibility of Bötticher's ideas with Semper's *Stoffwechseltheorie* see in particular *Tektonik*, Excursus 2, pp. 29f.

107. MS 150c, fol. 4.

108. *Stil* 2, p. 395.

109. MS 275, fol. 5.

110. *Schleudergeschosse*, p. 5; similar version, MS 122, fol. 25.

111. MS 141, fol. 4.

112. *Baustyle*, p. 27.

113. MS 144, fol. 37.

114. *Stil* 1, p. 485.

115. MS 34, fol. 11.

116. MS 262, fol. 28.

117. *Stil* 2, pp. 466, 477. On Semper's conflicting attitude see Ettlinger (1937), pp. 95f. Contrary to Ettlinger, I believe that Semper wanted the second part of the quotation to be understood in a general, not only a technical-historical, sense.

118. Semper to Vieweg, 25 July 1855.

119. MS 169, fol. 3; similarly in MS 168, fol. 3.

120. MSS 171, fols. 1f; 175, fols. 1f; 179, fols. 1, 8. Cf. *Tektonik* 1, p. XIV.

121. MS 171, fols. 3, 10; MS 175, fols. 2, 8.

122. MS 180, fol. 47.

123. MS 181.

124. MS 180, fol. 100.

125. MS 180, fol. 48.

126. MS 180, fol. 47. When revising MS 178 he changed on fol. 28 "tectonics" into "art," and "sphere of tectonics" into "sphere of Kunstformenlehre" (theory of art forms), and he did the same when transferring a sentence from MS 170, fol. 37, to *Stil* 1, p. VII.

127. Cf. Börsch-Supan (1976), p. 166.

128. As far as I can tell, only once, in a passage omitted from the printed text (MS 88, fol. 31), had Semper written of "conceptions of tectonics"; but he used the term as a synonym for "industrial art."

129. MS 52, fol. 29.

130. *4 El.*, p. 56; MS 97, fol. 12.

131. MS 97, fols. 30, 31.

132. *Tektonik* 1, p. 3.

133. Hettner, p. 40.

4. Semper's Position on Contemporary Architecture

1. MS 1, fol. 27.

2. *V.B.*, p. 11.

3. *V.B.*, p. 16.

4. MS 207, fol. 50 (draft for *Stil* 1, p. XX); see Eggert, p. 96.

5. He had originally added "and swore by everything he said" but then crossed it out.

6. MS 52, fol. 11, also MS 55, fol. 7 and MS 178, fol. 23 (where he changed "the domineering power of a late master's genius" into "the domineering influence of its founder and late master"). As can be gathered from Gau's reply (22 February 1835), Semper had complained to him about the "proliferation of Schinkel-like deformities." For Schinkel himself he expressed sincere admiration: see MS 25, fol. 259, and *Stil* 1, p. XVII. On Semper and Schinkel see the recent paper by Quitzsch (1982) and above, page 4.

7. MS 6, fol. 13.

8. MS 19, fol. 31: "the almost universal fault of facelessness . . . for which most modern buildings are rightly being blamed."

9. Hitchcock, p. 49.

10. Durand's style represents the last phase of the neoclassical movement that began in France toward the middle of the eighteenth century as a reaction against the exuberant decoration of the rococo and culminated before the turn of the century in the severe cubic forms of the so-called revolutionary style of a Ledoux or Boullée (the latter had been Durand's teacher at the Académie d'Architecture). Durand brought this trend toward simplification to its logical conclusion, permitting only basic geometrical figures such as the square and the circle for the ground plan and an abundance of rows of classical columns for the elevation. His influence was considerable and widespread through the publication of his lecture courses at the Ecole Polytechnique (*Précis des leçons d'architecture données à l'Ecole Polytechnique*, 2 vols. Paris, 1802–1809).

11. MS 6, fols. 22f. In print (*V.B.*, pp. vif), Semper shortened this sentence considerably and toned down the sarcasm without, however, modifying his clear rejection of Durand's system. Only later, during the years in Paris when he himself was working on a typology of buildings, did he appreciate Durand's achievements in this field and call his writings "still the most valuable handbooks for beginning architects;" although he blamed him for often getting lost "in lifeless schematism," he granted that this might have been due to "the then fashionable trend" (MS 55, fol. 4; also MS 52, fols. 5f). This makes it more justifiable to regard Semper's outburst of twenty years earlier as an attack directed mainly against the contemporary style. On Durand see Germann (1980), pp. 229–246; Milde (1981), pp. 60ff; Rykwert (1982); Szambien, with bibliography of recent works.

12. MS 25, fol. 53. The remarks are taken from a student's notebook. As numerous corrections in Semper's hand prove, he had looked it over and accepted it as an accurate rendering of his lectures.

13. MS 6, fols. 8, 6.

14. MS 6, fol. 14.

15. MS 2, fol. 7; cf. *4 El.*, pp. 1, 8.

16. MS 6, fol. 7.

17. MS 6, fol. 16; cf. *V.B.*, pp. 6, 12.

18. MS 19, fol. 23.

19. MS 6, fols. 7f; ibid., fol. 15: "The main cause of the decline of architecture . . . is probably the very fact that architecture exists as an independent art, complete in itself, and not sufficiently supported by all the other arts."; similarly in fol. 5.

20. MS 1, fol. 3.

21. MS 19, fols. 21, 24.

22. MS 171, fols. 9f; MS 175, fol. 8.

23. MS 195, fol. 5.

24. *Stil* 1, p. vii.

25. MS 207, fol. 4. Similarly in a London lecture: the main cause of the decline of architecture and "high" art was their separation from industrial art (MS 122, fol. 14).

26. MS 207, fol. 1.

27. *WIK*, p. 12; *Stil* 1, pp. 23, 191, 204; *Stil* 2, p. 185; see also MS 135, fol. 1, and MS 167, fol. 9.

28. MS 88, fol. 34.

29. MS 14, fol. 6.

30. MS 95, fol. 17.

31. *Stil* 1, p. xiv.

32. MS 52, fol. 8; MS 55, fol. 5; MS 178, fol. 17. A few years earlier, a French architect had expressed the same fear in almost identical terms: "Le doute règne partout, le sol manque sous les pieds, l'artiste ne sait plus à quoi se rattacher" (Jean-Baptiste Lassus, "De l'art et de l'archéologie," *Annales archéologiques* (1845) 2, p. 426 (cited in Jean-Michel Leniaud, *Jean-Baptiste Lassus [1807–1857]*, Geneva: Droz, 1980, p. 133).

33. MS 207, fols. 50f, Cf. *Stil* 1, pp. xiiif.

34. MS 52, fol. 3; similarly in MS 122, fols. 1f.

35. MS 14, fol. 5; cf. *E.K.*, p. 15.

36. *V.B.*, p. VIII.

37. *V.B.*, p. VII.

38. Germanisches Museum, Nuremberg. Klenze complained about it to Eduard Metzger, his pupil and Semper's friend; Metzger tried to mediate between them.

39. Semper wrote his letter on 4 April 1835.

40. Klenze's letter is dated 7 June 1835.

41. MS 20: on fol. 1 the bibliography lists Gau's "splendid edition," and on fol. 16 reference is made to his research.

42. Gau, p. VIII.

43. MS 25, fols, 258ff.

44. To Ottomar Glockner, 27 September 1840 (Sächsische Landesbibliothek, Dresden, App. 1191, No. 793): "Lack of spontaneity is the main reason why so many works of modern art with nothing really wrong with them make no impression on us, or at least not the powerful and rapturous impression of a revelation that the works of the past have on us." Semper used this sentence years later, almost unchanged, in *E.K.*, p. 15; see also MS 14, fol. 6.

45. Semper (1843/1904), p. 229.

46. *E.K.*, p. 14.

47. MS 8, fol. 2.

48. MS 55, fol. 9. In almost identical form in the preface of 1849 for "Vergleichende Baulehre" (MS 52, fols. 13, 15), and partly revised in MS 178, fol. 21.

49. MS 55, fol. 6.

50. MS 55, fol. 9.

51. MS 52, fol. 14.

52. MS 55, fol. 10. Similarly in MS 52, fol. 15; MS 170, fol. 31; MS 178, fol. 22.

53. MS 207, fols. 34, 35. On Semper's attitude toward eclecticism see Quitzsch (1962), p. 63.

54. MS 52, fols. 15, 16; similarly in MS 55, fol. 10; see also Klenze's letter quoted above (note 40).

55. MS 205, p. 7 (printed prospectus for *Stil*).

56. MS 8, fol. 2.

57. MS 264, fol. 1.

58. MS 281, fol. 24.

59. MS 281, fol. 24.

60. MS 281, fols. 24, 26; *Baustyle*, pp. 7ff. Meeting him one day in front of the Paris Opera House, his former pupil Lawrence Harvey asked him: " 'What do you think of this building, Professor Semper?' 'Sehr schlecht,' very bad, was his answer." Lawrence Harvey, "Semper's Theory of Evolution in Architectural Ornament," *Transactions of the Royal Institute of British Architects* (1885), p. 5.

61. *Stil* 1, p. v.

62. MS 170, fols. 1ff. (the last quotation on fols. 4, 5); slightly revised in MS 178, fols. 3f.

63. MS 55, fol. 10; MS 205, p. 7 (printed prospectus for *Stil*).

64. MS 178, fol. 26. Anthemius and Isidor were the architects of Hagia Sophia in Constantinople.

65. *4 El.*, p. 103; *Baustyle*, p. 31.

66. MS 178, fol. 4.

67. MS 180, fols. 70ff.

68. MS 180, fol. 92. (My italics, except *"evolutionary,"* which are Semper's.)

5. *Semper's Position on the Primitive Hut*

1. On the notion of the "hut" see the two comprehensive studies by Gaus and Rykwert (1972); also Middleton and Watkin, p. 377.

2. MS 31, fols. 8f.

3. MS 66, fol. 188.

4. *4 El.*, p. 56. See above, p. 140.

5. *4 El.*, p. 54; similarly in *Stil* 1, p. 2, where he cites as an example of "senseless speculations . . . the attempt, repeated a hundred times since Vitruvius, of tracing the Doric temple with its parts and members back to the wooden hut."

6. MS 67, fol. 245.

7. MS 208, fol. 30. Draft for *Stil* 1, p. 259.

8. *Stil* 2, p. 210.

9. MS 225, fol. 53, a note in the manuscript to *Stil* 2, p. 395, which, however, was not printed.

10. Hirt (1809); Hope (1835).

11. Cf. Lotze, pp. 523ff.

12. MS 25, fols. 109, 137.

13. MS 52, fol. 89.

14. MS 64, fol. 129.

15. MS 66, fol. 189A.

16. MS 67, fol. 243; cf. *Stil* 1, p. 258.

17. Ms 67, fol. 245. He then describes in detail the forms of stone pagodas that clearly derived from wooden structures.

18. MS 68, fols. 29, 76; also fol. 87. In this connection it should also be mentioned that in his opinion "many characteristic features of the Romanesque style of the Lower Rhine show the direct influence" of Scandinavian timber construction. This is discussed in detail by Frankl, pp. 592f.

19. MS 129, fol. 16.

20. MS 154, fol. 8.

21. *Stil* 2, pp. 393, 380.

22. MSS 55–68. An idea of the manuscript's wide range can be gained from the various students' notebooks of his lecture courses on this subject; in the lectures he was able to deal with almost all building types since he did not have the time to go into the detailed discussions that he planned for the book (MSS 25, 26, 28 from Dresden; MSS 257, 258, 260, 263, 264 from Zurich). The concept of such a typology

was not new. In Germany, Aloys Hirt had undertaken it, in England Joseph Gwilt (Hirt [1827] 3, Gwilt, pp. 782–818). It is quite probable that volume 3 of Hirt's work, subtitled *Die Lehre der Gebäude bei den Griechen und Römern*, was the stimulus to Semper's own, though far more comprehensive, "Lehre der Gebäude" (MSS 24–34), divided like Hirt's into eleven sections. Recently Pevsner (1976) made typology the subject of a major study.

23. MS 24, fol. 4, and the identical text in MS 25, fol. 8.

24. MS 31, fol. 8; repeated in MS 52, fol. 29, and in MS 58, fol. 17.

25. MS 52, fol. 34.

26. MS 31. fols. 13ff; MS 52, fols. 31ff; MS 58, fol. 24; MS 97, fol. 31. In the section on India (MS 67, fol. 222) he explains that "two basic types of dwelling have prevailed there from early times on . . . the oldest and simplest type still seems to exist today in the rural dwellings of Hindustan. They are simple reed-covered mountain huts."

27. MS 25, fol. 107.

28. MS 81b, fol. 85, a variant of *4 El.*, p. 73. Similarly in MS 97, fols. 33f, where he adds, "Yet the first appearance of architecture as *art* certainly did not arise from this rudimentary form."

29. MS 97, fol. 31.

30. *Stil* 2, p. 275. In the manuscript (MS 223, fol. 134) "not" is underlined twice. On this see Bletter, p. 149: "Semper's Caribbean hut . . . was an archetype used to describe the evolution of architectural elements, but it was not proposed as a model to be followed by contemporary architects."

31. MS 46, fol. 13; then in several manuscripts of "Vergleichende Baulehre": MSS 52, fol. 32; 58, fol. 24; 97, fol. 31. On funeral urns in the form of huts see Rykwert (1972), pp. 171ff.

32. MS 66, fol. 188; cf. MS 129, fol. 2; MS 138, fol. 14, and *4 El.*, pp. 73f.

33. MS 97, fol. 2: "The material for 'Vergleichende Baulehre' will consist not only of what the history of architecture provides; of great importance will also be what exists today, because through ethnography we will observe with our own eyes, as it were, how forms develop out of their first motifs."

34. MS 97, fol. 32. In the *Official Descriptive and Illustrated Catalogue of the Great Exhibition . . . 1851* (London, 1851) 2, p. 975, under Trinidad: "Model of an Indian hut, in the village of Arima 16 miles from the town of Port of Spain made by Manuel Sorzano." An enumeration follows of the utensils and tools displayed in the hut, which together with the lifesize figures of the Indian family presented a realistic picture of their way of life.

35. MS 129, fol. 1.

36. *Stil* 2, p. 276, and MS 141, fol. 4.

37. MS 66, fol. 188.

38. MS 141, fol. 11.

39. MS 283, fol. 3.

40. *Stil* 2, p. 250, Cf. Germann (1976), p. 226.

41. *Baustyle*, p. 13.

42. MS 141, fol. 10.

43. MS 262, fol. 51; also MS 58, fol. 38.

44. *Stil* 2, p. 210. For a comprehensive survey on the significance and dissemination of the sacred hut type, see Rykwert (1972), chapter 6.

45. *Stil* 2, p. 275. See Rykwert (1972), pp. 174f.

46. *Stil* 2, p. 275.

47. *Stil* 2, p. 275.

48. *Tektonik*, p. XIX, Excursus 6, pp. 101, 103.

49. *Stil* 2, p. 276.

50. Ettlinger (1964), p. 59; Gaus, pp. 36f; Rykwert (1976), p. 70; Vogt, p. 181.

51. MS 81b, fol. 117; cf. *4 El.*, p. 95.

6. Semper's Position on Iron as a Building Material

1. Paper read at the Technische Universität Dresden; published in *Gottfried Semper 1803–1879*, Schriftenreihe der Sektion Architektur, Technische Universität Dresden, 13 (1979), pp. 46–52.

2. *V.B.*, p. XI.

3. *V.B.*, pp. xf.

4. Summerson, p. 250.

5. Naturally—though in the context improbably—"simple" could equally refer to the French word spelled in the same way.

6. Some years later, he quoted Hope's *Historical Essay on Architecture*, which was published only the following year.

7. Semper, "Wintergarten" (1849), p. 521.

8. *Stil* 2, p. 551.

9. No doubt the architect Eduard Heuchler, professor at the Bergakademie Freiberg in Saxony.

10. On the tower of Rouen Cathedral, erected a few years earlier, only the helm roof is constructed in iron.

11. MS 7, fols. 9f. The report is not signed, but marginal notes in Semper's hand leave no doubt about his authorship.

12. Semper, "Wintergarten," pp. 522f. The source for the attribution of the Jardins d'Hiver to Théodore Charpentier is this article. In the art historical literature Hector Horeau is usually cited as architect, but this has been disputed by Middleton and Watkin, p. 404; they name an architect Rigolet, whom, however, I was unable to identify. Nor could I identify an architect, Meynadier, to whom Semper attributes the initial planning ("Wintergarten," p. 526).

13. *Stil* 2, pp. 263f.

14. *Stil* 2, p. 245; see also pp. 263, 382.

15. *Stil* 1, pp. 304, 366; *Stil* 2, p. 393.

16. Semper, "Wintergarten," p. 522.

17. *Stil* 2, pp. 265f.

18. *Stil* 2, p. 250.

19. *Stil* 2, p. 551. On the Bibliothèque Ste-Geneviève see Guy and the recent article by Neil Levine.

20. Semper, "Wintergarten," p. 521.

21. MS 7, fol. 10.

22. MS 94, fols. 4, 15. See above, p. 273, note 168, on this manuscript and Semper's articles about the Great Exhibition.

23. From Semper's article, published in English translation in the *Edinburgh Review* (1851) 44, pp. 576f. MS 94, fol. 15.

24. MS 94, fol. 9.

25. MS 87, fol. 1.

26. Bucher.

27. Hallmann, p. 71. On Anton Hallmann see Kimpel.

28. Metzger, pp. 176f.

29. Bötticher (1846), pp. 119f (reprint, pp. 23f).

30. *Stil* 1, p. 7; *Stil* 2, p. 550.

31. MS 262, fol. 2.

32. MS 7, fol. 11.

33. MS 171, fol. 18; similarly MS 179, fol. 13.

Semper's Literary Estate

1. Institut für Denkmalpflege, pp. 140ff, 162ff; Fröhlich, pp. 182ff; Milde (1981), pp. 274ff.

2. MS 195, fols. 6–19.

3. Institut für Denkmalpflege, pp. 88ff, 194ff; Fröhlich, pp. 186ff; Milde (1981), pp. 270ff.

1. Influence of Historical Research on Trends in Contemporary Architecture

1. Semper first wrote "and nineteenth century," then crossed it out but left "the Cuviers and Humboldts." In the revision of 1855 he replaced these two names with "and others."

2. See "Semper's Position on Contemporary Architecture," note 10.

2. The Basic Elements of Architecture

1. M. P. E. Botta, *Monument de Ninive* (Paris, 1849–1850), 5, p. 10.

4. The Attributes of Formal Beauty

1. Semper adopted the term "meloplastic" from Zeising, as he also followed fairly closely Zeising's classification of the fine arts into groups of three. Zeising probably coined the term of which he gives this definition: "The main task of Meloplastic is to display the movement of the human body . . . in compositions of seemingly living pictures and groups . . . underscored by rythm, melody, and harmony" (Zeising [1855], p. 531).

2. Zeising (1855), p. 181.

3. Realizing that no equivalent expression exists in the German language for the Latin "auctoritas," Semper chose the literal translation *Autorität*. Using the word in this context is as unusual and sounds as strange in German as does "authority" in English. Nevertheless, rather than convey its meaning by using a more common word like "supremacy" or "rule" or "dominance," it seemed better to follow Semper's idiosyncratic mode of expression and, like him, to translate it as "authority."

4. In the revision Semper changed "architecture" to "art."

5. *A Critical Analysis and Prognosis of Present-Day Artistic Production*

1. Semper alludes here to Gothic Revival architects, above all to those belonging to the Catholic faction in whose opinion the four centuries between the end of the Gothic style proper and its rebirth was an artistically unproductive and wasted time.

2. Semper wrote in great detail about this then-new material (*Stil* 1, pp. 112–119); see above, page 87.

3. Richard Redgrave had been art superintendent at the Department of Practical Art and Semper's superior. Semper was greatly impressed by Redgrave's "Supplementary Report on Design," in *Reports by the Juries on the Subjects in the Thirty Classes into Which the Exhibition Was Divided* (London, 1852), 4, pp. 1580–1682, and, judging from the frequent verbatim citations of long passages from the report, consulted it when writing the first volume of *Der Stil* (*Stil* 1, pp. 36, 125, 163, 191, 199).

4. Cf. Semper's remarks about the special character of French Gothic and Gothic Revival in his "Reise nach Belgien" (1849), p. 505; also *K.S.*, p. 481.

Bibliography

Selected Manuscripts in the Semper-Archiv (preceded by MS number)

1–6. "Vorläufige Bemerkungen über bemalte Architektur und Plastik bei den Alten" (Preliminary Remarks on Polychrome Architecture and Sculpture of the Ancients). 1834.

8–18. On the design and competition for St. Nicholas, Hamburg. 1844–1845.

19–36. Texts and transcriptions of Dresden lectures, 1834–1849. Includes "Lehre der Gebäude" (Theory of Building Types), 1840–1849, MSS 24–34.

43–45. "Das königliche Hoftheater zu Dresden" (The Royal Hoftheater in Dresden). 1849.

52–77. "Vergleichende Baulehre" (Comparative Building Theory). 1849–1850.

78–86. "Die vier Elemente der Baukunst" (The Four Elements of Architecture). 1850–1851.

87–91, 93. "Wissenschaft, Industrie und Kunst" (Science, Industry and Art). October 1851.

92, 94–96. Fragmentary drafts of articles on the Great Exhibition of 1851.

97–98. New drafts of "Vergleichende Baulehre."

99–106. Articles on archaeological subjects.

107–147. Manuscripts in connection with the Department of Practical Art, London, 1852–1854. Includes lectures: for a complete list see note 268 to "In Exile: Semper in Paris and London, 1849–1855."

156–162. "Über die Schleudergeschosse der Griechen" (On Greek Slingshot Missiles): first draft, 1853–1854. "Über die bleiernen Schleudergeschosse der Alten. . ." (On Lead Slingshot Missiles of the Ancients . . .): final version ready for press, 1854.

163–166. "Über die formelle Gesetzmässigkeit des Schmuckes" (On the Formal Uniformity of Adornment). 1856.

168–181. "Theorie des Formell-Schönen" (Theory of Formal Beauty). 1855–1859.

["Kunstformenlehre" (Theory of Art Forms). The only manuscript of this treatise that ever existed was the part that Semper sent to Vieweg in 1856. Vieweg refused to return it, and it was probably later destroyed. See pages 91 and 284n34.]

184–253. "Der Stil" (Style). 1859.

255–265. Texts and transcriptions of Zurich lectures, 1858–1869.

280–282. "Über Baustyle" (On Architectural Styles). Lecture read 4 March 1869.

283. Fragmentary draft of beginning of the third volume of "Der Stil."

Semper's Main Published Works

Vorläufige Bemerkungen über bemalte Architectur und Plastik bei den Alten. Altona: Johann Friedrich Hammerich, 1834.

Über den Bau evangelischer Kirchen. Leipzig: B. G. Teubner, 1845.

"Noch etwas über den St. Nikolai-Kirchenbau," *Neue Hamburgische Blätter*, 12 March 1845. Reprinted in *K.S.*, pp. 468–473.

Das königliche Hoftheater zu Dresden. Braunschweig: Friedrich Vieweg und Sohn, 1849.

"Reise nach Belgien im Monat Oktober 1849," *Zeitschrift für praktisches Bauwesen* 9 (1849), pp. 501–514. Reprinted in *K.S.*, pp. 474–483.

"Der Wintergarten zu Paris," *Zeitschrift für praktisches Bauwesen* 9 (1849), pp. 516–526. Reprinted in *K.S.*, pp. 484–490.

Die vier Elemente der Baukunst. Braunschweig: Friedrich Vieweg und Sohn, 1851.

"On the Study of Polychromy and Its Revival," *The Museum of Classical Antiquity* 1 (1851), pp. 228ff.

Wissenschaft, Industrie und Kunst. Braunschweig: Friedrich Vieweg und Sohn, 1852. For a modern reprint see Wingler, Hans, under "Secondary Sources."

"Briefe aus der Schweiz. Die neben den Propyläen aufgefundenen Inschrifttafeln," *Deutsches Kunstblatt* 6 (1855), nos. 38, 42–46.

Über die formelle Gesetzmässigkeit des Schmuckes. Zurich: Meyer & Zeller, 1856.

Über die bleiernen Schleudergeschosse der Alten und über zweckmässige Gestaltung der Wurfkörper im Allgemeinen. Frankfurt: Verlag für Kunst und Wissenschaft, 1859.

Der Stil in den technischen und tektonischen Künsten, oder praktische Aesthetik. Vol. 1, Frankfurt: Verlag für Kunst und Wissenschaft, 1860. Vol. 2, Munich: Friedrich Bruckmann, 1863.

Über Baustyle. Zurich: Friedrich Schulthess, 1869. Translated by John Root and Fritz Wagner, *Inland Architect* (December 1889, January–March 1890).

"Unmassgebliche Vorschläge zur Erhaltung und Wiederherstellung des Domes in Meissen," *Zentralblatt der Bauverwaltung* 24 (1904), pp. 229–230. Written in 1843.

Kleine Schriften, ed. Manfred and Hans Semper. Berlin and Stuttgart: W. Spemann, 1884.

Secondary Sources

Ames, Winslow. *Prince Albert and Victorian Taste.* London: Chapman and Hall, 1967.

Atterbury, Paul. *The Story of Minton from 1793 to the Present Day.* Stoke-on-Trent: Royal Doulton Tableware Ltd., 1976.

Bauer, Hermann. "Architektur als Kunst," *Kunstgeschichte und Kunsttheorie im 19. Jahrhundert.* Berlin: Walter de Gruyter, 1 (1963), pp. 133–171.

Bell, Quentin. *The Schools of Design.* London: Routledge & Kegan Paul, 1963.

Beust, Friedrich von. *Aus Drei-Viertel Jahrhunderten.* Stuttgart, 1887.

Biermann, Franz Benedikt. "Die Pläne für die Reform des Theaterbaus bei Karl Friedrich Schinkel und Gottfried Semper," *Schriften der Gesellschaft für Theatergeschichte* 38 (1928).

Binney, Marcus. "The Origins of the Albert Hall," *Country Life* 149 (1971), pp. 680–683.

Bletter, Rosemarie. "On Martin Fröhlich's Gottfried Semper," *Oppositions* 4 (1974), pp. 146–153.

Bøe, Alfred. *From Gothic Revival to Functional Form*. Oslo: Oslo University Press, 1957.

Boisserée, Sulpiz. *Geschichte und Beschreibung des Doms von Köln*. Stuttgart, 1823–1832.

Bonython, Elizabeth. *King Cole*. London: Victoria and Albert Musuem, n.d. [1982].

Börsch-Supan, Eva. "Der Renaissancebegriff der Berliner Schule im Vergleich zu Semper." In *Gottfried Semper und die Mitte des 19. Jahrhunderts*. Schriftenreihe des Instituts für Geschichte und Theorie der Architektur an der ETH Zürich, 18. Basel and Stuttgart: Birkhäuser, 1976, pp. 153–174.

Böttcher, Karl. "Das Prinzip der hellenischen und germanischen Bauweise . . . Rede an der Geburtstagsfeier Schinkels am 13. März 1846," *Allgemeine Bauzeitung* 11 (1846), pp. 111–125. Reprinted in *Festreden Schinkel zu Ehren 1846–1980*, ed. Architekten und Ingenieur Verein zu Berlin. Berlin, n.d., pp. 12–32.

————. *Die Tektonik der Hellenen*. 2 vols. Potsdam, 1852.

Bucher, Lothar. "Berichte über die Londoner Industrieausstellung," *National Zeitung* (Berlin), July 31, 1851.

Bunsen, Christian C. J. Freiherr von. *Die Basiliken des christlichen Roms*. Munich, 1842.

Bunsen, F. von. *Christian Carl Josias von Bunsen*. 3 vols. Leipzig, 1868–1871.

Chadwick, George F. *The Works of Sir Joseph Paxton*. London, 1961.

Clemens, Mellin, and Rosenthal. *Der Dom zu Magdeburg*. Magdeburg, 1837.

Cole, Henry. *Fifty Years of Public Work*. 2 vols. London, 1884.

Doering-Manteuffel, H. R. *Dresden und sein Geistesleben im Vormärz*. Dresden, 1835.

Dolgner, Dieter. "Gottfried Sempers Verhältnis zur mittelalterlichen Architektur." In *Gottfried Semper 1803–1879*. Schriftenreihe der Sektion Architektur, Technische Universität Dresden, 13. Dresden, 1979, pp. 81–87.

Eggert, Klaus. "Gottfried Semper. Carl von Hasenauer." In *Die Wiener Ringstrasse*, ed. Renate Wagner-Rieger, vol. 8, part 2. Wiesbaden: Steiner, 1978, pp. 79–225.

Ettlinger, Leopold. *Gottfried Semper und die Antike*. Halle, 1937.

————. "The Duke of Wellington's Funeral Car," *Journal of the Warburg and Courtauld Institutes* 3 (1939).

————. "On Science, Industry and Art. Some Thoughts of Gottfried Semper," *The Architectural Review* 136 (1964), pp. 57–60.

Faulwasser, Julius. *Die St. Nikolaikirche in Hamburg*. Hamburg, 1926.

Fehr, Max. *Richard Wagners Schweizer Zeit*. Aarau, 1934.

Fenger, L. *Dorische Polychromie*. Berlin, 1886.

Frankl, Paul. *The Gothic*. Princeton, N.J.: Princeton University Press, 1960.

Fröhlich, Martin. *Gottfried Semper: Zeichnerischer Nachlass an der ETH Zürich. Kritischer Katalog*. Schriftenreihe des Instituts für Geschichte und Theorie der Architektur an der ETH Zürich, 14. Basel and Stuttgart: Birkhäuser, 1974.

Gau, Franz Christian. *Antiquités de la Nubie*. Stuttgart and Paris, 1822.

Gaus, Joachim. "Die Urhütte. Über ein Modell in der Baukunst und ein Motiv in der bildenden Kunst," *Wallraf-Richartz Jahrbuch* 33 (1971), pp. 7–70.

Geiger, L. *Aus Adolf Stahrs Nachlass*. Oldenburg, 1903.

Germann, Georg. *Gothic Revival*. London: Lund Humphries, 1972.

———. "Gottfried Semper über Konvention und Innovation," *Zeitschrift für Schweizerische Archäologie und Kunstgeschichte* 33 (1976), pp. 224–228.

———. *Einführung in die Geschichte der Architekturtheorie*. Darmstadt: Wissenschaftliche Buchgesellschaft, 1980.

Gurlitt, Cornelius. "Gottfried Semper," *Deutsche Bauzeitung* 37 (1903), pp. 626–627, 637–639.

Guy, Michel, ed. "Exposition Labrouste," *Les Monuments historiques de la France* 6 (1975), pp. 22–25.

Gwilt, Joseph. *Encyclopedia of Architecture*. London, 1842.

Habel, Heinrich. "Sempers städtebauliche Planungen im Zusammenhang mit dem Richard-Wagner-Festspielhaus in München." In *Gottfried Semper und die Mitte des 19. Jahrhunderts*. Schriftenreihe des Instituts für Geschichte und Theorie der Architektur an der ETH Zürich, 18. Basel and Stuttgart: Birkhäuser, 1976, pp. 129–152.

Hallmann, Anton. *Kunstbestrebungen der Gegenwart*. Berlin, 1842.

Haltern, Lutz. *Die Londoner Weltausstellung von 1851*. Münster: Aschendorff, 1971.

Hammer, Karl. *Jakob Ignaz Hittorff*. Stuttgart: Hiersemann, 1968.

Hautecoeur, Louis. *Histoire de l'architecture classique en France*. 7 vols. Paris: Picard, 1943–1957.

Heeren, Arnold H. L. *Ideen über die Politik, den Verkehr und den Handel der vornehmsten Völker der alten Welt*. Historische Werke, 10.–15. Theil. Göttingen, 1824–1826.

Herrmann, Wolfgang. *Laugier and Eighteenth Century French Theory*. London: A. Zwemmer, 1962.

———. "Semper und Eduard Vieweg." In *Gottfried Semper und die Mitte des 19. Jahrhunderts*. Schriftenreihe des Instituts für Geschichte und Theorie der Architektur an der ETH Zürich, 18. Basel and Stuttgart: Birkhäuser, 1976, pp. 199–237.

———. *Gottfried Semper im Exil*. Schriftenreihe des Instituts für Geschichte und Theorie der Architektur an der ETH Zürich, 19. Basel and Stuttgart: Birkhäuser, 1978.

———. *Gottfried Semper: Theoretischer Nachlass an der ETH Zürich. Katalog und Kommentare*. Schriftenreihe des Instituts für Geschichte und Theorie der Architektur an der ETH Zürich, 15. Basel and Stuttgart: Birkhäuser, 1981.

Hettner, Hermann. *Vorschule der bildenden Kunst der Alten*. Oldenburg, 1848.

Hirt, Aloys. *Die Baukunst nach den Grundsätzen der Alten*. Berlin, 1809.

———. *Die Geschichte der Baukunst bei den Alten*. 3 vols. Berlin, 1821–1827.

Hitchcock, Henry-Russell. *Architecture: Nineteenth and Twentieth Centuries*. London: Penguin, 1971.

Hobhouse, Christopher. *1851 and the Crystal Palace*. London: John Murray, 1950.

Hoffstadt, Friedrich. *Gothisches ABC Buch*. Frankfurt, 1840.

Hope, Thomas. *Household Furniture and Interior Decoration*. London, 1807.

———. *An Historical Essay on Architecture*. London, 1835.

Huber, Ernst Rudolf. *Deutsche Verfassungsgeschichte seit 1789.* 3 vols. Stuttgart: Kohlhammer, 1960–1967.

Humboldt, Alexander von. *Kosmos.* 5 vols. Stuttgart and Tübingen, 1845–1862.

Institut für Denkmalpflege. *Gottfried Semper zum 100. Todestag: Ausstellung im Albertinum zu Dresden vom 15. Mai bis 29. August 1979.* Dresden, n.d. [1979].

Keller, Gottfried. *Briefe und Tagebücher,* ed. E. Ermatinger. Stuttgart and Berlin, 1916.

————. *Kellers Briefe an Vieweg,* ed. J. Fränkel. Zurich, 1938.

Kimpel, Sabine. "Der Maler-Architekt Anton Hallmann (1812–1845)." Ph.D. dissertation. Munich, 1974.

Knoepfli, Albert. "Zu den Zürcher Kreisen der frühen Semperzeit." In *Gottfried Semper und die Mitte des 19. Jahrhunderts.* Schriftenreihe des Instituts für Geschichte und Theorie der Architektur an der ETH Zürich, 18. Basel and Stuttgart: Birkhäuser, 1978, pp. 255–274.

Kobuch, Manfred. "Gottfried Semper's Berufung nach Dresden." In *Gottfried Semper 1803–1879.* Schriftenreihe der Sektion Architektur, Technische Universität Dresden, 13. Dresden, 1979, pp. 97–115.

Kühne, Hellmut. "Über die Beziehung Sempers zum Baumaterial." In *Gottfried Semper und die Mitte des 19. Jahrhunderts.* Schriftenreihe des Instituts für Geschichte und Theorie der Architektur an der ETH Zürich, 18. Basel and Stuttgart: Birkhäuser, 1979, pp. 109–117.

Kugler, Franz. *Handbuch der Kunstgeschichte.* Stuttgart, 1842.

Lankheit, Klaus. "Gottfried Semper und die Weltausstellung London 1851." In *Gottfried Semper und die Mitte des 19. Jahrhunderts.* Schriftenreihe des Instituts für Geschichte und Theorie der Architektur an der ETH Zürich, 18. Basel and Stuttgart: Birkhäuser, 1976, pp. 23–46.

Laudel, Heidrun. "Semper's Planungen für ein Zwingerforum in Dresden." In *Gottfried Semper 1803–1879.* Schriftenreihe der Sektion Architektur, Technische Universität Dresden, 13. Dresden, 1979, pp. 115–126.

Laugier, Marc-Antoine. *Observations sur l'architecture.* Paris, 1765.

Levine, Neil. "The Book and the Building: Hugo's Theory of Architecture and Labrouste's Bibliothèque Ste-Geneviève." In *The Beaux-Arts and Nineteenth-Century French Architecture,* ed. Robin Middleton. London: Thames and Hudson/Cambridge, Mass.: MIT Press, 1982, pp. 149–173.

Lewis, R. A. *Edwin Chadwick and the Public Health Movement 1832–1854.* London, 1952.

Lipsius, Constantin. *Gottfried Semper in seiner Bedeutung als Architekt.* Berlin, 1880.

Löffler, Fritz. *Das alte Dresden.* Dresden, 1955.

Lotze, Hermann. *Geschichte der Ästhetik in Deutschland.* Munich, 1868.

Lützow, Carl von. "Sempers Einfluss auf die Reorganisation der modernen Kunstindustrie," *Recensionen und Mittheilungen über bildende Kunst* 2 (Vienna, 1863), pp. 85f.

Macdonald, Stuart. *The History and Philosophy of Art Education.* London: University of London Press, 1970.

May, Walter. "Die grosse Ausstellung. Ein Aufsatz Gottfried Sempers über die Weltausstellung 1851." In *Gottfried Semper 1803–1879.* Schriftenreihe der Sektion Architektur, Technische Universität Dresden, 13. Dresden, 1979, pp. 53–66.

Metzger, Eduard. "Beitrag zur Zeitfrage: In welchem Stil man bauen soll!" *Allgemeine Bauzeitung* 10 (1845), pp. 169–179.

Middleton, Robin, ed. *The Beaux Arts and Nineteenth-Century French Architecture.* London: Thames and Hudson/Cambridge, Mass.: MIT Press, 1982.

————— and Watkin, David. *Neoclassical and Nineteenth-Century Architecture.* New York: Abrams, 1980.

Milde, Kurt. "Gottfried Sempers städtebauliche Leitgedanken," *Architektur der DDR* 28 (1979), pp. 218–233.

—————. *Neorenaissance in der deutschen Architektur des 19. Jahrhunderts.* Dresden: VEB, 1981.

Minihan, Janet. *The Nationalisation of Culture.* London: Hamilton, 1977.

Moller, Georg. *Denkmäler der deutschen Baukunst.* 3 vols. Darmstadt, 1815–1851.

Montbé, A. von. *Der Mai-Aufstand in Dresden.* Dresden, 1850.

Müller, Sebastian. *Kunst und Industrie.* Munich: Carl Hanser, 1974.

Mundt, Barbara. "Theorien zum Kunstgewerbe des Historismus in Deutschland." In *Beiträge zur Theorie der Künste im 19. Jahrhundert* 1 (Frankfurt, 1971), pp. 317–336.

—————. *Die deutschen Kunstgewerbemuseen im 19. Jahrhundert.* Munich: Prestel, 1974.

Newman, Ernest. *Richard Wagner.* 4 vols. London: Cassell, 1933–1947.

Pecht, Friedrich. *Deutsche Künstler des neunzehnten Jahrhunderts.* 3 parts. Nördlingen, 1877.

Pevsner, Nikolaus. *Academies of Art, Past and Present.* Cambridge: Cambridge University Press, 1940.

—————. *Matthew Digby Wyatt.* Cambridge: Cambridge University Press, 1950.

—————. *The Buildings of England: Hampshire.* London: Penguin, 1967.

—————. *Some Architectural Writers of the Nineteenth Century.* Oxford: Clarendon Press, 1972.

—————. *A History of Building Types.* London: Thames and Hudson, 1976.

Plagemann, Volker. *Das Deutsche Kunstmuseum 1790–1870.* Studien zur Kunst des 19. Jahrhunderts, 3. Munich: Prestel, 1967.

Pole, William. *The Life of Sir William Siemens.* London, 1888.

Polenz, Serafim. "Sempers Konkurrenzentwurf für den Umbau des Schlosses Schwerin." In *Gottfried Semper 1803–1879.* Schriftenreihe der Sektion Architektur, Technischen Universität Dresden, 13. Dresden, 1979, pp. 141–144.

Popp, J., and Bülau, Th. *Die Architektur des Mittelalters in Regensburg.* Regensburg, 1834.

Prinzhorn, H. *Gottfried Sempers ästhetische Grundanschauungen.* Stuttgart, 1909.

Quast, Ferdinand von. *Die alt-christlichen Bauwerke von Ravenna.* Berlin, 1842.

Quitzsch, Heinz. *Die ästhetischen Anschauungen Gottfried Sempers.* Berlin: Akademie Verlag, 1962.

—————. *Praktische Ästhetik und politischer Kampf. Im Anhang: Die vier Elemente der Baukunst.* Braunschweig/Wiesbaden: Friedrich Vieweg & Sohn, 1981.

—————. "Gottfried Semper und Karl Friedrich Schinkel." In *Karl Friedrich Schinkel 1781–1841.* Wissenschaftliche Zeitschrift der Ernst-Moritz-Arndt-Universität Greifswald, 31. Greifswald, 1982, pp. 69–71.

Redgrave, Richard. *A Memoir Compiled from His Diary.* London, 1891.

Redtenbacher, Rudolf. "Die moderne Kunst vor dem Forum der Kunstgeschichte," *Deutsche Bauzeitung* 19 (1885), nos. 43–47.

Reising, Gert. "Kunst, Industrie und Gesellschaft. Gottfried Semper in England." In *Gottfried Semper und die Mitte des 19. Jahrhunderts.* Schriftenreihe des Instituts für Geschichte und Theorie der Architektur an der ETH Zürich, 18. Basel and Stuttgart: Birkhäuser, 1976, pp. 49–66.

Robson-Scott, W. D. *The Literary Background of the Gothic Revival.* Oxford: Clarendon Press, 1965.

Rosenau, Helen. "Gottfried Semper and German Synagogue Architecture." In *Year Book of the Leo Baeck Institute*, 22 (1977), pp. 237–244.

Rumohr, Carl F. von. *Italienische Forschungen.* Berlin, 1827.

Rykwert, Joseph. *On Adam's House in Paradise.* New York: The Museum of Modern Art, 1972; Cambridge, Mass.: MIT Press, 1981.

————. "Semper and the Conception of Style." In *Gottfried Semper und die Mitte des 19. Jahrhunderts.* Schriftenreihe des Instituts für Geschichte und Theorie der Architektur an der ETH Zürich, 18. Basel and Stuttgart: Birkhäuser, 1976, pp. 67–81.

————. "Jean-Nicolas-Louis Durand or the Perils of Eclectic Indifference." In *Convegno Internazionale di Studi 1977*, 1 (Padua, 1982), pp. 27–47.

Sayn-Wittgenstein, Carolyne. *Aus der Glanzzeit der Weimarer Altenburg.* Leipzig, 1906.

Scherer, H. *Londoner Briefe über die Weltausstellung.* Leipzig, 1851.

Schnaase, Carl. *Briefe aus den Niederlanden.* Stuttgart, 1834.

————. *Geschichte der bildenden Künste.* 8 vols. Düsseldorf, 1843–1879.

Schubert, Gustav von. *Lebenserinnerungen.* Stuttgart, 1909.

Schumacher, Fritz. *Wie das Kunstwerk Hamburg nach dem grossen Brande entstand.* Hamburg: Hans Christians Verlag, 1969.

Semper, Hans. *Gottfried Semper.* Berlin, 1880.

Semper, Manfred. *Das Münchener Festspielhaus.* Hamburg, 1906.

Stieglitz, Christian Ludwig. *Von alt-deutscher Baukunst.* Leipzig, 1820.

Stockmeyer, E. "Gottfried Sempers Kunsttheorie." Dissertation, Universität Zürich. Glarus, 1939.

Summerson, Sir John. *Georgian London.* Harmondsworth: Penguin, 1978.

Survey of London, general ed. F. H. W. Sheppard. Volume 38: *The Museums Area of South Kensington and Westminster.* London: Athlone Press, 1975.

Szambien, Werner. "Durand and the Continuity of Tradition." In *The Beaux-Arts and Nineteenth-Century French Architecture*, ed. Robin Middleton. London: Thames and Hudson/Cambridge, Mass.: MIT Press, 1982, pp. 19–33.

Tietze, Hans. *Die Methode der Kunstgeschichte.* Leipzig, 1913.

Viollet-le-Duc, Eugène Emmanuel. *Dictionnaire raisonné de l'architecture française du XIe au XVIe siècle.* 10 vols. Paris, 1854–1868.

Vischer, Friedrich Theodor. *Ästhetik oder Wissenschaft des Schönen.* 3 vols. Reutlingen and Leipzig, 1846–1854.

Vogt, Adolf Max. "Gottfried Semper und Joseph Paxton." In *Gottfried Semper und die Mitte des 19. Jahrhunderts.* Schriftenreihe des Instituts für Geschichte und Theorie der Architektur an der ETH Zürich, 18. Basel and Stuttgart: Birkhäuser, 1976, pp. 175–197.

Wagner, Richard. *Richard Wagners gesammelte Briefe (1830–1850)*. ed. J. Kapp and E. Kastner. 2 vols. Leipzig, 1914.

————. *Mein Leben*. Munich: List Verlag, 1964.

Waldersee, Johann Gregor von. *Der Kampf in Dresden im Mai 1849*. Berlin, 1849.

Werner, Ernst. *Der Kristallpalast zu London 1851*. Düsseldorf: Werner Verlag, 1970.

Wingler, Hans, ed. *Wissenschaft, Industrie und Kunst*. Mainz and Berlin: Florian Kupferberg, 1966. Reprint.

Zanten, David van. "Architectural Polychromy: Life in Architecture." In *The Beaux-Arts and Nineteenth-Century French Architecture*, ed. Robin Middleton. London: Thames and Hudson/Cambridge, Mass.: MIT Press, 1982, pp. 196–215.

Zeising, Adolf. *Neue Lehre von den Proportionen des menschlichen Körpers*. Leipzig, 1854.

————. *Ästhetische Forschungen*. Frankfurt, 1855.

Name and Place Index

Subject Index